Holding Patterns: Air Transport and Foreign Policy in the Netherlands

Holding Patterns: Air Transport and Foreign Policy in the Netherlands

By

Marc Dierikx
Jean Guillaume Petit

BRILL

LEIDEN | BOSTON

Cover illustration: KLM world route network, 2023. Image courtesy of KLM Royal Dutch Airlines.

Library of Congress Cataloging-in-Publication Data

Names: Dierikx, M. L. J., author. | Petit, Jean Guillaume, author.
Title: Holding patterns : air transport and foreign policy in the Netherlands / by Marc Dierikx, Jean Guillaume Petit.
Description: Leiden ; Boston : Brill, [2025] | Includes bibliographical references and index.
Identifiers: LCCN 2024041977 (print) | LCCN 2024041978 (ebook) | ISBN 9789004694460 (hardback) | ISBN 9789004695245 (ebook)
Subjects: LCSH: Aeronautics, Commercial–Netherlands. | Aeronautics and state–Netherlands.
Classification: LCC HE9854.A4 D54 2025 (print) | LCC HE9854.A4 (ebook) | DDC 387.706/5492–dc23/eng/20241002
LC record available at https://lccn.loc.gov/2024041977
LC ebook record available at https://lccn.loc.gov/2024041978

Typeface for the Latin, Greek, and Cyrillic scripts: "Brill". See and download: brill.com/brill-typeface.

ISBN 978-90-04-69446-0 (hardback)
ISBN 978-90-04-69524-5 (e-book)
DOI 10.1163/9789004695245

This book is printed on acid-free paper and produced in a sustainable manner.

Contents

Preface

> People harboring doubts will not advance a good cause. (...) Why don't we make a start, here, in our own country? (...) The fact that (...) traffic by air has not been established long ago is truly surprising. (...) In the near future one should be able to travel from Amsterdam to Paris twice a day, and return just as often. Daily services must also be maintained to Berlin and to London.[1]

When the Dutch pilot officer Marinus Hofstee wrote these words in the spring of 1918, the first airplane had taken off less than fifteen years previously. Commercial use of the air for transportation was even more recent. The concept of civil air transport was in its infancy. Even before the return of peace, vistas of the civil use of airplanes developed in various European countries. A few months after the end of the First World War in November 1918, German, French and British pioneers were already considering scheduled commercial air services. The hope was that these services, heralds of a new age, might play a role in promoting peaceful international contacts. In countries with overseas possessions the idea of setting up air links to the colonies also beckoned. Nonetheless, the first actual air service took off in Germany, the nation that had just lost the war and its colonies. On 22 February 1919 the Deutsche Luft Reederei began scheduled flights from Berlin to Weimar, where the German National Assembly was meeting to define the country's new constitution. A month later, on 22 March, the French Lignes Farman launched the first international passenger service: from Paris to Brussels. Convinced that this new form of transport held the promise of a great future, proposals for the creation of commercial airline ventures were put forward in several European countries, including the Netherlands. Although these initial operations were all loss-making, investors were convinced of the immense potential of this new form of transport. They would prove right: over the ten decades covered in this book commercial aviation saw an amazing increase in passenger numbers, from around 10,000 worldwide in 1920 to nearly 3.8 billion in 2022.[2] This growth, particularly marked since the 1970s, both reflected and enabled global

1 M.L.J. Hofstee, *Nederland en het luchtverkeer in de toekomst* (Amsterdam: Swartsenburg, 1918) 26

2 Societé des Nations, *Etudes sur la Situation Economique, Administrative et Juridique de la Navigation Aérienne Internationale* (The Hague: Martinus Nijhoff, 1930). https://www.statista.com/statistics/564717/airline-industry-passenger-traffic-globally/ [2023].

economic spread, the internationalization of trade, industry and production, and the growth of tourism. Aviation has influenced patterns of migration and urbanization, and provided a stimulus to modern society's cultural mix.[3]

This new travel mode introduced new risks. Items might fall from an airplane and cause damage on the ground; indeed, the whole flying machine might come down inadvertently. To address these risks, supervision was clearly necessary. As with other forms of transport, this was a task taken on by governments and followed historical traditions. In the Netherlands, regulation of transport went back to the sixteenth century, when local city authorities issued permits to skippers who wished to operate boat services on the country's inland waterways. After the Netherlands became a unified state in 1813, the regulation of transport developed into a responsibility of the national government. State involvement with rail transport dated from 1839, the year the first train service became operational. When international rail connections became possible in the 1850s, the government assumed a role in not only financial matters and questions concerning safety, but also in support of Dutch economic interests. Parliament confirmed this in adopting a Railways Act in 1875. A decade after the invention of the motorized airplane, developments towards the regulation of flight followed a similar path.

The first proposals for a Dutch Aviation Law were issued in October 1911, at which time the country counted no more than a handful of airplanes. For the most part these were used for occasional public flying displays. Concerns over public safety prompted lawmakers to take action, but no legislation ensued because it proved impossible for Dutch jurists and politicians to keep up with the rapid technological development of aviation. Time and again legislative proposals were shelved for further consideration and the Aviation Law [Luchtvaartwet] was not passed until 1926. This slow start meant the Dutch were late in adopting legislation, outpaced by neighboring countries who embraced aeronautical laws around 1920 that supported both public safety and that of the passengers on board.

The absence of an Aviation Law made the Netherlands government reluctant to commit to cross-border air services when these were proposed in the early 1920s, especially where these involved some form of formal accord between governments. Nonetheless, as the governments of other countries assumed authority over activities in the airspace above their territory, it was inevitable that the Netherlands should follow suit. Despite the absence of legislation, the Dutch followed the practice of neighboring states in assuming

3 Saskia Sassen, *Globalisering: over mobiliteit van geld, mensen en informatie* (Amsterdam: Van Gennep, 1999)

aerial sovereignty. By extension, The Hague accepted that international air services required common ground rules.

International air services touched on the sovereign powers of the states flown over, a major concern in the early postwar years when memories of aerial bombardments were fresh and fears of air attack high. Airline operations themselves abounded in national sentiments. Airlines depended on public money to keep flying and international operations needed prior permission from foreign governments. Because of the high visibility of aviation as an exciting new technology, air services connected sovereignty and national prestige. Pilots landing at a foreign airport were instructed to proudly hoist the national flag from their cockpit window and show passengers, spectators and foreign airport officials that yet another envoy of their great nation had arrived.[4]

Although aviation was still young, the concept of sovereignty in the air already had a history. In May and June 1910 an international conference of legal specialists had gathered in Paris to consider this question. The Netherlands sent three observers to report on the discussions, instructing them to stay aloof from the contents of the conference. After six weeks of discussions, the eighteen delegations that did participate agreed on the principle of complete and absolute sovereignty of the ground state in the air column above its territory. Border crossing flights and the establishment of international air services, the conference decided, would be dependent on prior authorization by the states concerned.[5] Air transport between points within a national territory – cabotage, in legal terms – would be reserved exclusively for that nation's aircraft. After the conference these principles had remained, but in 1919 the sovereignty principle was confirmed in the form of an international treaty. As a result of the war, nationalism surged in Europe and prompted the defense of borders. Free trade, which was not unusual in the 19th century, was on the decline. In March 1919, representatives of 26 nations gathered in Paris to discuss an international legal and political regime for air transport. On 13 October 1919 they signed the Convention Relating to the Regulation of Aerial Navigation, subsequently known as the Paris Convention, one of the results of the Versailles Peace Conference.[6] The treaty was ultimately ratified by 32 nations.

---

4 Marc Dierikx, *Clipping the Clouds. How Air Travel Changed the World* (Westport CT: Preager, 2008), p. 11.

5 Article 21 of the proposed convention of 29 June 1910, in: Albert Roper, *La Convention Internationale du 13 Octobre 1919 portant Réglementation de la Naviqation* Aérienne. Son origine, son application, son avenir (Paris: Recueil Sirey, 1930), Annexe B.

6 For a comprehensive overview of the legal aspects of international air transport, see: Pablo Mendes de Leon, *Introduction to Air Law* [11th edition] (Alphen aan den Rijn: Kluwer Law International, 2022).

Although present at the negotiating table, the United States did not accede to the Convention, narrowing its involvement in international air contacts to bilateral dealings with Canada and issuing a (temporary) ban on civilian flying in the absence of federal legislation. Given the highly diverse recommendations from the various industry advisory bodies, the implications of the Convention's links with the League of Nations made that ratification was buried in Congress in 1926.[7] This created the need for a separate agreement for international aviation in the Americas. A special treaty was negotiated between 21 states from the Western Hemisphere, the Havana Convention, signed on 20 February 1928. The Paris and Havana conventions provided two regimes for international air transport in the inter-war period. The wartime circumstances of the 1940s brought an end to this situation. For a postwar world, where developments in aviation technology would likely lead to new conditions in global air transport, a single, new regime was desirable. In November 1944, the United States brought together representatives of 52 nations in Chicago to devise a new legal and political framework with global coverage. The new treaty was signed on 7 December 1944 as the Chicago Convention on International Civil Aviation.[8] It reconfirmed national sovereignty as the basis for international air services. Article 6 of the Convention specified:

> No scheduled international air service may be operated over or into the territory of a contracting State, except with the special permission or other authorization of that State, and in accordance with the terms of such permission or authorization.[9]

The Chicago Conference established the (Provisional) International Civil Aviation Organization (ICAO), which in October 1947 became an agency of the United Nations. The Chicago Conference also adopted two separate agreements intended to mitigate the implications of the sovereignty principle: the International Air Services Transit Agreement and the International Air Transport Agreement. These introduced the concept of 'Freedoms of the Air', a terminology inspired by President Roosevelt's famous call, in his annual message to Congress on 6 January 1941, for the general recognition of four freedoms: of expression, of religion, from want and from fear. The concept of the 'Freedoms

7 Sean Seyer, *Sovereign Skies. The Origins of American Civil Aviation Policy* (Baltimore: Johns Hopkins University Press, 2021), p. 40–42, 50–51, 61–63, 165–166, 171–172.

8 *Proceedings of the International Civil Aviation Conference Chicago, Illinois, November 1–December 7, 1944,* [2 volumes] (Washington DC: United States Printing Office, 1949).

9 Text of the Chicago Convention from: Nicolas M. Matte, *Treatise on Air-Aeronautical Law* (Toronto: Carswell, 1981), p. 606.

of the Air' had previously been discussed by the Americans and their British allies as a way to streamline discussions between governments on scheduled airline operations.

The International Air Services Transit Agreement created two so-called *technical* freedoms for scheduled international air services. As the First Freedom, each contracting state granted civil aircraft from signatory countries the right to fly across its territory without landing. The Second Freedom granted the privilege to land for non-traffic purposes, such as refuelling.

The International Air Transport Agreement next defined three *commercial* freedoms. The Third Freedom was defined as 'the right or privilege, in respect of scheduled international air services, granted by one State to another State to put down, in the territory of the first State, traffic coming from the home State of the carrier'. The Fourth Freedom was defined as 'the right or privilege, in respect of scheduled international air services, granted by one State to another State to take on, in the territory of the first State, traffic destined for the home State of the carrier'. The Fifth Freedom was defined as 'the right or privilege, in respect of scheduled international air services, granted by one State to another State to put down and to take on, in the territory of the first State, traffic coming from or destined to a third State'.[10]

While the Transit Agreement was immediately understood to be crucial for international airline operations, and therefore quickly signed by many ICAO members – in 2023 the tally stood at 135 – the International Air Transport Agreement was much less successful. Only 19 delegations signed the agreement (including the US), but ultimately only 11 states ratified the Agreement and opened their airspace to free commercial operations. These included the Netherlands.

Although not officially defined at the Chicago Conference, another 'freedom' developed in operational airline practice: the right or privilege, with respect to scheduled international air services, of transporting, via the home State of the carrier, traffic moving between two other States. This Sixth Freedom, tolerated in some cases but almost never officially granted, was to play an important role in negotiations on the operation of scheduled international air services. Over the years, the legal parlance expanded to encompass a total of nine freedoms.[11]

The acceptance and application of national sovereignty in the air and the system of freedom rights established a global regime for the negotiation of

10 ICAO Manual on the Regulation of International Air Transport (Doc 9626): https://www.icao.int/pages/freedomsair.aspx [2022].

11 Mendes de Leon, *Introduction to Air Law*, p. 77–79.

international air services.[12] Incorporating changes, this remained in effect as a normative framework to facilitate the making of international agreements until the late 1980s. This had important and far-reaching consequences for the development and operation of international air services. Sovereignty made air carriers dependent on their national government to negotiate traffic rights on their behalf with other countries. Thousands of such bilateral air transport agreements have been concluded worldwide since 1944. The importance of the regime delineating the playing field for bilateral negotiations has often been misunderstood or neglected in the historical literature on air transport, which tends to portray airline companies as the prime movers; examples of this approach are too numerous to list here. This book focuses on the role played by government diplomacy, using documented case studies that demonstrate the effects of the Dutch diplomatic effort to organize and operate scheduled international air services between the Netherlands and other countries. In particular, this book will examine the relationship between the Netherlands' government and the national airline, KLM, in procuring foreign landing rights, evaluating the extent to which airline interests dictated government policy towards Dutch international air transport.

Over the course of a century, The Hague has sent many hundreds of missions to negotiate bilateral air services agreements in foreign capitals and received a similar number of delegations from abroad. Such negotiations take weeks but they are often longer. In some cases discussions took years or even decades, for example the negotiations with the United States and with the People's Republic of China. More than once, the Dutch have found themselves stuck in a *holding pattern*, circling a foreign destination in the hope of receiving clearance to land, resembling, in a sense, the practice of commercial aviation operations. Hence the title of this book.

These patterns did not originate solely from the legal basics identified above. Over the years, agreements on air transport have become an important element within the larger outlines of bilateral political, economic and trade relations, with governments championing national self-interest. In the postwar world this national interest was often defined as the promotion of security, prestige, and prosperity, along with the well-being of the population.[13] Of these, security and prestige rank in the realm of high politics, while

12 On the theory of international air transport regimes and their implications for the development of international commercial aviation, see Christer Jönsson, *International Aviation and the Politics of Regime Change* (New York: St. Martin's Press, 1987).

13 Wetenschappelijke Raad voor het Regeringsbeleid, *Aan het buitenland gehecht. Over verankering en strategie van het Nederlands buitenlandbeleid* [WRR-report 85], (Amsterdam: AUP, 2010), p. 60.

prosperity and well-being are usually considered to belong to the sphere of low politics. What makes aviation interesting as a topic of research is that it combines the two fields. Prestige, as we shall see, played a major role in high politics as both an incentive and an obstacle for the development of international air services in the interwar period, when aircraft were seen as symbols of power and influence. After 1945, however, the low politics of economic and commercial interests shaped developments. At the same time commercial aircraft, which often displayed the national flag on their tail, continued as a symbol of identity and of global influence.[14] Such symbols carry considerable weight, placing air transport landing rights at the pinnacle of bilateral and international relations. In conflicts between nations, the suspension or even revoking of landing rights was and is used as one of the first ways to signal serious discord.

On the other hand, issuing or extending commercial landing rights to a foreign airline symbolizes fruitful economic relations. As one of the Dutch protagonists in the air transport negotiations depicted in this book wrote to its co-author, 'trade follows the flag' and 'traffic creates trade'.[15] Nonetheless, to achieve beneficial agreements in areas such as air services and trade, sovereignty, prestige and protectionism remain powerful factors to overcome, especially for a small nation like the Netherlands.[16]

Trading interests have been central to the Dutch quest for landing rights. In the Netherlands, the share of international trade in the nation's economy went up by around 60 per cent between 1920 and 2000 and has continued to increase.[17] In 2022 almost a third of the gross national product was generated by exports of goods and services.[18] KLM, the Dutch national airline, has played an important role in this development throughout the entire 100-year period covered in this book, despite a weak starting position as a consequence of its small home market. For those able to afford the price of an air ticket, KLM offered rapid travel and transport connections to locations around the world. The airline developed from a small, loss-making public service, dependent on government subsidies, to an international player in its own right. In the period since 1945 the airline's growth has reflected the increasingly strong links

---

14 Jenifer van Vleck, *Empire of the Air. Aviation and the American Ascendancy* (Cambridge MA: Harvard University Press, 2013), p. 3–15.

15 Letter Henri 'Or' Wassenbergh to Jean Petit, 4 March 2002: Collection Petit, The Hague.

16 Ruud van Dijk, Samuël Kruizinga, Vincent Kuitenbrouwer, Rimko van der Maar, *Shaping the International Relations of the Netherlands, 1815–2000: A Small Country on the Global Scene* (London: Routledge, 2020), Introduction.

17 Wetenschappelijke Raad voor het Regeringsbeleid, *Nederland Handelsland. Het perspectief van de transactiekosten* [WRR-report 66], (Den Haag: Sdu, 2003), p. 44–45.

18 Figures Central Bureau of Statistics: https://longreads.cbs.nl/nederland-handelsland-2022/nederlandse-verdiensten-aan-internationale-handel/ [2023].

between the Dutch economy and the world beyond its national borders. This connection through trade did not arise spontaneously, however; government bureaucracy played an important role by facilitating foreign contacts and contracts. Excelling in a specific area was one of the ways in which a medium-sized power like the Netherlands advanced its interests in the highly competitive global trading environment.[19] The development and expansion of international air services, necessitating close cooperation between the national airline and the government in the exchange of commercial landing rights, provides a clear example of this.

As early as 1943, Minister of Foreign Affairs Eelco van Kleffens phrased the need for an active foreign policy to further Dutch interests abroad.[20] As part of the response to this call for an engaged foreign policy effort, KLM president Albert Plesman took the initiative in 1945 to bring KLM executives and senior civil servants from the Ministry of Foreign Affairs to the table with representatives from the Ministry of Traffic and Waterworks to coordinate Dutch international air transport policy. Remarkably, the model was not copied in other areas of foreign trade and it remained unique in the Dutch government organization. Although Foreign Affairs also acted on behalf of Dutch agriculture and industry, their development as export sectors took place with no organized interdepartmental coordination unless the issues at hand had immediate and clear political overtones.[21] In 1945, Van Kleffens supported the initiative, emphasizing the importance of distributing the minutes of the coordinating meetings to Dutch legations around the world to encourage the diplomatic corps to engage with the process.[22] Mirroring this flow of information, the Ministry of Foreign Affairs put KLM on the standard distribution list for departmental papers that might have some relevance to air transport. The airline was the only non-governmental institution to enjoy this status, a clear indication that air transport was not regarded as a normal economic activity but as an endeavor that reflected the Dutch place in the world. From October 1945 until 1997, the Civil Aviation Meeting (BLV: burgerluchtvaartvergadering) met periodically under the chairmanship of the Foreign Affairs' departmental traffic advisor (VADV: Verkeers Adviseur Directie Vervoer). As a bureau, VADV was a semi-separate entity within the Ministry of Foreign Affairs, with direct hierarchical links to the departmental leadership.

---

19 WRR, *Nederland Handelsland.*, p. 20, 90–93. WRR, *Aan het buitenland gehecht*, p. 63–64.

20 *Documenten Betreffende de Buitenlandse Politiek van Nederland,* Series C, 1940–1945, Vol. 7, nr. 217, p. 351–354.

21 Johan Schot, Dick van Lente, Techniek, industrialisatie en de betwiste modernisering van Nederland, in: *Techniek in Nederland*, Vol. 7 (Zutphen: Walburg Pers, 2003), p. 257–283.

22 Historical overview of BLV activity by VADV Siem Nieuwenhuijsen: Minutes 160th BLV, 23 June 1981: NNA, 2.05.330, Archive BZ, 1975–1984, inv.nr. 24345.

Convened by VADV, the Civil Aviation Meetings were routinely attended by KLM's top management, accompanied by experts from the airline's own Bureau of Foreign Relations and Cooperation. The meetings covered Dutch bilateral and multilateral aviation relations, and pending or planned negotiations worldwide. The minutes of the Civil Aviation Meetings thus form the backbone material for this book. Through the years, the agendas of these meetings reflected the current wish list regarding KLM landing rights. It was evident to all involved that KLM's pursuits were to be treated as synonymous with the Dutch national interest and that KLM's interests would determine government policy.

The third leg of this cooperation consisted of representatives of the Ministry of Transport and Waterworks (Verkeer en Waterstaat), which held the primary responsibility for all technical aspects of Dutch civil aviation. In January 1930 a specialist branch of the ministry was established, the Government Aviation Service (RLD: Rijksluchtvaartdienst), supervised by its own Director-General. The RLD, which was central to aviation policy-making until its dissolution in the year 2000, also had a bureau for political, legal and economic affairs and for international air transport policy. In the words of Jan van Arkel, the Foreign Affairs' traffic advisor in 1982, the collective effort that came out of the Civil Aviation Meetings was so strong that the cooperation could be called the 'Iron Triangle'.[23] This 'Iron Triangle' was instrumental for attaining success in international commercial aviation diplomacy.

Changes in this institutional setting began to occur towards the end of the 1980s. Reorganizations in the government bureaucracy resulted in the responsibilities of the Government Aviation Service's bureau for political, legal and economic affairs being merged and tasked with looking after the Dutch aviation infrastructures. This introduced environmental concerns, which had hitherto been treated as a separate issue, into the policy equation, to the detriment of international air transport policy. The three actors in the field that had for so many years operated in unison found that they were no longer bonded by the singular interest of a liberal, growth-oriented air transport policy.[24] The responsibilities for air transport policy also began to shift; the ongoing process of European integration meant that these increasingly came under the purview of the European Commission.[25]

The latter development originated in ongoing legal reviews of the clauses of the 1957 EEC Treaty by the European Commission and by the European Court

23 Minutes 161th BLV, 7 January 1982: NNA, 2.05.330, Archive BZ, 1975–1984, inv.nr. 24345.

24 Minutes special meeting of RLD, VADV and KLM, 22 December 1998: Archive BZ, VADV.

25 *Luchtvaart gebonden. Een institutioneel onderzoek op het terrein van de burgerluchtvaart, 1945–1993* (The Hague: Rijksarchiefdienst/PIVOT, 1994), p. 7–16.

of Justice. Interpreting the treaty, the Court ruled that its provisions on free trade among member states extended to air transport. This new interpretation coincided with views already held in Brussels. In response, in February 1986 the European Community member states adopted the Single European Act, which set as its objective the creation of a truly integrated European market by 31 December 1992. The Single European Act encompassed commercial aviation, providing the European Commission with the legal basis necessary to liberalize air transport within the Community. Three packages of policy measures followed, the first in December 1987, the second in November 1990, and the third package in June 1992. Together, these effectively opened up the field of European air transport to free competition between airlines from member states, creating a level playing field within the European Union.[26] The European air transport market was liberalized from 1 January 1993.[27] In lieu of national sovereignty, the defining principle behind the organization of international air services, a European rule book was put forward.

These developments changed the fundamentals of Dutch air transport policy. The Hague prepared for the new situation that would come into effect in 1993 by negotiating agreements with third countries that would solidify Dutch commercial air transportation rights for the foreseeable future, when negotiating such rights would come to reside under competence of the European Commission.[28] While negotiations with countries outside Europe continued, the primary role of the government bureaucracy in The Hague shifted after 1993 from diplomatic promotion and the provision of political and legal support for KLM to pursuing less clearly defined Dutch interests in (international) aviation, such as issues of finance and corporate investment. After several more years in which the government perception of aviation changed further and domestic issues received increasing attention in aviation policy, in 2000 the Government Aviation Service (RLD) was replaced by a new administrative framework that would be more attentive to developments within the Netherlands. This change occurred to the detriment of involvement in international affairs. Given the increased role of the European Commission, the Ministry of Foreign Affairs dissolved VADV in 2005. In the Dutch perception, commercial air transport had clearly shed the special status it had enjoyed from the early days of flight to become a regular international economic activity.

26 Jaqueline Dutheil de la Rochère, Contribution of the ECJ to the Implementation of the EEC Treaty in the field of Air Transport, Past and Future, in: Tanja L. Masson-Zwaan, Pablo Mendes de Leon. (eds), Air and Space Law: *De Lege Ferenda. Essays in Honour of Henri A. Wassenbergh* (Dordrecht: Martinus Nijhoff, 1992) p. 161–172.

27 For a legal treatment of developments, see: Mendes de Leon, *Introduction to Air Law*, p. 115–130.

28 Minutes 184th BLV, 3 March 1992: NNA, 2.05.392, Archive BZ, 1985–1990, inv.nr. 126.

To trace these developments over time, the text of this book has been divided into five chapters that reconstruct the story on the basis of archival records. These chapters each correspond to major disruptions in the international environment in which Dutch air transport operated. They also chart the geographic spread of Dutch air services across the globe, radiating from Europe to East Asia, China, Australia, the United States, Brazil and Argentina, and Southern Africa. Together, they create an impression of the challenges and obstacles Dutch negotiators encountered around the world. This organization of the text inevitably involved some hard choices in order to prevent the book from running aground on an abundance of foreign shores. Some significant files have thus been left for future researchers to peruse, for example those related to Japan, Israel and the changing status and position of the Netherlands Antilles and Surinam, all of which would have resulted in a much more voluminous book. Finally, one more thing needs to be noted: this is not a book on the development of the Dutch airline industry. For such works the reader is referred to the titles in the footnote.[29]

Chapter 1 details the period 1919 to 1945 and traces the origins of Dutch air transport policy and the way it became part of international diplomacy. In so doing, the focus moves from diplomatic efforts related to the establishment of scheduled air services to neighboring countries in Europe to take in the development of the all-important Dutch national air service to the Netherlands East Indies and then Australia. Early encounters with United States' aviation diplomacy, which would come to dominate the postwar diplomatic effort in the field, are also discussed. The chapter ends with the impact of the war on Dutch air transport and how this affected air transport diplomacy.

Chapter 2 limits itself to the immediate postwar years, when Dutch air transport policy was totally dominated by the political and military events unfolding in the Netherlands East Indies that culminated in the signing of a treaty recognizing Indonesia's independence in December 1949. This chapter also continues the story of Dutch airline diplomacy in Europe, especially the effects of the emerging Cold War. Widening its geographic scope, the chapter also considers in detail the consequences of Dutch policy in Indonesia for the development of air services to the United States, South America and South Africa.

29 Marc Dierikx, *Blauw in de lucht. Koninklijke Luchtvaart Maatschappij 1919–1999* (Den Haag: Sdu, 1999)–English summary: *Blue in the Sky. KLM Royal Dutch Airlines 1919–1999* (The Hague: Sdu Publishers, 2000) – and Bram Bouwens, Frido Ogier, *Welcome Aboard! 100 years of KLM Royal Dutch Airlines* (Zwolle: WBooks, 2020). For a more journalistic account: Ties Joosten, *De Blauwe Fabel. Waarom we de KLM al een eeuw lang tegen elke prijs in de lucht houden* (Amsterdam: Follow the Money, 2022).

Chapter 3 encompasses the period from 1950 to the international Oil Crisis of 1973. Taking political developments in European aviation as a starting point, it examines the diplomacy involved in Dutch efforts to expand KLM's position in Europe, including air services that reached across the Iron Curtain. From here, attention shifts to pick up the ongoing story of the Dutch air transport relations with Indonesia and with Australia. Against this background, initial discussions on air services to the People's Republic of China are also examined before moving on to the negotiations regarding transatlantic services to the United States and to South America. Finally, attention turns to continue the story of Dutch air transport diplomacy in Southern Africa.

International developments in the 1970s and 1980s, the topic of chapter 4, were significantly influenced by emerging new, non-regulatory ideas regarding the relations between governments and the airline industry. Originating in the United States in the mid-1970s, new notions on stimulating competition among airlines found their way into European thinking in the years that followed. This had major consequences for Dutch air transport diplomacy in Europe when the Iron Curtain fell, towards the end of 1989. Suddenly a new European market came into existence, offering all sorts of challenges and opportunities. The feeder traffic for KLM's long-haul operations to China, Indonesia and Australia and across the Atlantic to the United States and South America expanded rapidly. Nonetheless, the diplomacy regarding these air services operations remained fraught with difficulties.

The fifth chapter then considers how the post-Cold War world that emerged from the political developments of 1989 influenced ideas on competition and liberalization, and how this process has affected Dutch air transport policy. First and foremost, these changes not only had a major impact on the organization and operation of the internal air transport market in the European Union, but also affected services and agreements between the European Union and the countries discussed in the earlier chapters.

The book's concluding chapter brings the various developments reviewed together, focusing in particular on the challenges and problems a small nation like the Netherlands encountered in its diplomatic efforts to promote and strengthen its international position by supporting the development of scheduled air services from its territory.

Acknowledgements

This book could – and would – not have been written without the endeavors of Jean Petit, former adjunct transport advisor (Plv. VADV, in the departmental parlance) at the Ministry of Foreign Affairs in The Hague. Throughout his involvement in Dutch international air transport policy, and continuing after his retirement, Jean has accumulated an absolutely impressive collection of photocopied policy documents, far more than was needed for this book. Indeed, his collection is so extensive that it would keep a researcher occupied for a decade simply to read the material in its entirety. I cannot thank Jean enough for his generosity in sharing the fruits of his endeavors, and am proud to share co-authorship of this book with him.

Others have also generously assigned time and expertise. I am indebted to the thoughtful comments of my British colleague Alan Dobson, honorary professor at Swansea University, a renowned specialist in the history of international air transport politics, and above all a good friend. Sadly, Alan passed away in 2022 and did not see this book completed.

I am much indebted to emeritus professor Pablo Mendes de Leon of the International Institute of Air and Space Law at Leiden University. Pablo was kind enough to offer his expertise and comment on the text. Having read the book, I wonder if he will agree with his famous predecessor Daniël Goedhuis that 'international aviation relations take place in an atmosphere of conflicting interests and incompatible aspirations, above which no law extends.'[1]

I would also like to devote a special word of thanks to Peter van Fenema, adjunct professor of law at the Institute of Air and Space Law, McGill University, Montreal. Peter read several of the draft chapters and I owe much to his comments, suggestions, legal insights and expertise. Peter came to KLM Royal Dutch Airlines in 1973. For the better part of twenty-five years, he was active in the field of negotiating bilateral air transport agreements, rising to become Vice President of Foreign Relations and Cooperation between 1990 and 1997.

At the Directorate-General for Aviation and Maritime Affairs of the Ministry of Infrastructure and Water Management, senior policy advisor Jeroen Mauritz took time from his busy agenda to read chapter 5 of this book, and offered helpful comments.

1 Quote Goedhuis from the text of his *Dies* speech at Leiden University, February 1953, *in:* Marc Dierikx, Frappez toujours. De diplomaat en het luchtvervoer, in: Bob de Graaff, Duco Hellema, *Instrumenten van buitenlandse politiek. Achtergronden en praktijk van de Nederlandse diplomatie* (Amsterdam: Boom, 2007), p.77. Translation by the author.

Others also advised on the text. At Groningen University Hans Meijer explained some of the intricacies to do with KLM's role in Garuda in the 1950s, and Emile van Konijnenburg's efforts in restoring KLM landing rights in Jakarta in 1963. I also owe thanks to my colleagues of the research group on Political Culture and History at the Huygens Institute of the Royal Netherlands Academy of Arts and Sciences KNAW to read and comment on earlier drafts of various chapters. At the Ministry of Foreign Affairs Bert van der Zwan read and commented on the draft of this book. Hans den Hollander and Harold Zee guided me through the various procedures for access to archival records. Foreign Affairs' in-house historian Cees Heere steered me through the procedure to get the Ministry's permission to publish this text where it is based on sources that are not yet open to the public. KLM's corporate archivist Dick Jansen kindly arranged permission to reproduce the map that features on the cover. My contact at Brill Publishers in Leiden, Alessandra Giliberto, made sure I kept on track to produce this book. She also engaged the expertise of three anonymous reviewers. I am much indebted to their thoughtful comments, suggestions and advice on the draft text. The final result has definitely benefitted from their insights. The clarity and consistency of the text has gained significantly by the efforts of my trusted editor Jan Szechi from New Mills in the United Kingdom.

Since the first discussions about a joint project that Jean Petit and I had in 2015 it has taken several sequences of *holding patterns* to find the time to write this book. Unavoidably, various other projects and duties in academia had to take priority, but 35 years after my dissertation on the origins of Dutch air diplomacy, completing the present project does provide a sense of closure.

Marc Dierikx

Abbreviations

ABC	Advanced Booking Charter
Alitalia	Aerolinee Italiane Internazionali (IT)
AOA	American Overseas Airlines (USA)
APEX	Advanced Passenger Excursion fare
ASEAN	Association of South East Asian Nations
AT&T	Air Transport & Travel (UK)
BA	British Airways (UK)
BEA	British European Airways (UK)
BLV	Burgerluchtvaartvergadering (Civil Aviation Meeting – NL)
BOAC	British Overseas Airways Corporation (UK)
BWI	Baltimore-Washington International airport (USA)
CAAC	Civil Aviation Administration of China (CN)
CAB	Civil Aeronautics Board (USA)
CAL	China Air Lines (Taiwan)
CEO	Chief Executive Officer
CERNAI	Comissão de Estudos Relativos à Navegação Aérea Internacional (BR)
CIS	Commonwealth of Independent States (ex-USSR)
CMA	Compagnie des Messageries Aérienne (F)
CNAC	China National Aviation Corporation (CN)
ČSA	Československé Státní Aerolinie (CZ)
DEZ	Directie Economische Zaken (Directorate of Economic Affairs – NL)
DLH	Deutsche Luft Hansa (D)
DLR	Deutsche Luft Reederei (D)
EAC	East African Community
EASCO	East African Common Services Organization
ECAC	European Civil Aviation Conference
ECSC	European Coal and Steel Community
EEC	European Economic Community
EU	European Union
FAMA	Flota Aérea Mercante Argentina (ARG)
FRG	Federal Republic of Germany (West Germany)
GDR	German Democratic Republic (East Germany)
HEES	Helliniki Eteria Enaerion Synghinonion (GR)
IA	Imperial Airways (UK)
IATA	International Air Traffic Association / International Air Transport Association
ICAO	International Civil Aviation Organization (UN)
IGGI	Inter-Governmental Group on Indonesia

JAL	Japan Air Lines (JP)
JAA	Japan Asia Airlines (JP)
KLM	Koninklijke Luchtvaart Maatschappij (Royal Dutch Airlines)
KNILM	Koninklijke Nederlandsch-Indische Luchtvaart Maatschappij (Royal Netherlands-Indies Airlines)
KPM	Koninklijke Paketvaart Maatschappij (NL)
MCA	Ministry of Civil Aviation (UK)
NATO	North Atlantic Treaty Organization
NGAT	Netherlands Government Air Transport (NL)
NLM	Nederlandse Luchtvaart Maatschappij (KLM subsidiary – NL)
NWA	Northwest Airlines (USA)
OEEC	Organization for European Economic Cooperation
OPEC	Organization of Petroleum Exporting Countries
PanAm	Pan American Airways (USA)
PRC	People's Republic of China
QANTAS	Queensland and Northern Territories Air Services (AUS)
QEA	Qantas Empire Airways (UK / AUS)
RAAF	Royal Australian Air Force (AUS)
RAF	Royal Air Force (UK)
RDM	Rotterdamsche Droogdok Maatschappij (NL)
RLD	Rijks Luchtvaart Dienst (Government Aviation Service – NL)
RSV	Rijn-Schelde Verolme (NL)
SAA	South African Airways (ZA)
SABENA	Société Anonyme Belge d'Exploitation de la Navigation Aérienne (B)
SARS	Severe Acute Respiratory Syndrome
SAS	Scandinavian Airlines System
SNETA	Société Nationale pour l'Etude des Transports Aériens (B)
TAI	Transports Aériens Intercontinentaux (F)
TAM	Transportes Aéreos Meridionais (BR)
TAP	Transportes Aéreos Portugueses (P)
TWA	Trans World Airlines (USA)
UN	United Nations Organization
US-BIAS	United States Airports for Better International Air Services (USA)
USSR	Union of Soviet Socialist Republics (Russia)
VADV	Verkeers Adviseur Directie Vervoer (Foreign Affairs Transport Advisor – NL)
VARIG	Viação Aérea Rio Grandense (BR)
VASP	Viação Aérea São Paulo (BR)

CHAPTER 1

1919–1945: Aviation Policy in the Making

1 Introduction

Benevolently, the 'Koninklijke Luchtvaart Maatschappij voor Nederland en Koloniën' [KLM: Royal Aviation Company for the Netherlands and its Colonies] from The Hague had assured me a place in their airplane, which maintains a daily service between Amsterdam and London. And so we raced in the car of the 'Air Express' through the low polders to the 'Schiphol' aerodrome, from where the machines depart. 'You are out of luck', one of the company's representatives said in the car. 'It's rather cloudy today. In clear weather it is much more interesting'. I can't judge that, because I've only flown in cloudy skies, but it is impossible to imagine that it might be even more interesting than it has been. Let me confess right away: I had high expectations, but they have been far exceeded by reality. It has become the greatest sensation I remember ever experiencing. Everything about such a journey is under the aegis of the speed. The car ride to Schiphol aerodrome was a frenzy. Trees, farms, meadows, everything flashed past. The road itself leaped up, dashed right under us, was devoured by the roaring car. At the aerodrome, you jump out. Your passport and luggage are checked quickly, and then you find yourself with the friendly manager in his office. You get a flying cap, dust (or storm) glasses, a long coat and leather gloves. Then they put a life jacket on you … and a few seconds later they sit you in your small, padded seat, which you won't leave until you land at Croydon, near London … in a few hours … A couple of mechanics jump from the wings to the ground right in front of you, you press someone's hand, who, smiling, wishes you a 'good trip'. The engine starts in a deafening roar, the propeller becomes invisible and suddenly the machine rolls, bumps and jolts over the unevenness of the terrain. Faster and faster it goes, the engine bellows louder, like a shimmer you see horses in a neighboring pasture run away, tails in the air and heads low to the ground, then the machine jumps up, gently touches the ground again once, twice, and then reality ends and the dream begins …[1]

1 De J., 'Per vliegtuig naar Londen' [To London by plane], in: *Het volk: Dagblad voor de Arbeiderspartij*, 29 July 1920. Translation by the author.

 | DOI:10.1163/9789004695245_002

After the war ended in November 1918 it was an appealing thought to many that the technology of flight would come to manifest itself as a force for the good that would bring people and countries together. The idea was that aviation might generate a new sense of linkage between nations united by a common air medium. An alluring vista, although the realities of international politics pointed in a different direction. For the big powers in the world the return to peace was, first of all, an opportunity to re-establish themselves politically. The Peace Conference at Versailles offered the setting for this. Britain and France used the opportunities that victory on the battlefield delivered to re-draw European borders and to exert themselves as colonial empires. To the east Russia engulfed itself in a civil war that led to a complete restructuring of its society and an exit from international relations. In Central Europe new nations rose from the rubble of four years of conflict. Between 1918 and the mid-1920s Europe went from 19 to 28 countries, bringing new sovereign borders to respect. Much of this development was at the cost of the defeated Central Powers, particularly Austria-Hungary, which lost over 60 per cent of its prewar territory. Germany was forced to part with around 13 per cent, plus all of its colonial possessions. The German army and navy were cut drastically and the production of warplanes was forbidden. Forced reparations left the country destitute, struggling with the economic effects of the peace. Not only in Germany, but in France and all over Europe protectionist tariffs went up to the detriment of international trade, an unfavorable development for liberally oriented nations such as the Netherlands.[2]

The victors Britain and France withdrew in part from European politics and focused instead on their respective overseas territories. Aviation played no small role in this. The British became front-runners in pioneering air power as a new means to control their vast empire. The Royal Air Force (RAF) built airfields and landing strips throughout Africa and Asia to enable aerial operations in support of the colonial status quo. Throughout the 1920s aircraft were a cost-effective way to exert power, even partially replacing ground troops.[3] The French employed a similar strategy in North Africa. Postwar developments at home and in the colonies meant that communication with overseas territories rapidly became more important.

2 James Foreman-Peck, *A History of the World Economy. International Relations Since 1850* (New York: Harvester Wheatsheaf, 1995), p. 175–207. Hein Klemann, Een handelsnatie in de twintigste eeuw, in: Bob de Graaff, Duco Hellema, Bert van der Zwan (eds.), *De Nederlandse buitenlandse politiek in de twintigste eeuw* (Amsterdam: Boom, 2003), p. 105–129.

3 David E. Omissi, *Air Power and Colonial Control. The Royal Air Force, 1919–1939* (Manchester: MUP, 1990), p. 52–59.

Sailing by their traditional compass of detachment, the Netherlands steered away from the larger political processes in Europe, seeking refuge instead in developing stronger ties with the neutral Scandinavian countries and Switzerland. Having kept to the middle ground in the war, Dutch foreign policy found itself in a tight spot after 1918 as diplomats struggled to align pro-German and pro-British sentiments. In terms of trade, Britain and Germany were more or less of equal importance for the Netherlands, each accounting for about a quarter of Dutch imports and exports.[4] The Netherlands' geographical position meant that these trade flows continued throughout the interwar period, despite the declining share of trade in European national incomes during the 1920s. Because economic relations were becoming increasingly important for Dutch foreign policy, the Ministry of Foreign Affairs was expanded, with a new section dealing specifically with economic affairs. Overseeing international trade was no easy matter. Traditionally, Dutch diplomats had stayed away from economic issues, preferring instead to focus on legal questions. But in the interest of expanding trade, change was now called for. Starting in 1919, the Ministry of Foreign Affairs, not the strongest of government departments to begin with, went through a process of reorganization. This was initiated by Minister Herman van Karnebeek, who sought to end the habitual passivity that had characterized the Dutch diplomatic service in favor of a more proactive attitude.[5] One of the prime issues that a more proactive diplomacy needed to focus on was aviation.

The return to peacetime conditions at the end of 1918 had brought several questions about aviation to the fore, particularly how to ensure that foreign aircraft would not present a threat to the territorial integrity of the state flown over, and how to provide for international safety standards to protect aircraft passengers and people on the ground. The world war that had just ended had led to aerial bombardments of French, British and German cities, causing many European countries to prioritize the principle of national sovereignty in the skies, as had been proposed at a conference of legal specialists in Paris in 1910. The idea had quickly been accepted in The Netherlands, supported by the

4 Hein Klemann, The 'Tommies' or the 'Jerries': Dutch Trade Problems in the Inter-War Period, in: Nigel John Ashton, Duco Hellema (eds.), *Unspoken Allies: Anglo-Dutch Relations Since 1780* (Amsterdam: AUP, 2001), p. 101–120. Hein Klemann, Een handelsnatie in de twintigste eeuw, in: De Graaff, Hellema, Van der Zwan (eds.), *De Nederlandse buitenlandse politiek in de twintigste eeuw*,, p. 105–129 (107–109).

5 Albert Kersten, Een woud van verandering. Ontwikkeling van taak en organisatie van het ministerie, in: R.E. van Ditzhuyzen, A.E. Kersten, A.L.M. van Zeeland, A.C. van der Zwan (eds.), *Tweehonderd jaar Ministerie van Buitenlandse Zaken* (Den Haag: Sdu, 1998), p. 62–65.

Dutch scholar Jenny Lycklama à Nijeholt.[6] Sovereignty necessitated national legislation as well as an international regime to govern activities in the air. In the wake of the peace negotiations in Versailles an international conference was called in March 1919 to deal with these issues.

For six months, delegations debated the outline of a legal regime for international civil aviation. Participants needed to bridge serious differences between the British and French approaches, with London pressing for a framework that would serve future air services to colonial outposts, while Paris prioritized safeguards that the air would not be used for attack from above. This difference was reflected in the treaty that resulted from the talks. The starting point, article 1, enshrined the absolute and unrestricted sovereignty of each ground state in the air column above its territory. In contrast, Article 2 contained a clause supporting the peaceful passage of aircraft, although this was subordinate to the principle of sovereignty. Connecting these two provisions, article 15 of the treaty opened up the possibility of allowing individual international flights. However, the establishment of scheduled air services would require prior authorization from the states flown over (article 15, section 3). On 13 October 1919, the delegates present committed themselves to a treaty, the Paris Convention.[7]

Several of the provisions of the Convention caused additional problems. For example, Article 5 stipulated that Member States would not allow non-Treaty-State aircraft into their airspace, unless by singular and temporary exception. This was a French demand to create an instrument to keep German aircraft out – a punishment for the vanquished.

As a neutral country, the Netherlands did not take part in the negotiations on the treaty as it had such obvious links with the outcome of the war. Continuing its middle course between German, British and French interests, Dutch foreign policy aimed at remaining aloof. Thinking was that the convention's clauses would infringe on Dutch sovereignty and neutrality. Besides, the widespread recognition in government circles of the concept of 'passive neutrality' precluded acceding to the treaty.[8] This placed the Netherlands and its newly

6 J.F. Lycklama à Nijeholt, *Air Sovereignty* (The Hague: Martinus Nijhoff, 1910). I.H.Ph. Diederiks-Verschoor, Dr. J.F. Lycklama à Nijeholt (1876–1947), in: *Air & Space Law*, Vol. XIX, 1994, nr.1, p. 8–9.

7 Albert Roper, *La Convention Internationale du 13 Octobre 1919 portant Réglementation de la Navigation Aérienne. Son Origine, son application, son avenir* (Paris: Recueil Sirey, 1930). For a concise treatment of the convention, see: Pablo Mendes de Leon, *Introduction to Air Law* [11th edition] (Alphen aan den Rijn: Kluwer Law International, 2022), p. 8.

8 Duco Hellema, *Nederland in de wereld. Buitenlandse politiek van Nederland* (Utrecht: Het Spectrum, 2016), p. 79–81.

established airline, KLM, outside the scope of the treaty's provisions. The question then arose as to what, if any, penalties non-adherence to the convention would have for international flights from the Netherlands: would these even be possible and would Dutch aircraft be admitted into the airspace of the Contracting States? It was not until 1 May 1920 that the signatories provided clarity. A conference of the Treaty States agreed on a protocol in which aircraft from non-member states would henceforth be welcome on a basis of other than singular temporary exceptions.[9] Nonetheless, a prior bilateral agreement would be required for a license to fly.

In 1920, being transported by air was a new and unprecedented sensation, reserved for those few who were wealthy and brave enough to board a plane. An air trip stood for adventure and was not without risk. Passengers were mostly businessmen with a full agenda and a 'sense of modern times' and affluent tourists looking for a unique new experience. If they wished, they could receive a signed statement from the pilot to prove that they had actually flown. That air services from the Netherlands would exist was special, given the Dutch refusal to adhere to the convention. In The Hague, investors sought to be part of the new transport mode. The case was special at a time in which no more than a dozen airlines existed in the world. Airline companies were set up with money from visionary businessmen and investors who saw a new market for international travel by air.

Coming so soon after a devastating war, air services aroused interest and the press followed developments closely. In the first year of peace, more than 1,000 newspaper articles about the new transport mode appeared in the Netherlands and its overseas territories. Roaring headlines like 'The Flying Future', 'World Air Traffic', and 'Across the Atlantic' were common.[10] In the Dutch East Indies, Governor-General Johan van Limburg Stirum promised 10,000 guilders for the first Dutch pilot to fly from the Netherlands to Java before 1 September 1920, which he believed could be done within 14 days.[11] The call appeared in the newspapers on 7 October 1919, the day that a select group of investors gathered in The Hague at the office of notary Hendrik Stoop to sign the founding papers of the Royal Aviation Company for the Netherlands and its Colonies (Koninklijke Luchtvaart Maatschappij voor Nederland en Koloniën), KLM

9 'Gemengde berichten' [Mixed news], in: *Het Vliegveld* 4(1920) nr. 14, 240. Also: Roper, *La Convention Internationale*, p. 63.

10 'De vliegende toekomst', in: *Sumatra Post*, 4 Jan. 1919. 'Het wereld-luchtverkeer', in: *De Telegraaf*, 8 Jan. 1919, 'Over den Atlantischen Oceaan', in: *Algemeen Handelsblad*, 14 June 1919.

11 'Luchtverkeer Nederland-Java', in: *De Tijd*, 7 Oct. 1919.

for short. The list of signatories represented a roll-call of the country's prime investment bankers and financial entrepreneurs. They ensured that the predicate 'royal' was granted prior to the company's actual foundation. The idea was that this epitaph would make the new enterprise exude reliability. Although preparations had been going on for more than six months, the signing of the foundation documents was hardly a newsworthy event.[12] The newspapers did not report on it until three weeks later.[13] The company's investors put up an initial sum of 1,015,000 guilders. Total share issue was set at a maximum of 5.1 million guilders.[14] It was a considerable sum at the time. Taking into account the prospects, it was clear from the outset that there would be no money to be made in the short term.

How to become remunerative was foremost in the minds of the three person staff at the small KLM office located above the Odeon Theatre in The Hague. Finding an answer was not easy. In the weeks after its creation, the fledgling company tried selling short air tours from its hangar tent at the Maaldrift airstrip north of town, but without much success. Clearly, this was not the way to go forward and the board of the company started developing other plans. Although admitting that there was not a single aerodrome in Holland suitable for scheduled flying, they hoped to participate in an air link to connect London and Copenhagen, via The Hague and Hamburg.[15] The envisaged route reflected Dutch trading interests in Europe at the time. Participating in the air service was costly, which was why KLM's founders joined the International Air Traffic Association (IATA), a cooperative venture between early air transport companies. IATA had been established in The Hague just two months earlier, on 25 August 1919, an initiative of George Holt Thomas, the director of Britain's Air Transport & Travel Ltd. (AT&T). In addition to AT&T, the initial circle of members was comprised of Det Danske Luftfartselskab, Svenska Lufttrafik Aktiebolaget, and KLM, then still in the process of formation. Together, they hoped to bring a new form of transport to Europe, and at the same time regulate future competition.

It was at this point, seven months after KLM's founding, that the Netherlands sought to become an active participant in international air transport. The first service, jointly operated by AT&T and KLM, was between London and

12 Ariëtte Dekker, *Leven op krediet: Anton Kröller, 1862–1941* (Amsterdam: Prometheus, 2015), p. 384–386.

13 *Algemeen Handelsblad*, 28 Oct. 1919.

14 Official Notary Act of the founding of Koninklijke Luchtvaart Maatschappij voor Nederland en Koloniën, 7 Oct. 1919: KLM Archive, Amstelveen, Corporate Documents (Algemeen Secretariaat, 05–01–01–01).

15 *Dagblad van Zuid-Holland en 's-Gravenhage*, 13 Nov. 1919.

Amsterdam. As KLM had no aircraft of its own, the company depended on AT&T to fly. At 10 a.m. on 17 May 1920, a de Havilland biplane took off from London's Croydon Airport with two journalists aboard and about a hundred kilos of that morning's newspapers.[16] The Friday before, KLM's young administrator Albert Plesman had announced this inaugural flight at a small press conference. At 12:40 p.m., the machine landed at Schiphol aerodrome near Amsterdam. Once on the ground, the two passengers – a third had arrived late and missed the flight – clambered out of the plane, limbs stiff from the long cold sojourn on uncomfortable seats.[17] They were met by a delegation of dignitaries led by the director of the Dutch state-owned Postal Services and Telegraph Company, Evert Westerveld. It was he who sponsored the service with a contract for the carriage of mail and provided the financial backbone of the operation. For the Netherlands, the great future of air transport had arrived, although very few passengers came forward, averaging less than two on a normal flying day. In its first year, KLM carried only 345 passengers, despite expensive advertising campaigns.[18]

Although the Netherlands had now become part of the nascent network of European air services, the government took a long time to relate to the Paris Convention. It was only on 22 August 1928 that The Hague ratified the treaty, after the anti-German clauses in article 5 had been toned down.[19] Part of the Dutch reluctance resided in the absence of an Aviation Act. KLM's early services remained without a national legal basis until the act was finally passed in July 1926 and entered into effect in February 1929.[20] Moreover, the government ruled that the absence of an Aviation Act precluded bilateral agreements in the field. This underlined the exceptional status of Dutch aviation in Europe.

Dutch government bureaucracy added to this problem. In The Hague, international aviation was regarded through a legalistic lens with officials arguing that neutrality precluded joining the Paris Convention. Added impediments

---

16 *The Times* (London), Tuesday, 18 May 1920; p. 14.

17 *Nieuwe Rotterdamsche Courant* (NRC), 17 May 1920.

18 Marc Dierikx, *Blauw in de lucht. Koninklijke Luchtvaart Maatschappij 1919–1999* (Den Haag: Sdu, 1999), p. 22–24.

19 *Staatsblad* nr. 226 of 1928. Letter F. Beelaerts van Blokland re. Treaty Ratification, 28 Nov. 1928: Netherlands National Archive (NNA), 2.05.37, Archive Ministry of Foreign Affairs, 1919–1940, inv.nr. 4323.

20 Marc Dierikx, *Begrensde Horizonten. De internationale burgerluchtvaartpolitiek van Nederland in het interbellum* (Zwolle: Tjeenk Willink, 1988), p. 44–70. Marc Dierikx, Hoofd in de wolken of benen op de grond? De ontwikkeling van het toezicht op de luchtvaart, in: *150 jaar toezicht Verkeer en Waterstaat. Rampen, wetten en inspectiediensten* (Den Haag: Sdu, 2004), p. 67–115.

were the mentality and outlook of the civil servants in charge. The primary responsibility for civil aviation resided with the Ministry of Water Management, a government department with an extensive set of existing responsibilities, including the supervision of dikes along major rivers; the construction and maintenance of canals; the regulation of inland shipping; the management and maintenance of sea barriers and ports; controlling land reclamation, dike construction and peat extraction; and the building and maintenance of roads.[21] Within this broad set of tasks, aviation was a new topic in which there was no expertise in 1920. For the first ten years of civil air transport, responsibilities resided with a handful of employees in the department's tiny Aviation Bureau, led by former navy lieutenant Emile de Veer, who had run the administration of the Navy Air Arm (Marine Luchtvaart Dienst). De Veer was a formalistic man, an insecure official who needed considerable time to develop and implement policy. In spite of this, the tasks and responsibilities of the Aviation Bureau developed fast, determined by the rapidly changing technology of flight, issues such as public safety around airports, radio communications, meteorology and the distribution of messages to aviators, and the medical aspects of flying. In 1930, the organizational structure was reinforced by the formation of a dedicated civil service branch, the Aviation Service (Luchtvaartdienst). It was a modest set-up, with a staff of fifteen. De Veer became its first director.

It would have been logical to develop policies on the international aspects of aviation in cooperation with the Ministry of Foreign Affairs, but in everyday practice contacts between the two government departments were weak. Added to this was the circumstance that the Foreign Ministry's new Directorate of Economic Affairs (DEZ) needed time to develop its own working procedures. DEZ's primary task was the wider field of Dutch international economic contacts and it took a long time to appreciate the urgency of regulating aviation.[22] More than a few issues were not dealt with at all. This was not entirely surprising. Appointed in 1921, the head of DEZ, the economist Johan Nederbragt, was an advocate of the legalistic approach to foreign affairs and agreed with De Veer at the Ministry of Water Management's Aviation Bureau that the absence of an Aviation Act precluded the conclusion of aviation agreements, including provisional ones.[23] Added to this mental outlook, was a problem of

21 NNA, 2.16.05, Inventory Archive Ministry of Water Management [Waterstaat]: Waterstaat A, 1906–1929 (Den Haag: Nationaal Archief, 1979), p. 5.

22 Albert Kersten, Een woud van verandering. Ontwikkeling van taak en organisatie van het ministerie, in: Van Ditzhuyzen, Kersten, Van Zeeland, Van der Zwan (eds.), *Tweehonderd jaar Ministerie van Buitenlandse Zaken*, p. 62–65.

23 Letter König to Van Karnebeek, 22 Apr. 1921: NNA, 2.05.37, Archive Ministry of Foreign Affairs, inv.nr. 4281.

staffing, as it was 1927 before Nederbragt's small unit expanded and the young lawyer Peter Witte was brought in to oversee the aviation portfolio. Contrary to expectations, this staff increase had no impact on air transport policy. Like Nederbragt, Witte excelled in finding legalistic impediments that prevented taking action, even on files that urgently required it.

2 Setting up Air Services in Europe

The inaction on the part of the government meant that the few international services that KLM operated were all based on provisional arrangements. First and foremost was the service to London. A temporary aviation arrangement was discussed as early as July 1919 to allow British aircraft to take part in Amsterdam's major civil air traffic exhibition, the ELTA, which was held in August and September of that year. Informal consultations resulted in a verbal agreement under which British aircraft were allowed to fly over Dutch soil to participate in the month-long airshow.

With an eye on future developments, on 30 August 1919 the British envoy in The Hague, Arnold Robertson, proposed putting this verbal arrangement into writing. This might then form the basis for future scheduled air services between London and Amsterdam.[24] Given the absence of an Aviation Act, The Hague found it impossible to formulate a reply, however, and no formal agreement ensued. Nonetheless, AT&T and KLM started their provisional air service on 17 May 1920. This prompted London to come up with a new, more formal proposal for a bilateral air transport agreement, as intended in the Paris Convention.[25] In The Hague, Water Management and Foreign Affairs needed six months to formulate a noncommittal response in which they referred to the unresolved status of the Dutch Aviation Act as a reason to remain idle.[26] The British initiatives therefore led to naught, which was surprising given that KLM had been vainly knocking on government doors with requests for subsidies since April 1920, before the air service to London had even started.[27] As far as international arrangements were concerned, The Hague remained passive.

24 Letter Robertsen to Van Karnebeek, dd. 27 Oct. 1919: NNA, 2.16.19.39, Archive Waterworks: Aviation Bureau (Waterstaat: Bureau Luchtvaart, (1911) 1920–1929), inv.nr. 1.

25 Provisional agreement relating to air navigation between Holland and Great Britain, undated (18 June 1920): art. 1 and 7: KLM Archive, series R-5.

26 Air Ministry report (by W.O. Raikes) re. Anglo-Dutch contacts over a bilateral air services agreement, 22 June 1922: NNA, 2.16.19.39, Waterworks, Aviation Bureau (1911) 1920–1929, inv.nr. 20.

27 Letter König to KLM, 24 Nov. 1920: KLM Archive, series R-502.

Customs arrangements were not dealt with before April 1921, when KLM came to an understanding with Britain on this.[28] Despite repeated British reminders, Dutch foot dragging meant that a bilateral air services arrangement could not be drawn up before July 1923; as long as London allowed operations to continue, the civil servants in The Hague sat on their hands.[29]

Meanwhile, KLM had also started issuing tickets for flights to Hamburg and Copenhagen. Like the air service to London, services to Hamburg were arranged on a provisional basis. The initial, informal agreement dated from 27 April 1920. The willingness of KLM to participate in operations to Hamburg must have pleased Foreign Minister Van Karnebeek, who was convinced of the importance of stimulating trade relations with Germany in the interest of economic recovery and reconstructing the prewar power balance in Europe. However, Allied measures under the Versailles Treaty made the legal status of air services to Germany uncertain. Versailles entailed the application of restrictions on German aviation, with German operators being excluded from air traffic to countries that adhered to the Paris Convention. For German companies, the only option open in the field of air transport was the organization of domestic services, and air links with neutral neighboring countries such as Denmark, the Netherlands and Switzerland. Berlin initially left the planning of services to the airlines themselves and preferred not to interfere.[30] This matched the view in The Hague that formal air transport agreements were to be avoided. In the absence of bilateral arrangements, the air service to Hamburg was organized on the basis of private contracts between the Deutsche Luft Reederei (DLR) and KLM. Facing considerable operational losses, KLM was happy it did not have to operate beyond Hamburg, where passengers transferred to a German plane. Mail and goods carried were also reloaded.[31]

In its first years of operations, KLM airplanes flew on only two routes, to London and Hamburg. Conditions were very basic. There was no reliable weather service and radio connections were completely absent. To navigate routes, pilots had to fly low and follow visible landmarks on the ground.[32]

---

28 Dierikx, *Begrensde Horizonten*, p. 65.

29 Draft Bill to endorse the provisional agreement with Britain [Ontwerp van wet tot goedkeuring van de op 11 juli 1923 te 1 s-Gravenhage getroffen voorloopige luchtvaartschikking tusschen Nederland en Groot-Brittannië en Ierland]: *Handelingen der Staten-Generaal* (HSG) 1923–1924, Bijlage 316, nr. 2.

30 Lutz Budrass, *Adler und Kranich. Die Lufthansa und ihre Geschichte 1926–1955* (München: Blessing, 2016), p. 19–82.

31 Dierikx, *Begrensde Horizonten*, p. 69–70.

32 Per Högselius, Arne Kaijser, Erik van der Vleuten, *Europe's Infrastructure Transition. Economy, War, Nature* (Basingstoke: Palgrave Macmillan, 2016), p. 331–333.

With subsidies that were insufficient to allow them to break even, finances remained in the red. It was a feeble basis for a business. Although a service to Paris, after London the most promising destination, could potentially improve turnover, this required international arrangements with Belgium and France, both of which strictly adhered to the Paris Convention. Hoping to initiate a service to Paris, KLM submitted a request for the overflight of French territory on 21 January 1921. However, France indicated that Article 5 of the Paris Convention precluded an agreement. KLM would be welcome only if the Netherlands signed the treaty.[33] This was a disappointing response. Left to its own devices, KLM tried to improve its chances for a permit and pointed out that the companies that had thus far actually operated the route, the French Compagnie des Messageries Aériennes (CMA) and the Belgian Syndicat National pour l'Etude des Transports Aériens (SNETA), were notoriously unreliable. Negating the issue of Dutch international aviation policy, KLM's acting director Albert Plesman claimed his company could do better.[34] In search of additional income, he urged both Water Management and Foreign Affairs to double their efforts to enable some form of operations on the Paris route.

On the face of it, the prospects for negotiating an easy arrangement with Belgium appeared unfavorable. Since the return of peace in 1918, bilateral relations with Belgium had been problematic. Belgium claimed various territories in the southern provinces of the Netherlands as compensation for alleged Dutch pro-German policies during the war and relations suffered as a consequence. However, aviation turned out to offer an exception. When an air service from Amsterdam via Brussels to Paris was first discussed in March 1921, the Belgians were cooperative and even proposed a provisional agreement that would give KLM freedom to fly over Belgian soil.[35] Typically, a Dutch response was not forthcoming and the pending status of the Aviation Act again prevented action. It was good news, therefore, that Brussels granted KLM a special license, regardless of the lack of progress on the diplomatic front. Parties looked for a settlement and The Hague was persuaded to sign a provisional accord on 8 July 1922.

This left a decision on the French case. KLM repeatedly tried to pressure its government into action, but to no avail. In a desperate attempt to force the

---

33 Letter French under-secretary for Aviation to the Dutch consul in Dunkirk, 10 March 1921: NNA, 2.05.37, Archive Ministry of Foreign Affairs, 1919–1940, inv.nr. 4345.

34 Letter Plesman to Minister of Waterworks, König, 1 July 1921: NNA, 2.16.19.39, Waterworks, Aviation Bureau, inv.nr. 3.

35 Letter Belgian envoy in The Hague, Albert, prince de Ligne, to Van Karnebeek, 26 March 1921: NNA, 2.05.37, Archive Ministry of Foreign Affairs, 1919–1940, inv.nr. 1723.

issue, Plesman sent one of KLM's Fokker F.III airliners, with passengers that had booked passage on CMA and SNETA, to Le Bourget Airport in Paris on 15 June 1921. The French protested against this flagrant breach of air sovereignty, but refrained from lodging a formal complaint.[36] Nonetheless, KLM's move had the desired effect: it prompted The Hague into action. The Ministry of Foreign Affairs decided that it would cooperate in establishing bilateral arrangements, as long as these were of an informal nature. On 8 July 1921, the date the accord with Belgium was signed, the Foreign Ministry instructed its envoys to take steps towards concluding provisional understandings on air services.

In keeping with the more active foreign policy advocated by Minister Van Karnebeek, the Dutch now also approached Berlin with a request for a formal bilateral settlement for air services. But if The Hague had been slow off the mark, the Germans were in even less of a hurry to strike a deal. Their diplomats were instead focusing on lifting the ban on international air services from Germany, then under discussion among the signatory states of the Paris Convention. It took until March 1922 before bilateral talks could even be scheduled. These resulted in a provisional settlement signed by Van Karnebeek and the German envoy Helmuth Lucius von Stoedten on 22 July. They agreed on the liberalization of air traffic between the two countries.[37]

There was also progress in the French case. A few weeks later a Dutch draft proposal arrived at the Quai d'Orsay in Paris. The Hague hoped that France would agree on complete freedom of passage for civil airliners on the route to Paris.[38] Indeed, the French sent a counter proposal with only minor textual changes, and generally appeared willing to go along with the Dutch draft. While The Hague took time to study the various documents, KLM managed to get permission to carry out incidental flights on the route, on behalf of CMA and SNETA. In June 1922, the Dutch started participating, with Brussels as final destination. KLM thus replaced SNETA, which had primarily been set up to gain experience and now ceased operations. A month later, Brussels and The Hague signed a provisional settlement covering the new set-up. It appeared in The Hague that the matter of the air service to Brussels and Paris was now 'in the bag'. As a result, all sense of urgency again evaporated. It took De Veers Aviation Bureau no less than eight months to advise Water Management's

36 Letter Eynac to Labouchère, 8 July 1921: NNA, 2.05.102, Netherlands Legation in Paris, inv. nr. 653.

37 Bilateral Aviation Agreement Netherlands-Germany, 24 July 1922: NNA, 2.16.5240, Government Aviation Service (Rijksluchtvaartdienst: RLD), inv.nr. 7337.

38 Projet d'accord provisoire concernant la navigation aérienne entre la France et les Pays-Bas, 12 Sept. 1921: NNA, 2.05.37 Archive Ministry of Foreign Affairs, 1919–1940, inv.nr. 1723.

Minister Adriaan König to agree to the French response, while the Ministry of Foreign Affairs also shrouded itself in silence. This proved fatal to a speedy conclusion of a deal, which, in the French view, hinged on a formal bilateral agreement. It was not until the end of January 1923, again under pressure from KLM, that progress was made. On 18 April 1923 a Franco-Dutch bilateral agreement finally entered into force. Six weeks later, and two and a half years after KLM's initial request to fly, the Dutch airline was able to start its own service to the French capital on 4 June 1923.[39]

Conditions for international air transport in Europe were changing. On 1 January 1923, Germany regained its air sovereignty from the Allies on the basis of the Treaty of Versailles. This was the precursor of a number of mergers in German air transport and of a stronger German air presence generally.[40] This was evidenced on 6 January 1926, when the two major German airlines, Junkers Luftverkehr and Deutsche Aero Lloyd, merged into a largely state-funded national carrier, Deutsche Luft Hansa (DLH). Four months later, on 21 May, Germany and France concluded a bilateral aviation agreement that put an end to the Allied restrictions on German aircraft construction. Germany was now free to develop its own aviation policy to put the country back on the air map and the government in Berlin became a major actor furthering German air transport. As a consequence, Deutsche Luft Hansa attained a significant role in European air traffic.[41]

Notwithstanding these developments, aviation relations between Germany and the Netherlands continued along the lines of the informal agreement of July 1922. Although the German operating rights for KLM were not secure, The Hague had been happy to bide its time. However, after the formation of Deutsche Luft Hansa, Berlin indicated that the moment had come to formalize arrangements. In The Hague, where inertia still prevailed, the matter was allowed to drift for years. Towards the end of 1927 Berlin made a renewed request to draw up a settlement, but although no major points remained to be resolved it was August 1928 before signatures could be exchanged.[42] Despite the institutional inertia at The Hague , by the end of the 1920s the Netherlands had signed air transport agreements with Belgium (in 1922), Britain and France

39 Telegram Loudon to Van Karnebeek, 17 Apr. 1923: NNA, 2.05.37, Archive Ministry of Foreign Affairs, 1919–1940, inv.nr. 4345.

40 Budras, *Adler und Kranich*, p. 101–102.

41 Letter Reichsverkehrsministerium (Wegerdt) to De Veer, 19 Dec. 1927: NNA, 2.16.5240, RLD, inv.nr. 7404.

42 Dierikx, *Begrensde Horizonten*, p. 70.

(in 1923), Poland, Norway, Switzerland and Sweden (all in 1926), Denmark (in 1927) and Germany (in 1928).

Changes in the air transport environment also came about as a result of technological and operational developments that made aircraft more reliable. The length of the air network increased. The Netherlands was a case in point. Although KLM's founders had assumed that the airline would one day offer flights to the Netherlands East Indies, this remained far beyond the horizon in the first years of operations. There were simply no aircraft in existence capable of safely operating scheduled flights across continents. At the root of the problem was the lack of reliable aircraft engines. In 1924, KLM still prided itself in the fact that 'only 33 percent' of the flights announced in the airline's winter schedule had been cancelled.[43]

In Holland the engine problem was highlighted later that year when the first trial flight to the Dutch East Indies experienced engine trouble over Bulgaria, resulting in an emergency landing. A new power plant had to be brought in from the Netherlands by train and horse cart. Including repairs, the airplane took 54 days to reach its destination. In the mid-1920s, however, new air cooled aircraft engines came onto the market that proved better suited to tropical conditions. As a result, reliability increased. In the mid-1920s the Netherlands own aircraft producer, Fokker, was working on the development of multi-engine airliners, which again contributed to greater reliability.

Proof of this was provided by two flights to the Dutch East Indies undertaken in 1927. In June, American millionaire Van Lear Black, owner of the Baltimore Sun newspaper, chartered a KLM plane for a very special travel adventure: a return flight to Batavia, capital of the Dutch East Indies. The endeavor was organized at very short notice and hinged on British cooperation. As this was a singular charter flight, under private contract, diplomatic arrangements between governments were deemed unnecessary. Practically no formal paperwork was drawn up to ensure the smooth operation of the flight. On 15 June KLM's Fokker F.VIIA airliner departed from Amsterdam's Schiphol Airport, after no more than two weeks of preparation. The risks taken were enormous. But seven years into operations, KLM, like all other early airlines, had so far only incurred losses. Subsidies averted the worst, but deficits had increased over the years, paralleling the expansion of KLM's network. In The Hague doubts against the airline's financial policy were on the rise. By 1927 the string of red figures had brought KLM to the verge of bankruptcy, since government money covered only part of the losses and immediate collapse loomed.

43 Minutes 75th meeting of delegates from the KLM Board of Directors, 15 Febr. 1924: KLM Archive, series R-5.

KLM's management gambled that a favorable outcome of the charter flight to Batavia might contribute to a continuation of subsidy that was vital for the airline's survival.[44] To the immense relief of KLM's management, the aircraft, crew and passengers completed the return flight without major incidents and arrived back in Amsterdam safe and sound on 23 July. This led to a deluge of news coverage – more than 1,500 newspaper articles – and an exuberant public reception at Schiphol Airport. This public acclaim ensured the continuation of KLM's subsidy.

Two and a half months later the Dutch undertook a second return flight, this time with mail on board. The aircraft, the three-engine version of the Fokker F.VIIA airliner, was appropriately christened *Postduif* [Carrier Pigeon]. The flight was intended to test the waters for a scheduled postal air service to the Dutch East Indies. To the dismay of Britain's colonial authorities, the plane made mail deliveries at various points in India. This had not been discussed or agreed to previously. Both London and Delhi were not amused to see a foreign plane be the first to deliver airmail to destinations along the route in British India. At KLM, on the other hand, the flights brought reason for celebration: in order to promote a national air route to Batavia, the government drew up a multi-year subsidy agreement. Now that the technical feasibility of the service had been proven, The Hague set out to develop a more active policy in the field of landing rights.

3 Negotiating the Air Route to the Dutch East Indies and Beyond

To prepare for scheduled flights to the Dutch East Indies, arrangements had to be made with a number of countries across Europe to obtain overflight rights. Towards the end of 1927 a plan was drawn up in The Hague to organize a series of trial flights with mail destined for Batavia. These flights represented a vital national interest, namely speeding up communications with the Dutch colonial possessions.[45] They also served to justify the government's increased financial involvement in KLM. A more proactive approach to aviation diplomacy also resulted. Dutch envoys in Berlin, Prague, Vienna, Budapest, Belgrade, Bucharest, Istanbul, Paris, London, Tehran and Bangkok received instructions to make the necessary arrangements.

44 Marc Dierikx, *Vliegende Hollanders. Het ware verhaal van Anthony Fokker & Albert Plesman* (Amsterdam: Boom, 2020), p. 81–83.

45 Bob de Graaff, *Kalm temidden van woedende golven. Het ministerie van Koloniën en zijn taakomgeving, 1912–1940* (Den Haag: Sdu, 1997), p. 130–134, 300–304.

The first door the Dutch knocked on was German, as KLM planned to make an overnight stop in Leipzig to refuel. Discussions on flights across Germany were held in the spring of 1928. Since the Dutch plans were neither politically nor prestige sensitive, Berlin was happy to cooperate and a basic agreement was signed on 17 August 1928. After further contacts, The Hague received a permit on 21 January 1929.[46]

Prague seemed to be the next logical stopover location. Contacts with the Czechs had been in place for some time as part of KLM's developing European network of air services, much encouraged by the Czechoslovak Republic.[47] On 17 February 1927, Plesman was in Prague to plead for cooperation that would enable a Dutch trial mail service to the East Indies. The Dutch envoy, who also saw this as an opportunity to promote the export of flowers, was very supportive.[48] Talks rapidly advanced towards a quid pro quo, in which the Czech authorities asked for rights in exchange. Their interest was to set up an air service via Rotterdam to London. The perspective of reaching an agreement seemed favorable, especially since the Czechs were also negotiating with KLM about buying two second hand Fokker planes to operate their own Rotterdam service.[49] Czech plans pictured some form of cooperation with KLM, but nothing came of this. Facing continued financial shortages, KLM could not afford to participate in the envisaged Czech service. The company had instead to focus on its own flights to the Dutch East Indies, which held a promise of additional subsidies. In the end no formal agreement resulted, but the Dutch did receive permission for trial flights. In 1928 four of these were undertaken with aircraft ordered by KLM's newly founded colonial sister company, the Royal Netherlands Indies Airline Company (KNILM: Koninklijke Nederlandsch-Indische Luchtvaart Maatschappij), and one by KLM itself.

Meanwhile KLM's board discussed where the airline's priorities should lie: in developing a service of its own to the East Indies, or in expanding scheduled services in Europe. For the time being, the answer remained inconclusive. For the Czechs, who hoped to cooperate on European routes, this was disappointing.

---

46 Letter Auswärtiges Amt to Netherlands Envoy in Berlin, 21 Jan. 1929: NNA, 2.16.19.39, Waterworks, Aviation Bureau (1911) 1920–1929, inv.nr. 16.

47 Peter Svik, *Civil Aviation and the Globalization of the Cold War* (Cham (CH): Palgrave Macmillan, 2020), p. 26–29.

48 Letter Netherlands Envoy in Prague to Ministry of Foreign Affairs, 17 Feb. 1927: NNA, 2.05.37, Archive Ministry of Foreign Affairs, 1919–1940, inv.nr. 4411.

49 Note Czechoslovak Legation in The Hague to Ministry of Foreign Affairs, 3 Sept. 1927: NNA, 2.05.37, Archive Ministry of Foreign Affairs, 1919–1940, inv.nr. 4411. René de Leeuw (ed.), *Fokker Verkeersvliegtuigen. Van de F.I uit 1918 tot en met de Fokker 100 van nu* (Amsterdam: NV Koninklijke Nederlandse Vliegtuigenfabriek Fokker, 1989), p. 181.

Looking for opportunities to expand their international trade contacts and become a part of the European air services network, they offered KLM postal guarantees and even free use of the facilities at Prague's Kbely airport.[50] For the Netherlands, however, only the national colonial air link counted. Taking Czechoslovak mail would just complicate matters, was the prevailing thought.

The next Dutch trial flight destined for Batavia took off from Amsterdam's Schiphol Airport at six o'clock in the morning on Friday 13 September 1928, with 276 kilos of mail on board. The machine was intended to be used by KNILM after arrival in the East Indies, as were the three planes that followed, departing at one-week intervals to test the solidity of the ground organization. The fifth plane, the first that was owned and operated by KLM, would make a return flight. Only the first two machines made it to Batavia. The next two suffered damage to the landing gear along the way and had to be transported by ship. The fifth machine was also damaged, but could be repaired and continued by air. Clearly, the risks involved were considerable, even without taking politics into account.

Chance ruled the diplomatic front. On 24 July 1929, the Austrian Government granted permission for the flights to Batavia without much discussion.[51] But across the border, the Dutch encountered demands from Hungary in return for cooperation. The Hungarian government wished to obtain landing rights in the Netherlands for its own airline, Malért. Moreover, Budapest was not prepared to enter into a bilateral aviation agreement, as this would limit its freedom of action in future aviation matters. Consequently, permission for a technical stopover in Budapest was the best result that could be obtained from the discussions. Commercial rights for the transport of passengers, cargo and mail remained under negotiation until 10 November 1933.[52]

The Indies route was initially conceived to continue through Belgrade and Sofia to Istanbul. To those involved in The Hague it appeared that more hurdles went up as the route stretched further east. Yugoslavia required that each airplane follow an exact course over its territory and that every subsequent plane be registered with the Yugoslav authorities two weeks prior to take-off in Amsterdam.[53] Bulgaria also issued a similar conditional permit: each flight

---

50 Letter Secretary-General Ministry of Foreign Affairs to Minister of Water Management, 20 May 1930: NNA, 5.016.5240, RLD, inv.nr. 6271.

51 Memorandum Austrian Minister of Foreign Affairs to the Dutch envoy in Vienna (Michiels van Verduynen), 24 July 1929. Bilateral agreement Netherlands-Austria, 31 Dec. 1929: NNA, 2.16.5240, RLD, inv.nr. 1512.

52 Hungarian concession for KLM, 10 Nov. 1933: NNA, 2.16.5240, RLD, inv.nr. 6270.

53 Diplomatic notes Yugoslav Ministry of Foreign Affairs to the Dutch legation in Belgrade, 4 July and 29 August 1929: NNA, 2.05.37 Archive Ministry of Foreign Affairs, 1919–1940, inv. nr. 4304.

had to be formally notified at least two weeks in advance, listing all individual cargo items on board.[54] These restrictions were not made public by The Hague, for fear that countries would copy specific clauses from each other when negotiating overflight rights.[55]

Initially, The Hague assumed that the air link with the East Indies would hinge on aviation technology and mail subsidies. A scheduled service over vast areas that lacked anything resembling an air traffic infrastructure was without precedent. The mail service was made financially possible by an additional subsidy from the government and a generous arrangement with the Dutch postal authorities. Overall, the Dutch focus was on technology. The role that national prestige and international political factors might play was underestimated and recognized late. Even so, the element of prestige would turn out to be crucial. To varying degrees, the combination of prestige and commerce played out everywhere.

The first non-European country where the Dutch planes to Batavia planned to land was Turkey. At the beginning of December 1928, KLM approached the Turkish government in Angora [Ankara] to ask for cooperation. This initial approach soon ran aground. Afraid to lose control over the air traffic crossing its territory, Angora refused to issue a blank permit.[56] Each individual flight would require special advance permission. Dutch pleas to ease this requirement were summarily dismissed.[57] As a result, the route via Turkey turned out to be impracticable. Nevertheless, the technical preparations continued.

In the original plan, KLM had hoped to fly via Istanbul to Aleppo in Syria. Here the French exercised authority since 1919 under a mandate from the League of Nations. This meant the Dutch needed to apply in Paris for a Syrian operating permit. At first it appeared this would not present a problem. In September 1928, Paris granted unreserved authorization for a series of 12 trial flights with mail in the period up to 31 December 1929. But the French attitude changed when the Dutch mentioned their intention to extend the test flights into a scheduled service, carrying mail and also passengers. For a scheduled passenger service Paris applied different standards. After all, KLM would probably gain a head start in air traffic to south-east Asia as a result. This could

54 Memorandum Bulgarian Ministry of Foreign Affairs to the Netherlands legation in Istanbul, 26 June 1929: NNA, 2.16.5240, RLD, inv.nr. 6274. (There was no Dutch legation in Sofia at the time).

55 Internal memo Ministry of Foreign Affairs, 17 Apr. 1935: NNA, 2.05.37, Archive Ministry of Foreign Affairs, 1919–1940, inv.nr. 4372.

56 Letter De Veer to KLM, 14 Dec. 1928: NNA, 2.16.19.39, Waterworks, Aviation Bureau, inv. nr. 16.

57 Letter Snouck Hurgronje to Van de Vegte, 11 July 1929: NNA, 2.16.5240, RLD, inv.nr. 7320.

show up French aviation as second rate. Paris proposed instead to set up the envisaged service as an Anglo-Franco-Dutch joint venture, involving Britain's Imperial Airways, France's Air Orient and KLM. Air Orient had recently started flying from Marseille to Beirut and Damascus and the French plan was to extend this service to Baghdad in the British mandate region of Mesopotamia in 1930. With reference to geopolitics, Paris proposed that Imperial Airways operate the route between Baghdad and Rangoon, leaving KLM to fly the Rangoon to Batavia segment. The Hague, by now fully intent on creating its own national air connection, saw nothing positive in this proposal. After all, acceptance of the French plan would mean the end of the envisaged *Dutch* service to Batavia.[58]

To find a solution, talks were held in Paris in September 1929. On paper, the chances of reaching a compromise seemed fair. Three months earlier, another French airline, Aéropostale, had applied to the Ministry of Colonies in The Hague for a permit to land in Paramaribo in the Dutch colony of Surinam on a projected transatlantic route to the French territories in the Caribbean, Martinique and Guadeloupe. The Dutch therefore held a negotiating gambit. Indeed, playing the Surinam card, The Hague secured permission for an air service via Aleppo to the Dutch East Indies.[59] In return, the Dutch would permit Aéropostale to land in Paramaribo. However, the license for KLM was subject to conditions. On the trial flights Paris claimed KLM should reserve cargo capacity for French mail destined for Indo-China. Moreover, a scheduled service would only be allowed

> … le jour ou la route des Indes sera libre pour la France pour assurer une exploitation régulière de France en Indo-Chine.[60]

Until then, KLM was only allowed to operate on a temporary basis. Paris demanded that the Netherlands join in a cooperative air service with Air Orient and Imperial Airways.[61] Given these demands, the delegations failed to reach an agreement. The weakness of the Dutch position was evident; The

58 Letter Dutch Chargé d'Affaires in Paris, to Minister of Foreign Affairs, 9 Aug. 1929: NNA, 2.05.37, Archive Ministry of Foreign Affairs, 1919–1940, inv.nr. 4311.

59 Letter Minister of Water Management to Minister of Colonial Affairs, 3 July 1929; Letter minister of Colonial Affairs to Minister of Water Management, 1 Oct. 1929: NNA, 2.16.19.39, Waterworks, Aviation Bureau, inv.nr. 6.

60 Proces-verbal de la réunion du 16 Septembre 1929, by Campana (Ministère des Affaires Etrangères), 16 Sept. 1929: NNA, 2.05.102, Netherlands Legation in Paris, inv.nr. 2038.

61 Letter Minister of Colonial Affairs to Minister of Water Management, 1 Oct. 1929: NNA, 2.16.19.39, Waterworks, Aviation Bureau, inv.nr. 6.

Hague simply held no cards in the game. As Angora did not permit flights after 30 September 1930, the route via Turkey and Syria was blocked and KLM used the Syrian route only once. The machine that was flown out to Batavia from 25 September to 4 October 1930 landed for an intermediate technical stop in Aleppo, but it was clear that a proper route would have to run through Greece and Egypt.

Ideally situated on the route across the Mediterranean, Greece had a standing conflict with Turkey after losing a three year war over territories around Smyrna [Izmir] on Turkey's west coast in 1922. Against this background the Greeks were willing to step in after Turkey denied landing rights for the Dutch service. In October 1930, a temporary permit to allow the flights to go ahead did not present a problem, but for a more permanent agreement Greece demanded a price, as was provided for in article 15 of the Paris Convention. Well aware of their excellent negotiating position now that the route via Turkey was barred, the Greeks sought to extract a promise that Athens would become a permanent stopover on all KLM services across the Mediterranean. This would mean the Greek capital would come to feature prominently in the world air network. A promise to this effect was easily extracted from the Dutch.

However, when KLM's route inspector Matthijs Moes, accompanied by the Dutch envoy in Athens, Christiaan Schuller tot Peursum, arrived at the Greek Ministry of Foreign Affairs to discuss details of the arrangement, they were unpleasantly surprised to find that Greece also demanded that KLM pay a special compensation to the newly founded Greek airline Helliniki Eteria Enaerion Synghinonion (HEES) for revenues KLM might derive from transit flights across Greece. Moes and Schuller could not accept such a condition. KLM's finances were in a bad state to begin with and giving in to the Greek demands would increase the costs of the air service – already substantial – and set a dangerous precedent. Against this background, the Dutch decided to adopt a low profile in Athens and try to continue to operate under the provisions of the temporary permit, rather than starting talks on a formal agreement. The hope was that discussions that were also ongoing between Athens and Imperial Airways and Air Orient would mellow Greek demands. Perhaps if HEES developed a network of its own, enabling reciprocity to be introduced into the negotiations, this would put an effective brake on Greek demands.[62] In these circumstances the Dutch diplomats reverted to their preferred state of idleness to wait and see what would happen.

---

62 Miscellaneous correspondence between Moes and Schuller tot Peursum, Nov. 1930: NNA, 2.16.5240 RLD, inv.nr. 1607.

In April 1931 Greece tabled a new proposal for a bilateral aviation agreement. By now it was clear that Turkey was maintaining its ban on foreign air services so The Hague could not afford to lose Athens as a stopover location. The Greeks knew this and demanded that the Dutch promised landings in Athens would continue indefinitely. KLM would have to refrain from all transport between Greece and Yugoslavia, Bulgaria, Italy and Turkey. Air transport between Athens and Egypt was allowed, but only on a temporary basis. Mail could be taken, but KLM was to carry one kilo of Greek mail for free on each flight, regardless of the destination. These demands were potentially detrimental to remunerative operations and talks dragged on until December 1932. Meanwhile the Greeks allowed KLM to continue to fly under the temporary permit of 1930.[63] In these circumstances Greek demands were silently shelved, along with run-of-the-mill practicalities to do with the air service, of which there were plenty. Passengers, for example, not only needed a special visa and health certificates, but Greece also required official documental 'proof of good moral behavior' from each traveler.[64]

From Athens, KLM flew to its first destination outside Europe, Mersa Matruh on the Egyptian coast. The flight across open sea took a little over three hours. Egypt had become 'independent' in 1922, but its former colonial power Britain still controlled foreign and defense policy, and the Suez Canal. As in the Greek case, consultations on a temporary arrangement for commercial flights started in October 1930 when the envisaged route via Turkey fell through and an alternative arrangement had to be found. Without much discussion London allowed KLM to land at two RAF bases, Mersa Matruh and Heliopolis, near Cairo as a stop-gap provision. With this solution, The Hague lost interest in the case – a recurring pattern – and no formal agreement with either Britain or Egypt ensued. This created irritations. Although the matter had been settled in London, Egypt wished to be recognized as a party with its own rights and conveyed this in a diplomatic message. Not responding, The Hague bided its time, hoping the situation would resolve itself. Then, in August 1933, Egypt came with a demand to skip Mersa Matruh and exchange it for landings at Cairo's new civil airport Almaza. This turned out to be technically infeasible as the range of KLM's Fokker F.XII airliners was not sufficient to cover the distance between Athens and Cairo without a refuelling stop. The

63 Concept bilateral agreement between Greece and the Netherlands, 12 Dec. 1932: : NNA, 2.16.5240, RLD, inv.nr. 1607.

64 Bilateral Agreement between Greece and the Netherlands on air services, June 1933: NNA, 2.05.37, Archive Ministry of Foreign Affairs, 1919–1940, inv.nr. 4346. Further: Dierikx, *Begrensde Horizonten*, p. 103–106, 111–113.

topic was subsequently dropped from the discussions, but Egypt introduced a new element when it asked that KLM give Egyptian officials a special discount on tickets.[65]

The demand met with resistance in The Hague. Officials at the Ministry of Foreign Affairs now woke up to the fact that the important air service to the East Indies hinged on various informal agreements and was vulnerable to all sorts of demands in exchange for landing rights. While KLM continued to fly, discussions continued intermittently until the Italian invasion of Abyssinia [Ethiopia] in October 1935 meant that the RAF closed its base at Mersa Matruh to civilian flights. KLM, by then operating Douglas DC-2 aircraft which had a greater range than the Fokkers, duly changed its schedule. Flights now went directly from Athens to Cairo, although this reduced the payload and increased dependence on Egyptian good will. Consequently, The Hague had little option but to accept the Egyptian demand for a rebate on ticket prices to secure long-term operating rights in Cairo. These were finally granted in November 1936.[66]

For flights to Asia, the RAF facilities in Baghdad represented the next important staging point after Cairo. Under the terms of the League of Nations mandate for Mesopotamia and the Anglo-Iraqi Treaty of October 1922, landing rights were controlled by Britain. Contacts between The Hague and London dated from September 1928, when the Dutch asked for cooperation for the trial flights with mail that were then under preparation. Although there was a strong sentiment in London to see scheduled Imperial Airways' services to India firmly established before KLM began to fly the route, the Dutch received permission to land at Baghdad. To the Dutch, it was self-evident that part of the mail carried on these flights would be delivered at destinations along the route. However, neither the Dutch Postal Services, nor the Ministry of Foreign Affairs had communicated this to London and the British authorities were thus unpleasantly surprised to learn about the planned deliveries. At this point, Imperial Airways did not operate beyond Baghdad, whereas the Dutch aircraft intended to continue all the way to Singapore and Batavia. The service thus infringed on British imperial prestige. When The Hague next came with a follow-up request for an additional return flight with Christmas mail in December 1928, to be followed by twelve mail flights in 1929, the head of British

65 Note of the Egyptian Ministry of Foreign Affairs to the Dutch chargé d'affaires in Cairo, 20 Aug. 1933: NNA, 2.05.37 Archive Ministry of Foreign Affairs, 1919–1940, inv.nr. 4312.

66 Letter Van Lith de Jeude (Minister of Waterworks) to De Graeff (Minister of Foreign Affairs), with bilateral concept agreement, 20 Feb. 1936: NNA, 2.05.37, Archive Ministry of Foreign Affairs, 1919–1940, inv.nr. 4312.

civil aviation, Sir William Sefton Brancker, felt the Dutch had overstepped their mark. He wrote to Plesman:

> This has done a lot of harm. The Secretary of State is very angry, and everyone will tell me: "I told you so!" It is going to make the difficulties in obtaining agreement to 12 regular flights next year considerably greater.[67]

Sefton Brancker advised that the matter be taken up directly with the Secretary of State for Air, Sir Samuel Hoare. On 7 December 1928, the Dutch envoy to London, Reneke de Marees van Swinderen, spoke with Hoare who offered a deal: he would allow the extra Christmas flight to go ahead, but after that KLM would have to stay off the route until 'improvements' to the ground organization could be made in Baghdad and at various airports in British India. This would take till the end of April 1929.[68] It was no coincidence that this corresponded exactly with the time frame in which Imperial Airways planned to extend its own service from Baghdad to Karachi. As soon as Imperial Airways began flights, KLM would once again be welcome.[69]

In The Hague, Plesman was disappointed. He had spent considerable funds ordering new aircraft for the trial flights planned in 1929 and felt the envoy had failed to promote KLM's interests.[70] How a few Dutch mailplanes could pose a problem for ground organization was beyond all those involved in The Hague. There was a sense of urgency to see the matter settled, as the next sequence of trial flights was planned to take place before the summer to avoid the heavy monsoon rains over the British territories in Asia. After some hesitation, London allowed KLM to use Baghdad Airport from the end of March 1929. A complicating factor was that control over the airport was being turned over to the Iraqis, who were scheduled to gain independence in 1932. Remarkably, given the importance of Baghdad for the Dutch service, the consequences of Iraq's approaching independence – i.e. that a new Iraqi permit would be required – only hit Foreign Affairs in The Hague in the summer of 1931. Baghdad now demanded that KLM transport Iraqi mail at a special, reduced rate. The Hague

67 Letter Brancker to Plesman, 14 Sep. 1928: NNA, 2.05.37, Archive Ministry of Foreign Affairs, 1919–1940, inv.nr. 4311.

68 Letter De Marees van Swinderen to the Netherlands' Minister of Foreign Affairs, 7 Dec. 1928: NNA, 2.05.37, Archive Ministry of Foreign Affairs, 1919–1940, inv.nr. 4345.

69 Letter Brancker to Plesman, 17 Sep. 1928: NNA, 2.05.37, Archive Ministry of Foreign Affairs, 1919–1940, inv.nr. 4311.

70 Letter Plesman to the Minister of Water Management, 18 Dec. 1928: NNA, 2.05.37, Archive Ministry of Foreign Affairs, 1919–1940, inv.nr. 4342.

dragged its feet as long as possible, but had to accept the inevitable in August 1931: here too, operating permits came at a cost in mail carriage.[71]

Beyond Baghdad, KLM wanted to fly via Bushire in Persia [Iran] to the coastal towns of Bandar Abbas and Jask on the Persian Gulf. After brief consultations with the Persian authorities, the Dutch obtained permission from Tehran in July 1928 for the five trial flights. Reaching agreement with Persia on a scheduled service, however, would take some doing.

Late in 1925, Persia had initiated a modest domestic air network, maintained by Junkers Luftverkehr Persien. Under the influence of these German interests, anti-imperial sentiments, and disagreements with London over old war debts, the Persians demanded that Britain's carrier Imperial Airways route its service to Karachi via the capital Tehran, rather than Bushire on the Persian Gulf coast. This presented a huge detour compared to the more logical and shorter route along the Persian Gulf. When the British indicated in 1927 that they much preferred to use the coastal route Persia cancelled Imperial's landing rights, meaning the service had to divert its itinerary towards the end of 1929 and fly via British-dominated sheikhdoms on the south shore of the Persian Gulf.[72]

Compared to Imperial Airways, the Dutch were in a better position. The Dutch chargé d'affaires in Tehran, Leendert de Decker, who had joined the diplomatic service after a career in commerce, enjoyed excellent contacts with the Persian authorities and knew how to use them. In June 1929 he managed to get authorization for the second batch of Dutch mail flights planned later that year. Tehran even expressed a willingness to extend KLM's permit to use the coastal route until 1 January 1932, although the Persian government did express the hope that KLM would come to land in Tehran after that time.[73] As a token of good will, Persia offered KLM a multi-year concession agreement with only two conditions: First, Tehran wanted to fix the number of flights per year. Second, mail offered by Persia would have to be carried free of charge. De Decker, aware of the outcome of discussions with Greece and Iraq, tried to avoid or at least lower the demand for free mail carriage. In the end he got the volume of free mail reduced to a mere seven kilos per flight, an acceptable outcome; De Decker also managed to have Persia raise the number of permitted flights to

71 Letter Martin (KLM) to De Veer and Damme (Director-General of the Dutch Postal Services), 21 Dec. 1931: NNA, 2.16.5240, RLD, inv.nr. 1605.

72 Gordon Pirie, *Air Empire. British Imperial Civil Aviation 1919–1939* (Manchester: Manchester Univ. Press, 2009), p. 145–148. Robin Higham, *Britain's Imperial Air Routes 1918–1939. The Story of Britain's Overseas Airlines* (Stroud: Fonthill Media, 2016), p. 94–96.

73 Letters Neth. Chargé d'Affaires in Tehran (L.P.J. de Decker) to Minister of Foreign Affairs, 6 and 17 July 1929: NNA, 2.05.37, Archive Ministry of Foreign Affairs, 1919–1940, inv.nr. 4311.

104 per year. This made a weekly scheduled service possible without the need to apply for a new concession.[74]

In The Hague, Persia's *quid-pro-quo* demand met with concern. Foreign Affairs feared that if it agreed, and word got out, there would be no stopping similar claims. In the end it was KLM that gave in. On balance, the transportation of Persian mail also generated revenue.[75] After KLM's general secretary, Hans Martin, had visited Tehran at the beginning of August 1930 to take care of the details of the service – and had lain sick for three weeks in the Dutch legation due to water poisoning – the KLM contract was put in writing at the end of August by diplomatic exchange of notes.[76]

From the Persian coastal town of Jask, KLM's route continued to Karachi, the first stopover in British India. Karachi was approximately halfway between Amsterdam and Batavia. Operationally this was an important stop, because Karachi was the only airport in British India where planes could be parked overnight in a fully equipped hangar, which facilitated maintenance. Crews and passengers were accommodated at the Dutch-owned Hotel Bristol. Initially, KLM was the only airline flying east out of Karachi, but this did not mean that British mail could be taken. London's planning was to extend the Imperial Airways network to Calcutta and Rangoon in 1933. Until then, British mail would be carried by train and other surface transportation. Nonetheless, the fact that KLM operated an air service from Europe to major centers in British India caused some anxiety in London. Several officials expressed the view that the Dutch were taking advantage of British investments in infrastructure for their own benefit.[77] The loss of prestige involved was also noted at the Ministry of Industry and Labor in Delhi, where it contributed to practical obstructions being raised against KLM.[78]

Meanwhile, British reservations about the Dutch air service across India increased and The Hague took steps to mollify them. At a conference in June 1929 where amendments to the Paris Convention were discussed, the Dutch

74 Letter De Decker to Beelaerts van Blokland, 28 Feb. 1930: NNA, 2.05.37, Archive Ministry of Foreign Affairs, 1919–1940, inv.nr. 4311.

75 Minutes 62nd KLM Board Meeting, 22 Apr. 1930: KLM Archive, series R-5.

76 Interview with Hans Martin, in: *De Nieuwe Vorstenlanden*, 12 Nov. 1930. Persian memorandum (Foroughi) to the (new) Neth. Chargé d'Affaires in Tehran (P.A. v. Buttingha Wichers), 21 Aug. 1930; memorandum Van Buttingha Wichers to Foroughi, 29 Aug. 1930: NNA, 2.16.5240, RLD, inv.nr. 7605.

77 Pirie, *Air Empire*, p. 145.

78 Confidential Foreign Office note Alexander Leeper on the question of KLM services across India, 14 Dec. 1929, British National Archive (BNA), Foreign Office Papers, FO 371, inv.nr. 14095.

delegation supported a British plea for greater freedom in the air. However, to the secret relief of those in London, a considerable majority of the participating countries opposed a relaxation of sovereignty. Instead, the conference decided to strengthen the conditions of Article 15 of the convention, restricting the scope of international air services.[79] In retrospect, this strengthening of sovereignty turned out to be advantageous for Britain. On 17 June 1929, Sefton Brancker noted in an internal memorandum:

> We are now in a very strong position as regards art. 15, because, although we have pleaded for liberty, all the European nations, except Holland and Sweden, have voted against us. This can be borne in mind when negotiating with the French ["and the Dutch", Deputy Director Francis Bertram added] regarding the passage over India.[80]

Such signals were welcomed by the British colonial administration in Delhi, where prestige played an even bigger role than in London. In a telegram to the India Office, Delhi proposed to revoke KLM's license, citing the latest interpretation of Article 15 of the Paris Convention.[81] However, the British Foreign Office, protecting the interests of good bilateral relations, felt this would go too far. Instead, it was decided to allow the Dutch trial flights to go ahead until the end of 1929. After that, the Dutch would have to wait for the ground organization in British India to be brought to order. To underline the logic of this decision, The Hague was reminded that two of the Dutch trial flights undertaken in 1928 had suffered accidents and had been cut short.

Nonetheless, the Foreign Office felt uncomfortable about the matter and put pressure on the British-Indian government to come up with funding to enable Imperial Airways to reach Rangoon earlier than planned, preferably within a year. The problem was that Rangoon had no airport. To the displeasure of the local equestrian society, landings had to be arranged on the city's horse racetrack. Constructing a real airport would take time.[82] Consequently, KLM was instructed to interrupt its trial flights in January 1930. Although the

---

79 Protocol relating to the amendment of the Articles 3, 5, 7, 15, 34, 41,42 and the final clauses of the Convention relating to Air Navigation of 13 October 1919 (Article 15), 15 June 1929: *Handelingen der Staten-Generaal*, 1929 – 1930, Tweede Kamer, Bijlage 284.

80 Memorandum Sir William Sefton Brancker, added to the file of the conference on international air navigation of June 1929, 17 June 1929: BNA, Air Ministry, AVIA2, inv.nr. 1863.

81 Department of Industries and Labour to India Office, 13 June 1929: BNA, Foreign Office, FO 371, inv.nr. 14095.

82 Summary of radio consultation with Netherlands East Indies' Authorities in Bandung, 27 Nov. 1928: NNA, 2.16.19.39, Waterworks, Aviation Bureau, inv.nr. 16.

setback was expected, this greatly displeased the Dutch envoy De Marees van Swinderen. He believed the whole thing was an all-too-transparent excuse for protectionism – and thus the reverse of the free trade that London publicly said it stood for. In a note to Foreign Minister Arthur Henderson, Van Swinderen added that, in his opinion, the Foreign Office was using the motive of insufficient ground organization for lack of a better argument.[83] But although Henderson adhered to general British protectionist trade policy, he eventually handed KLM the coveted permission for its scheduled Amsterdam-Batavia service, starting from 1 October 1930. However, the authorization, in a note dated 7 April, came at a price:

> In return for these facilities the Netherlands Government shall undertake to grant reciprocal facilities, when applied for later, for a British service across Netherlands territory to Australia.[84]

In The Hague, where the Dutch civil service was preoccupied obtaining permission for the Batavia air route, the implication of Henderson's words was not picked up. In January 1929, KNILM had notified the colonial authorities in Batavia that it would like to operate international routes from the Dutch East Indies, especially to Australia. At the time the only means of transport between the Dutch East Indies and Australia were the ships of the Koninklijke Paketvaart Maatschappij (KPM), which sailed from Surabaya to Brisbane once a month. Air services within Australia were almost entirely limited to operations along the west coast, the larger cities in New South Wales and air taxi flights by the Queensland and Northern Territories Air Services (Qantas). Thus, from a Dutch perspective the prospects for an air service from Batavia looked promising. The Dutch put out feelers in London and in Canberra.

However, the idea of a foreign air service did not go down at all well with the Australian government. In a letter to the Dutch Consul General in Sydney, Prime Minister Stanley Bruce, a personal friend of Imperial Airways' chief executive Sir Eric Geddes, cut short the Dutch plans. He bluntly stated that air services operated to and from Australia by any carrier other than Imperial

83 Note De Marees van Swinderen to Henderson, 9 Dec. 1929: BNA, Foreign Office, FO 371, inv. nr. 14095.

84 Henderson to De Marees van Swinderen, 7 April 1930: NNA, 2.05.44, Netherlands Legation in London, inv.nr. 940.

Airways, or an Australian company, were unthinkable.[85] The first contacts about a KNILM service to Australia hit a brick wall.

Meanwhile, the Dutch envoy in London, De Marees van Swinderen, had communicated his government's consent to Henderson's note of 7 April on 3 June 1930. Thus, a bilateral agreement had been reached. The Hague was proud to receive commercial rights. In return, Van Swinderen agreed 'to grant the same facilities as are now accorded to the Netherlands–Batavia service for a British service across The Netherlands territory to Australia.'[86] The exchange of notes had the markings of an arrangement that satisfied both parties. On 2 October 1930, KLM was able to convert its trial flights to Batavia into a scheduled service, carrying passengers, freight and mail and operating every two weeks. The service was an instant success. Just over a year later, KLM saw fit to double the frequency of flights to a weekly basis in response to pleas from the Dutch business community. Thanks to the continued subsidies from the government and the postal services, the first full year of operations even showed a profit: 292,812 guilders.[87]

The competing British service to Australia was now also in preparation. On 1 April 1931, the Post Office in London announced that Imperial Airways and Qantas were to conduct two trial flights with mail to Sydney later that month. The plan was for Imperial Airways to fly from London to Port Darwin on Australia's north coast, where a Qantas plane would pick up the mail and continue to Sydney. However, the first flight out was stranded on the island of Timor in the Dutch East Indies, where the pilot had to make an emergency landing due to a fuel shortage. Before the end of the year, two more British aircraft crashed en route. Meanwhile, the postal authorities in London and in Delhi argued over the conditions of carriage and the setting up of air services in British India.[88]

The pace of progress in Britain was therefore slow and this put a strain on Anglo-Dutch aviation relations. In addition, KNILM had a long-standing wish to operate a Batavia-Sydney service of its own. As KLM's successes found acclaim internationally, this strengthened London's and Canberra's stance of keeping the Australian sky closed to the Dutch. This also aligned with the protectionist preferences discussed between Britain and various Commonwealth

---

85 Letter Bruce to the Dutch Consul-General Teppema, 15 Apr. 1929: NNA, 2.05.37, Archive Ministry of Foreign Affairs, 1919–1940, inv.nr. 4332.

86 Note De Marees van Swinderen to Henderson, 3 juni 1930: NNA, 2.05.44, Netherlands Legation in London, inv.nr. 940.

87 Balance Account KLM on the year 1939 (with financial overview of the period 1921–1939): KLM Archive, series R-5.

88 Higham, *Britain's Imperial Air Routes*, p. 132–135.

members at the Imperial Conference of 1930. There was indeed ground for Commonwealth concern: airline figures showed that Dutch traffic was booming. In 1932, KLM's Indies route already carried seven times the number of passengers welcomed in 1931 and further growth was expected.[89] This toughened resistance against the Dutch. From Canberra, Australia's Prime Minister Joseph Lyons assured the Dominion Office in London

> that consideration will not be given to any suggestion for inclusion of foreign interests until the possibility of a co-operative British-Australian service will be fully exhausted.[90]

On 18 January 1934, Imperial Airways and Qantas set up a joint venture, Qantas Empire Airways (QEA), to operate the air service to Sydney. Careful legal study of the Anglo-Dutch aviation agreement of April/June 1930 preceded this. In the agreement, the Dutch promised rights for a future British service to Australia. It was therefore crucial to present QEA as British. Indeed, Imperial Airways in London took 51 per cent of the shares. In this way, QEA could operate on the basis of the bilateral agreement and would not need prior approval from the Dutch authorities. A possible claim for reciprocity of services did not come into the equation and Australia thus kept its airspace closed.

QEA was registered as an Australian company, operating with Australian registered aircraft and Australian personnel. Management resided with Qantas and the service was marketed as the final leg of the Empire Air Route to connect Britain and Australia. However, the distribution of the shareholding made that QEA could legally be portrayed as British, even though the company's place of business and statutes were Australian. This was a debatable interpretation of nationality, but the Dutch were unable to raise this as it would jeopardize the 1930 agreement on which KLM's all-important Amsterdam-Batavia service was built.

Meanwhile, the modern, faster aircraft that were replacing the biplanes which Imperial Airways and QEA operated had the effect that KLM drew the lion's share of its passengers on the East Indies' route from Britain: about 40 per cent were British compared to 25 per cent who were Dutch. Even British mail was taken. This was first sent to the Netherlands, where Dutch stamps were affixed before the mail items were carried on board KLM's aircraft.

In The Hague, Plesman was convinced that KLM's operational performance should be a reason to grant landing rights in Australia. To force a breakthrough,

89 KLM statistics Amsterdam-Batavia Service [author's collection].

90 Letter Lyons to Dominions Office, 8 June 1932, BNA, Foreign Office, FO 371, inv.nr. 16413.

he came up with a bold plan in February 1934. Plesman decided to enroll KLM in the big international air race to Melbourne that was being organized in October of that year. His gamble involved the deployment of a brand new, ultramodern airplane that KLM had on order in the United States at the time, the Douglas DC-2. When Plesman announced his plans to participate in the air race, the DC-2 prototype was still to make its first flight. Delivery to KLM was scheduled for early September 1934. The risks taken with this brand new, unfamiliar airplane were enormous. On 20 October, just four weeks after the machine had arrived by ship for assembly in Rotterdam, the KLM machine appeared at the starting line at Mildenhall aerodrome in the United Kingdom. Within four days, the crew flew the plane, christened *Uiver* [Stork], to Australia. Despite the handicap of taking passengers and mail, KLM's DC-2 finished second in the speed race and winning the handicap classification. It was a remarkable feat that stunned the public the world over. In the Netherlands newspapers bulged with chauvinistic superlatives. Festivities continued for weeks and KLM became a national icon.[91]

However, in the field of aviation policy the Melbourne Race turned out to be counterproductive. KLM's achievement bolstered chauvinistic refusals in London and in Canberra.[92] KLM and KNILM were forced to watch the first aircraft of the joint Imperial Airways/QEA service take off from London's Croydon Airport on 8 December 1934. It took Imperial Airways and QEA twelve days to deliver the mail. The air service proved non-remunerative. Despite being heavily subsidized, QEA struggled to stay out of the red. Allowing competition would have a negative impact on QEA's finances, so the Dutch desire to be allowed to fly the route did not stand a chance.[93] Prestige was paramount. Despite poor finances, QEA doubled the frequency of its services in 1936, leaving the Dutch still at square one.

It was not until 1938 that the situation changed. A little more than three years earlier, a plan had been adopted in London to equip Imperial Airways and QEA with luxury flying boats, very large four engine aircraft that operated from water and did not require purpose-built runways. The Melbourne Race had provided the impetus for this remarkable changeover. The new flying boat service was named the Empire Air Mail Scheme.

91 Marc Dierikx, *Vliegende Hollanders*, p. 117–127.

92 Correspondence between Foreign Office, Dominions Office, Air Ministry and the Australian Liaison Officer in London, October-December 1934, BNA, Foreign Office, FO 371, 18495.

93 Report of conversation with Sir Robert Parkhill, Australia's Defense Secretary, by the Netherlands' Consul-General in Sydney, Tom Elink Schuurman, 17 Jan. 1936, NNA, 2.05.37, Archive Ministry of Foreign Affairs, 1919–1940, inv.nr. 4332.

The scheme's authors, the Director of Civil Aviation Francis Shelmerdine and Postmaster-General Sir Donald Banks, needed more than a year to convert the skeptical leadership of Imperial Airways to the new set-up. The Australians also needed convincing. The idea was that from the beginning of 1937, all first-class mail would be transported by flying boat, boosting unity in the British Empire. The surplus transport capacity on board these large aircraft would then be used to take passengers and upgrade the level of comfort on board.[94]

Somewhat surprisingly, it was only after these decisions had been taken and the construction of the flying boats initiated that London and Canberra realized that the decision to operate from water had not only practical implications, but also international political and legal aspects. For example, the use of flying boats required special servicing stations in the Dutch East Indies. For The Hague, the request for the construction of facilities was a godsend after years of fruitless pleading for landing rights. It was decided to use the additional costs associated with the construction of fuel depots and other facilities as leverage to finally obtain rights on the route to Sydney.[95]

The bastion that Britain and Australia had put up now began to show cracks. London had also adjusted Britain's own aviation policy to enable Imperial Airways to operate between Singapore and Brisbane, alongside QEA. This underlined the British character of the Empire Air Mail Scheme. In legal terms this meant that Imperial Airways would be using the rights granted in 1930 for a *British* service to Australia. The consequence was that QEA would no longer be able to operate under the umbrella of the existing agreement. The Dutch indicated that if Australia wanted QEA to continue to operate across the Dutch East Indies, Canberra would have to meet the long-standing wish of KNILM to have its own service to Sydney.[96] And so, after nine years of frustrating negotiations, The Hague was finally able to secure the Australian rights it had sought for so long. On 22 February 1938 Canberra granted permission.[97]

In terms of diplomacy this was a major breakthrough, but financially it proved to be a pyrrhic victory. With Imperial Airways and QEA flying, there was insufficient demand to warrant a parallel Dutch service. Moreover, KNILM did

---

94 Leigh Edmonds, Australia, Britain and the Empire Air Mail Scheme, 1934–1938, in: *Journal of Transport History* 20 (1999), p. 91–106.

95 Letter Colijn to Gouvernor-General in Batavia, 5 Nov. 1936, NNA, 2.05.37, Archive Ministry of Foreign Affairs, 1919–1940, inv.nr. 4332.

96 Letter Patijn (Netherlands' Minister of Foreign Affairs) to the British envoy in The Hague, 31 Jan. 1938, NNA, 2.05.37, Archive Ministry of Foreign Affairs, 1919–1940, inv.nr. 4333.

97 Letter Australian Minister for External Affairs, William Hughes, to the Netherlands' Consul-General in Sydney, Tom Elink Schuurman, 22 Feb. 1938: NNA, 2.05.48.14, Consulate-General Sydney, inv.nr. 76.

not possess the right aircraft. The long flight segments on the route to Sydney required the carriage of extra fuel, at the expense of the available capacity in KNILM's Lockheed L-14 aircraft. In order to take (Dutch) mail, there was room for only six, rather than twelve, passengers per flight.[98] But prestige made it unthinkable that KNILM would not fly. The Hague put pressure on the colonial government in Batavia to grant a special subsidy for the Australia service.[99]

The first KNILM machine left for Sydney on 3 July 1938, but there was no reason to party. The air service was bleeding money from day one, while Australia continued to hinder the Dutch whenever possible. To spread the burden and make the service more remunerative, KNILM hoped to bring in KLM. This was immediately blocked in Canberra. The Australian Foreign Minister Henry Gullett even told the Dutch Consul-General Tom Elink Schuurman that he did not feel bound by an aviation agreement concluded by his predecessor. Gullett argued that Australia would never have granted the KNILM rights in the first place if it had been clear that the Netherlands would try and introduce KLM to Australia. Elink Schuurman reacted furiously: that Australia regretted the agreement was Canberra's own fault and surely the matter had been discussed long enough. Nonetheless, he agreed to a joint review of the issue.[100]

This left the matter of KLM's involvement. The Hague proposed that KLM participate in the air service under a charter contract with KNILM. Even KNILM was strongly opposed to this, since it would provide KLM an opportunity to fly within the Dutch East Indies, operations that had been reserved for KNILM since 1927. It took concerted pressure from the Ministers of Colonies and of Water Management to have the boards of the two companies agree on a compromise: KNILM was to operate the Australia link under a common brand name *Intercontinental Airways. Combined Netherlands Indies and Dutch Lines KNILM-KLM*.[101]

In Canberra no one was happy about this. If Australia continued its obstructions, QEA ran the risk of losing its permission to fly over the Dutch East Indies. On the other hand, a Dutch revocation of the permit might also jeopardize KLM's position on the air route to the East Indies. The result was a stalemate. While QEA plodded along with its unremunerative flying boat service, KNILM

98 KNILM Annual Report 1938 [author's collection].

99 Letter Colijn to Governor-General in Batavia, 5 Nov. 1936, NNA, 2.05.37, Archive Ministry of Foreign Affairs, 1919–1940, inv.nr. 4332.

100 Letter Elink Schuurman to Patijn, 12 May 1939: NNA, 2.05.48.14, Consulate-General Sydney, inv.nr. 76.

101 Concept agreement KLM-KNILM re. Australia service, 9 Jan. 1939: KLM Archive, series R-5.

was forced to operate its own loss-making flights to Sydney. The colonial government's subsidy did not cover the costs.[102]

Although operating on government money, KNILM was forced to reduce the frequency of its services by half in August 1939. With international tensions rising in the Pacific region, its aircraft were needed elsewhere. Elink Schuurman made several attempts to have Gullett change his position, but to no avail. By now, personal animosity between Australia's Minister for External Affairs and the Dutch Consul-General also stood in the way of any constructive approach.

The outbreak of war in Europe did not solve the controversy, although Imperial Airways withdrew from the Singapore to Sydney route in June as its aircraft were needed elsewhere. This did not mean that there was space for Dutch flights. Even the unexpected death of Henry Gullett and two other cabinet members in a plane crash near Canberra on 13 August 1940 did not change anything. Allied or not, Australia persisted in its obstructive aviation policy towards its colonial neighbor.

4 Discussing Air Services to the United States

Aviation contacts between the Netherlands and the United States dated from 1929. The initiative was American and came in the wake of flights operated by Pan American Airways (PanAm) in the Caribbean. From 21 June 1929, a PanAm airplane with mail arrived every week in Willemstad on the Dutch island of Curaçao. In keeping with PanAm's operational model, there was no prior application for a landing permit. The idea was that becoming part of the 'world air network' would be so attractive to Curaçao that PanAm would be issued such a permit forthwith.[103] In several Latin American countries this had worked well and the Dutch territories in the Caribbean were no exception. Three months into PanAm's operations to Curaçao, on 25 September 1929, one of their machines touched down on the Surinam River at Paramaribo. It was piloted by none other than aviation legend Charles Lindbergh. He had been sent from Washington as a flying envoy to strengthen ties with Latin America.[104] Apart from Lindbergh, the plane also carried PanAm's chief executive Juan Trippe.

---

102 Letter Nieuwenhuis to the Board of KLM, 31 July 1939: KLM Archive, series R-5.

103 Jenifer van Vleck, *Empire of the Air. Aviation and the American Ascendancy* (Cambridge: Harvard UP, 2013), p. 64–71.

104 Van Vleck, *Empire of the Air*, p. 53–60.

That very same day, Trippe and Surinam's Governor Bram Rutgers signed a contract for the transportation of air mail.[105]

In between these two events, US Secretary of State Henry Stimson approached the Dutch envoy in Washington, Jan van Roijen, with a proposal for a bilateral aviation agreement that would include the overseas territories. The agreement extended to Cuba, Puerto Rico, Guam and the Philippines. Washington wished to exchange 'general rights' for commercial operations. Only with regard to cabotage did Stimson wish to make a proviso.[106]

In The Hague the proposal arrived wholly unexpectedly. Due to poor communication between the Ministry of Colonies, the Ministry of Water Management, and Foreign Affairs, the latter department had little previous knowledge of aviation contacts in the Caribbean. Because the document referred to air transport in Surinam, the Ministry of Colonies was considered leading, though the other departments were asked for advice.[107] Characteristically, it took Foreign Affairs months to arrive at a preliminary conclusion, which was that the appropriate thing to do was to cooperate with the American plans, since Dutch interests were perceived as limited. After all, the issue primarily played out in the Caribbean and did not appear to touch on Dutch interests as such.[108]

Washington's proposal was built on the ideas of the Havana Convention (1928) and provided for freedom for aviation, including the establishment of scheduled (American) air services. Consequently, the document did not include any provision for a bilateral exchange transport rights. In Washington's view a formula that recognized the general possibility that airlines of both countries might wish to offer international flights sufficed. Referring to the Havana Convention, Washington insisted such flights would be operated on the basis of permits drawn up for each flight.[109] The proposed agreement as such applied only to the transportation of passengers and goods. Carriage of mail by non-American companies was ruled out and PanAm's interests would be safeguarded.[110]

---

105 Letter Rutgers to Minister S. de Graaff, 26 Sep. 1929 (with overview of postal contract with PanAm): NNA, 2.10.54, Ministry for the Colonies, Dossier archive, inv.nr. 598.

106 Letter Stimson to the Netherlands envoy, 22 July 1929: NNA, 2.05.13 Archive Legation Washington, 1814–1940, inv.nr. 758.

107 Letter Reymer to Beelaerts van Blokland, 13 Sep. 1929: NNA, 2.05.37, Archive Ministry of Foreign Affairs, 1919–1940, inv.nr. 4328.

108 Memorandum Beelaerts van Blokland to Reymer, 29 Apr. 1930: NNA, 2.05.37, Archive Ministry of Foreign Affairs, 1919–1940, inv.nr. 4328.

109 Nicolas Mateesco Matte, *Treatise on Air-Aeronautical Law* (Toronto: Carswell, 1981), p. 121.

110 Memorandum Van Royen to State Department, 13 March 1931: NNA, 2.05.13 Legation Washington 1814–1940, inv.nr. 758.

Neither at Foreign Affairs, nor at Colonies or at Water Management were the consequences of the American proposal recognized. Moreover, The Hague believed it had nothing to gain or lose from an agreement with the United States. This attitude was not entirely surprising, since PanAm ceased its service to Curaçao in July 1931, due to disappointing results. Thus, the need for a settlement appeared to have gone. Nonetheless, Ambassador Van Roijen informed the State Department that the Netherlands agreed to the terms of the proposed bilateral. The formal exchanges of signatures were carried out on 16 November 1932.[111]

For the Dutch ratification of the agreement, one of the bodies to be consulted was the Netherlands East Indies' Council [Volksraad]. In view of possible future air links between the Dutch East Indies and the Philippines, at the time under American administration, the arrangement also touched upon the interests of the Dutch East Indies. This induced delay: the treaty documents were not sent to Batavia until March 1933. The East Indies Council then needed five months to deliver a positive opinion.

This delay would have unforeseen consequences, not only for the agreement but for aviation relations with the United States generally. On 20 September 1933, the new American envoy in The Hague, Laurits Swenson, unexpectedly requested the withdrawal of the aviation agreement as such. On reflection, Washington wanted to keep the Philippines, Hawaii and the Panama Canal Zone outside the scope of this type of bilateral agreement. No direct reason for this was given. Swenson referred only to the fact that his government had also excluded territories from other bilateral agreements.[112] Ever since the Japanese occupation of Manchuria late in 1931 and the attack on Shanghai in the following year, the Americans had banned foreign aircraft from flying over areas of perceived strategic importance.[113]

In The Hague, reactions to this development held middle ground between bewilderment and indignation. Only now did the government realize the opportunities missed since 1929. The new American take on aviation was likely to result in a restrictive agreement that would only strengthen PanAm's position, offering no benefits for the Netherlands. Small wonder then that KLM and

111 Memorandum State Department (White) to L.G. van Hoorn (Neth. Chargé d'Affaires in Washington), 16 Nov. 1932 and memorandum Van Hoorn to US Secretary of State, 16 Nov. 1932: NNA, 2.05.13 Legation Washington 1814–1940, inv.nr. 758.

112 Letter Swenson to De Graeff, 20 Sep. 1933: NNA, 2.05.37, Archive Ministry of Foreign Affairs, 1919–1940, inv.nr. 4328.

113 Correspondence between State Department and the American legation in The Hague re. aviation negotiations with the Netherlands, 17 Oct. 1933 – 31 Dec. 1934: United States National Archives, Record Group 59, State Decimal File 1930–1939, 711.5627/69-711.5627/73.

KNILM opposed the proposals. It was typical of many aspects of Dutch foreign policy at the time that both Water Management and Foreign Affairs concluded that the best thing to do was not to respond at all. Maybe the whole issue would blow over.[114] Nine months passed before the new US envoy in The Hague, Grenville Emmet, issued a note stating that he presumed that the Netherlands, by not answering, agreed to Swenson's proposal.[115] The gap between parties widened. If the agreement held no provision for a future Dutch air service in Manila, The Hague saw no reason to play along.[116]

Less than two months later the setting for the negotiations changed. On 19 January 1935, KLM opened a small West Indies Branch [KLM West-Indisch Bedrijf] in Curaçao. Henceforth two aircraft would provide services between the Dutch islands in the Caribbean, Venezuela and Surinam. A future Dutch air link from Curaçao to the United States was also on the cards, and informal consultations were taking place between representatives of PanAm and of KLM about a possible PanAm service in the Pacific between Manila and Surabaya. Then, in September 1935, envoy Emmet came up with a newly amended, more restrictive proposal that expressly stated that the Philippines remained outside the scope of the agreement. Washington claimed full and unrestricted sovereign authority to deny landing rights of foreign operators – even on other than the 'reasonable grounds' that had featured in earlier discussions. Although not a party to the Paris Convention, Washington referred to the outcome of the June 1929 conference of the convention's member states, which had created an opportunity for such 'unreasonable' restrictions. Like the European States adhering to the convention, Washington reserved the right to refuse any operating permit.[117]

This restricted proposal was not acceptable to the Dutch. KLM and KNILM noted they would rather have no bilateral agreement than this agreement, if the Philippines remained outside its scope. Added to this were objections to the licensing regime proposed by Washington.[118] The Hague concluded that the negotiations would likely remain unproductive. Perhaps a settlement

114 Summary De Veer re. steps taken after the US memo of 20 Sep. 1933, undated (Dec. 1933).: NNA, 2.16.5240, RLD, inv.nr. 12680.

115 Memorandum Emmet to De Graeff, 3 Aug. 1934: NNA, 2.10.54, Ministry for the Colonies, Dossier archive, inv.nr. 321.

116 Letter De Graeff to US Chargé d'Affaires in The Hague, 20 Nov. 1934. NNA, 2.10.54, Ministry for the Colonies, Dossier archive, inv.nr. 321.

117 Memorandum Emmet to De Graeff, 10 Sep. 1935 (with draft proposal): NNA, 2.10.54, Ministry for the Colonies, Dossier archive, inv.nr. 321.

118 Letter Slotemaker to Van Lith de Jeude, 13 Dec. 1935; letter Rendorp to Van Lith de Jeude, 17 Dec. 1935: NNA, 2.16.5240, RLD, inv.nr. 12680.

outside the scope of a formal bilateral agreement would be an option? KNILM hoped for leeway that would make operations between the cities of Surabaya, Tarakan (North Borneo) and Manila possible.[119]

After lengthy interdepartmental deliberations, the Ministry of Water Management advised on 6 January 1938 that maintaining Dutch silence again appeared to be the best option.[120] Indeed, this appeared to have the desired effect. Washington did not return to the issue and the whole matter was allowed to disappear from the agenda as general political tensions in the world mounted. In 1940 and 1941 KNILM made 36 charter flights to Manila on which mail was carried for delivery in the United States.

Meanwhile, the activities of KLM's West Indies Branch had expanded. Now operating two planes, new regional air connections were in preparation. In the fall of 1936, the idea arose to open a service to Miami, the closest city in the United States. After all, PanAm's service to Curaçao had been on hold for five years. In Miami KLM hoped to connect to the network of Eastern Airlines, one of America's largest domestic carriers. After some months of preparation, the Dutch envoy in Washington, Hendrik van Haersma de With, submitted an application for a permit with the State Department on 23 February 1937.[121]

As was the case in the discussions over a general bilateral agreement, the prospects of American cooperation for the envisaged service to Miami were not favorable. Not only was Miami home to Eastern Airlines, but it was also the main operating base of PanAm. In recent years, America's chosen instrument had acquired a monopoly in air traffic to Central and South America with the support of the government agencies in Washington.[122] PanAm was dead set against foreign competition and did what it could to stall talks. What was more, the Dutch application came at an unfortunate time, coming shortly after the request for the KNILM air service to Manila, which was already a thorny issue. Besides, the Dutch silence with regard to the latest American proposal for a bilateral aviation agreement had not been appreciated in Washington.

Three weeks after van Haersma de With submitted the application, Secretary of State Cordell Hull informed him that the permit for Miami had been rejected by the Commerce Department. Hull did not give a reason. Plesman, who happened to be in Washington at the time, was convinced that the

119 Letter Van Arkel to De Graeff, 24 Dec. 1935; letter Colijn to De Graeff, 2 Jan. 1936: NNA, 2.10.54, Ministry for the Colonies, Dossier archive, inv.nr. 321.

120 Memorandum Van Ede van der Pals and J. Kan to Van Buuren, 6 Jan. 1938.: NNA, 2.16.5240, RLD, inv.nr. 5614.

121 Memorandum Van Haersma de With to Secretary of State Cordell Hull, 23 Feb. 1937: NNA, 2.05.13 Legation Washington 1814–1940, inv.nr. 720.

122 Van Vleck, *Empire of the Air*, p. 64–77.

rejection was due to lobbying by PanAm.[123] After further consultations the State Department agreed to review the Miami case in the context of the development of transatlantic air traffic, but a policy for this had yet to be adopted and a decision would therefore not be forthcoming in the short term.[124]

By 1940, the war had put an end to the discussions but the Dutch still held out hope. However, the chances of a service to Miami did not improve when KLM's West Indies Branch fell into disrepute that spring because of an alleged espionage affair. Several KLM staff members had engaged in the transportation of private mail from Trinidad, outside the scope of the British Postal Service and the newly imposed wartime censorship. As a punitive measure, Britain withdrew KLM's landing rights in Trinidad, a snub that dealt the company's prestige a serious blow in Washington.[125] The matter of a Dutch air service to Miami was temporarily dropped.

To the dismay of the Dutch, who saw repeated evidence of the way Washington used PanAm as a tool for economic and political penetration in Latin America, it took until 1942 before any possibility of an accord over the air service presented itself.[126] After years of futile reminders, KLM was finally granted permission to operate a series of charter flights for America's Standard Oil Company. From 18 June 1942, KLM aircraft made flights ferrying oil refinery staff between Curaçao and Miami. This gave KLM a toehold on US territory, but when it came to regular landing rights, PanAm remained an obstacle. Juan Trippe made efforts to obtain a permit for a refuelling stop in Curaçao on PanAm's service to the city of La Guaira in Venezuela. The Dutch were willing to cooperate because of the wartime conditions, but in return again demanded commercial landing rights in Miami. Washington's negotiator Adolf Berle found it an odd request, since PanAm was already operating the route. He proposed to deal with the issue in the corridors of the big international aviation conference in Chicago that he was organizing.[127] Meanwhile PanAm wanted to expand its rights in Curaçao, converting its technical stop into a commercial one. The Netherlands Antilles' governor Piet Kasteel felt he had little option

---

123 Memorandum Cordell Hull to Van Haersma de With, 16 March 1937: NNA, 2.05.13 Legation Washington 1814–1940, inv.nr. 720. Telegram Van Haersma de With to De Graeff, 18 March 1937: NNA, 2.05.37, Archive Ministry of Foreign Affairs, 1919–1940, inv.nr. 4408.

124 Letter Loudon to Patijn, 22 May 1939: NNA, 2.16.5240, RLD, inv.nr. 12680.

125 Jan Hagens, *Londen of Berlijn? De KLM en haar personeel in oorlogstijd,* Vol. 1, *1939–1941* (Bergen: Bonneville, 2000), p. 184–192.

126 Short preview re. PanAm policy, 2 Oct. 1942: NNA, 2.05.80, Foreign Affairs, London Archive, inv.nr. 3351.

127 Letter Van Boetzelaer to Van Kleffens, 26 Nov. 1943: NNA, 2.05.80 Foreign Affairs, London Archive, inv.nr. 3351. Van Vleck, *Empire of the Air*, p. 175–180.

but to go along with this.[128] Nonetheless, Kasteel and the Netherlands' government in London regretted that it was not possible to refuse, knowing full well that a PanAm service would diminish KLM's chances of obtaining a permanent American authorization for a service to Miami.[129] Nonetheless, there was something of a small success to celebrate in the end for the Dutch. Wartime conditions meant that Washington decided to honor the request for a KLM service to Miami on 6 May 1943 and the charter flights for Standard Oil were upgraded to a scheduled service. Until six months after the end of the war KLM would be allowed to fly to Miami twice a week.[130] Despite competition from PanAm, KLM's service opened on 17 August 1943.

5 Air Transport Politics in Wartime

From 1938 onwards, the political tensions in Europe, and subsequently the conditions of war, left their mark on air transport. In September 1938, airlines shuttled diplomats across Europe to mediate in the developing international crisis over Czechoslovakia. The British ambassador in Berlin, Neville Henderson, commuted between Berlin and London aboard KLM's aircraft. As the pressures on Czechoslovakia increased, KLM, Sabena, and Air France scheduled extra flights to Prague from 22 September to meet the steep rise in demand for tickets to destinations in Western Europe. The Czech airline ČLS also operated additional flights, delivering refugees – often Jews seeking asylum – at its Dutch stop in Rotterdam.[131] On the return flights East they carried Czechs hurrying to return home before borders might close. In the weeks leading up to the Munich Conference late in September, operational conditions deteriorated. Telegraph and telephone connections became problematic. Flights, most of them fully booked with people on urgent business, were closely monitored by the secret services and at least one machine was forced to land in Germany to have its passengers and cargo checked.[132] Other flights were cancelled.[133] On 24 September, the Czechs mobilized their army.

128 Letter Kasteel to PanAm in New York, 30 July 1943: NNA, 2.16.36, Waterworks, London Archive, inv.nr. 307.

129 Telegram Netherlands Ministry of Foreign Affairs in London to Kasteel, 21 Dec. 1942: NNA, 2.16.36, Waterworks, London Archive, inv.nr. 307.

130 Netherlands Ministry of Foreign Affairs in London to Minister for Water Management, J.W. Albarda, 26 May 1943: NNA, 2.16.36, Waterworks, London Archive, inv.nr. 307.

131 *Haagsche Courant*, 23 Sept. 1938.

132 *Het Vaderland*, 22 Sept. 1938. *De Volkskrant*, 23 Sept. 1938.

133 *De Standaard*, 24 Sept. 1938.

KLM, which had applied to lay in extra aircraft, saw itself forced to discontinue its service to Prague for the next two days. When flights were resumed on 26 September, passengers expressed anxiety about flying over Germany for fear that their machine might be grounded there. Services to Vienna and Budapest were suspended completely.[134] On 29 and 30 September an emergency summit conference of European powers took place in Munich, resulting in an agreement to give up Czechoslovakian territory to appease Germany.

After 'Munich' nothing in European aviation was as it had been. As a precaution against surprise air attacks, most countries closed all or parts of their airspace. When Britain and France issued guarantees in March 1939 to assure Poland's independence in response to Germany's military occupation of Czechoslovakia, London put pressure on The Hague to adopt a restrictive regime on German flights over Dutch territory. All over Europe civilian air traffic collapsed and what remained was tied to narrowly defined air corridors.

For the Dutch, one of the pressing problems of the new situation was whether and how it would be possible to keep the vital air service to Batavia going. Here too, European political tensions caused a surge in demand and in September 1938 KLM operated several extra flights. Plans to acquire new, high flying, long-range aircraft to operate the service, avoiding the need to pass over parts of Europe, now received urgency. However, technological development could not be rushed and KLM was forced to ponder a number of different options to keep its Indies' service going.

In July 1939 initial preparations were made to split the route into two operational segments: flying the Amsterdam-Cairo section with DC-2 aircraft, which used more readily available low octane fuel, then switching to the DC-3s, which burned high octane fuel, for the Cairo-Batavia section.[135] Dutch diplomats were sent out to secure Britain's cooperation for a possible alternative route to Batavia across the British-held territories in Africa. This, however, proved not to be an option, as the local fuel reserves along the projected route were not sufficient to provide for KLM's weekly flights. An alternative was to secure Italian cooperation for a service that would have Naples as its European operating base. But how to get there? Both routes and pilots were few. On 22 August 1939, the Netherlands' government called for a general mobilization, decimating KLM's pilot corps, which included quite a few reservists. The domestic network had to be discontinued. Services to and via Germany were terminated.

134 *De Volkskrant*, 24 Sept. 1938. *Het Volk*, 26 Sept. 1938.

135 Letter Hans Martin to Minister of Water Management, 29 Aug. 1939: NNA, 2.05.37, Archive Ministry of Foreign Affairs, 1919–1940, inv.nr. 4308.

On the very first day of the war, 1 September 1939, the Dutch envoy in Paris, John Loudon, deposited an urgent request at the French Foreign Office at the Quay d'Orsay to allow KLM to operate flights to Naples via France. Envisaging refueling stops in Bordeaux and Marseilles, KLM planned to fly the European sections of the Indies route over water whenever possible, avoiding the various forbidden French zones. A few flights were made, but in early September two KLM aircraft were fired upon by French air defenses, which caused grave concern. By mid-September it was no longer possible to maintain the service, as Paris closed its airspace completely. At Schiphol Airport, unsent mail was accumulating. Through contacts in Germany, Switzerland and Italy, an arrangement for the carriage of mail and passengers was worked out with the German railways, but under wartime conditions this deal proved unstable. The German authorities put up hurdles for transit visas to foreigners. Besides, Britons, the majority of passengers on KLM's Batavia service, were no longer allowed to travel via Germany and Italy after September 1939. This caused a serious drop in ticket sales. Given the uncertain international situation the transportation of colonials on leave also fell sharply. Even the carriage of mail shrank by one third.

With the exception of Brussels – Belgium reopened its airspace and airport to international flights on 20 September – only a few destinations that could be reached over water remained for KLM: Copenhagen, Malmö, and Oslo. On instructions from the RAF, the service to London had to be diverted to Shoreham by Sea near Brighton on the English South Coast. Many air travelers could not leave or return home as visas were revoked. As far as possible, air services were kept going from day to day, week to week, on the basis of temporary permissions. This was not without risk and Dutch neutrality provided no protection. Incidents were common. To increase safety, the fuselage, wings and tail surfaces of KLM aircraft were labelled 'HOLLAND' in large, easily recognizable black lettering. It turned out not to be enough. On 24 September 1939, KLM's DC-3 PH-ASM *Mees*, en route from Copenhagen to Amsterdam over the North Sea, was attacked by a German patrol plane. It cost one of the nine passengers his life, while the plane itself suffered significant damage. After landing at Schiphol, some 80 bullet holes were counted.[136] The incident led to the decision, in October, to paint all commercial airliners from the Netherlands, Belgium, Sweden and Denmark orange, starting with KLM's *Mees*. From 1 December 1939, KLM set about respraying the rest of its thirty-six aircraft – a

136 J.J. Moll, *Langs de hoge weg. Herinneringen uit een vliegersleven* (Den Haag: Van Hoeve, 1959), p. 114–123.

task that was still under way when the Germans invaded the country on 10 May 1940.[137]

In the final months of 1939, an increasing number of KLM aircraft were grounded, which prompted Plesman to come up with a new idea in October. He launched a plan to set up a subsidiary in Portugal that would operate charter flights for the Portuguese Government, serving Portugal's West African colony Angola. This was less of a wild plan than it seemed: in Lisbon Dutch technicians were involved in the construction of a new airport, Cintra, for which Schiphol served as a model. KLM's board did not really warm to the idea, but, given the special circumstances, went along with it. As part of the preparations, a DC-2 was stationed in Lisbon. This aircraft, KLM's only DC-2 to survive the war, landed there on 29 December. Plans were also being developed for a transatlantic postal service to Paramaribo, flown with stripped DC-3 aircraft that would receive an additional fuel tank. The idea was to fly non-stop from Amsterdam over the open sea to Lisbon, take on fuel there and then make the crossing to Surinam. In the period up to 10 May 1940, 12 return mail flights were made to Lisbon, but nothing came of the envisaged transatlantic service.[138]

Problems increased by the month. Equipping an operating base in Naples for the East Indies service became an urgent requirement. Repeated appeals to Berlin resulted in permission to fly three DC-3 aircraft to Naples carrying spare parts and supplies, via a roundabout route over Denmark, Germany and Austria. The three aircraft left from Schiphol on 2 November 1939. But the problem remained how to get passengers and mail to Naples in an effective manner. Renewed pleas to France to allow KLM to operate via Marseilles were to no avail. However, KLM secured an alternative arrangement early in 1940 whereby passengers and mail would be transported by rail via Paris.[139]

Significant operational problems continued. To keep the Batavia service going amid the belligerents, KLM relied on accumulated goodwill. The acquisition of fuel was a major concern: it was only through the intervention of the government and Royal Dutch Shell that KLM was able to secure enough high octane aviation fuel to feed the engines of its DC-3 aircraft and keep the Indies service going at all. Early in May 1940, tensions in Europe ramped up further and KLM decided to close its base in Naples by the end of the month. Three of KLM's four DC-3 aircraft stationed there were ordered to take off for Batavia immediately. The service would henceforth be operated from the Netherlands

137 Hagens, *Londen of Berlijn?* Vol. 1, *1939–1941*, p. 48–50.

138 Marc Dierikx, *Bevlogen Jaren. Nederlandse burgerluchtvaart tussen de wereldoorlogen* (Houten: Unieboek, 1986), p. 155–160. Hagens, *Londen of Berlijn*, Vol. 1, *1939–1941*, p. 72–75.

139 Hagens, *Londen of Berlijn, 1939–1941*, p. 45–52.

East Indies. A fourth machine left for England with technical staff and spare parts.[140]

In June and July 1940, a handful of KLM staff who had managed to travel to England after the Netherlands were invaded on 10 May negotiated through their British station manager at Croydon Airport, Henry Spry Leverton, the possibility of deploying the six KLM aircraft present in the British Isles for the Allied cause. Initially, the idea was to organize an air service from London, via Lisbon, Casablanca and Khartoum to Lydda [Lod], near Tel Aviv, as had already been discussed in the summer of 1939. Lydda would thus become the western terminus of what was left of the East Indies service. However, no agreement was reached with the British government on the finances of the operation. The Batavia service was shifted to Lydda nonetheless. Politics meant that the route itself had to be diverted from Iran (as Persia had been named since March 1935) to the British protectorates on the southern shore of the Persian Gulf, because Iran closed its airspace to civilian aircraft. In exchange for cooperation to enable them to continue flying, London requested Dutch consent for the possibility of requisitioning KLM aircraft for war purposes in November 1940. No objections were raised.[141] Until the fall of Singapore and the Dutch East Indies in February and March 1942 made the continuation of the service impossible, the shortened Batavia route was maintained, even though cooperation with the British remained at times problematic.[142] Nevertheless, in June 1941 an agreement was reached under which KLM was allowed to carry British mail. However, the hoped-for extension of the service from Lydda to Cairo did not materialize due to opposition from the Egyptian authorities.[143]

On the other end of the line, the air service from the Dutch East Indies to Australia also remained an issue. Pulling out all the stops, KLM and KNILM managed to keep the air route going in the first years of the war. Just like the Lydda-Batavia service, flights took place under KNILM's aegis. From early February 1942, the pressure of war necessitated a reduction of operational frequency to one flight per week, since the Dutch East Indies were under Japanese attack. On Sunday 15 February 1942, the last machine of KLM's flagship service landed in Batavia.[144] Thereafter, and in the light of the worsening military situation, most of the civilian air traffic in the East Indies consisted of

140 Hagens, *Londen of Berlijn, 1939–1941*, p. 158–166.

141 Letter Van Kleffens to Michiels van Verduynen, 15 Nov. 1940: NNA, 2.05.80 Foreign Affairs, London Archive, inv.nr. 3332.

142 Dierikx, *Bevlogen Jaren*, p. 164–168. Hagens, *Londen of Berlijn, 1939–1941*, p. 300–302.

143 Letter Harold Balfour to Albarda, 2 June 1941: NNA, 2.05.80 Foreign Affairs, London Archive, inv.nr. 3332.

144 Jan Hagens, *Londen of Berlijn*, dl.2, p. 61–70.

evacuation flights to Australia. The eleven aircraft that made it to Sydney at the time of the Dutch military collapse in March 1942 were sold to the US Air Force in May. In the Indonesian archipelago, KNILM's properties were confiscated by the Japanese.[145] At the end of the war in August 1945, KNILM existed only on paper.

Unrelated to the developments above, talks had been held in London in the summer of 1940 on organizing a KLM service from Britain to neutral Lisbon, carried out as a charter for the British Overseas Airways Corporation (BOAC). Flights would be made from Bristol, the operating base that the RAF had assigned to KLM. In August 1940, operations started with about forty staff using the five aircraft that remained. Until the termination of the service in January 1946, KLM would carry 18,108 passengers and an unknown quantity of mail and cargo on the route.

But the Dutch plans went beyond that. From September 1943 onwards, talks were initiated with Portugal on setting up an air service from Lisbon across the Atlantic to Paramaribo in Surinam.[146] KLM's plans even extended to Rio de Janeiro and Buenos Aires. The Dutch envoy, Peter Teppema, already envisaged such a service.[147] Before the war, Air France and Italy's Ala Littoria had also been planning a service to Brazil and therefore some of the basic groundwork had already been done. However, the Dutch lacked aircraft to operate the route and the discussions made little progress.

It appeared easier to expand Dutch airline operations from Curaçao and Paramaribo. In the spring of 1943, the airline Panair do Brasil, a subsidiary of PanAm, had applied for a permit in Surinam to set up a connection from Brazil to the United States, via Paramaribo. Progress was slow, but in July 1943, the Dutch became convinced that an agreement on the Panair service should be made dependent on KLM obtaining reciprocal rights in Rio de Janeiro.[148] Brazil promised these on 2 October, but domestic entanglements in Brazil led Panair

---

145 Chronologic report on KNILM developments since 8 December 1941, undated (presumably March 1945): NNA, 2.10.45, Colonies, London Archive, inv.nr. 107. For a detailed account of KNILM-operations in 1941 and 1942, see G.J. Hagens, *De KNILM vloog door...* (Haarlem: Uitgeverij Bakkenes, 1972) and Jan Hagens, *Londen of Berlijn*, dl. 2, *1942–1945*, p. 35–114, 177–196.

146 Letter Albarda to Van Kleffens, 24 July 1944: NNA, 2.05.80, Foreign Affairs, London Archive, inv.nr. 3364.

147 Letter Teppema to Plesman, 20 Apr. 1940: NNA, 2.05.80, Foreign Affairs, London Archive, inv.nr. 3336.

148 Code message Van Kleffens to the Dutch envoy in Rio de Janeiro (Willem Daniëls), in: *Documenten Betreffende de Buitenlandse Politiek van Nederland*, 1940–1945, Vol. 7, nr. 35.

to abandon its plans later that year.[149] Although these discussions lead to naught, in January 1944 the Dutch again proposed the issue. In the absence of suitable aircraft talks stalled and no actual flights were made.

Contacts with Argentina developed along similar lines. These too largely remained on the back burner. In March 1944 the Dutch tried to revive the air services issue as the end of the war appeared to draw nearer, assuming that Brazil and Argentina might wish to escape from PanAm's aviation dominance and be willing to do business.[150] However, Dutch diplomats were proved to be not particularly well informed and talks soon ran aground. In any case, in May 1945 Argentina issued a decree stating that all aviation in and to the country should have an exclusively national Argentinian character.[151]

This Argentinian decree resulted from the outcome of the big international aviation conference organized by the United States in Chicago in November 1944. Under the chairmanship of Assistant Secretary of State Adolf Berle, the aim of the conference was to establish a general world-wide regulatory system and set technical standards for post-war international air transport. American policy makers hoped to reach agreement on 'an increase in existing services and on the early establishment of international air routes (…) by general agreement to be reached at the Conference.'[152]

The starting point was to establish a global legal regime for aviation based on liberalism and the granting of 'freedoms' that would enable international commercial air services.[153] However, the American point of departure was not uncontroversial. In November 1944 the United States was the only country in the world to possess a functional civilian air transport system. And what was more: America alone had the industrial capacity to build the aircraft that would be needed to operate international routes. This gave American air carriers a huge advantage in the postwar world and meant they were likely to capture the lion's share of international traffic.

---

149 Letter envoy in Rio de Janeiro (Daniëls) to Governor of Surinam, 21 Oct. 1943: NNA, 2.05.80, Foreign Affairs, London Archive, inv.nr. 3353.

150 Memorandum Foreign Affairs for Ministry of Water Management, March 1944: NNA, 2.05.80, Foreign Affairs, London Archive, inv.nr. 3336.

151 Chargé d'Affaires in Buenos Aires to Foreign Ministry in London, 4 May 1945: NNA, 2.05.80, Foreign Affairs, London Archive, inv.nr. 3336.

152 Note American embassy in London to Neth. Foreign Ministry, 14 Sept. 1944: NNA, 2.05.80 Foreign Affairs, London Archive, inv.nr. 3377.

153 Alan Dobson, *A History of International Civil Aviation. From its Origins through Transformative Evolution* (London: Routledge, 2017), p. 37–51. Marc Dierikx, Shaping World Aviation: Anglo-American Civil Aviation Relations, 1944–1946, in: *Journal of Air Law and Commerce* 57 (1992) nr. 4, p. 795–840. N.M. Matte, *Treatise on Air-Aeronautical Law* (Toronto: Carswell, 1981), p. 125–130.

Britain, supported to some extent by Canada and other Commonwealth countries, feared American dominance in post-war aviation and voiced serious reservations. From early on London put forward its view that some form of regulation of international aviation was desirable to create an equal playing field. In the British view this could best be achieved through the institution of some form of international authority that would oversee the orderly development of air transport and prevent undue competition between the various national carriers. London had good reason to be concerned, given Washington's role in the development of PanAm.[154] In contrast to Washington's premise of liberalism, London put forward a plan for a supranational organization that would oversee the most important international air services. The idea was that each country should be entitled to a proportion of the traffic.[155] Thus, liberalism and supranationality became each other's opposites at the Chicago conference.

In September 1944, the Netherlands' exiled government in London had also received an invitation. It seemed the right time to make a strong point about freedom for international air traffic, especially since past contacts with Washington over Dutch operating rights to Manila and Miami had fed doubts about the American motives for promoting liberalism. In order to suppress a conflict of opinions at the Chicago Conference, the Dutch embassy in Washington gave out warnings 'not to cause any unnecessary difficulties' that might damage relations with the Netherlands' most powerful ally.[156] In Chicago, the Dutch delegation therefore supported the American objectives and prided itself on being involved in drawing up technical standards. The Dutch oversaw the editing process for Committee III, which concerned itself with establishing the standards for international air services agreements. This was, however, not the most influential role in Chicago. And although the Dutch had serious reservations about the way chairman Berle was wheeling and dealing to get America's interests across, the political instructions from the exiled government in London and the embassy in Washington ensured that the Dutch voice was no more than a whisper in the corridors of the Stevens Hotel in Chicago, where the conference was held.[157]

---

154 Alan P. Dobson, *Peaceful Air Warfare. The United States, Britain and the Politics of International Aviation* (Oxford: Oxford University Press, 1991), p. 188–191. Jennifer van Vleck, *Empire of the Air* (2013).

155 Dierikx, Shaping World Aviation, p. 803–808.

156 Memorandum Van Boetzelaer, substitute envoy Washington, 21 Sep. 1944: NNA, 2.05.80, Foreign Affairs, London Archive, inv.nr. 3377.

157 David MacKenzie, *ICAO: A History of the International Civil Aviation Organization* (Toronto: University of Toronto Press, 2010) does not even mention the Dutch efforts to contribute to the Chicago conference.

Given the political, military and economic power shown by the United States in the war, the American points of view were leading the course of discussions in Chicago. President Roosevelt was known to be an advocate of freedom in the air and indeed it appeared that the conference would bring greater freedom in international air transport than the Paris Convention had allowed. But beyond the view of the Dutch delegates, the chairman of the American Civil Aeronautics Board (CAB), Lloyd Welch Pogue, schemed to limit the freedom concept, thus protecting the future commercial interests of the American airline industry and keep foreign, subsidized competitors at bay.[158] The Dutch delegates were in blissful ignorance of this agenda and went home satisfied with the results.[159]

The South American countries also supported Washington's proposals on freedom in the air, although caveats were heard from Brazil. Australia, Canada, France, Belgium, Norway, Portugal and Turkey supported the British position.[160] Nonetheless, the delegations in Chicago agreed on one point: the absolute sovereignty of national states in the air was not conducive to the rapid development of air transport. Only the Soviet Union fundamentally disagreed, but its delegates had left before the conference opened.

After a month of discussions, the Chicago Convention on International Civil Aviation was signed on 7 December 1944. The British objections to American liberalism were, however, registered. As in the Paris Convention, article 1 set out complete and exclusive sovereignty of states in the airspace above their territory. Only aircraft that did not operate according to a specified public timetable, such as charter flights, would be permitted to fly without bilaterally agreed traffic rights granted beforehand. Under the regime provided in article 5 of the Convention, such flights could operate on the basis of ad hoc consent by the landing state. Next, article 6 of the Chicago Convention dealt with International scheduled air services. Such services would remain dependent on special permission or other prior authorization by the states involved, to be confirmed in air services agreements between them. States were entitled to reserve cabotage, defined as the transportation of passengers or goods for remuneration within the territory or territories of a state, for aircraft registered in that particular state (article 7). The treaty's more liberal aspects were

---

158 I am indebted to my late friend professor Alan Dobson (†2022) for pointing this out.

159 Report of the Netherlands' delegation at the International Civil Aviation Conference, held in Chicago from 1 November to 8 December 1944, 15 December 1944: NNA, 2.05.80, Foreign Affairs, London Archive, inv.nr 3375.

160 Telegram Lord Swinton, (chair of the British delegation) to Sir Edward Bridges, Secretary of the War Cabinet, 4 Nov. 1944: BNA, Foreign Office, FO371, inv.nr. 42580.

expressed in the two important agreements that were also committed to paper at the Chicago Conference: the International Air Services Transit Agreement and the International Air Transport Agreement. The first, crucial for international operations, recognized the right of peaceful passage through the airspace of Treaty States and land there for the purpose of technical stops (e.g. to take on fuel). It was signed by all the states present in Chicago. The second, the International Air Transport Agreement, provided for the exchange of five specified commercial freedoms for the operation of scheduled air services between Treaty States. Only ten states signed this second annex, among whom were the United States and the Netherlands. Together, the two international agreements defined the five 'Freedoms of the Air' identified in the preface of this book.[161] In doing so, the die was cast for the development of post-war aviation.

6 In Conclusion

The origins and development of the relationship between air transport and government can be traced to the early days of flight, when national states first claimed control over the airspace above their territory. After the end of World War I, such ideas were reflected in an international regulatory regime for civil aviation, the Paris Convention. In subsequent years this treaty provided the backdrop to the emergence of a new field of international foreign relations, aviation policy. The field linked national interests with the prestige emanating from the exciting new technology of civil air transport, then very much in the public eye.

The Netherlands woke up late to this new field in foreign relations. The government took ten years to adopt aerial legislation, and shunned international commitments as a consequence. Nonetheless, in the early 1930s, it became clear that it was necessary to develop an international aviation policy. Generally ill-prepared, The Hague lacked awareness of the various international problems that presented themselves when it came to the development of the national airline KLM. As a consequence, Dutch international air transport ran into all sorts of unexpected troubles.

161 Matte, *Treatise on Air-Aeronautical Law.* Text Chicago Convention, plus annexes and agreements, p. 605–632; interpretation and explication: p. 140–157. See also: Mendes de Leon, *Introduction to Air Law*, p. 9–47.

CHAPTER 2

1945–1949: Reorientation

1 Introduction

> London, Paris, Copenhagen have come to be 'next door'. Batavia, New York, Tehran, Curaçao, Johannesburg, we now speak of them as if they were destinations for family outings. In 1920, a KLM machine flew little faster than 100 km per hour; and now, in 1949, it's already 450 km per hour. Flying is no longer an adventure for the tourist and the businessman. We now sit back in the soft cushions of an easy armchair, even more comfortable than in a Pullman train, and allow ourselves to be served by handsome flight attendants, so that we hardly get to peer out of the window to the world below us. Cotton ear waddings and disposal bags have gone out of fashion. Our KLM machines, quiet four-engine giants, drone across mountains and oceans, from airport to airport, which are no longer mazes for curious newspaper people, but business stations where tens of thousands of 'ordinary' journeys begin and end every year and where therefore tighter control than before has become necessary. But … the nostalgia in commemorating how it once was: not easily forgotten![1]

If modern aviation, to some Dutch observers, gave cause for nostalgia after the war, general conditions in the Netherlands did not. With widespread devastation, housing was a problem for many. Agricultural areas had been laid waste and livestock decimated. Industry was virtually paralyzed. The transport infrastructure lay in ruins as roads and bridges had been damaged and private cars, lorries and buses had largely disappeared. A considerable portion of the railways' rolling stock had been seized by the Germans.[2] Consumer goods were rationed, and economic necessity drove the government to freeze wages while reconstruction plans were drawn up. The government was necessarily the central actor driving efforts to rebuild the economy. Across the border, Germany lay in ruins. International economic contacts and trade were at a standstill, handicapped by the non-convertibility of national currencies. Further away in Europe a rift between West and East was developing, with Allied

1 *Algemeen Handelsblad*, 5 Oct. 1949. Translation by the author.

2 Marc Dierikx, Bram Bouwens, *Building castles of the air. Schiphol Amsterdam and the development of airport infrastructure in Europe* (The Hague: Sdu Publishers, 1997), p. 73–75.

 | DOI:10.1163/9789004695245_003

and Soviet troops garrisoned on different sides of a de facto divide. In Western Europe this military and political split was reflected in American programs for political adhesion and economic reconstruction that gained in strength as time progressed, with the Truman Doctrine and the Marshall Aid program both introduced in 1947. Western European governments rallied to underwrite this evidence of American leadership, to the detriment of Britain and France. The old order of colonial empires on which British and French power had been built was crumbling. The war and its moral connotations had driven demands for independence in areas hitherto ruled from Europe. By extension, the Dutch position as a medium sized colonial power was also under pressure.

A new world order beckoned, led by the new superpower, the United States, with its nuclear weapons, its thriving economy and above all its prosperity shining as a beacon of hope across the Atlantic. By contrast, the Dutch economy was in urgent need of reconstitution and a change from its prewar orientation based on labor intensive agriculture to one in which industrial production played a more central role. This was reflected in government programs for mechanization, industrialization and the promotion of exports. In many ways the new outlook of these programs was in direct conflict with nostalgia and traditional forces to restore tradition. Colonial relations were a case in point. After centuries of Dutch presence in Asia it was unthinkable for many that the war had changed the checkerboard of global power relations. It took the Dutch years to come to terms with the new realities, gruesomely evidenced in a bloody colonial war in the Dutch East Indies, which worked to the detriment of one of the prime instruments that represented the new Dutch outlook on the postwar world: air transport. KLM, as the national carrier, had a role to play in the increasingly international orientation that the Netherlands embraced after 1945. Nonetheless, colonial nostalgia and war had considerable consequences for Dutch aviation and air transport policy.

In 1945 the changed state of international relations required The Hague to push forward the new, active foreign policy that Van Kleffens had announced in 1943. In the years that followed, the traditional close relations with Britain gave way to the need to take into account the interests of the United States as the world's leading nation. Although Dutch postwar governments continued to claim a status of 'middle power', this was seldom recognized abroad. In international affairs the big powers ruled. By necessity, foreign policy began to steer away from the traditions of independence and neutrality, instead being reinvented with a far greater focus on stimulating international trade and finances.[3] Subsequent governments embarked upon an economic policy

3 Hellema, *Nederland in de wereld*, p. 115–120.

aimed at fostering industrialization and exports. The development of new markets was considered of prime importance for a country forced to relinquish its colonial status and adapt itself to a reduced international ranking. Export promotion to boost the economy and combat the balance of payments deficits that existed since 1945 became a core component of economic and of foreign policy.[4] This is where air transport came in.

The war itself acted as a watershed for aviation technology, with innovations in aerodynamics and enormous advances in engine performance. Transport airplanes had become bigger and were able to fly faster and further. This put the clauses of the new Chicago Convention and of its related international agreements to an immediate test. How would they hold up in practice: would air transport be able to develop more freely than had been the case before the war, or would the principles of sovereignty again prove decisive? And would the fears of the European countries become a reality, with American aviation, using the 'freedoms of the air' defined in the agreements attached to the Chicago Convention, as a set-up to take over world air transport? The first signs were not hopeful. On 3 February 1945, the US and Ireland signed an agreement that granted American aircraft general operating rights between the United States, Ireland, and points beyond.[5] In its wake Washington commenced negotiations for bilateral civil aviation agreements with Greece, Egypt, Iraq, Iran, and Lebanon. In July 1945, the State Department informed its European allies of American intentions to operate six transatlantic air routes to various capitals in Europe.[6] Washington appeared to be in a hurry to acquire a lead in international air transport at a time when Britain was still focusing on avoiding competition. It appeared in Washington that London might gear up to obstruct the spread of American commercial air services.[7] London's Ministry of Civil Aviation in particular regarded fifth freedom rights as an intrusion of uncontrollable commercialism into the predominantly political and strategic business of maintaining overseas air routes.[8] For the Dutch, staunch believers of the principle of freedom in the air, such differences spelled trouble. Rallying

4 White Paper Minister of Economic Affairs J.R.M. Van den Brink to the Netherlands Council for Economic Affairs, 19 Oct. 1949: NNA (Netherlands National Archive), 2.02.05.02, Council of Ministers, nr. 582.

5 Agreement between the United States of America and Ireland Relating to Air Transport Services, 3 Feb. 1945, United States National Archives, Department of State, Record Group 59, inv. nr. 1402.

6 Telegram State Department to Netherlands Embassy in London, 5 July 1945: NNA, 2.05.80, Foreign Affairs, London Archive, inv.nr. 3386.

7 MacKenzie, *ICAO. A History*, p. 62.

8 Note from Sir George Cribbett, Deputy Secretary Ministry of Civil Aviation, to the Minister of Civil Aviation, 15 June 1945: BNA (British National Archive), Air Ministry, AVIA 2, 2759.

behind the American point of view would mean accepting a role for KLM that would at best be secondary compared to that of the American airlines. Accepting the British take on things meant that KLM's transport rights might come to depend on the judgement of an international authority. Clearly, The Hague needed to develop and uphold its own point of view.

At the end of the war, civil aviation had to be reinvented. Initially there was no room for civilian operations and for those airlines that had more or less survived the war, obtaining aircraft was an immediate problem. As was the case elsewhere, KLM depended on the government for equipment, as wartime circumstances made it impossible to place orders of its own. Since 1943, the Dutch government-in-exile had been considering the purchase of transport aircraft. Decision making revolved around airplanes that could be used after the return to peace to operate the air connection with the Dutch East Indies. The government-in-exile placed an order for the Douglas C-54 Skymaster, the military version of the DC-4 airliner. To be able to fly in the uncertain environment after the cessation of hostilities, a semi-military government air transport service was set up. The actual operation of the service was entrusted to KLM.[9] This structure had several advantages. KLM could use the aircraft that the government obtained from the US on a lend-lease basis as part of the war effort. Flying in the guise of a government service, rather than as a commercial airline, also provided protection against the British policy to postpone the restoration of civil air traffic for at least a year after the war, which would allow British airline companies time to procure aircraft and assume a prominent role. As early as 1943, one of Britain's leading politicians, Lord Beaverbrook, had noted that its geographical position and its vital interests overseas meant that Britain 'can become and should become a dominating factor in the air transport system of the Continent.'[10] This point of view was echoed by George Cribbett, the senior official at London's Ministry of Civil Aviation.[11]

British policy spelled trouble for Dutch hopes of a speedy restoration of international air transport. Moreover, KLM had seen its fleet diminish over the war. In October 1944, the government-in-exile requisitioned two of KLM's remaining six machines to set up an air link from England to Eindhoven in the liberated south of the Netherlands.[12] The aircraft were adorned with military

9 Hagens, *Londen of Berlijn*, dl. 2, *1942–1945*, p. 208–209.

10 Minute Beaverbrook to Churchill, 14 Oct. 1943: BNA, Cabinet Office files (CAB) 87, 61129.

11 Memorandum Cribbett to William Hildred, Director-General of Civil Aviation, 25 June 1945: BNA, Ministry of Civil Aviation, BT217, 126.

12 Ben van Eysselsteijn, *Naar breeder vlucht. Van vrede tot vrede*, (Den Haag: Leopolds, 1946), p. 427.

registrations and call signs. KLM's management in London was not happy about this arrangement and lobbied for permission to set up a civil air service of its own from Croydon Airport.[13] The plea went unheeded: London banned civil flying operations for the time being. Only the Swedish airline ABA was exempted. In the summer of 1945, it was the only carrier permitted to operate a commercial service to Europe.[14] Other than this, London's airports were not released for civil use until February 1946. As had been the case during the war, air travel was reserved for military and government officials in possession of special priority papers. Obtaining the necessary visa was a problem in itself. In the first year after the war, it repeatedly happened that people were not allowed on or off aircraft because the relevant paperwork or the correct stamps were missing.[15]

Air services to the makeshift facilities at Amsterdam's Schiphol Airport were barely possible after Liberation. Of the airport itself, little more than a large plain littered with bomb craters remained. Bombed-out hangars and a few makeshift wooden barracks lined the perimeter. To operate as an airport the site required extensive repairs and the construction of new buildings, yet many of the things needed for such improvements were lacking. Building materials and their supply were a particular problem. About 70 percent of the transport equipment in the country had been destroyed or taken away by the Germans.[16] Aviation seemed to be back where it started in 1920 and it was two months after Liberation before the first civilian machine, a DC-3 from ABA, landed at Schiphol Airport on 28 July 1945. Not until the end of September was KLM ready to set up a few provisional domestic services using six De Havilland Dominie biplanes that the government put at its disposal and the shortage of aircraft meant that only a few flights per day could be made. Meanwhile it was considered important to become part of the resurgent international air network. Despite the dire state of the national finances, plans for airport reconstruction received priority as one of the ways to reconnect a war isolated economy with international developments.

Although the airline continued to struggle with a shortage of aircraft, KLM's chief executive Albert Plesman promoted ambitious plans for rapid expansion. He was adamant that the Netherlands could and should claim a significant

13 Letter H. Spry Leverton, KLM's London Station Manager, to Sir William Hildred, 5 May 1945: BNA, Ministry of Civil Aviation, BT217, 610.

14 Report Tromp on meeting with Swinton in London on 24 July 1945: NNA, 2.05.117, Foreign Affairs 1945–1954, inv.nr. 9862.

15 Minutes 2nd BLV (Civil Aviation Meeting: BLV), 3 Dec. 1945: NNA, 2.05.117, Foreign Affairs 1945–1954, inv.nr. 1689.

16 Pieter Lieftinck, *Herinneringen* (Utrecht/Antwerpen: Veen, 1989), p. 88.

role in world air transport. With Plesman as the prime mover, The Hague was charged to prioritize the international hunt for landing rights. Such a policy required focus at the level of the ministries involved, plus a pro-active attitude by the Dutch diplomatic service. At Plesman's behest a consultative body, the Civil Aviation Meeting [Burgerluchtvaartvergadering], was established in October 1945. This initiative was supported by the traffic advisor at the Ministry of Foreign Affairs, Carel Schaepman. Three Ministries were involved initially: Foreign Affairs, Traffic, and Overseas Territories. Government officials gathered on a regular basis with senior representatives of KLM and KNILM to coordinate policy. In addition to Schaepman as chairman, two of his Foreign Affairs colleagues, Peter Witte and Johan (Siem) Nieuwenhuijsen, served as delegates. They were joined by Henri van Ede van der Pals and Henk Spanjaard, director and chief official, respectively, of the newly formed National Aviation Service [Rijksluchtvaartdienst], and M. van Loon and Daniël van der Meulen of the Ministry of Overseas Territories. On behalf of KLM Albert Plesman sat on the committee, assisted by the airline's general secretary Hans van der Wiel. Hendrik Nieuwenhuis represented KNILM.[17]

The Civil Aviation Meeting united corporate and public interests and was highly innovative in an era in which tradition was still strong at Foreign Affairs. The promotion of trade interests was not something that came naturally to the diplomatic corps. To further promote Dutch air transport the government decided to appoint a special aviation attaché to the legations in the two most prominent foreign capitals, London and Washington, a move that was indicative of the importance The Hague ascribed to aviation as a foreign policy issue. The Netherlands had only a limited number of attaché posts at the various legations in foreign capitals. On 9 November 1945, Daniël Goedhuis, professor of Air Law at Leiden University, was appointed to serve in this capacity in London. Goedhuis had earned his doctorate in 1933 with a dissertation on the application of international private law in the air.[18] He subsequently taught air law at Leiden until the war led him to flee to Britain in 1944. Initially, his main tasks as a diplomat focused on preventing American and British aviation interests from combining to the detriment of the Dutch. In the years that followed, Goedhuis became involved in virtually all negotiations on KLM landing rights anywhere in the world.[19]

17 Minutes 1st BLV, 29 Oct. 1945: NNA, 2.05.117, Foreign Affairs 1945–1954, inv.nr: 1689.

18 Daniël Goedhuis, *National Airlegislations and the Warsaw Convention* (The Hague: Nijhoff, 1937).

19 Marc Dierikx, Frappez Toujours. De diplomaat en het luchtvervoer, in: Bob de Graaff, Duco Hellema (eds.), *Instrumenten van buitenlandse politiek. Achtergronden en praktijk van de Nederlandse diplomatie* (Amsterdam: Boom, 2007), p. 71–78.

If the general purpose of the Civil Aviation Meeting was to coordinate Dutch policy on landing rights, its initial priorities were more narrowly defined, with reinstatement of the old pre-war rights to fly to the Dutch East Indies firmly at the top of the list. Along with the desire to open a new air connection to New York, KLM also hoped to operate services to the Dutch territories in the Caribbean and fly from the Caribbean to South America, while KNILM worked on plans for air links from the Dutch East Indies to China, the United States and Australia.[20] The problem with this 'wish list' was that the Netherlands did not have the aircraft to provide such services. The Dutch situation was not exceptional. After five years of war, all the airlines in Europe were in a bad state, with aircraft deliveries depending entirely on the US. The first of the 14 Douglas C-54 transport aircraft the Dutch obtained in lend-lease from the United States landed at Schiphol Airport on 17 September 1945. Airlines in the surrounding countries were in no better shape. In Belgium, Sabena had only a pair of Lockheed Lodestar aircraft located in the Congo,[21] while Deutsche Luft Hansa had completely ceased to exist.[22] Only Air France had more, about 30 planes, most of them dating from before the war, supplemented by a dozen Junkers Ju-52s left over from the German occupation.[23] Small wonder then that American intentions in the air were regarded with suspicion in Europe. The outcome of the US-Irish agreement of 1945 appeared to confirm this.

Meanwhile, The Hague regarded American intentions in the air with suspicion, which was only made worse by the bilateral discussions underway between Washington and London. To the dismay of the British, the US wished to procure 5th freedom rights in the United Kingdom, which would give their carriers a huge push to build a dominant position in air transport to Europe. In Washington, the CAB argued for using deliveries of ex-military transport aircraft as leverage to secure these rights.[24] More weight still was carried by Washington's threat to hold up the Loan Agreement that was pending in Congress and which London desperately needed to finance its postwar

20 Minutes 1st BLV, 29 Oct. 1945: NNA, 2.05.117, Foreign Affairs 1945–1954, inv.nr: 1689.

21 Guy Vanthemsche, *La Sabena. L'Aviation commerciale Belge 1923–2001. Des origines au crash* (Brussel: De Boeck, 2002), p. 104–107.

22 Lutz Budrass, *Adler und Kranich. Die Lufthansa und ihre Geschichte 1926–1955* (München: Blessing, 2016), p. 433–438.

23 Robert Espérou, Gérard Maoui, *Air France. Des origins à nos jours* (Paris: Le Cherche Midi, 1997), p. 38–39. Nicolas Neiertz, Air France: an elephant in an evening suit, in: Hans Dienel, Peter Lyth (eds.), *Flying the Flag. European Commercial Air Transport since 1945* (Basingstoke: MacMillan, 1998), p. 26.

24 Letter CAB chairman L. Welch Pogue to the Secretary of State, 16 July 1945: Harry S. Truman Presidential Library, CAB, General, C7 (box 10).

reconstruction, unless Britain would come to an agreement on a bilateral settlement concerning civil aviation.[25]

To find a solution, Britain and the United States agreed in November 1945 to convene a special bilateral conference to discuss matters. The Bermuda Islands were chosen as the venue, with delegations meeting between 15 January and 11 February 1946. The British negotiators found themselves in a tight spot: the need to secure a crucial American loan for Britain's economic reconstruction in Congress forced them to give America's airlines more freedom than London had wanted. Nonetheless, the delegations reached agreement on a standard model for bilateral exchanges of traffic and landing rights, henceforth known as the Bermuda Agreement.[26] The accord was in effect a balance in mutual air transport capacity on the transatlantic route, with a provision to escalate an airline's capacity on the basis of traffic results achieved. In return for an agreement that curbed free competition, US airlines were allowed to fly to Britain and let 5th freedom passengers destined for points beyond the United Kingdom board in London. Both parties agreed that the price of air tickets would be determined and approved by the two governments concerned. This way London could prevent its national carrier BOAC from being wiped out by American competition and put a stop to the predatory pricing of tickets.[27] It was agreed that both countries would henceforth promote 'Bermuda' as a model for other bilateral agreements.

2 Re-Developing Dutch Air Services in Europe

For various reasons, Britain was at the top of the list of countries with which the Netherlands wanted to reach air traffic agreements as soon as possible. In the early postwar years Britain represented some 10 per cent of the total volume of Dutch foreign trade, although at a deficit to The Hague.[28] As early as 4 May 1945, Plesman arrived in London to plead to allow KLM services from Amsterdam.[29] However, the Air Ministry was not receptive to an exchange

---

25 Telegram British Embassy, Washington, to Foreign Office, London, 17 Nov. 1945: BNA, Foreign Office, FO371, 50,267.

26 Dierikx, Shaping World Aviation, p. 829–840. Dobson, *Peaceful air warfare*, p. 173–210.

27 Alan Dobson, *A History of International Civil Aviation. From its Origins through Transformative Evolution* (London: Routledge, 2017), p. 52–73.

28 Wendy Asbeek Brusse, Dutch-British Commercial Relations in a European Context, in: Nigel John Ashton, Duco Hellema (eds.), *Unspoken Allies: Anglo-Dutch Relations Since 1780* (Amsterdam: AUP, 2001), p. 204, 207.

29 Letter J.W. Sefton Brancker (BOAC) to Plesman, 4 May 1945: BNA, MCA, BT217, 64.

of rights. Although London had the transport airplanes needed to operate a reciprocal service, the terms of the Lend-lease Agreement under which the US had supplied the aircraft stipulated they could only be used for military purposes. This meant the resumption of commercial air traffic had to be put on hold for the time being.[30] While regular airline companies were not operating, London used 110 Wing of RAF Transport Command as the military guise under which BOAC provided air transport to the continent.[31]

Nonetheless, KLM kept knocking on doors to be allowed to fly. Less than a week after the signing of the Bermuda Agreement a Dutch delegation sat down in London to consult with the Foreign Office and the new Ministry of Civil Aviation. They found the British committed to an equal distribution of capacity following the 'Bermuda' example. London also wanted bilateral agreements on the tariffs to be applied. The Hague was strongly opposed to this, as it would prevent normal commercial operations and make KLM dependent on policies made in London.[32]

The talks were intense, but after three days of discussions the Dutch managed to persuade their British counterparts to agree to a more liberal deal. Given the sorry state of Britain's airlines, this was surprising. However, the ink was barely dry before London had second thoughts, because the Ministry of Civil Aviation felt that KLM had received too much freedom. They tabled a new proposal that again held a fifty-fifty division of capacity. When the Dutch did not warm to this idea the Ministry of Civil Aviation warned they might withhold transport rights at Prestwick in Scotland and at Gander, Newfoundland (at the time a British dominion), for KLM's envisaged transatlantic service to New York.[33] While Goedhuis, himself an Anglophile and well acquainted in London thanks to his British spouse, could understand this point of view, the officials at Foreign Affairs in The Hague were less accommodating. Transport advisor Schaepman noted: 'This is a great disappointment, to which we should not resign.' Goedhuis was instructed to hand over a sharp protest note.[34] After all, 5th freedom traffic was vital if KLM was to operate profitably.

30 Memorandum Cribbett to Hildred on civil aviation development in Europe, 25 June 1945: BNA, MCA, BT217, 126.

31 (Secret and Personal) letter Swinton to Sir Archibald Sinclair, 20 April 1945: BNA, MCA, BT217, 90.

32 Report on negotiations, 18–21 Feb. 1946: NNA, 2.05.117, Foreign Affairs 1945–1954, inv.nr. 9925.

33 Letter Gallop to Michiels van Verduynen, 4 June 1946: NNA, 2.05.117, Foreign Affairs 1945–1954, inv.nr. 9925.

34 Office memo Nieuwenhuijsen, 19 March with comment Schaepman, 22 March 1946: NNA, 2.05.117, Foreign Affairs 1945–1954, inv.nr. 9925.

In the end the matter was settled after a realignment within the British government that gave the Foreign Office the full prerogative in international affairs.[35] To the relief of the Dutch, London's diplomats factored in the interests of good relations with neighboring countries and KLM received permission for a temporary service from Maastricht in the south of the Netherlands to London. Scheduled flights from Amsterdam were also welcomed, and the Dutch received rights to operate to New York and Curaçao via a northern route through Gander, Newfoundland, and a southern route stopping in the Bermuda Islands.[36]

But for KLM, in a hurry to rebuild its former position in European air transport, these concessions were not enough. The airline was seeking an air mail service to Prague, across the British occupation zone in Germany, trial flights to Johannesburg via the British colonies in Africa, and commercial rights in Lydda and in Singapore.[37] On top of this, Plesman complained that KLM did not have rights for a commercial stop in London on its transatlantic route, as Britain had allowed the American carriers.[38] KLM's appetite for air services was insatiable. By 1947 a pattern was emerging in which the lion's share of air transport between Britain and the Netherlands was carried by KLM, offering seven times the number of seats per week that British European Airlines (BEA), the struggling corporation responsible for most of Britain's short-haul routes, was able to offer.[39] Clearly, this was a recipe for future bilateral disputes.

While the first postwar aviation contacts with Britain were marred by the lack of civil transport aircraft, which precluded commercial operations, the first contacts with France went smoothly. In August 1945, Paris settled on a restoration of the pre-war agreements. These would enable airlines from both countries to fly pending official notification of the end of hostilities. The Hague was glad to cooperate and licensed Air France for a service to Amsterdam. In further talks, Paris was particularly accommodating, even offering to make two

35 Letter Gallop to Michiels van Verduynen, 4 June 1946: NNA, 2.05.117, Foreign Affairs 1945–1954, inv.nr. 9925.,

36 Agreement between government of the United Kingdom and government of the Netherlands for certain air services, 13 Aug. 1946: NNA, 2.05.117, Foreign Affairs 1945–1954, inv.nr. 9925.

37 Letters to the Foreign Office by Dutch Embassy, London, 11 and 15 June 46: BNA, FO, FO371, 54520.

38 Letter Backer (RLD) to Cribbett (MCA), 10 Oct. 1946: BNA, FO, FO371, 54520.

39 Draft MCA report on operations of BEA and competitors, 2 May 1948: BNA, MCA, BT217, 68.

airplanes available to KLM, although Air France itself was forced to make do with captured German Junkers Ju-52s transports for lack of suitable aircraft.[40]

A little over a year later, however, the French enthusiasm for a settlement with the Netherlands had diminished considerably after London and Paris reached agreement on the coordination of their mutual air traffic. The cooperative spirit of 1945 was on the way out and The Hague feared that France might even revert to the restrictive policies it had pursued in the 1930s. From a Dutch perspective, this was disconcerting. The plan was not just to apply for KLM rights to fly to Paris, but also for permission to see KNILM operate to Saigon and Hanoi in French Indo-China. When further exploratory talks were held in Paris in July 1946, the French negotiators indicated they felt that the Dutch had come to the table with excessive demands, against which stood relatively small French interests.[41] Besides, with its increasing foreign policy focus on the United States and on transatlantic concerns, the Netherlands had relatively little clout in Europe's political arena.[42] It took until February 1948 before negotiators from both sides met again in Paris. Goedhuis, presiding over the Dutch delegation, was somber about the prospects, largely because KLM indicated it hoped to establish an air service via France to Tunis, then a French protectorate in North Africa. Paris saw the KLM plan as an infringement on French colonial interests. On top of this, the Dutch repeated their wish for air services from Batavia to Saigon and Hanoi. This dampened French enthusiasm even further. The Dutch position in East Asia was under increasing pressure as a result of the colonial war in Indonesia,[43] and the French considered KLM to be far too eager to build its position in Europe's air network.[44] As a consequence, a bilateral agreement remained out of reach.

Germany presented a case onto itself. In the immediate postwar years, the country was the focal point of Dutch foreign and economic policies. Anxious to avoid the mistakes of 1918 that had crippled the German economy, The Hague came out in favor of mitigating reparation payments, although Dutch influence on the course of events was minimal. Nonetheless, Germany continued as the biggest trading partner of the Netherlands and exercised considerable

---

40 Telegram Van Haersma de With (Embassy Paris) to Netherlands Foreign Ministry, Londen, 14 Aug. 1945: NNA, 2.05.80, Foreign Affairs, London Archive, inv.nr. 3382.

41 Letter Goedhuis to Director-General Govt. Aviation Service RLD, 15 July 1946: NNA, 2.05.117 Foreign Affairs 1945–1954, inv.nr. 9890.

42 Hellema, *Nederland in de wereld*, p. 123–127.

43 Report Goedhuis on negotiations in Paris, 25–28 Feb. 1948: NNA, 2.05.117, Foreign Affairs 1945–1954, inv.nr. 9890.

44 Memorandum Goedhuis re. discussions in Paris, 20–22 July 1949: NNA, 2.05.117, Foreign Affairs 1945–1954, inv.nr. 9958.

influence on the Dutch economy as a major recipient of transit goods shipped through the port of Rotterdam. This meant the reconstruction of the German economy and its foreign trade was also a Dutch concern.[45]

The provision of air services was a good fit for these interests, especially because the German airline Luft Hansa had been grounded by the Allies. Because Germany was divided into four occupation zones, aviation was not a bilateral issue, but rather a topic for discussion with the four occupying powers. Permission for air services depended on the Civil Aeronautics Board of the Allied High Commission for Germany. In May 1947, KLM applied for a license to fly between Amsterdam and Berlin. The Russians did not warm to the idea, but after repeated pleas, Moscow decided to grant permission for a service to Schönefeld Airport in the Soviet occupation sector.[46] KLM, however, saw better prospects in landings at Tempelhof in the American sector, but was not allowed to do so. For once, the Dutch did not press the case, as KLM was wary of incurring financial losses on a service to war-stricken Berlin. Germany was impoverished and its economy lay in tatters. For the time being the Berlin plan was traded for an air service to Copenhagen and Stockholm via Bremen and Hamburg in the British occupation zone. In September 1947, London granted permission for this route, although it came at a price: BEA was to be involved as KLM's sole sales agent in Germany.[47] The Dutch reluctantly agreed as the route through Bremen and Hamburg would strengthen KLM's foothold in Germany. Further south, in the American sector, KLM also improved its position, receiving permission for services to and from Frankfurt, Munich, Düsseldorf, Stuttgart and Nuremberg.[48] Things changed in June 1948, when the Soviet blockade of Berlin and the Allied airlift that followed changed conditions, pulling Germany's western sectors closer to the Western Alliance.[49]

KLM also hoped to expand its services further east. The first thoughts in this direction dated back to the end of 1944. Plesman had repeatedly returned to the idea of operating to the USSR as it harmonized with old echoes of Dutch neutrality as The Hague continued to try to bridge the widening rift between the Anglo-Saxon and the Soviet spheres. Thus, Moscow was high on KLM's

45 Hellema, *Nederland in de wereld*, p. 126–135. Friso Wielenga, *West-Duitsland: partner uit noodzaak. Nederland en de Bondsrepubliek 1949–1955* (Utrecht: Spectrum, 1989), p. 21–42.

46 Telegram British Mission, Berlin, to Foreign Office, London, 5 Sept. 1947: BNA, FO, FO371, 65478.

47 Letter Van der Tuuk Adriani to Netherlands Ministry of Foreign Affairs, 4 June 1948: NNA, 2.05–117, Foreign Affairs 1945–1954, inv.nr. 9983.

48 Survey of rights given to KLM, Sept. 1953: NNA, 2.05.117, Foreign Affairs 1945–1954, inv.nr. 9883.

49 Minutes 39th BLV, 19 July 1949: NNA, 2.05.117, Foreign Affairs 1945–1954, inv.nr. 21391.

list. However, prospects appeared bleak. In 1944 the Soviets had chosen not to participate in the Chicago Conference and had indicated that, as a matter of principle, the operation of air routes over Soviet territory should be carried out by Soviet planes only.[50]

Since the end of the war, general political relations between the Western Allies and the Soviets had deteriorated. Inevitably, this left a mark on air transport. Plesman had little eye for this. Despite the rising tensions, he continued to hope to develop a market for commercial air travel to Moscow. At the same time, ambassador baron Casper van Breugel Douglas, no friend of the Soviets to begin with, warned him that the USSR was no ordinary country and that it was not clear whether KLM would be able to develop any meaningful cooperation. In any case, he believed the acquisition of Soviet landing rights was likely to be a long-term affair.[51] Indeed talks continued without much progress, as the Russians remained adamant that they did not want foreign aircraft in their airspace. Instead, the Soviets proposed a 'switchboard service' that entailed a change of plane in the Russian occupation zone of Berlin. For KLM such an arrangement entailed technical problems. The runway at Schönefeld airport was too short for the Convair CV-240s that KLM planned to use, hence flights to Schönefeld would have to be operated with older, slower and less comfortable Douglas Dakotas.[52] However, official confirmation of the agreement was slow in coming. Meanwhile, the Dutch were pressured by the Americans and by the British not to do business with the Soviets and thus preserve the existing isolation by the Western Powers of the Russian-occupied part of Europe.[53] Undeterred, The Hague chose to side with KLM's commercial interest and decided to go along with the 'switchboard service' that the Soviets proposed. So as not to ruffle Allied diplomatic feathers, The Hague adopted a low profile: the conditions for the service were put in a private agreement between KLM and the Russian airline Aeroflot.[54] On 27 September 1947, the first KLM machine landed in East Berlin, but a regular scheduled service never got off the

50 Peter Svik, *Civil Aviation and the Globalization of the Cold War* (Cham (CH): Palgrave Macmillan, 2020), p. 22.

51 Letter Van Breugel Douglas to Plesman, 1 Feb. 1946: NNA, 2.05.117, Foreign Affairs 1945–1954, inv.nr. 9915.

52 Report on negotiations, 10–14 June 1947: NNA, 2.05.118, Foreign Affairs 1955–1964, inv.nr. 8727. Letter Neth. Ambassador, Moscow, to Neth. Ministry of Foreign Affairs, 25 June 1947: NNA, 2.05.117, Foreign Affairs 1945–1954, inv.nr. 9915.

53 Memorandum US embassy The Hague to Foreign Affairs, 1 July 1947: NNA, 2.05.117, Foreign Affairs 1945–1954, inv.nr. 9915.

54 Code message Boetzelaer to Neth. embassy Moscow, 18 July 1947: NNA, 2.05.117, Foreign Affairs 1945–1954, inv.nr. 9915.

ground. KLM only operated a few individual flights, for which prior permission had to be applied for with the Russian authorities. This arrangement proved unsatisfactory; the Soviets withdrew KLM's landing permit several times at the last minute, without giving reasons. In 1948, the escalating tensions over Berlin brought an end to the flights.

Contacts with Czechoslovakia, the most open economy in Eastern Europe, appeared to hold more promise. Before the war, Prague had been an important destination for KLM and the airline hoped that this might be the case again in the future. At this point, Czechoslovakia was in flux, with a government dominated by the communist party, although the country had a strong democratic and parliamentary tradition. The Dutch hoped to build on this and foster bilateral relations, despite the rising political differences. The idea was to set up a joint service with the Czechoslovak airline ČSA (Československé Státní Aerolinie); a similar service to Prague had existed in the 1930s. KLM hoped to get permission for connecting flights to Vienna and Budapest and to this end exploratory talks were held in Prague and with the Hungarian envoy to the Netherlands, Rudolf Polonyi. From the outset, however, there were reservations about the Hungarian willingness to cooperate because of historical sensitivities between Hungarians and Czechs that had affected air services in the past.[55] Then, in July 1947, Stalin blocked Czech participation in the Marshall Plan, which caused political turmoil. Hence it was no surprise that the air service got off to a difficult start. The Dutch were partly to blame for this. After a bilateral agreement was signed on 1 September 1947, the Dutch envoy, Allard Merens, failed to arrange the corresponding exchange of diplomatic notes. As a result, the air services issue was overtaken by the political upheavals in Czechoslovakia late in 1947 and early in 1948, when the communists took power. Air services across the incipient Iron Curtain became an issue. The Americans in particular feared that ČSA was in fact a Soviet vehicle to gather intelligence, facilitate the placement of agents in the West, and provide communist parties in Western Europe with a rapid air link to Moscow.[56] In June of 1948, the Berlin crisis only added to the uncertainty. Washington, which had asked Pan American to end its service to Prague as early as October 1946, tried to halt all air traffic to countries in the Soviet sphere of influence by applying

55 Letter Secretary-General Ministry of Traffic and Energy to Foreign Affairs, 17 July 1946: NNA, 2.05.117, Foreign Affairs 1945–1954, inv.nr. 10064.

56 Memorandum "Some Considerations Involved in US Aviation Policy toward the Soviet Union and Its Satellites," 28 May 1948; United States National Archives, Record Group 59, State Department, Policy Planning Staff, Subject File Aviation, Box 7.

political pressure on western European allies.[57] It took until the autumn of 1949 before KLM started flying. ČSA participated in the service, while SABENA was added as a third party. Of the other Western airlines, only Swissair and SAS operated flights to the Czechoslovakian capital. Nonetheless, Prague became the major hub for air travel between West and East.

KLM also wanted to fly south. The proposed route initially ran through Switzerland, the peaceful and wealthy refuge on a burning continent, where industry and infrastructure had remained intact. Switzerland was one of the few locations where there was enough money in the early post-war years to constitute a real market for air travel. The country experienced rapid economic growth, which showed in the statistics. In 1946 the average seat occupancy on flights to and from Switzerland was double that in 1939.

In April 1946 KLM received provisional permission to operate through Geneva. An informal, liberal arrangement was made with the Swiss and signed on 28 March 1947.[58] Because KLM promised not to transport Swiss passport holders, the Dutch were granted commercial rights for destinations beyond Geneva. Switzerland's national airline Swissair acted as a booking agent, which meant they shared the revenue. From Geneva, KLM wanted to operate westward to Barcelona, Madrid and Lisbon, and southward to Rome.

In 1947 the route through Spain continued across the South Atlantic. This was possible because of a peculiar laxity on the part of the Swiss customs and border officials. As long as foreign passengers who boarded in Geneva could show a South American entry visa, the Swiss did not ask too many questions. This opened the door for people with a dubious war record who were in possession of the necessary financial means to book passage.[59] Thanks, in part, to such ticket sales, KLM's South America flights from Geneva became a profitable operation worth more than one million Swiss francs per year, about 10 percent of KLM's annual turnover.[60] Although KLM was the first, it was not the only operator. The market potential of the air service was also recognized by Swissair. In the summer of 1948, the Swiss approached Brazil and Uruguay with the request to operate their own air service to Rio de Janeiro and Montevideo.

---

57 Minutes 29th BLV, 4 May 1948: NNA, 2.05.117 BZ, Foreign Affairs 1945–1954, inv.nr: 1689. Svik, *Civil Aviation and the Globalization of the Cold War*, p. 32–39.

58 Letter Slotemaker to Director-General RLD, 4 Dec, 1946: NNA, 2.05.117, Foreign Affairs 1945–1954, inv.nr. 9935. Further: File aviation negotiations Switzerland: NNA, 5.016.5240, RLD, inv.nr. 5615.

59 Luc van Dongen, *Un Purgatoire Très Discret. La Transition Helvétique d'Anciens Nazis, Fascistes et Collaborateurs après 1945* (Paris: Perrin, 2008).

60 Correspondence in file NNA, 5.16.5240, RLD, inv.nr. 5615. KLM, *Annual Report 1948*.

Talks proceeded without difficulties and agreements were duly signed.[61] However, a formal arrangement with the Netherlands, confirming KLM's commercial stop in Geneva, had more to it. Once Swissair was flying the South Atlantic, the Swiss found that KLM operated more services than they liked and thus skimmed their home market in Geneva. Resolving this dissatisfaction took months, but a bilateral aviation agreement was eventually signed in March 1949.[62]

From Geneva KLM flew to Spain, where Franco's fascist government had survived the war on the basis of non-intervention. The fascists pursued a particularly protectionist aviation policy to preserve the monopoly of the national airline Iberia. Foreign air services were not welcome in Madrid. However, given Spain's internationally isolated position in the postwar antifascist world, the Franco government could not completely block foreign air services.

At the end of March 1946, Goedhuis arrived in Madrid for talks, followed by Henri van Ede van der Pals of the National Aviation Service, Foreign Affairs' representative Siem Nieuwenhuijsen, and Bert Slotemaker on behalf of KLM. Dutch expectations ran high, although the schedule for the talks was tight. The entire Spanish civil service corps had the week off from 16 April for the religious and festive celebrations of the *Semana Santa*. To the surprise of the Dutch, however, the Spanish readily gave away the sought-after traffic rights. Within a day, delegates were on their way home, feeling very pleased. KLM would receive permission for both a direct service from Amsterdam via Madrid to Lisbon and for a second service with stops in Geneva and Barcelona.[63] Ratification by the Spanish Council of Ministers appeared a formality.[64] Not so: under pressure from the national airline Iberia, which saw a foreign competitor on the rise in its own backyard, the Spanish cabinet withheld its signature. Indeed, word was sent that Madrid regretted granting KLM 5th freedom rights at all. In retrospect, foreign passenger pickup in Spain was undesirable and the cabinet now labelled traffic between Madrid and Lisbon as 'Iberian cabotage' which should be reserved for Spanish and Portuguese air carriers only. Indeed,

61 Accord aéronautique avec le Brésil. Bundesratsprotokoll, 26 July 1948. Antrag EPED/Proposition DFPCF), 5 Aug. 1948: dodis.ch/2920 [2019]. Accord aéronautique avec l'Argentine. Bundesratsprotokoll, 16 Nov. 1948. Antrag EPED/Proposition DFPCF), 19 Nov. 1948: dodis.ch/ 2989 [2022].

62 Letter KLM (H.M.C. van Eck Duymaer van Twist) to E. Groh (Swissair), 10 Aug. 1949: NNA, 2.05.117, Foreign Affairs 1945–1954, inv.nr. 9935.,

63 Draft text bilateral agreement Netherlands-Spain (undated: April 1946): NNA, 2.05.117, Foreign Affairs 1945–1954, inv.nr. 9917.

64 Code message ambassador Teppema to Ministry of Foreign Affairs, 17 Apr. 1946: NNA, 2.05.117, Foreign Affairs 1945–1954, inv.nr. 9917.

Madrid now rejected any idea of foreign traffic rights over Spanish territory.[65] Suddenly agreement appeared out of the question. The Dutch, who had thought that an accord had been reached, were perplexed.[66] At KLM, Plesman and Van der Wiel were at a loss to understand what had gone wrong.[67]

An answer came in a roundabout fashion. For the transatlantic service to South America, the Dutch Embassy in Portugal had approached the authorities at the end of 1945 with a request to renew the pre-war arrangements. Because the Portuguese were still setting up their own air services and had no short-term plans for long-haul routes, they agreed that KLM could stopover in Lisbon. As long as the national airline TAP (Transportes Aéreos Portugueses) did not operate flights to Madrid, the Portuguese also allowed KLM to carry passengers between Madrid and Lisbon.[68] While the discussions with Spain were ongoing, an agreement with Portugal was reached on 8 June 1946. This enabled KLM to fly, if not from Spain.[69] The Portuguese also granted permission to fly between Lisbon and Madrid, albeit without transport regional transport rights for the Iberian section.[70] Subsequently, KLM and its operational partner Swissair signed a deal with Iberia that allowed the Spanish airline a share in the revenues of the flights from Geneva, after which Madrid dropped its objections.[71]

Nonetheless, the situation still had to be formalized. At a cocktail party in Madrid, Slotemaker managed to persuade Spain's negotiator Ruiz Morales to agree to a one-year provisional arrangement – the usual way KLM tried to get a foot in the door. Morales gave permission to take on passengers in Madrid for destinations in South America. However, the entry of KLM to the Spanish market also gave rise to resentment, particularly in the armed forces where

65 Javier Vidal Olivares, *Las Alas de España. Iberia, Lineas* Aéreas (1940–2005) (Valencia: Universidad de Valencia Press, 2008), p. 76, 118–121. Also: Minutes 14th BLV, 2 Dec. 1946: NNA, 2.05.117, Foreign Affairs 1945–1954, inv.nr. 21391.

66 Code message Teppema to Ministry of Foreign Affairs, 31 May 1946: NNA, 2.05.117, Foreign Affairs 1945–1954, inv.nr. 9917.

67 Code message Foreign Affairs (Van Royen) to Madrid, 21 May 1946: NNA, 2.05.117, Foreign Affairs 1945–1954, inv.nr. 9917.

68 Letter Minister of Foreign Affairs to ambassador Madrid, 20 March 1946; Letter Foreign Affairs to embassy Madrid, 20 May 1946: NNA, 2.05.117, Foreign Affairs 1945–1954, inv.nr. 9917.

69 Letter Van Buttingha Wichers to Minister of Foreign Affairs, 20 June 1946: NNA, 2.05.117, Foreign Affairs 1945–1954, inv.nr. 9912.

70 Report on incident with PH-TCL on 25 Sept. 1946: NNA, 2.05.117, Foreign Affairs 1945–1954, inv.nr. 10038.

71 Note Ministerio de Asuntos Exteriores (No. 24), 29 Jan. 1947: NNA, 2.05.117, Foreign Affairs 1945–1954, inv.nr. 9917.

nationalist feelings ran high. Just how high became clear on 25 September 1946. A KLM DC-4 en route from Geneva was intercepted by two Messerschmitt fighters of the Spanish Air Force and, without a clear reason for this action, forced to land at Bañoles (Banyoles) airport in north-eastern Spain, after a warning salvo had been fired at the airliner. Miraculously, no-one was hurt in the incident.[72] At first the Dutch wanted to lodge a formal diplomatic complaint, but this was swallowed in the interest of good relations.

Meanwhile Iberia had established itself in international aviation, starting its own service to Buenos Aires in October 1946.[73] It was not until September of the following year that bilateral discussions were resumed. In the relaxed atmosphere of San Sebastian on Spain's northern seacoast, the negotiators sat down. The Dutch delegates, Van Ede van der Pals, Spanjaard and Slotemaker, hoped to use the international-political isolation in which Franco's Spain had become trapped to persuade the Spaniards to work with them. Still, aviation remained a complicated issue between Madrid and The Hague, which showed in the fact that the Netherlands supported a proposal in ICAO to deprive fascist Spain of membership.[74]

Unsurprisingly, the bilateral talks were not successful. In response to anti-fascist international politics Spain backtracked on its bilateral aviation deals. In the summer of 1947, Madrid announced that it would rescind the Spanish-Dutch bilateral accord on 26 August 1948.[75] New objections to the Dutch South America service were also raised.[76] With Iberia now operating along the South Atlantic route, strong factions in the Spanish government and political circles found it unacceptable that any part of air traffic between Spain and what was dubbed 'Spanish America' should be transported by an airline from a third country.[77] If KLM wished to maintain its commercial stop in Spain, a new agreement would be needed. After all, the transatlantic route had become Iberia's main money maker. The Hague saw no other option but to use the changing political conditions in Europe – the unfolding Cold War in 1948 – and information obtained from trade contacts to push for improvements.[78]

---

72 Report on incident with PH-TCL on 25 Sept. 1946: NNA, 2.05.117, Foreign Affairs 1945–1954, inv.nr. 10038.

73 Javier Vidal Olivares, *Las Alas de* España, p. 76, 118–121. Also: Minutes 14th BLV, 2-12-1946.

74 Report Dutch delegates to Foreign Affairs, 2 Oct. 1947: NNA, 2.05.117, Foreign Affairs 1945–1954, inv.nr. 9917.

75 Letter Van Ede van der Pals to Foreign Affairs, 12 Sept. 1947: NNA, 2.05.117, Foreign Affairs 1945–1954, inv.nr. 9917.

76 Minutes 19th BLV, 3 Apr. 1947: NNA, 2.05.117, Foreign Affairs, inv.nr. 21391.

77 Vidal Olivares, *Las Alas de España*, p. 76.

78 Minutes 27th BLV, 27 Jan. 1948: NNA, 2.05.117, Foreign Affairs 1945–1954, inv.nr. 21391.

Resolving the deadlock proved difficult. The Spaniards were reluctant to talk. The situation was further complicated because Iberia ran into considerable difficulties in paying for spare parts for its aircraft due to a lack of hard currency revenues.[79] Although the former head of the Spanish air transport delegation, Emilio de Navasqüés, was appointed ambassador to The Hague, Madrid had the Dutch wait until 1948 before reopening discussions. In September talks continued in Madrid, helped along because the Netherlands was now cautiously pledging support for Spain's efforts to undo the country's exclusion from the United Nations and ICAO. To appease the Spaniards further, KLM offered to sell a DC-4 to Iberia on favorable terms, while the Dutch Ministry of Economic Affairs expressed willingness to make a special gesture concerning bilateral trade and the balance of payments.[80] Fearing that this would still not be enough to land the operating rights for the South America service, KLM promised Iberia additional financial compensation.[81] This gesture eventually pulled Madrid over the line. A new agreement was drawn up on 8 October 1948, although it was not signed until 20 June 1950.

The other European route KLM hoped to operate beyond Geneva, was to Rome. Italy presented another special case. Pending talks on a peace treaty with the Allies, doing business with Rome was nigh impossible. In September 1946, just after a new Italian national airline, Aerolinee Italiane Internazionali (Alitalia), was founded in cooperation with British European Airways (BEA), a KLM delegation visited the Italian capital to establish new contacts. Embassy council Willem Gevers went out of his way to create an opening. While the Italians were not flying themselves, he had his interlocutors agree that KLM could make a technical stopover in Rome on the route to Batavia. In November, Italian permission was gained for an Amsterdam-Basel/Geneva-Rome service. However, an aviation agreement was not signed because Italy found itself undergoing an administrative transition while setting up a democratic government. This transient state suited the Dutch just fine, since a regular agreement would likely entail restrictions for KLM.[82]

It was October 1947 before the Italians were ready for discussions. Alitalia had started operations of its own five months earlier. As was the case with

79 Letter Chargé d'Affaires Van Voorst tot Voorst to Foreign Affairs, 11 Feb. 1948: NNA, 2.05.117, Foreign Affairs 1945–1954, inv.nr. 9917.

80 Code message Foreign Affairs to legation Madrid, 20 Sept. 1948: NNA, 2.05.117, Foreign Affairs 1945–1954, inv.nr. 9917. Report on negotiations with Spain, 21 Sept – 3 Oct. 1948: NNA, 2.05.117, Foreign Affairs 1945–1954, inv.nr. 9917.

81 Minutes 31th BLV, 2 Sept. 1948: NNA, 2.05.117, Foreign Affairs, inv.nr. 21391.

82 Minutes 14th BLV, 2 Dec. 1946 and 15th BLV, 16 Dec. 1946. Correspondence Oct–Dec. 1946, in: NNA, 2.05.117, Foreign Affairs 1945–1954, inv.nr. 9902.

Madrid, Rome was not only attractive as a European destination, but also as a commercial stop on KLM's intercontinental routes. Eyes were on operations via Rome to South America and KLM hoped to cash in on Italy's emigration links. However, the Italians did not grant 5th freedom rights in Rome, which was what the Dutch were after, as Alitalia considered the connection belonged to a declared Italian-South American sphere of interest. Besides, the Dutch claim that a KLM service to South America via Rome was a logical route met with skepticism. While the admission of Argentinian and Brazilian airlines would be logical, agreeing to a role for KLM was not. The Dutch airline was perceived as being much too aggressive commercially. It took until October 1948 before the Netherlands and Italy reached a settlement. To bring this about Plesman personally approved a pool agreement with Alitalia in which revenues could be shared.

Two months later, on 31 December 1948, Italy revoked KLM's permit anyway, after the Italians discovered that more than 60 per cent of KLM's passengers for South America boarded in Rome.[83] Alitalia announced it regarded all such traffic as reserved for these three countries and their respective national carriers. If KLM wished to continue to operate, it would have to pay a hefty price: the provision of a Douglas DC-6 airplane for free. Fearing that the Italians might be in cahoots with the Brazilians, since Rio also created obstructions for the Dutch, KLM offered Alitalia guarantees for a 70 per cent occupancy rate on its own flights to South America, provided it operated the service in a new pool agreement. This was a significant gesture: Alitalia used outdated aircraft that were not very attractive to passengers and incurred heavy operational losses, flying old converted Lancaster bombers for lack of more suitable equipment.[84]

The Dutch, meanwhile, considered the Italian demands a violation of the Chicago principles in which airplanes were allowed to make stops en route for traffic purposes. In KLM's view, accepting the exclusion from traffic between Rome and Rio would ultimately make the development of new trunk routes impossible for lack of a sound economic basis.[85] Slotemaker, who stayed in Rome on behalf of KLM in mid-December to try to smooth things over, did not have it easy. Moreover, he had to convince his interlocutors that a free DC-6 was not an option. KLM possessed less than a handful of DC-6 aircraft itself,

83 Minutes 33rd BLV, 22 Nov. 1948: NNA, 2.05.117, Foreign Affairs, inv.nr. 21391.

84 Minutes extra meeting BLV, 8 Dec. 1948: NNA, 2.05.117, Foreign Affairs, inv.nr.21391. Amilcare Mantegazza, Alitalia and Commercial Aviation in Italy, in: Hans-Liudger Dienel, Peter Lyth, *Flying the Flag. European Commercial Air Transport since 1945* (Basingstoke: Macmillan, 1997), p. 161–167.

85 Minutes 36th BLV, 8 March 1949: NNA, 2.05.117, Foreign Affairs, inv.nr. 21391.

which had only been delivered after the summer of 1947. However, KLM was prepared to sell one of its older DC-4 aircraft on very favorable terms.[86] The Italians were not satisfied. It was only when Slotemaker came up with a whole package of commitments, including a second DC-4, with eight spare engines, training for pilots and maintenance technicians at Schiphol, and assistance in setting up workshops at Rome's Ciampino Airport, that the Italians gave in.[87] For KLM flights from Rome, a special regime was conceived in the airline's legal department: these were labelled as traffic on an ad hoc basis, so that they would fall under the Chicago clauses for irregular flights in article 5 of the convention – and hence remain outside the restrictive regime of bilateral arrangements. The Italians were prepared to accept this, provided KLM paid further financial compensations. The Brazilians also considered this a reasonable option. Patience and prudence were thus rewarded and on 4 March 1949 the signatures were inked under a bilateral agreement. The air route to South America appeared open.

3 The Struggle to Maintain the Air Route to the Dutch East Indies and Australia

In 1945, restoration of the air connection between Amsterdam and Batavia was considered a vital national interest for The Netherlands. Permission for the service had never been an easy matter, but in the post-war situation, with Asian nationalism on the rise, it became clear that The Hague would need to invest extra diplomatic effort to obtain clearance to resume operations. As before, flying depended on British cooperation. The end of the war had created considerable unrest in parts of British India, reason why the RAF remained in control of the former civil landing grounds. Given the unstable conditions, London initially withheld the approval needed to reinstate KLM's pre-war commercial rights. A complicating factor was that the Government of British India in Delhi indicated it wanted a separate aviation agreement with the Netherlands now that independence was in the works. The Hague worried whether it would even be possible to operate the old route after an absence of over three years. Nobody knew what, if anything, was left of KLM's prewar ground organization

86 Letter Slotemaker to Minister Traffic and Waterworks, 28 Dec. 1948: NNA, 2.05.117, Foreign Affairs, 1945–1954, inv.nr. 9902.

87 Letter Spanjaard to Schaepman, 26 Feb. 1949: NNA, 2.05.117 Foreign Affairs, 1945–1954, inv. nr. 9902.

in British India and the feasibility of servicing aircraft along the route was a serious cause for concern.

The Dutch planned to use the new four engine Douglas C-54 Skymasters on the route, instead of the DC-3s that KLM had operated before. Because of the need to use RAF facilities, The Hague donned the air service as the semi-military Netherlands Government Air Transport (NGAT). This went back to a decision taken by the exiled Dutch government in London in December 1943 to set up a military air transport service after the British model of 110 Wing RAF. Because NGAT was a government organization and not an airline company, it could operate under the guise of allied wartime cooperation and did not need the prior permission required under article 6 of the Chicago Convention.[88] The NGAT organization was confirmed by the cabinet on 28 September 1945.[89] The government supplied the airplanes, freshly delivered from the USA, while KLM acted as the 'contract carrier' and provided crews and maintenance. The papers were signed in The Hague on 6 October. The first C-54 arrived at Schiphol eleven days later, on 17 October.

Just over three weeks later, on the morning of Saturday, 10 November 1945, the Amsterdam-Batavia service reopened. On board the first aircraft were 20 passengers, a British and an American liaison officer, and 120,000 letters. About a thousand people saw the airplane take off, piloted by KLM's celebrated captain Koene Parmentier. It took him six days to reach Batavia. The flight itinerary was via Naples, with stops in Cairo, Karachi, Colombo, and the Cocos Islands, because there was not enough aviation fuel available on Java.[90] The machine arrived in Batavia on the afternoon of 15 November, finding an unruly city largely in the hands of the Indonesian nationalists who had declared independence twelve weeks before, on 17 August.[91] Against this background NGAT, headed by a committee under navy commander Floris Heeris, would operate the service for the foreseeable future. Before the year was out, twelve more flights followed. It was months before the old commercial route via Karachi, Calcutta, Bangkok and Singapore could be used again.[92] The management of NGAT was transferred to KLM on 28 December 1945, although flight operations continued under the NGAT banner.

88 KLM, *Overzicht van het bedrijf over de jaren 1941 tot en met 1946*, p. 40.

89 Hagens, *Londen of Berlijn*, Vol. 2, p. 209, 360–361.

90 Leo van Maare, *De Mauritius Route. KLM Constellations in het kielzog van Abel Tasman* (Hilversum: All Media Productions, 2005), p. 13.

91 Hagens, *Londen of Berlijn*, Vol. 2, p. 362–369.

92 Van Maare, *De Mauritius Route*, p. 13.

The Dutch service was closely scrutinized. In the spring of 1946, protests were registered in British India that the way the NGAT operated looked more like a commercial airline than like a government service. However, when Goedhuis subsequently submitted a diplomatic request in London to allow operations to be handed over to KLM and commence regular, commercial flying again in August 1947, this met with objections.[93] The Government of British India, led by Jawaharlal Nehru, who sailed a distinctly anticolonial course, refused to cooperate. While Nehru was willing to allow NGAT to continue flying, this was on the basis of a provisional permit only.[94] Along the air route, trouble was brewing. To continue flying, the Netherlands would have to negotiate a bilateral aviation agreement with the government of India. As a condition, Nehru demanded that the Dutch submit a declaration of no objection issued by the provisional Republic of Indonesia. To The Hague this was an affront and the demand was found unpalatable. After all, the Netherlands were involved in an armed conflict with what The Hague saw as insurgents.[95] Discussions took until 31 May 1947 before an aviation agreement was eventually reached.

Beyond Batavia, things were also complicated. The Hague hoped it would finally be possible to extend the Batavia service to Australia, with reference to the old air transport agreement of 1938, as aviation relations with Australia had improved during the war. In 1944, a joint Dutch-Australian military transport service had been set up, which in August 1945 became 19 squadron of the Royal Australian Air Force (RAAF). After the end of hostilities, the squadron performed both military and civilian tasks in the Dutch East Indies and from November 1946, passenger tickets were sold.[96] On 1 January 1947, the squadron was transferred to Dutch command, part of the Military Aviation branch of the Royal Netherlands East Indies Army. Next the squadron's services were reorganized as civilian operations in the spring of 1947, after which Australia and the Netherlands returned to the practice of civil air transport separated along national lines. However, it soon became apparent that the Australians were involved in the planning of flights with relief supplies to the areas on Java controlled by the provisional Indonesian Republic. This caused alarm in The Hague.[97] With public opinion in Australia supporting the Republic and

93 Dierikx, Frappez Toujours, p. 75.

94 Correspondence Foreign Office with Netherlands' embassy, London, 11 and 15 June 1946: BNA, FO, FO371, 54520.

95 *Officiële bescheiden betreffende de Nederlands-Indonesische betrekkingen, 1945–1950*, Vol. 7 (The Hague: Nijhoff, 1978), p. 389–390.

96 *The West Australian*, 19 Nov. 1946: https://trove.nla.gov.au/newspaper/article/46184676.

97 Letter De Ranitz to Foreign Affairs, 10 July 1947: NNA, 2.05.117, Foreign Affairs 1945–1954, inv.nr: 1689.

its leader Sukarno, relations deteriorated. Australian trade unions clamored for a boycott of Dutch ships and aircraft. In Batavia, voices called for a cut in oil supplies to Australia to retaliate. The wish to see KLM operate to Australia evaporated.[98] Added to this it became clear that Canberra fostered plans for a scheduled air service that would land in Republican areas of Java.[99] Discussions with The Hague were deliberately frustrated.

The situation in the Dutch East Indies changed for the worse in July 1947, a period when political relations in South Asia were on edge anyway because of the decolonization of British India. London agreed to split the Indian subcontinent into separate Hindu and a Muslim states, India and Pakistan, respectively. In this volatile period, three and a half weeks before the planned independence of India and Pakistan, the Netherlands began a big military offensive against the Indonesian nationalists on Java on 21 July, euphemistically dubbed 'police action' in the Dutch news media. Not surprisingly, the Dutch action did not remain without consequences. The United Nations Security Council called for a ceasefire. Lacking international support, the Dutch standing in Asia suffered considerably. What was worse from The Hague's perspective: the crucial air connection to Batavia now proved extremely vulnerable.[100] When on 29 July Dutch fighter aircraft shot down a British-Indian Dakota over Java, carrying supplies for Sukarno's nationalists, the Nehru government revoked KLM's landing rights in India the same day. Following a visit by one of Indonesia's prominent politicians, Sutan Shahrir, to Pakistan's political leader, Muhammad Ali Jinnah, Pakistan followed suit. As a result, the Dutch stopovers in Karachi and in Calcutta were suddenly barred. To give legal substance to the sanctions, Delhi terminated the aviation agreement with The Netherlands, signed just two months before. Effective immediately, aircraft in NGAT colors were no longer welcome. The objection of the Dutch Foreign Affairs' Minister Carel van Boetzelaer that the NGAT service had, in fact, already been taken over by KLM and was now operated on a civilian, commercial basis, was to no avail.[101] Across the religious divide the Nehru government, itself facing huge flows of religious refugees on the move on the Indian subcontinent, contended KLM

98 Letter Hein Vos (Minister Traffic and Waterworks) to Van Boetzelaer, 24 Sep. 1947: NNA, 2.05.117, Foreign Affairs 1945–1954, inv.nr: 1689.

99 Letter Dutch Envoy, Canberra to Foreign Affairs, 10 July 1947: NNA, 2.05.117 Foreign Affairs 1945–1954, inv.nr: 1689.

100 Minutes 52nd meeting Commission-General, 15 Feb. 1947: *Officiële bescheiden betreffende de Nederlands-Indonesische betrekkingen, 1945–1950*, Vol. 7, p. 454.

101 Code message Overseas Territories to govt. In Batavia, 1 Aug. 1947: NNA, 2.10.14, Alg. Secretarie Nederlands-Indische Regering 1942–1950, inv.nr. 3473.

was transporting soldiers and equipment that were then deployed in 'battering (…) fellow Muslims on Java'.[102]

Before the start of the military offensive there had been some discussion on the Dutch side about the risk of disruption of the air connection, but it took until 31 July before Goedhuis reported to the Foreign Office in London with an urgent request to allow KLM to change its route and avoid flying over Pakistan and India. Goedhuis requested emergency permission for a technical stopover at the RAF airbase Sharjah, located in the British-controlled Sultanate of Muscat and Oman, on the south side of the Persian Gulf. The plan was that KLM would fly non-stop from Sharjah to Negombo, an RAF base north of Colombo on Ceylon [Sri Lanka], which was also used by BOAC as a refuelling station. From there, the normal route via Bangkok and Singapore was to be resumed. Pakistani and Indian airspace could thus be avoided, although it was clear that the longer flying distance would reduce the payload carried by about 60 per cent.[103] The first aircraft for the diverted service was by now ready to depart from Schiphol. This put Britain in a difficult position: cooperating with the Dutch request might develop into an obstacle for the progress of discussions with the Nehru government on India's independence. Moreover, London was reluctant to do anything for KLM in Ceylon that could influence the talks there about the island's upcoming dominion status.[104] On the other hand, there were no direct legal arguments to reject the Dutch request since it only asked for a technical stopover, as defined by the International Air Services Transit Agreement, signed by Britain in Chicago.[105]

These developments spelled serious trouble for KLM. In the night of 2 to 3 August, the outbound flight to Batavia was stopped in Karachi by order of the British Indian government, while the inbound machine to Amsterdam was grounded in Calcutta. The next westbound flight had to be aborted in Bangkok. On 4 August, the Dutch government decided to try and keep the air service going at all costs and do everything in its power to obtain British permission to land at Sharjah and on Ceylon. To underline the urgency of the matter, the

---

102 Foreign Office (Eastern Department) memorandum, 31 July 1947: BNA, FO, FO371, 65478. Chargé dÁffaires New Delhi (Bas Backer) to Minister Van Boetzelaer van Oosterhout), 29 July 1947, in: *Officiële bescheiden betreffende de Nederlands-Indonesische betrekkingen, 1945–1950*, Vol. 10 (The Hague: Nijhof, 1982).

103 Code message Van Boetzelaer van Oosterhout to ambassador New Delhi (Lamping), 26 Aug. 1947, in: *Officiële bescheiden betreffende de Nederlands-Indonesische betrekkingen, 1945–1950*, Vol. 10, nr. 372, note 4. Also: Van Maare, *De Mauritius Route*, p. 14–19.

104 Foreign Office minute (by Dening), 31 July 1947: BNA, FO, FO371, 65478.

105 Foreign Office minute (by Edden), 31 July 1947: BNA, FO, FO371, 65478; Minute Foreign Office legal advisor (Evans), 2 Aug. 1947: BNA, FO, FO371, 65478.

government specifically instructed KLM to fly, despite the risks that could be associated with this.[106]

Meanwhile the airplane grounded in Bangkok was fitted with additional fuel tanks, at the personal initiative of captain Ton van Ulsen. This would enable the DC-4 to fly from Bangkok to Ceylon in a single stage. Without advance warning to the British, Van Ulsen took off for the long flight to Ceylon on 5 August, the day the military offensive on Java and Sumatra came to an end. It was only when approaching the island that Van Ulsen requested permission over the radio for a technical landing at Negombo. Van Ulsen made his request referring to the International Air Services Transit Agreement. At Negombo, the RAF base commander saw no other option but to allow the Dutch plane to land. Thus a precedent was created.[107]

Indeed, KLM did receive permission from London for the temporary use of Sharjah and Negombo shortly afterwards, on condition that no weapons or ammunition would be carried. The British stipulated that the use of the two RAF bases would be entirely at KLM's own risk. The Sharjah airstrip was very short for operations with large four-engine aircraft and the runway consisted only of rolled sand. Fuel stocks were also lacking.[108] With the help of the Royal Dutch Shell oil company these were brought up to standard.

The Dutch Minister of Reconstruction and Housing, Lambert Neher, who had been appointed mediator in the Dutch-Indonesian conflict, travelled to Batavia via Sharjah and Negombo on 9 August on the next outbound flight. Ceylonese protests that no permission had been given for the route to be relocated were ignored by The Hague on legal grounds. In view of Ceylon's formal status at that time as a British colony, The Hague maintained that diplomatic agreement with London sufficed for a technical stop at Negombo, as defined in the International Air Services Transit Agreement. It was a good thing for all parties involved that the diversion of the route was temporary. The Nehru government revoked the landing ban on 7 October. However, the British subsequently insisted on KLM's departure from Negombo. Thereafter, and lacking alternatives, the original route via Karachi and Calcutta was restored. But not everything ended on a bright note. The Dutch military action and the way KLM had circumvented the Indian and Pakistani overflight bans, caused bad blood

106 Van Boetzelaer van Oosterhout to ambassador Washington (Van Kleffens), 5 Aug. 1947, in: *Officiële bescheiden betreffende de Nederlands-Indonesische betrekkingen, 1945–1950*, Vol. 10, nr. 163.

107 Foreign Office (Edden) to Ratcliffe-Cousins (Ministry of Civil Aviation), 7 Aug. 1947: BNA, FO, FO371, 65478.

108 Foreign Office memorandum (by Edden), 13 Aug. 1947: BNA, FO, FO371, 65478.

with governments supporting the Indonesian cause. To signal its displeasure, Australia terminated the 1938 aviation agreement in December 1947.[109] It was not until 9 December 1951 that the first scheduled KLM flight landed in Sydney.

Meanwhile, the vulnerability of the Indies route had been revealed at a time when tensions in Indonesia were high and the end of colonial rule was perceptively closer. The Dutch were in dire straits once it became evident that the USA did not support Dutch colonial policy. The Netherlands became isolated internationally. In Indonesia, Dutch entrepreneurs began to lose confidence in a positive outcome of the conflict and started to leave the colony. In June 1948, there was already a waiting list in Batavia of some 600 people trying to get an air ticket to the Netherlands. At KLM, Plesman prepared for the eventuality of a new blockade. After all, the service to Batavia accounted for more than 44 percent of KLM's total passenger transport and its revenues were vital for the company's bottom line. Strangely, the Ministry of Foreign Affairs did not share Plesman's concerns, even though talks with Ceylon, which had received independence on 4 February 1948, about a permanent landing permit stagnated.[110]

Just how vulnerable the air service was became evident when Dutch troops started a new military offensive on Java between 19 December 1948 and 5 January 1949. This second 'police action' was a military success, resulting in Dutch territorial advances and the capture of members of the republican government. Politically, however, it was a disaster that cost The Hague much sympathy and further isolated the Netherlands internationally. Reprisals against Dutch policy were aimed at KLM's Amsterdam-Batavia service and Dutch landing rights were called into question. Nonetheless, the airline had prepared for this eventuality. While officials at the Ministry of Foreign Affairs sat on their hands, KLM had investigated several operational alternatives. One possibility seemed to be to cooperate with the French Transports Aériens Intercontinentaux (TAI) in providing flights to Batavia via New York, Los Angeles and the French possessions in the Pacific and East Asia. Non-stop flights from the British colony of Aden on the Red Sea were also investigated. Throughout all of this, the Ministry of Foreign Affairs kept a curiously low profile. Despite the institutionalization of policy coordination in the Civil Aviation Meetings in The Hague, Dutch diplomacy hardly played a role.[111]

---

109 Telegram Teppema to Foreign Affairs, 4 Dec. 1947: NNA, 2.05.117, Foreign Affairs 1945–1954, inv.nr: 1689.

110 Minutes 29^e^ BLV, 4 May 1948: NNA, 2.05.117 Foreign Affairs 1945–1954, inv.nr: 1689. Van Maare, *KLM Constellations*, p. 19–21.

111 Second bulletin Indies' route Ministry of Foreign Affairs, 27 Dec. 1948; Thirteenth bulletin Indies' route Foreign Affairs, 13 Jan. 1949, in: *Officiële bescheiden betreffende de*

Three days after the start of the second military offensive, on 22 December 1948, the Government of India stopped a KLM Constellation in Calcutta on its return flight from Batavia for a check of cargo and passenger luggage. The outbound plane to Batavia received a similar treatment. After inspection, both aircraft were allowed to continue their journey, but the next day India revoked the permit for the air service indefinitely. The Government of Ceylon instantly took similar steps. Another KLM flight, on its way to Batavia with civil servants returning from leave in Holland, was stranded in Basra, Iraq. After a full week on the ground, the machine eventually returned to Amsterdam. Aviation sanctions from Pakistan and Burma followed on 24 and 25 December. On Christmas Day 1948, the air connection with the Dutch East Indies again ground to a halt.[112] At the United Nations, the Security Council met to discuss Indonesia's decolonization despite the Christmas recess. The Dutch came under great pressure. In front of the whole world, the Netherlands was hung out to dry by the United States, which publicly disapproved of Dutch policy and used America's influence to reverse the course of action.

As mentioned earlier, KLM had prepared for service disruptions. One of the scenarios that had been discussed beforehand was an emergency route via Khartoum in Sudan and the British island of Mauritius in the Indian Ocean. An alternative solution was to fly from Aden directly to Sabang or Medan on Sumatra, but this proved unfeasible in the short term. This left Khartoum-Mauritius-Batavia as the only option. To the government's great satisfaction, KLM's technical services had already prepared one airplane that stood ready to depart from Amsterdam as soon as the necessary landing permits arrived. Prime Minister Willem Drees, who happened to have a visit to Batavia planned, decided to travel on the first flight out, despite objections from civil servants in The Hague, where considerable anxiety existed about the risks of the very long flight over the Indian Ocean.[113] However, arranging London's permission for the Mauritius route took time. KLM therefore pleaded for an emergency arrangement for the flight with Prime Minister Drees on 4 January 1949.[114]

Nederlands-Indonesische betrekkingen, 1945–1950, Vol. 16 (The Hague: ING, 1991) nr. 294, resp. 464, note 10. Van Maare, *KLM Constellations*, p. 23–27.

112 Lamping (Ambassador New Delhi) to Stikker (Minister of Foreign Affairs) and Elink Schuurman, 23 Dec. 1948, in: *Officiële bescheiden betreffende de Nederlands-Indonesische betrekkingen, 1945–1950,* Vol. 16, nr. 232.

113 Second bulletin Indies' route Ministry of Foreign Affairs, 27 Dec. 1948; Sixth bulletin Indies' route, 29 Dec. 1948, in: *Officiële bescheiden betreffende de Nederlands-Indonesische betrekkingen, 1945–1950,* Vol. 16, nr. 294, note 8.

114 Telegram High Representative Louis Beel to Minister Sassen, 30 Dec. 1948, in: *Officiële bescheiden betreffende de Nederlands-Indonesische betrekkingen, 1945–1950,* Vol. 16, nr. 339. Reporting in *de Volkskrant*, 4, 5 and 7 January 1949.

Because of the non-scheduled character of the flight with the Prime Minister, this particular departure received special permission from Pakistan and India after mediation by UN Secretary-General Trygve Lie. The permission stipulated that the route followed had to remain secret to prevent public outcry. Captain Leendert Sillevis managed to reach Batavia with only three stopovers landing his Lockheed Constellation only in Malta, Sharjah and Bangkok. Airports in Pakistan, India, Ceylon and Burma were thus avoided.

Meanwhile, KLM also tried to make an emergency provision for the transportation of mail. An hour after Drees' flight left, captain Adriaan Viruly took off for Batavia with a second Constellation. On board this aircraft were some 3,000 kilos of mail, a route inspector from KLM and an observer from the Government Aviation Service. While in the air Viruly received radio instructions not to land in Sharjah, but instead to divert to Dahran, Saudi Arabia. The reason for this diversion was unclear, but in Dahran his airplane was immediately impounded and the occupants interned by the Saudis. Effecting their release took three days. Viruly then continued along the customary route towards Batavia, but without reporting his position to India's air traffic control. At high altitude and in radio silence, the KLM machine covertly passed through the airspace of Pakistan and India and made it to Ceylon and Bangkok. Nonetheless, this state of affairs added urgency to the Mauritius option.[115]

The situation around mail, freight and passengers was now becoming more problematic by the day. However, the Indian and Pakistani confidentiality clause for the flight with Prime Minister Drees and the quiet success of Viruly's flight gave KLM an idea: would it be possible to make more secret passages across the Indian subcontinent? To prevent losing the crucial connection with the Dutch East Indies, KLM aircraft made nine clandestine night flights through India's airspace between 4 January and 6 February 1949, carrying vital supplies and mail despite a reduced payload. Pilots flew with extinguished navigation lights, observed radio silence and registered false flight plans. KLM's Constellations could just cover the distance between Sharjah and Bangkok without refuelling. In the event of difficulties, the crews were instructed to invoke the 1944 International Air Services Transit Agreement, which granted the signatories the right of peaceful overflight. The agreement had been signed by Britain on India's behalf. KLM gambled that its high-flying aircraft would not be detected, as India did not possess the necessary radar installations. Nonetheless, the set-up was not entirely successful. On both sides of the Indian subcontinent, KLM aircraft were spotted at take-off and landing. The Dutch diplomatic representative in India, Arnold Lamping, who had been deliberately kept in the dark

115 Van Maare, *KLM Constellations*, p. 33–36. Wim Adriaansen, *Jons Viruly. 1905–1986. Vlieger en schrijver* (Zaltbommel: Aprilis, 2008), p. 237–240.

so that he could deny all knowledge when called upon by the authorities in Delhi, had some uncomfortable moments, facing difficult questions from the Indian government to which he had no answer. It was only after the ninth and final clandestine flight had left Indian airspace that Lamping was instructed on 10 February 1949 to solemnly promise that no further violations of India's airspace would take place.[116]

Four days after learning in London on 22 January that Britain had agreed to a Dutch emergency route via Mauritius, KLM was ready to undertake a first trial flight. However, the new makeshift service did not commence until 14 March. Before that, half a dozen trial flights were made to determine the risks involved. All the aircraft that were to fly the Mauritius route had to be completely stripped inside to save weight. Operating at a greatly reduced payload and providing only six to ten passenger seats, KLM's Lockheed L-749 Constellations were just able to bridge the distance between Mauritius and Batavia. In an era in which navigation depended on dead reckoning, this was a major achievement. It was also an expensive operation, paid for by special government funds. The aviation boycott and the blockade of the regular air route continued until 20 July 1949. In total, 130 flights were made, carrying 210,328 kilos of mail and 2,034 passengers, costing the government a total of 27.2 million guilders.

Before reinstating KLM's operating rights, the Indian and Pakistani governments insisted that hostilities on Java must end and the Indonesian government's position be restored.[117] In view of the international rejection of Dutch policy in Indonesia concessions were inescapable, although The Hague continued to state its position via-à-vis independence on the basis of legalistic principles that stemmed from another era. This did not contribute to a rapid solution. Under American pressure to stop Marshall Aid to the Netherlands and covert threats to go as far as blocking Dutch accession to NATO, a political agreement was reached with the Indonesian Republic. The Van Roijen-Roem Agreement was signed on 5 May 1949. It brought a perspective of peace and promised a Round Table Conference on Indonesian independence.[118] What made aviation diplomacy especially complex was that at the same time, India was lobbying The Hague to agree to the introduction of an Air India service via Batavia to Australia, BOAC was seeking to ramp up its own Australia route.

---

116 Van Maare, *KLM Constellations*, p. 36–38. Dierikx, Frappez Toujours, p, 76–77.

117 Code messages Lamping (New Delhi) and Van Karnebeek (Karachi) to Foreign Affairs, 17 May and 7 June 1949: NNA, 2.10.14, General Secretariat Dutch East Indies (Algemene Secretarie van de Nederlands-Indische Regering), 1922–1950, inv.nr. 3473.

118 Van Maare, *KLM Constellations*, p. 44–45, 60–66.

The Hague had a hard time defining its position on these issues now that KLM was not allowed to fly these routes.[119] The last machine for Mauritius left Amsterdam on 13 July 1949; five days later the final return flight departed from Batavia.[120] Pakistan revoked its landing ban on 14 July and India and Ceylon followed. On 20 July, the first KLM machine to fly the normal route again took off from Amsterdam.

These developments did not affect the need to settle relations between the Netherlands and the government of Indonesia, including issues related to aviation. From 23 August to 2 November 1949, consultations were held in The Hague as part of the Round Table Conference on Indonesian Independence. The aviation issue was deliberately avoided. At the beginning of November, the delegations agreed to discuss aviation relations in separate bilateral consultations to take place before 1 March 1950. Things became even more complicated beforehand, as American money enabled Indonesia to prepare for the creation of its own national airline, Indonesian Airways.[121] After the transfer of sovereignty, this new company would take over air transport in the Indonesian archipelago, covering the routes that KLM had operated since August 1947.

Apart from finances and operations, aviation policy was also a topic of discussion, as a new relationship had to be defined between the Netherlands and the Republic of Indonesia. In this specific case, reaching agreement proved easier than anticipated. Aviation was one of the few subjects on which the Netherlands and Indonesia agreed, and the contacts between KLM and the Indonesians were characterized by an atmosphere of good will. This resulted in the signing of a cooperation agreement with the new government in Jakarta on 31 March 1950. This stipulated that KLM would take a 50 per cent share in Garuda International Airways, the new Indonesian national air carrier. For a period of ten years, KLM was to supervise Garuda's development. The funds for this participation were made available by the government in The Hague.[122]

The agreement served several purposes. On the one hand, KLM was able to keep its existing contacts and make arrangements for the transfer of members of its staff in Indonesia to Garuda. On the other hand, cooperation provided a certain degree of protection against the possible weakening of KLM's position by the Sukarno Government, which was of considerable importance to compensate for the decline in the market for air transport between Amsterdam

119 Minutes 36th-38th BLV, 8 March 1949–11 May 1949: NNA, 2.05.117 Foreign Affairs, 1945–1954, inv.nr: 1689.

120 Van Maare, *KLM Constellations*, p. 69–72.

121 Minutes 41st BLV, 1 Nov. 1949: NNA, 2.05.117, Foreign Affairs, 1945–1954, inv.nr: 1689.

122 KLM, *Annual Report 1950*, p. 4. Dierikx, *Blauw in de lucht*, p. 128–129.

and Jakarta that was expected to follow independence. In December 1949, preparations were made to establish a bilateral air transport agreement and a wider accord on cooperation in the field of aviation as such.[123]

4 Transatlantic Air Services to New York

The political, military, economic and diplomatic status of the United States had increased enormously during the course of World War Two. America had become a superpower, a leader in almost every area imaginable. Aviation evidenced the technological leaps that had been taken in the course of hostilities. Suddenly the 25-year old vision of flying passengers across the Atlantic became a reality in the shape of transport aircraft capable of crossing the ocean's vast expanse. In the second half of 1945 as many as 30,000 decommissioned US servicemen flew home across the Atlantic each month. A whole new travel market appeared to be there for the taking. Almost overnight, New York became a hub for global air transport.

As soon as the first Douglas Skymasters arrived in Amsterdam, KLM started preparing for air services to New York, eager to claim a share of this emerging new market. From the perspective of flight technology, it was a bonus that a number of KLM pilots had been part of the North Atlantic Return Ferry Service that BOAC had maintained for the RAF during the war. The Return Ferry Service flew aircrews and priority passengers across the Atlantic, completing several thousand flights. Crews had gained a wealth of experience and now all that was needed were aircraft.[124]

The Americans, on the other hand, had airplanes in abundance. On 1 June 1945, the CAB ruled on the North Atlantic Route Case, which arranged for the admission of American airline companies to transatlantic air traffic. Three airlines were designated to fly six routes to Europe: PanAm, American Overseas Airlines (AOA), and Trans World Airlines (TWA).[125] Air route number 4, flown by AOA, ran via London, Amsterdam, Berlin and Warsaw to Moscow.[126] The initial flights all took place under a military guise.

---

123 Minutes 42nd BLV, 6 December 1949: NNA, 2.05.117 Foreign Affairs, 1945–1954, inv.nr: 1689.

124 R.E.G. Davies, *A History of the World's Airlines* (London: Oxford University Press, 1964), 325. Adriaansen, *Jons Viruly*, p. 194–205.

125 "Opinion and order adopted by the Civil Aeronautics Board on 1 June 1945, the North Atlantic Route Case, Docket No. 855: Harry S. Truman Presidential Library, Independence, Ml, file 6, CAB, North Atlantic Route Case, CAB 319 (1945).

126 Telegram State Department to Netherlands embassy London, 5 July 1945: NNA, 2.05.80, Foreign Affairs, London Archive, inv.nr. 3386.

In October 1945, The Hague was approached by the US Military Air Transport Service to cooperate on the air route. Grateful for the sacrifices the United States had made for the liberation of the Netherlands, the government granted permission to use Schiphol Airport that same day.[127] A subsequent application from AOA to begin a commercial service via Amsterdam to Germany was also approved without delay. The head of the Government Aviation Service, Henri van Ede van der Pals, needed all of 15 minutes to endorse the request.[128] Now only an American permit for KLM remained to be settled.

Preliminary plans for a Dutch service to New York had been put forward in October 1945.[129] In preparation, a KLM delegation led by Bert Slotemaker visited Washington two months later for a hearing by the CAB.[130] No immediate decision was taken, but The Hague expected American consent to be a formality between friends and allies. After all, both the United States and the Netherlands had spoken out in favor of liberalism at the Chicago Conference. Nonetheless, there were some doubts at KLM regarding the American position. With the 1930s negotiations in mind, Plesman felt a sense of urgency in pushing for an agreement. He believed it possible that only early applicants would receive a license easily.[131]

Freely accommodating foreign aircraft in New York was not in line with American aviation interests, however, and although former assistant Secretary of State Adolf Berle had promoted an 'open sky', his primary reference was that of the first two 'freedoms of the air': overflight and technical stops. The ultimate goal of his policy was to achieve a dominant position for the United States in international aviation, starting in Latin America.[132] From April 1945, the new Truman Administration implemented a policy that would offer American airline companies some form of protection against subsidized foreign competition. Meanwhile, KLM tried to build up brand awareness in the US with an advertising campaign in the *New York Times* to promote its flights between Miami and Curaçao. These efforts did not go down well at the CAB. At the behest of its chairman Lloyd Welch Pogue, the CAB restricted access for

127 Minutes meeting of the interdepartmental committee on civil aviation, 24 Oct. 1945: NNA, 2.05.117, Foreign Affairs 1945–1954, inv.nr. 9864.

128 Preliminaries and report on the discussions held in The Hague, 17–20 September 1946, undated (Sept. 1946), NNA, 2.05.117, Foreign Affairs 1945–1954, inv.nr. 9864.

129 Minutes 1st BLV, 29 Oct. 1945: NNA, 2.05.117 Foreign Affairs 1945–1954, inv.nr: 1689.

130 Minutes 3rd BLV, 7 Jan. 1946: NNA, 2.05.117 Foreign Affairs 1945–1954, inv.nr: 1689.

131 Minutes 1st BLV, 29 Oct. 1945: NNA, 2.05.117 Foreign Affairs 1945–1954, inv.nr: 1689.

132 Van Vleck, *Empire of the Air*, p. 169–171; 175–180.

foreign air services to a single point of entry, New York. At the beginning of 1946 promoting American interests took center stage in aviation policy.[133]

In The Hague this was not recognized. Indeed, the government saw no reason to push for a formal bilateral agreement on the exchange of landing rights. After all, both nations had signed the International Air Transport Agreement that promised liberalism.[134] As a result, KLM was happy to receive a simple provisional operating license. It came in April 1946 in the shape of a Foreign Air Carrier Permit, valid for a period of three years. The Dutch were granted two such provisional permits: one for a twice weekly service between Amsterdam and New York, and one for Curaçao-Miami.[135]

Early in May 1946 KLM started advertising its transatlantic service. The first scheduled flight, flown with the DC-4 *Rotterdam*, arrived in New York on 22 May 1946. It was met ceremonially by a festive party adorned with flags and with lots of Dutch cheese in readiness. However, upon landing, something went wrong. At La Guardia Airport there was a second airplane on the runway, forcing captain Evert van Dijk to apply full brakes as soon as his wheels touched the ground. Two tires blew out and the airplane came to a stop at a considerable distance from the welcoming party, which caused the planned festivities to end abruptly.[136] Nonetheless, Dutch newspapers reported in superlatives about 'a historic departure' and 'a national event'. Even the communist daily *De Waarheid* [The Truth] could not suppress a sense of chauvinism and reported extensively on KLM's pioneering work.[137] A radio reporter on the flight ensured that listeners in the Netherlands could tune in live and a filmed report featured in the weekly *Polygoon* cinema newsreel.[138]

The *Rotterdam* had needed some 25 hours to reach New York, including four hours spent on the ground for refuelling. From take-off in Amsterdam at half past two in the afternoon the route first ran to Prestwick in Scotland (where the plane landed at four o'clock, local time) and then on to Gander on Newfoundland (landing at half past one at night, local time), arriving in New York at nine o'clock in the morning, local time. The crossing 'within a day' represented a significant reduction in travel time compared to the crossing by

133 Interview by the author with Lloyd Welch Pogue in Washington DC, 10 Feb. 1989. Van Vleck, *Empire of the Air*, p. 193; 195. Dierikx, Spel zonder kaarten, p. 15.

134 Minutes 1st BLV, 29 Oct. 1945: NNA, 2.05.117, Foreign Affairs 1945–1954, inv.nr: 1689.

135 CAB Docket 1187, 14 March 1946: United States National Archives, State Dept., Record Group 59, inv.nr. 711.5627/4–846.

136 *De Tijd*, 23 May 1946.

137 *Het Parool*, 6 May 1946, *Algemeen Handelsblad*, 22 May 1946, *De Waarheid*, 22 May 1946.

138 *Polygoon* journaal, 1946: https://www.youtube.com/watch?v=C2MFVmZg2Cg [accessed 2018].

ship, which usually took five days. However, tickets were anything but cheap, costing 1050 Dutch guilders each way. Meals were served during stopovers on the ground while the machine was being refueled. In the air, passengers were pampered with chocolates, sweets and biscuits, and a small jug of gin. Liquor consumption was free of charge, as were reading materials and maps indicating the route.[139] The return service was proudly advertised as 'the Royal Route New York to Europe'.[140] Success seemed assured.

However, on 25 July 1946, Washington announced that it would withdraw from the International Air Transport Agreement in July 1947. The message took The Hague completely by surprise, although Dutch diplomats had warned about the possibility of such a policy change. The CAB wished to protect American carriers and was also opposed to the expansion plans that KLM voiced repeatedly. If KLM's service to New York was to continue after the three-year permit expired, a bilateral air transport agreement with the United States would be necessary. Unfortunately, while Washington pursued liberalism in almost every other area of economic activity, civil aviation was the exception. In this area, the United States sought to enforce American power and influence through restrictive bilateral agreements.[141] The Netherlands would need to initiate talks.[142]

From the outset, things went awry in the negotiations. In September 1946, the Dutch were still optimistic that the conclusion of a bilateral agreement would not pose problems. This nonchalance caused irritation in the American camp, where US interests ruled. In particular, the Dutch desire to be granted 5th freedom rights for services from New York to Curaçao encountered fierce resistance. To allow this would mean that KLM could compete with American domestic carriers on this route. The CAB qualified the very idea as 'preposterous'.[143]

The American reservations and objectives made no sense to the Dutch. Surely it could not be the case that superpower America was erecting a barrier to block the development of an impoverished small allied nation like the Netherlands, which badly needed the dollar-generating air service. Moreover,

139 De Volkskrant, 8 May 1946.

140 *New York Times*, 18 June 1946.

141 Giles Scott-Smith, David J. Snyder, "A Test of Sentiments": Civil Aviation, Alliance Politics, and the KLM Challenge in Dutch-American Relations, in: *Diplomatic History* 37(2013). Downloaded from http://dh.oxfordjournals.org.

142 Aide memoire Reuchlin (Neth. Embassy Washington) to State Department, 7 Apr. 1947: United States National Archives, State Dept., Record Group 59, inv.nr. 711.5627/4-747.

143 Letter CAB to State Dept., 26 Nov. 1946: United States National Archives, State Department, Record Group 59, 711.5627/11-2646.

The Hague had just freed a significant part of its scarce dollar reserves to buy no less than 26 new airliners from Douglas and Lockheed. Indignant Dutch negotiators put on the brakes, saying it would be better to hang on to the temporary permit than sign for the restrictions the CAB was insisting on. This attitude spoiled the atmosphere in the talks. The Dutch delegates packed their bags, leaving the American team, led by the CAB, annoyed at what they saw as a total incomprehension of legitimate American interests, an attitude that reeked of colonial arrogance.[144]

Nonetheless, the Dutch had a point. The treatment of KLM was in sharp contrast to the way other West-European airlines were hailed in the United States. To welcome Air France, TWA chief executive Jack Frye had even put a big ad in the New York Times: '... it is like welcoming an old friend to our own home to see these wings over American Soil'.[145] What made the Dutch case different was that KLM not only aimed at providing services to New York, but admitted it also hoped to fly to other cities on the American continent via New York and Curaçao.[146]

On the American side, the case was rooted in a fundamental difference of opinion between the State Department and the CAB. The CAB was there to promote the interests of the American airline industry, placing no value on the liberal principles to which the State Department was partial. State, however, was engrained in strategic and geopolitical concepts, as the divide in Europe between the West and the Soviets was widening. To the disbelief of the State Department, which wished to strengthen transatlantic cooperation, the CAB dug in. In London, the American civil air attaché Livingstone Satterthwaite even apologized to Daniël Goedhuis, saying that things in Washington had got out of hand. He believed that the CAB's attitude would ultimately relax and that the next round of talks would lead to an agreement.[147] In any case, the diplomats at State were more receptive towards the Dutch desire to be treated the same as the other Western European countries.[148] After all, Air France had

144 Report Goedhuis re. US-Dutch negotiations in Washington on 15, 16, 24 and 25 October 1946, 31 Oct. 1946; secret report Goedhuis of his after-dinner conversation with the US air attaché in London, Livingstone Satterthwaite, 31 Oct. 1946: NNA, 2.05.117, Foreign Affairs 1945–1954, inv.nr. 9927.

145 *New York Times* 25 June 1946.

146 Minutes 4th BLV, 4 Feb. 1946; 6th BLV, 1 Apr. 1946 and 12th BLV, 16 Sep. 1946: NNA, 2.05.117, Foreign Affairs 1945–1954, inv.nr. 21391.

147 Secret report by Goedhuis of his meeting with Satterthwaite in London, 31 Oct. 1946: NNA, 2.05.117, Foreign Affairs 1945–1954, inv.nr. 9927.

148 Memo J.H. Morgan to Walstrom (Aviation Division), 8 Nov. 1946: United States National Archives, State Department, Record Group 59, 711.5627/11-846.

been granted rights in New York and in Boston, and BOAC was allowed to land in several US cities.[149]

The Hague's hope to be treated on an equal footing to its European neighbors turned out to be a misconception. After 1945 Dutch foreign policy needed to adapt to the radically changed circumstances in the world. By 1947, the Dutch international position had shrunk to that of a small country, misguidedly clinging to its former colonial grandeur to Washington's discontent. In these circumstances there appeared to be little reason to allow the Dutch preferential treatment. After the walk-out in October 1946, the Dutch were unable to entice their American interlocutors to a new round of consultations. In March 1947 Plesman made a special three-week trip to America, but failed to effect a breakthrough. On both sides of the Atlantic, the positions hardened. Seemingly oblivious to Washington's anti-colonialist inclination in world affairs, especially America's attitude to Dutch policy in Indonesia, The Hague set about preparing a new package of wishes regarding routes and rights for KLM as if all was well.[150]

The controversy between the Netherlands and the United States over Dutch policy towards Indonesia was particularly unhelpful for bilateral relations; such differences were grist to the mill, reinforcing the CAB's restrictive attitude. In Holland, the implicit links between international politics and air transport were ill understood. The Hague even worked on an application for a KNILM service from Batavia to Los Angeles, and demanded that KLM should be allowed to use 5th freedom rights in New York for flights to Mexico and Cuba.[151] Those involved in aviation policy spoke about landing rights as if the broader political context did not exist.[152] This fed irritation in Washington, where the CAB became increasingly verbal about KLM's growing practice of transporting passengers from abroad – especially from Germany – via a transfer in Amsterdam to New York, a practice that became known as 6th freedom

149 Nicolas Neiertz, Air France: an elephant in an evening suit, in: Hans Dienel, Peter Lyth (red.), *Flying the Flag. European Commercial Air Transport since 1945* (Basingstoke: MacMillan, 1998), p. 27. Peter Lyth, Chosen Instruments: the Evolution of British Airways, in: *ibid.*, p. 61.

150 Internal minute Ministry of Foreign Affairs, 21 Aug. 1947: NNA, 2.05.117, Foreign Affairs 1945–1954, inv.nr. 9927.

151 Telegram consul-general New York to Ministry of Foreign Affairs, 8 Feb. 1947: NNA, 2.05.117, Foreign Affairs 1945–1954, inv.nr. 9927. Minutes 42nd BLV, 6 Dec. 1949: NNA, 2.05.117, Foreign Affairs 1945–1954, inv.nr. 21391.

152 Minutes 22nd and 23rd BLV, 4 Aug. 1947 and 8 Sept. 1947: NNA, 2.05.117, Foreign Affairs 1945–1954, inv.nr. 21391.

carriage.[153] Fortunately for KLM, which had been operating to New York four times a week since April 1947, the CAB was willing to renew the provisional permit of 1946 despite the differences of opinion. Given the American reservations about the Dutch Indonesia policy, this was the best deal The Hague could hope for. Nonetheless the Dutch were dissatisfied and continued to ask that the US confirm the rights they had granted in a formal bilateral agreement. From its side, KLM hoped to approach the Americans again about 5th freedom rights between New York and Curaçao. For the Dutch diplomats there was little other option but to press on in aviation matters, regardless of the fact that American patience with Dutch policies was dwindling. They hoped that the Brussels defense Pact of March 1948, and the Berlin Airlift in place since June of that year, would provide an incentive for increased collaboration that might hold benefits for KLM.[154] This was unrealistic. Early in 1949 the Truman administration made it clear that the US was displeased with Dutch conduct in Indonesia and that aid to the Netherlands under the Marshall Plan might be suspended unless The Hague changed its attitude. The Dutch Foreign Minister Dirk Stikker voiced his irritation about this threat in no uncertain terms.[155] The chances of reaching a satisfactory deal with Washington over landing rights were smaller than ever.

5 Negotiating Air Services to South America

In The Hague, interest in air services to South America dated from the end of the 1930s, following an expansion of trade in agriculture. Plans were launched for a postal air link to the Dutch overseas territories in the West Indies and for a cautious expansion of KLM's West Indies Division on Curaçao.[156] Other South American services were also contemplated; in October 1939 KLM had considered starting a service from Curaçao via Surinam to Buenos Aires for example.[157] The war meant that none of these plans came to fruition however. The idea of an air route to South America was reintroduced in 1943 when Brazil's airline Panair do Brasil, then a subsidiary of PanAm, expressed an interest in flying

153 Minutes 30th BLV, 25 June 1948: NNA, 2.05.117, Foreign Affairs 1945–1954, inv.nr. 21391.
154 Minutes 32nd and 33rd BLV, 20 Oct. and 22 Nov. 1948: NNA, 2.05.117, Foreign Affairs 1945–1954, inv.nr. 21391.
155 Hellema, *Nederland in de wereld*, p. 158–160.
156 Dierikx, *Blauw in de Lucht*, p. 93.
157 Letter P.E. Teppema to Plesman, 4 Nov. 1939: NNA, 2.05.80, Foreign Affairs, London Archive, inv.nr. 3336.

to Surinam. In return, the Dutch hoped for permission for a service to Rio de Janeiro. These early contacts seemed promising, but eventually led to nothing.[158]

The plan for a Dutch South America route ran through Madrid, Lisbon, Dakar, Natal and Rio de Janeiro to end in Buenos Aires. Such a service appeared attractive in the context of Dutch postwar reconstruction, because it could promote trading contacts with Latin America.[159] Moreover, the potential passenger transport market was significant. Travel from Europe to South America was growing, partly as a result of the outcome of the war: in the first couple of years after 1945, some 300,000 Germans left, especially for Argentina.[160] No wonder KLM wanted a piece of the cake. In anticipation of increased trade, it was important to develop new routes to destinations that could replace revenue from the traditional service to the Dutch East Indies.

An air link from Amsterdam to the major cities on the east coast of South America hinged on the conclusion of bilateral agreements with Brazil, Uruguay and Argentina. Brazil was first approached, in March 1946. The Dutch initiated discussions in the corridors of the Provisional International Civil Aviation Organization (PICAO) that met in Montreal, but the Brazilians showed little interest. As long as there were no plans for Brazilian air services to Europe there appeared to be no reason to accommodate a foreign air service.[161] As an additional complication, the Brazilians felt indebted to the US policy of reserving air transport in the Western Hemisphere for airlines that had their roots in the Americas.[162]

In advance of Brazilian responses, the Dutch had also approached Argentina. Unlike Brazil which had joined the allied cause in 1942, Argentina had long remained neutral in the war, although it sympathized with the Axis powers. After Pearl Harbor, when the US became involved in the war, an American

---

158 Letter Dutch envoy in Rio, Willem Daniëls, to Governor of Surinam, Johan Kielstra, 21 Oct. 1943: NNA, 2.05.80, Foreign Affairs, London Archive, inv.nr. 3353. Further: *Documenten betreffende de buitenlandse politiek van Nederland, 1919–1945. Periode C : 1940–1945*, Vol. 7 (The Hague: Instituut voor Nederlandse Geschiedenis, 2004), nr. 35; *Documenten betreffende de buitenlandse politiek van Nederland, 1919–1945. Periode C : 1940–1945*, Vol. 8, (The Hague: Instituut voor Nederlandse Geschiedenis, 2004), nr. 29.

159 Documents in file at NNA, RLD, 5.016.5240, inv.nr. 1507.

160 Anne Saint Sauveur-Henn, Die deutsche Migration nach Argentinien (1870–1945), in: Peter Birle (red.), *Die Beziehungen zwischen Deutschland und Argentinien* (Frankfurt: Vervuert Verlag [Bibliotheca Ibero-Americana], 2010), p. 21–52 (p.51). http://publications.iai.spk-berlin.de/receive/reposis-iai_mods_00000772 (2018).

161 Minutes 4th BLV, 4 Feb. 1946: NNA, 2.05.117, Foreign Affairs 1945–1954, inv.nr. 21391.

162 Telegram Chargé d'Affaires in Brazil to the Secretary of State, 28 May 1946: *Foreign Relations of the United States, 1946, The American Republics*, Volume XI, (Washington: United States Government Printing Office, 1969), docs. 420 and 426.

trade embargo had a serious effect on Argentina's domestic affairs and in June 1943, a coup brought a military dictatorship to power in Buenos Aires. Argentina had since gradually moved towards the Allied camp.[163] At a very late stage in the war, the country joined the Allied cause in March 1945, although this had little impact on Argentine foreign policy, which generally sought to steer clear of American interests.[164] Because Washington repeatedly meddled in Argentine affairs, keeping its distance was a sensitive issue, especially as the US Ambassador, Spruille Braden, worked to prevent the central figure in the Argentine junta, Juan Perón, from taking power in Buenos Aires.[165]

Against this background, opening discussions in Argentina on air transport proved more difficult for the Dutch than initiating such talks had been in Rio. After all, the Netherlands was an American ally, and this made Argentina suspicious. When the Dutch negotiators arrived in Buenos Aires in August 1946, two months after Argentina's new national airline FAMA [Flota Aérea Mercante Argentina] had started operating, they found the Argentines reluctant to meet with them. Moreover, language turned out to be a problem. Neither Henri van Ede van der Pals nor Bert Slotemaker spoke Spanish, while the Argentinians indicated that they only wished to have conversations in their own language.[166] In any case, Argentina was dead set against the idea of opening its airspace to foreign aircraft; some months earlier Argentina's president Juan Perón had initiated an ambitious nationwide program focused on using Argentine aviation as a means to rally and modernize the nation. In September 1946 this culminated in a national Aviation Week, with festivities in Buenos Aires.[167] Generally ill-prepared and unaware of the centrality of aviation in the political

163 Mario Rapoport, Foreign and domestic policy in Argentina during the Second World War: the traditional political parties and the military regime, 1943–1945, in: Guido di Tella, Donald C. Watt (eds.), *Argentina between the Great Powers, 1939–46* (Basingstoke: Macmillan, 1989), p. 77–105.

164 Memorandum Prepared in the Department of State, 2 Jan. 1945: *Foreign Relations of the United States: Diplomatic Papers, 1945, The American Republics, Volume IX*, (Washington: United States Government Printing Office, 1969), no. 242.

165 Carlos Escudé, US Destabilization and Economic Boycott of Argentina, in: Guido di Tella, Donald C. Watt (eds.), *Argentina between the Great Powers, 1939–46* (Basingstoke: Macmillan, 1989), p. 62–63. Soledad Altrudi, *Of Personalities and Democratization in US Public Diplomacy: The Case of the Blue Book on Argentina*: University of Southern California, Center on Public Diplomacy, Annenberg School, https://www.uscpublicdiplomacy.org/student-paper/personalities-and-democratization-us-public-diplomacy-case-blue-book-argentina-0 2015 [accessed 2020].

166 Code message Pallandt to Foreign Affairs, 16 Aug. 1946: NNA, 2.05.117, Foreign Affairs 1945–1954, inv.nr. 9873.

167 Marc J. Alsina, Aviation for the People: Class and State Aviation in Perón's 'New Argentina' 1946–55, in: *Technology and Culture*, Volume 63, Nr. 1, January 2022, p. 153–181 (153–161).

and economic processes going on in Argentina, the Dutch achieved no results. Siem Nieuwenhuijsen, who had been added to the delegation by the Ministry of Foreign Affairs at the last minute, told his colleague Peter Witte that he saw no prospects for a settlement. Argentina appeared to be under the spell of protectionism.[168] Perón's program of promoting a national *conciencia aeronáutica* [aeronautical consciousness] had political implications. Argentina insisted on strict control of aviation and the prevention of foreign competition, the very opposite of what the Dutch stood for.[169] Hoping to manoeuver things along in spite of Argentine obstruction, the Dutch decided to ask only for permission to organize a limited number of trial flights.[170] To this, Buenos Aires agreed. Nine such flights were carried out between 6 August and 11 December 1946, before Argentina revoked its permit.[171]

Because some competitors were already operating scheduled services to Brazil, KLM was in need of negotiating results. Rather than wait for an opportunity to continue discussions in Argentina, the Dutch chose to fly back to Rio, hoping to wrest permission for trial flights to Brazil. The Brazilians did not object, and on 25 September 1946, the first KLM DC-4 landed in Rio de Janeiro, after a three-day trip from Amsterdam. It carried technical staff and a team of five negotiators, including Plesman. This time talks went more smoothly and in the days that followed the contours of a bilateral accord were drawn up. As the licensing party, the Brazilians held the better cards at the table and the draft agreement reflected this. The guiding principles of the accord held Bermuda-like clauses for restricting capacity and tariffs. The Dutch team tried in vain to steer towards more liberal terms, but got nowhere. This was no surprise: while the talks with the Dutch were ongoing, Brazil signed a Bermuda-type bilateral agreement with the United States on 2 October 1946.[172]

Liberalism clearly held no central place in Brazilian or Argentine thinking, although the KLM trial flights were allowed to continue. They generated over one-and-a-quarter million guilders in revenues, an incentive for KLM to continue operations.[173] To achieve this, it would be helpful if KLM could be presented as a company rooted in the Americas. Indeed, Rio was waiting for

168 Office memo Nieuwenhuijsen to Witte, 30 Oct. 1946: NNA, RLD, 5.016.5240, inv.nr. 6282.

169 Melina Piglia, Carry our colors and defend our interests under the skies of other Continents. Argentinian Commercial aviation policy in the Peronista decade (Argentina 1945–1955), in: *Journal of Transport History* 40(2019) nr. 1, p. 44–61 (51–52).

170 Code message Pallandt to Foreign Affairs, 4 Sep. 1946: NNA, 2.05.117, Foreign Affairs 1945–1954, inv.nr. 9873.

171 KLM, *Overzicht van het bedrijf over de Jaren 1941 tot en met 1946*, p. 46–47.

172 R.E.G. Davies, *Airlines of Latin America*, p. 451.

173 KLM, *Annual Report 1946*, p.5.

a sign from Washington that a KLM service from Curaçao, would not be detrimental to American-Brazilian aviation relations, while Aerovias Brasil and Cruzeiro do Sul were in the process of seeking permission to operate services to the United States.[174]

Washington did its best to persuade the Brazil not to give The Hague what it wanted. After all, the Dutch had walked out of the negotiations with the US in Washington, which had caused some irritation. And there was more: rumor had it that on the outbound flights from Switzerland KLM's planes carried not only regular bona fide passengers, but also German citizens with dodgy papers. American officials were keen to stop this traffic.[175] Meanwhile, it was clear that the Dutch were aiming for a liberal agreement with Brazil, outside the confines of the Bermuda clauses that Washington embraced.[176] However, achieving progress proved difficult. Brazil objected to the Dutch proposal of a second KLM service, Curaçao-Rio, in addition to the transatlantic flights already under discussion. The Brazilian negotiators voiced (American inspired) concern that such a service would create excessive competition for indigenous carriers operating in the Americas. In the end only the transatlantic route from Amsterdam remained on the table. KLM was granted a provisional license. The Dutch negotiating team returned home feeling that they had finally achieved something. KLM would be able to open a service of sorts. But the Netherlands envoy in Rio was of a different opinion: was the rejected second service, from Curaçao, not just as much an air service of the Western Hemisphere? He feared the results of the Brazilian negotiations spelled trouble for the development potential of KLM's West-Indies Branch.[177]

The outcome of the talks with Brazil underlined the need to push for proper landing rights in Argentina. To reach Buenos Aires, KLM needed permission to fly over Uruguay, and this was where the Dutch negotiators went next. In contrast to the difficulties experienced in the neighboring countries, the Uruguayans welcomed the idea of a Dutch air service that would land in Montevideo

174 Code message Kleyn Molenkamp, 7 Oct. 1946: NNA, 2.05.117, BZ 1945–1954, inv.nr. 9867.

175 Letter US Consul General in Zurich, Samuel B. Woods, to US ambassador in The Hague, Herman Baruch, 30 Dec. 1947: United States National Archives, Record Group 319, Army Intelligence Document Files, 1/1944 – 1955, NM3 85A (box 2882).

176 Report Goedhuis re. US-Dutch negotiations in Washington on 15, 16, 24 and 25 October 1946, 31 Oct. 1946. Secret report Goedhuis of conversation with Livingstone Satterthwaite, 31 Oct. 1946: NNA, 2.05.117, Foreign Affairs 1945–1954, inv.nr. 9927.

177 Code message Van Boetzelaer to Rio, 25 Oct. 1946: NNA, 2.05.117, Foreign Affairs 1945–1954, inv.nr. 9867. Minutes 13th BLV 11/12 Nov. 1946: NNA, 2.05.117, Foreign Affairs 1945–1954, inv. nr. 21391.

straight away.[178] Although delineating the precise wording took time, a bilateral agreement was signed on 6 February 1947. Now only Argentina remained. However, the Perón Government considered all air transport in Argentina to be national property and took the view that international air transport, if admitted at all, should be strictly bilateral: a service between a point of departure in one nation, and the aircraft's final destination in the other. Commercial stopovers along the route were considered undesirable by the Argentines.[179] This proved a serious obstacle in the talks with the Netherlands.

For Argentina, the interests of its flag carrier were paramount.[180] FAMA was all about showing the Argentine colors abroad, and generating revenue came second. A year passed before Buenos Aires even considered sending negotiators to The Hague.[181] There was little room for discussion. Argentina's aims hardly extended beyond continuing FAMA's transatlantic service and showing the blue and white flag in Madrid. As in the Brazilian case, the United States meddled. The Dutch were told that the US Embassy in Buenos Aires objected to the Argentine-Dutch accord, as the Dutch proposals deviated from the Bermuda formula.[182] Ultimately, no agreement was reached, which meant that KLM flights had to end in Montevideo. Passengers bound for Buenos Aires were advised to disembark there and cross the Rio de la Plata by boat. It was not until 29 October 1948 that the negotiators reached agreement. Thereafter things moved along speedily and the inaugural flight to Buenos Aires took off on 29 November 1948.

Meanwhile, the talks in Brazil had run into difficulties, despite the provisional license KLM had received for the trial flights. In the hope of effecting a breakthrough, KLM's representative in Rio, Frans van der Vliet, engaged the services of a first-class intermediary: Osvaldo Aranha, a former Foreign Minister of Brazil and head of the Brazilian delegation to the United Nations. Van der Vliet believed that Aranha's influence would bring KLM's case to the personal attention of the Minister of Aviation Armando Figueira Trompowsky de Almeida. Following advice from Aranha, the Dutch deliberately delayed their request for a new round of discussions until after the Brazilian aviation negotiating team had left for discussions in Portugal in January 1947. Aranha then

178 Minutes 13th BLV, 11/12 Nov. 1946: NNA, 2.05.117, Foreign Affairs 1945–1954, inv.nr. 21391.

179 Piglia, Carry our colors and defend our interests, p. 51–52.

180 Code message V.d. Plas (Kleyn Molenkamp) to Foreign Affairs (Schaepman), 25 Oct. 1946: NNA, 2.05.117, BZ 1945–1954, inv.nr. 9873. Piglia, Carry our colors and defend our interests, p. 55–56.

181 Code message Van Pallandt (written by Slotemaker) to Foreign Affairs, 24 Oct. 1947: NNA, 2.05.117, BZ 1945–1954, inv.nr. 9873.

182 Minutes 30th BLV, 25 June 1948: NNA, 2.05.117, Foreign Affairs 1945–1954, inv.nr. 21391.

called on the minister. This surprise strategy worked. Thanks to Aranha's clout, a text for a bilateral agreement was drawn up on the basis of Dutch proposals.[183] The agreement secured the legal basis for KLM's weekly flights to Rio and Montevideo. Despite some lingering reservations on the part of the Brazilians, a bilateral air transport agreement was signed 11 months later on 6 November 1947. This provided for a weekly scheduled KLM service. It was also agreed that Brazil would now allow KLM to explore a second route from Curaçao.[184]

The agreement with Brazil had a significant and unexpected side effect: it alerted the authorities in Rio to the peculiar route followed by KLM's aircraft in Europe. Inspired by Italian policy towards KLM, Rio withdrew permission to transport 5th freedom passengers between Rome and Rio on 31 December 1948. It was only after much discussion that the Dutch persuaded their Brazilian counterparts to allow a provision for such carriage. By then, another problem was emerging: the commercial stops KLM also made in Frankfurt and in Geneva. Brazil demanded that KLM give up its rights in Geneva and make room for a service of their own.[185] It appeared that the ranks were closing against the ever-demanding Dutch, but the issue remained unresolved. In the end, the Brazilians allowed KLM's 5th freedom stops and the bilateral agreement was ratified on 4 July 1949.[186] KLM was authorized to carry out scheduled services via Geneva and/or Zurich, Madrid and/or Lisbon. A special facility was agreed for 35 'individual flights' to be carried out in 1949 that would make a commercial stop in Rome.[187]

6 The Long Air Route to South Africa

In the spring of 1946, Plesman asked the Ministry of Foreign Affairs to investigate possible Dutch air services to Johannesburg from Amsterdam and from Batavia.[188] This idea, popular in the Dutch East Indies, was in keeping with the

183 Letter F. van der Vliet to Plesman, 18 Jan. 1947: NNA, 2.05.117, Foreign Affairs 1945–1954, inv. nr. 9867.

184 Letter Kleyn Molenkamp to Foreign Affairs, 6 Dec. 1947: NNA, 2.05.117, Foreign Affairs 1945–1954, inv.nr. 9867.

185 Minutes 38th BLV, 11-5-1949: NNA, 2.05.117, Foreign Affairs 1945–1954, inv.nr. 21391.

186 Code message Kleyn Molenkamp to Foreign Affairs, 4 July 1949: NNA, 2.05.117, Foreign Affairs 1945–1954, inv.nr. 9867.

187 Minutes 39th BLV, 19-7-1949: NNA, 2.05.117, Foreign Affairs 1945–1954, inv.nr. 21391.

188 Code message envoy Cape Town (Ph.C. Visser), to Foreign Affairs, 14 May 1946: NNA, 2.0.117 Foreign Affairs, 1945–1954, inv.nr. 9930.

colonial mindset of Dutch-Afrikaans kinship.[189] To reconnoiter the long route across the African continent a trial flight had been undertaken in December 1938, before the war, named the *Dingaansvlucht* (named after a famous 19th century Zulu king). With this proposed new service The Hague hoped to build on the historic and cultural ties between the Netherlands and South Africa.

In May 1946, The Dutch set about drafting an agreement that might serve as a basis for a scheduled service. Meanwhile KLM prepared for a second trial flight, planned to depart on 6 October. Four months prior to this, Adolph Bentinck van Schoonheten, the Dutch special envoy in London, had announced the plans in a letter to Britain's Foreign Secretary Ernest Bevin. Although fully sovereign since 1934, South Africa was a member of the Commonwealth and informing London made sense. Bevin had no objections against a trial flight, but indicated he would not support passenger carriage. This presented a drawback for the Dutch. Without passengers, the South African endeavor made no economic sense. The Hague therefore invoked article 5 of the Chicago Convention, which provided for the right to pick up and discharge passengers on non-scheduled international flights. London rejected this argument. It was obvious that KLM hoped to use the trials to initiate a regular service across British-held Africa at a later stage. But upon further consideration, the Ministry of Civil Aviation came to the conclusion that it could not deny its cooperation, or the commercial rights, as they would indeed fall under the regime of article 5 of the Chicago Convention.[190]

In the hope of speeding things along, the Dutch plan was to send a team of negotiators with the new trial flight, the hope being that South Africa might well view an air connection with the Netherlands as a modern, visible representation of historic and cultural ties. However, the Dutch were ill informed. As it turned out, the South African government was not at all ready for an exchange of traffic rights.[191]

Chaired by diplomat Abraham Steenstra Toussaint, a small party of Dutch negotiators gathered at Schiphol Airport late on 5 October 1946 for the flight via Rome, Tunis, Kano (Nigeria) and Leopoldville (Belgian Congo) to Johannesburg. Plesman and a group of officials saw the plane off in the middle of the night, again with Parmentier at the controls. The DC-4 carried 23 passengers, cargo and mail. The Government Aviation Service RLD was represented by

189 Minutes 11th BLV, 5 Aug. 1946: NNA, 2.05.117, Foreign Affairs 1945–1954, inv.nr. 21391.

190 Letter Bentinck van Schoonheten to Bevin, 21 June 1946; internal minute sheets MCA June-Sept. 1946: BNA, MCA, BT217, 599.

191 Letter Schaepman to Embassy Paris, 24 Sept. 1946: NNA, 2.0.117, Foreign Affairs 1945–1954, inv.nr.: 9930.

Henk Spanjaard, the Indies' government by colonel B.H.F. van Lent, and KLM by Henri Taudin Chabot. The idea was to quickly hammer out an agreement, using the enthusiasm that the flight might generate among the Afrikaans speaking population. The plane arrived in Johannesburg on 10 October. Meanwhile KLM had begun preparations for a further trial flight in December.

However, it was already apparent from the first contacts in Pretoria that the South African Government focused on London for its international aviation policy, not on The Hague. A speedy exchange of traffic rights hardly fit in with this. Moreover, in the Dutch proposal full freedom for the operation of air services took center stage, including 5th freedom rights. The proposed accord would therefore differ considerably from the Bermuda principles embraced in London. This made the Dutch proposal unacceptable and the delegation flew home with the returning KLM plane.[192] Eight weeks later, the South African government rejected the draft agreement, but instead proposed an accord similar to the one The Hague had signed with London in August.[193] A more detailed South African proposal that carefully laid down the conditions for scheduled flights was put forward in June 1947.[194] This time the parties agreed and a Bermuda-based agreement was signed. In August, KLM was able to start a weekly Amsterdam-Johannesburg service, stopping in Tunis, Kano and Leopoldville. There was a sense of urgency involved in these negotiations, as Plesman feared KLM would miss new international air transport opportunities unless action was taken promptly.[195]

Passenger and cargo figures developed fairly well on the new route, which was in line with the trade policy of the incumbent South African Government of Daniël Malan that replaced Smuts' after the general election of May 1948. Malan aimed at expanding existing trade connections and encouraging new ones.[196] At the same time South-Africa was regarded as a prospective market for emigrants from the Netherlands. Plans were made to transport at least part of the emigrants by air. Against this background, KLM wanted to increase its

---

192 Letter Steenstra Toussaint to Foreign Affairs, 25 Oct. 1946: NNA, 2.0.117, Foreign Affairs 1945–1954, inv.nr.: 9930.

193 Code message Visser (Cape Town) to Foreign Affairs, 6 Dec. 1946: NNA, 2.0.117, Foreign Affairs 1945–1954, inv.nr.: 9930. Agreement between the government of the United Kingdom and the government of the Netherlands for certain air services, 13 Aug. 1946: NNA, 2.05.117, Foreign Affairs 1945–1954, inv.nr. 9925.

194 Letter minister Vos (Traffic) to Foreign Affairs, 5 June 1947: NNA, 2.0.117, Foreign Affairs 1945–1954, inv.nr.: 9930.

195 Minutes 11th BLV, 5 Aug. 1946: NNA, 2.05.117, Foreign Affairs 1945–1954, inv.nr. 21391.

196 Letter Chargé d'Affaires Pretoria (Van Kleffens) to Foreign Affairs, 28 June 1948: NNA, 2.0.117, Foreign Affairs 1945–1954, inv.nr.: 11329.

services from two to three times a week in September 1948. According to the provisions of the agreement of July 1947, this needed no prior consultation, because the capacity deployed would be reviewed afterwards – ex post facto, in aviation legal terms.[197] Relations became complicated, however, and the Malan government adopted protectionist trade barriers and threatened to terminate the air services agreement unless KLM reduced its number of flights.[198] The reason for this policy change was simple: since the opening of the service, KLM had sucked traffic away from South African Airways (SAA), which provided flights to London. Pretoria wished to put a stop to ticket sales through Amsterdam, worth about 12 million guilders a year in revenues, which was substantially more than SAA made.

The Hague sent negotiators to try to patch things up, but their mission was not easy. They found the South African government in the midst of moving its seat from Cape Town to Pretoria, which made it hard to get hold of various officials. There was no incentive to accommodate the Dutch. The South-Africans also identified the recurring pattern in KLM's operations: transporting passengers via a transfer in Amsterdam, the so-called 6th freedom carriage. South Africa insisted that KLM provide figures on how many passengers had a connecting ticket for transportation between Amsterdam and London.[199] It was estimated in London that no less than 61 per cent of KLM's passengers on the route were effectively flying between Britain and South Africa.[200]

As was often the case in such disputes, however, the figures at KLM's head office remained under lock and key. The airline simply could not afford to share them because it would open the floodgates to all sorts of restrictions throughout KLM's network. Instead, KLM smoothed over the difference of opinions with a promise of financial cooperation. KLM and SAA signed an agreement on an even distribution of the proceeds of the third weekly flight.[201] This pooling arrangement was confirmed in a diplomatic exchange of notes in March 1949.

The exchange of notes and the cooperation with SAA were, however, overtaken by a curious incident. In the autumn of 1948, The Hague had opposed the appointment of the former journalist Josias Otto du Plessis as South Africa's

197 Code message Foreign Affairs to Cape Town, 30 Sept. 1948: NNA, 2.0.117, Foreign Affairs 1945–1954, inv.nr.: 9930.

198 Letter envoy Pretoria to Foreign Affairs, 9 Nov. 1948: NNA, 2.0.117, Foreign Affairs 1945–1954, inv.nr.: 11329.

199 Report Piet van der Tuuk Adriani to Schaepman (Foreign Affairs), 19 Oct. 1948: NNA, 2.0.117, Foreign Affairs 1945–1954, inv.nr.: 9930.

200 Note on discussions at Ariel House, 17 May 1949: BNA, MCA, BT245, 1026.

201 Copy telegram exchange KLM-SAA, Oc–Nov. 1948: NNA, 2.0.117, Foreign Affairs 1945–1954, inv.nr.: 9930.

new envoy to the Netherlands. The right wing Du Plessis was known for his pro-German sympathies during the war and this had gone down badly in the Netherlands. Once the press picked up the story of Du Plessis' Nazi sympathies, his prospective appointment became tainted. The Hague refused to grant *agrément*. This was taken as an affront by the Malan government and the issue developed into a major chasm in bilateral relations. To retaliate, Malan postponed acceptance of the letters of credence of the newly appointed Dutch envoy in Pretoria and also called KLM's position in air traffic to South Africa into question.[202] Malan and his Undersecretary of Transport Gibson threatened to curtail KLM's landing rights, beginning with the third weekly service. The fuss this caused was serious enough that Plesman personally flew to South Africa to plead the interests of his airline in a meeting with Prime Minister Malan. He came back with mixed feelings; according to Malan, KLM had forfeited its credit by its self-righteous increase in the number of flights.[203] To make matters worse, KLM had also applied for rights to carry 5th freedom passengers from its stops in Kano and Leopoldville.[204] Prompted by its government, SAA thereupon terminated the otherwise beneficial pool agreement with KLM.[205] To avoid further ruffling feathers unnecessarily, as South Africa's foreign trade was already under pressure and sensitivities were high, KLM dropped the contested third weekly flight in October 1949. Nonetheless, relations took a downhill slide. South Africa protested against KLM's practice of offering passengers from Johannesburg connecting flights in Rome to destinations in the KLM world network.[206] It took the Dutch envoy in Pretoria, Jan van den Berg, months to improve relations and bring about a more relaxed diplomatic environment.

7 In Conclusion

World War II had made aviation a global activity, in need of a worldwide regulatory framework. In the Chicago Convention of 1944, developed to address this

202 Letter Minister D.U. Stikker to Legation in Pretoria, 22 March 1949: NNA, 2.0.117, Foreign Affairs 1945–1954, inv.nr.: 9930.

203 Notes Schaepman on his visit to Malan, 28 Apr. 1949: NNA, 2.0.117, Foreign Affairs 1945–1954, inv.nr.: 9930.

204 Letter Plesman to J. Zeegers (Neth. consul), 25 Apr. 1949: NNA, 2.05.117, Foreign Affairs 1945–1954, inv.nr. 9869.

205 Letter Venter (SAA) to Plesman, 30 June 1949: NNA, 2.0.117, Foreign Affairs 1945–1954, inv. nr.: 9930.

206 Letter J.D. van Karnebeek (Chargé d'Affaires Pretoria) to Foreign Affairs, 23 Dec. 1949: NNA, 2.0.117, Foreign Affairs 1945–1954, inv.nr.: 9930.

need, Governments agreed on a set of ground rules for international air transport. In the period before the war, a general lack of passengers meant there was no money to be made in air transport. This changed after 1945, when business communities discovered the use of the airplane. Although finances for most airlines were tight, the arrival of monetary concerns complicated negotiations on foreign traffic rights. In many cases such rights came at a price. Commercially oriented carriers such as KLM discovered this early on, both in Europe and on its intercontinental routes.

Over and above finances, aviation relations in this period were increasingly marred by political issues. If colonial prestige had dominated air transport relations in the interwar period, now current events on the world stage became a major factor to be reckoned with. In the Dutch case, the effects of the Indonesian conflict played out not just on the air route to East Asia, but also in dealings with the United States and other countries. As representatives of what was now a small nation, Dutch negotiators found their position inherently weak. Coming to grips with this reality took years and it underlined the necessity to coordinate all aspects of Dutch foreign air transport policy in the nation's interdepartmental Civil Aviation Meeting, set up in 1945.

CHAPTER 3

1950–1973: Landing Rights, Please!

1 Introduction

> After a few hundred thousand kilometers of air travel, I am certain that an onboard kitchen will never receive a star in the Michelin Guide, not with any airline. (…) We're in the sky in the middle of the ocean, it is ten thirty-five, and we are almost forty kilometers to the left of our mapped route at eleven kilometers altitude and we are five minutes ahead of schedule. The sky is blue, the sun is behind us and the cloudscape below is flat, empty and white. Just to our right is a straight dark shadow on the cloud carpet of a plane that passed before between the new world and the old. The shadow is from the condensation stripes that the burned gases leave in the atmosphere. (…) While our 'eight' [DC-8] is now navigating the 12 mile-wide air corridor between Iceland and London, we will fly for a while in the company of a BOAC Jumbo. It draws thick white stripes and flies past us. (…) It stays quiet in the long cylinder. The 177 passengers are youthful and relatively young; they have plenty of space, drink their own whisky and plunder the kitchen for a coke. Quiet people, in the opinion of our hostesses, though here and there a little uncivilized perhaps. Some sweet girls stroll by to take a look up front in the cockpit. They think it is 'great' when we pass Belfast. Thanks to a 'sharp guy' from ground air traffic control we arrive at London Airport without too much effort. We get many 'Good mornings' once on the ground, although it hasn't been morning for us all that long. We have our own time clock, set within our bodies. We've been getting in the way of our health for six hours, but enjoying it. It's been a good flight.[1]

Such a vista of relaxed transatlantic travel for a group of young people was still on the horizon in 1950 when airlines strictly catered to the well-to-do. Five years after the end of the war, the worst of the damage had been cleared. Recovery was under way and in Western Europe economic expectations were looking up thanks to America's Marshall Aid, designed to export American goods as well as American influence. National incomes expanded. The US pleaded

1 Wim Kroese, Charterpiloot houdt van zijn ongeregeld bestaan, in: *De Telegraaf*, 27 Apr. 1973. Translation by the author.

 | DOI:10.1163/9789004695245_004

international cooperation for maximal effect. Trade restrictions were reduced. In an effort to speed things along an Organization for European Economic Cooperation (OEEC) was founded in April 1948. Nonetheless, international affairs beyond Western Europe remained volatile, as relations between the two big power blocks, led by the United States and the Soviet Union, respectively, were on the decline. On the Eastern side of the Iron Curtain Soviet dominance had taken root, while the West had rallied around America's leadership and the NATO alliance of 1949. These developments contributed to a drive towards greater European cooperation, not just in economics, but also in political affairs. In May 1950 France's Foreign Minister Robert Schuman came up with a plan to collaborate in the fields of coal and steel. Within a year his initiative resulted in the founding of a European Coal and Steel Community (ECSC), the treaty for which was signed by six nations in April 1951. In joining the ECSC the new state of West Germany secured its allegiance to the West. In subsequent years France, West Germany, Belgium, the Netherlands, Luxemburg and Italy expanded cooperation, which was formalized in 1957 in the Treaty of Rome, which established the European Economic Community (EEC). With its intention to create a common market, the EEC aimed to stimulate trade among its members, while protecting agriculture, important for all, from cheap imports produced outside the Community. The EEC was to foster long-term economic growth and help realize old dreams of bringing Europe closer together by stimulating the development of infrastructures and means of communication, including air transport.[2] For the Netherlands, European cooperation was of paramount importance in the development of industrialization and trade.

General relations across the world appeared to evolve from the confrontation between the two major power blocks jockeying for position before achieving some form of coexistence. In 1956 the handling of conflicts over Suez and over the Soviet intervention in Hungary seemed to prove this. Dialogue and trade relations across the Iron Curtain appeared possible, and in September 1959 the Soviet leader Nikita Khrushchev visited the United States to conduct talks aimed to reduce tensions between the superpowers. Then, in May 1960, the downing of an American U-2 spy plane over the Soviet Union prompted a marked deterioration in relations, exacerbated by the construction of the Berlin Wall in August 1961 and the Cuban Missile Crisis in October 1962. Rebuilding basic confidence took years. In Asia relations were also strained, as American involvement in the conflict in Vietnam intensified. Against these

2 Per Högselius, Arne Kaijser, Erik van der Vleuten, *Europe's Infrastructure Transition. Economy, War, Nature* (Basingstoke: Palgrave Macmillan, 2016), p. 357–360.

complex backgrounds, The Hague had to deal with the loss of its last colony in Asia, New Guinea, to Indonesia in January 1963. However, the settlement of the Dutch-Indonesian dispute opened doors to improve bilateral relations between The Hague and Jakarta. After almost six years with no air connections, aviation was one of the first areas in which rapprochement was achieved. In its wake, the idea of lowering trade barriers to stimulate bilateral economic relations was also endorsed. This was in line with general Dutch policy to promote exports. Over the course of the 1960s such economic aspects became increasingly important in Dutch foreign policy, evidenced by an ever-expanding number of aviation agreements across the globe.

In the political field, Atlanticism and NATO membership continued to be cornerstones of Dutch foreign policy, even as EEC cooperation gained momentum. This was not without its issues. The Dutch were wary of French influence and its protectionist connotations as it sought to develop the EEC into a continental trading block. Economic integration, on the other hand, suited The Hague. The establishment of a joint European agriculture policy was of great importance in this respect. Possessing an open economy, the Netherlands was in favor of integration and removing obstacles to trade. The Netherlands was also keen to guard the trading status it had acquired in Germany since 1945, including its special position in air transport.[3]

In 1969 the EEC Member States agreed to establish an economic and monetary union in which cooperation in the political domain would also become closer. The Netherlands somewhat reluctantly agreed.[4] There was more enthusiasm for geographic expansion of the Community, however. The Hague, in keeping with its Atlantic orientation, was a fervent protagonist throughout the 1960s of an EEC that would include the United Kingdom. In December 1969, it was decided to open negotiations with Britain, Ireland and Denmark about joining the Community. The enlargement from six to nine Member States was completed in 1973. It formed the backdrop for discussions between Britain and the Netherlands on liberalization of the bilateral air transport market.

By this time, the makeshift barracks from which air passengers departed in 1950 had long since been replaced by luxury pavilions constructed for the purpose. For Schiphol Airport an ambitious expansion plan had been put in place in April 1949. This resided in an elaborate scheme to construct 'the ideal

3 Matthieu Segers, *Reis naar het continent. Nederland en de Europese integratie, 1950 tot heden* (Amsterdam: Bert Bakker, 2013), p. 133–160.

4 M. Dierikx, The Dutch 'Contribution' to the Werner Plan, in: Elena Danescu, Susana Muñoz (eds.), *Pierre Werner et l'Europe: pensee, action, enseignements: Pierre Werner and Europe: His Approach, Action and Legacy* (Brussels: P.I.E. Peter Lang, 2015), p. 217–230.

airport' that had the potential to help generate long-term growth for commercial aviation in the Netherlands and would, protagonists believed, attract international air traffic on the basis of its excellent facilities.[5] The success of the investment in these facilities depended largely on KLM so the airline *had* to grow. Plesman's policy provided for this, expedited by government money. From 1945 onwards, The Hague made financial sacrifices to enable KLM's redevelopment, for example, by diverting part of the Marshall Aid to the Netherlands to finance the airline's new fleet. Despite the scarcity of the country's dollar resources and the continued non-convertibility of the Dutch guilder, a lingering effect of the war, the Dutch prided themselves on being America's largest foreign customer for new commercial aircraft. To put these to the best possible use, an array of foreign landing rights and operating permits had to be procured or extended. Coordinated at the level of the Civil Aviation Meeting that assembled at the Ministry of Foreign Affairs in The Hague every other month, teams of negotiators crisscrossed the globe. Dutch wishes often met with delays and rebuffs, linked to the ups and downs in the Netherlands' international standing. In 1950 it was obvious that the Dutch colonial days were a thing of the past. With Indonesia independent, a reorientation of policy was inevitable, though in 1950 echoes from yesteryear still resounded. There was, for example, the Dutch belief that the Netherlands and Indonesia might conduct a joint international air transport policy.[6] Discussions were held with Indonesia on founding a bilateral airline consortium, but these were unsuccessful. Consequently, KLM changed its focus to the transatlantic arena. To finance its redevelopment as a commercial airline operating in a global market, the government invested over 100 million guilders.[7] Part of these funds had to be drawn from other government programs.[8]

Thus, the airport on the one hand, and KLM on the other, were tasked with putting the Netherlands on the postcolonial world map as an aeronautical center. Capturing such a position was deemed necessary in a situation in which the focus of Dutch air transport was shifting from a colonial perspective to a commercial mindset. This involved addressing the government's aspiration of creating an export orientated economy in the Netherlands, as delineated in a whitepaper on industrialization that appeared in September 1949.[9] For this to

5 Dierikx and Bouwens, *Building Castles of the Air*, p. 112–122.

6 Minutes 44th BLV, 10 March 1950: NNA, 2.05.117, Foreign Affairs 1945–1954, inv.nr. 21391.

7 Dierikx, *Blauw in de lucht*, p. 149.

8 Ties Joosten, *De Blauwe Fabel. Waarom we de KLM al een eeuw lang tegen elke prijs in de lucht houden* (Amsterdam: Follow the Money, 2022), p. 61–62.

9 Report Van den Brink to Raad voor Economische Aangelegenheden (Council for Economic Affairs), 19 Oct. 1949: NNA 2.02.05.02, Council of Ministers, inv.nr. 582.

be successful, an active civil aviation policy was a *conditio sine qua non*. This coincided with a far reaching reorganization of the Ministry of Foreign Affairs and of the Dutch diplomatic service.

Adopting a pro-active policy in aviation took time, as the tradition of aloofness lingered. At ICAO's fourth general session in May and June 1950 Dutch diplomats quietly went along when its members abandoned the idea of a multilateral agreement on the untrammeled exchange of commercial landing rights by postponing the issue.[10] Three years later the concept was declared dead as there was no prospect of achieving an accord on freedom for international air services.[11] For the Netherlands, already forced to accept the end of its colonial presence in Indonesia, it was another confirmation that the international developments of the 1940s had created new political realities. Sovereign control of the air had again become a prominent instrument in international affairs, just as it had been in the past. As a consequence, commercial air transport, a foreign currency earner, entered the sphere of bilateral trade relations.[12] Meanwhile, KLM's interests continued to serve as one of the cornerstones of Dutch foreign aviation policy. It was the task of the Civil Aviation Meeting to take stock of the wishes and plans for the expansion of the airline's international network, supporting and coordinating its implementation by Dutch diplomats and air transport negotiators.

The first issue that presented itself was that of redefining the aviation relationship between the Netherlands and Indonesia. In The Hague, Plesman argued that the Netherlands and Indonesia should continue to work together in aviation matters. Nonetheless, it soon transpired that KLM's interests and those of the newly founded Garuda Indonesian Airways, established on 31 March 1950, did not run in parallel. The proclamation of the unitary state of the Republik Indonesia in August of 1950 was a clear sign of things to come.[13] At the Round Table Conference on independence, concluded only ten months before in November 1949, the Netherlands and Indonesia had agreed on a federal statehood model for Indonesia that included a lasting and close relationship with the Netherlands. The concept came to naught. The Republik Indonesia immediately set its own international course and the joint foreign

---

10 ICAO-Resolution A4-16, 20 June 1950: ICAO doc. 7016-5 A4-P/2, p. 98 at https://www.icao.int/Meetings/AMC/Pages/Archived-Assembly.aspx?Assembly=a04 [accessed April 2022].

11 MacKenzie, *ICAO. A History*, p. 127.

12 Martin Staniland, *Government Birds. Air Transport and the State in Western Europe* (Lanham: Rowman & Littlefield, 2003), p. 105–108. Minutes 46th BLV, 4 July 1950: NNA, 2.05.117, Foreign Affairs 1945–1954, inv.nr. 21391.

13 Minutes 44th and 45th BLV, 10 March 1950, and May 1950: NNA, 2.05.117, Foreign Affairs 1945–1954, inv.nr. 21391.

policy that parties had agreed on turned out to be an empty shell. In the 1950s, both countries went their separate ways in the world.[14]

The Hague was thus forced to consider a future that would be largely defined within a European and North Atlantic context. The presentation in May 1950 of the plan for a European Coal and Steel Community by the French Foreign Minister Robert Schuman did not only provide for cooperation in the field of industrial commodities, but also opened up new opportunities for cooperation in European aviation. KLM participated in exploratory talks with BOAC, Air France, SAS and Swissair on possible ways to strengthen the European position vis-à-vis the American airline industry. In The Hague the Civil Aviation Meeting supported this, although KLM chief Plesman was skeptical.[15] He refused to listen to cooperative ideas, opposing a proposal put forward at the Council of Europe in Strasbourg by the Italian Foreign Minister, Count Carlo Sforza, to create a single European sky, regulated by a European counterpart of the American Civil Aeronautics Board (CAB). Plesman believed such ideas would push aviation into the power game of international politics, which was certain to restrict KLM's freedom to compete.[16] Already, the West Germans claimed a future market share of 20 percent, although at the time there was no German airline.[17] French and British carriers struggled to offer competitive services as they were obliged to use outdated equipment from their domestic aircraft industries. KLM feared cooperation would force the Dutch airline to share in subsidizing these less economic modes of operation.[18] Cooperation, Plesman believed, would have to be voluntary, with no role for national authorities.[19] On the other hand, he was prepared to support a Belgian initiative whereby Sabena, Swissair, Air France and KLM would together purchase sixty aircraft for joint operation of the European air network. Discussions on this were held in Maastricht under the leadership of economist and politician Paul de Groote, Belgium's former Minister of Economic Coordination and National

14 Hans Meijer, *Den Haag-Djakarta. De Nederlands-Indonesische betrekkingen 1950–1962* (Utrecht: Spectrum, 1994), p. 276–279. Tjalling Bouma, *Naar een federaal Indonesië. De geschiedenis van de totstandkoming van de Republiek der Verenigde Staten van Indonesië en de bijdrage van federale Indonesische nationalisten aan de Indonesische onafhankelijkheid 1917–1949* (Hilversum: Verloren, 2020), p. 298–356.

15 Minutes 48th BLV, 4 Oct. 1950: NNA, 2.05.117, Foreign Affairs 1945–1954, inv.nr. 21391.

16 Minutes 50th BLV, 15 Jan. 1951: NNA, 2.05.117, Foreign Affairs 1945–1954, inv.nr. 21392. Further: Martin Staniland, *A Europe of the Air? The Airline Industry and European Integration* (Lanham MD: Rowman & Littlefield, 2008), p. 43–44.

17 Lutz Budrass, *Adler und Kranich. Die Lufthansa und ihre Geschichte 1926–1955* (München: Blessing, 2016), p. 455–456.

18 Minutes 51st BLV, 20 Feb. 1951: NNA, 2.05.117, Foreign Affairs 1945–1954, inv.nr. 21392.

19 Minutes 56th BLV, 23 Nov. 1951: NNA, 2.05.117, Foreign Affairs 1945–1954, inv.nr. 21392.

Re-Equipment.[20] The talks culminated in the establishment of an Air Research Bureau in Brussels in October 1952 to delineate the perceived joint future. De Groote wrote an exploratory report for the intended cooperation.[21] It listed the main problems in European aviation arising from the geographic and sovereign divisions of the continent, and indicated possible solutions.[22] However, the plans for joint aircraft purchases and operations never made it beyond the paper they were written on.

Meanwhile, the aviation discussions at the Council of Europe in Strasbourg continued. From the outset The Hague was a lukewarm participant only, fearing the talks would end like those at ICAO, where freedom in the air had been quietly buried as a topic of discussion. Indeed, the Dutch ideas for an aviation regime based on liberalism in the air did not stand a chance. Conference after conference, Dutch representatives reported back to The Hague the disappointment they felt.[23]

Within the wider ECSC-context the three Benelux countries worked on a memorandum on consultations regarding economic cooperation, including air transport.[24] This was adopted at the Messina Conference in June 1955, where the Foreign Ministers of the six ECSC countries supported a resolution put forward by Belgium's Foreign Minister Paul-Henri Spaak on re-energizing their cooperation through the liberalization of transport, including air transport.[25] An official study group was set up. Hoping to build on this new mood, the Director-General of the Dutch National Aviation Service, Jan Backer, presented a proposal to establish a European partnership of national airlines. In the best of civil service traditions, he believed in setting up a single, integrated intra-European air network to avoid competition between national airlines.[26]

20 Minutes 58th BLV, 14 March 1952; minutes 62nd BLV 8 Oct. 1952: NNA, 2.05.117, Foreign Affairs 1945–1954, inv.nr. 21392.

21 Henri Wassenbergh, *Post-War International Civil Aviation Policy and the Law of the Air* (Den Haag: Martinus Nijhoff, 1957), p. 83–84.

22 Minutes 67th BLV, 15 July 1953: NNA, 2.05.117, Foreign Affairs 1945–1954, inv.nr. 21392. Christian Heinrich-Franke, From a Supranational Air Authority to the Founding of the ECAC, in: *Journal of European Integration History* 13 (2007) nr. 1, p. 69–89 (80–81).

23 Air Research Bureau, Interim report on the co-ordination of air transport in Europe, Sep. 1953: NNA, 2.05.117, Foreign Affairs 1945–1954, inv.nr. 9956.

24 Memorandum J.W. Beyen re. European integration, 29 Apr. 1955: NNA, 2.02.05.02, Council of Ministers, inv.nr. 510.

25 Staniland, *A Europe of the Air?*, p. 47–48.

26 Minutes 79th BLV, 13 June 1955, with text memorandum Backer: NNA, 2.05.118, Foreign Affairs 1955–1964, inv.nr. 27493.

Much to Backer's disappointment KLM's new chief executive Alphons Aler, did not support his views.[27]

The European consultations on cooperation continued nonetheless and a new conference was convened in Strasbourg in November 1955. This set up a new intergovernmental body, the European Civil Aviation Conference (ECAC), with the overarching task of harmonizing member states' policies.[28] Within months, the new organization put forward a proposal for freedom for unscheduled flights, while also granting greater freedom for the transportation of air cargo.[29] For scheduled passenger transport a European regulatory body was recommended, modelled on the American CAB. Air France President Max Hymans was its main supporter.[30]

These ideas found little or no support in The Hague. However, informal consultations were held between Air France, Sabena, Lufthansa, Alitalia and KLM in the autumn of 1958 on the possibility of setting up a joint partnership called Europair.[31] In April 1959 the talks between the five companies involved ran aground over the allocation of capacity. KLM, which was large for its home market and the only one of the airlines concerned that was making a profit, found it was expected to gradually hand a third of its European market share to Lufthansa and Alitalia, companies that had only recently been (re)established. For the Dutch, this was a distinctly unfavorable scenario. They were not the only ones to oppose it; neither Paris nor Bonn wanted to commit to the plans. The contemporary relaunch of the earlier ECAC initiative on a multilateral treaty for the exchange of 3rd and 4th freedom rights received more sympathy.[32] The Hague believed that embracing more freedom would enable KLM to flourish beyond the confines of Europair agreements. But in the short term, axing Europair could mean that KLM's rights in France, Germany and Italy would be in jeopardy.[33] In The Hague, the possible use of the terms of the

27 Minutes 80th BLV, 17 July 1955: NNA, 2.05.118, Foreign Affairs 1955–1964, inv.nr. 27493.

28 Minutes 83rd BLV, 10 Jan. 1956: NNA, 2.05.118, Foreign Affairs 1955–1964, inv.nr. 27493. Heinrich-Franke, From a Supranational Air Authority to the Founding of the ECAC (2007). Hussein Kassim, Handley Stevens, *Air Transport and the European Union: Europeanization and its Limits* (Basingstoke: Palgrave Macmillan, 2010), p. 61–62.

29 ECAC document 7695, Multilateral Agreement on Commercial Rights for Non-Scheduled Air Services in Europe, 30 Apr. 1956: https://www.ecac-ceac.org/documents/10202/74122/Multilateral+Agreement+1956.pdf/f6194048-1021-4724-8ea7-d5136c20700c [accessed October 2020].

30 Minutes 89th BLV, 16 July 1957: NNA, 2.05.118, Foreign Affairs 1955–1964, inv.nr. 27493.

31 Minutes 95th BLV, 17 Feb. 1959: NNA, 2.05.118, Foreign Affairs 1955–1964, inv.nr. 27494.

32 Minutes 95th BLV, 17 Feb. 1959; minutes 96th BLV, 5 May 1959: NNA, 2.05.118, Foreign Affairs 1955–1964, inv.nr. 27494.

33 Minutes 96th BLV, 5 May 1959: NNA, 2.05.118, Foreign Affairs 1955–1964, inv.nr. 27494.

1957 EEC Treaty was considered to prevent KLM's landing rights from being curtailed as a result of a possible Dutch dismissal of Europair.[34]

Meanwhile, consultations continued. Air France, Lufthansa, Alitalia and Sabena proposed a new vehicle, Air Union, as a cooperative structure between airline companies that extended beyond the scope of direct government policies. The basic idea was that the airlines of the six EEC members would coordinate Europe's air transport capacity between them.[35] Feelers were put out to see if the Dutch might wish to participate. Initially this was not the case, although it was recognized in The Hague that KLM's position in Europe would become vulnerable should Air Union proceed without Dutch participation. On the other hand, participation inevitably meant giving up part of KLM's market share in favor of the other partners.[36] Disconcerting sounds emerged from Bonn. To advance the interests of Lufthansa, German Transport Minister Hans Seebohm made a case for the containment of KLM.[37] Not only in the corridors of European diplomacy the adage sounded *Beaucoup d'Air et peu d'Union*.[38] The Dutch were nervous that the Air Union project would be taken over by politics. Former State Secretary for Foreign Affairs Ernst van der Beugel, deputy chief executive of KLM since 1959, wrote to Foreign Minister Joseph Luns that the proposals 'assign a place to the governments, which in our initial opinion is not compatible with the open and commercial character of our company'.[39] Van der Beugel, no supporter of the plans to begin with, was among those in The Hague who felt relief when Air Union seemed to be a non-starter the moment the respective governments claimed a role in the talks, thus highlighting politics and nationalism.[40]

34 Office Memorandum re. the question whether reference by France, Germany, Italy and/or Belgium to the EC-Treaty would be possible to justify restrictive measures against KLM, June 1959: NNA, 2.05.118, Foreign Affairs 1955–1964, inv.nr. 8819.

35 Nicolas Neiertz, Air France: an Elephant in an Evening Suit, in: Dienel, Lyth, *Flying the Flag*, p. 43. Staniland, *A Europe of the Air?*, p. 47–52.

36 Office memo VADV for Council of Ministers re. Europair, June 1959. Memo Van der Beugel to KLM Board re. conversation with Max Hymans, 4 Nov. 1959: NNA, 2.05.118, Foreign Affairs 1955–1964, inv.nr. 8819.

37 Letter Dutch Ambassador Bonn to Foreign Affairs, 27 May 1960: NNA, 2.05.118, Foreign Affairs 1955–1964, inv.nr. 8819.

38 Christiane Delepierre-Nys, *Air Europe. La politique de coopération entre les compagnies aériennes de l'Europe des Six* (Bruxelles: Éd. de l'Université, 1975), p. xxxvii.

39 Letter Van der Beugel to Luns, 11 July 1960: NNA, 2.05.118, Foreign Affairs 1955–1964, inv.nr. 8819.

40 Minutes 101st BLV, 1 Dec. 1960: NNA, 2.05.118, Foreign Affairs 1955–1964, inv.nr. 27494.

In The Hague Backer again declared support, but KLM kept its distance.[41] This changed in 1961. Pushed on by the need to compete with the latest equipment, the purchase of expensive new jet aircraft pushed airlines worldwide deep into the red. To make things worse, the jets created overcapacity in the industry. Like the other airlines, KLM was heading for a disastrous financial result. To compensate, new destinations were badly needed, but the Dutch dismissal of Air Union translated into opposition from the EEC partners towards extending KLM's landing rights.[42] Meanwhile, France embraced the concept of Air Union and pushed towards a European treaty with Italy, the German Federal Republic and Belgium. The Hague, however, persisted in its role of nonparticipant observer, though Foreign Minister Joseph Luns did try to keep a foot in the door.[43] Eventually no agreement on Air Union was reached as the parties could not agree on the division of transport quotas for Lufthansa and Alitalia.[44] Still, given the tradition of cooperation between the airlines ever since the inception of IATA in 1919, the idea of an overarching European airline struck a chord with many. By the end of 1963 the governments involved in the Air Union discussions indicated that Dutch participation would still be appreciated.

The renewed Dutch contribution to the discussions remained extremely marginal, however. The Hague hardly ventured beyond the role of observer. It was clear that KLM, which managed to reduce its losses in 1964, still did not warm to Air Union. Late that year, the European discussions stalled again – as before over the degree of government influence. At one end of the negotiating table Paris, seeking protection for Air France, wanted a bigger say than the other participants. On the other end the Dutch stressed the importance of efficiency and competition. A general conference of Foreign and Transport Ministers of the six EEC governments appeared necessary to break the deadlock.[45] This conference never took place. In July 1965, the EEC itself ran into crisis, when France refused to agree to majority decision-making in the Council of EEC Ministers and started boycotting its meetings. France stuck to strict unanimity in decision-making, in effect giving each member state a veto,

41 Letter Backer to Foreign Affairs, 10 Aug. 1961: NNA, 2.05.118, Foreign Affairs 1955–1964, inv. nr. 27494.

42 KLM, Survey of aviation policy in 1961, No. 72 (HAG/AF/M.1576), 6 Feb. 1962: NNA, 2.05.118, Foreign Affairs 1955–1964, inv.nr. 27494.

43 Code message Luns (from Brussels to Korthals and Stijkel (Traffic and Water Management), 16 Jan. 1963: NNA, 2.05.118, Foreign Affairs 1955–1964, inv.nr. 27494.

44 Minutes 106th BLV, 15 Oct. 1963: NNA, 2.05.118, Foreign Affairs 1955–1964, inv.nr. 27494.

45 Minutes 110th BLV, 17 Nov. 1964: NNA, 2.05.118, Foreign Affairs 1955–1964, inv.nr. 27494.

and withdrew from all EEC institutions for six months.[46] In January 1966, a compromise was signed in Luxembourg resolving the impasse, but by then the momentum for the formation of Air Union had gone. A sigh of relief sounded in The Hague.

The European perspective on cooperation in air services disappeared into the background of policy development. Instead, at the beginning of 1966, new ideas emerged, this time for cooperation in the European aircraft industry. In December 1970 these crystallized in the formation of Airbus Industries. This development also set thinking in motion again about the possibilities of cooperation in air services. At the end of 1971, the European Commission put aviation back on its agenda. The aim was now to bring users and industry together at the table. As before, KLM was skeptical.[47] Nonetheless the European Commission argued that air traffic in the EEC was not coherently organized and took the first steps towards adopting a role in the organization of air services within the Community.[48] The European Parliament supported this.[49]

2 Expanding the European Air Services Network

The forced farewell to the East Indies had profound consequences for Dutch commercial aviation. KLM expected a decline in revenues, so in an effort to reorient itself the airline invested in an advertising campaign in 1950 to recruit additional passengers for flights within Europe and across the North Atlantic. With the slogan 'Flying is cheaper than you think', tickets were marketed with reference to comfort, speed and moderate pricing.[50]

Air travel to and from Britain was the oldest market in which KLM competed. In the early postwar years, when the Netherlands struggled to get its economy running again, negotiations were held with Britain on ways to reduce the existing Dutch trade deficit.[51] Air transport was one area in which this might be

46 Luuk van Middelaar, *De passage naar Europa. Geschiedenis van een begin* (Groningen: Historische Uitgeverij, 2009), p. 86–96. Wim van Meurs, Robin de Bruin, Carla Hoetink, Karin van Leeuwen, Carlos Reijnen, Liesbeth van de Grift, *Europa in alle staten. Zestig jaar geschiedenis van de Europese integratie* (Nijmegen: Vantilt, 2013), p. 116–119.

47 Minutes 133rd BLV, 6 Dec. 1971: NNA, 2.05.313, Foreign Affairs 1965–1974, inv.nr. 25175.

48 Minutes 135th BLV, 29 Aug. 1972: NNA, 2.05.313, Foreign Affairs 1965–1974, inv.nr. 25175.

49 *De Volkskrant*, 9 Jan. 1973. Alan Dobson, *Globalization and Regional Integration. The Origins, Development and Impact of the Single European Aviation Market* (London: Routledge, 2007), p. 18–20.

50 Advertisements in *De Telegraaf* and *De Tijd*, May 1950.

51 Asbeek Brusse, Dutch-British Commercial Relations, in: Nigel John Ashton, Duco Hellema (eds.), *Unspoken Allies: Anglo-Dutch Relations Since 1780* (Amsterdam: AUP, 2001), p. 206.

accomplished. However, by 1950 it was unclear how much opportunity there could be for the Dutch to grow. On the route between Amsterdam and London KLM offered six flights a day, compared to a single daily flight by its counterpart BEA. The British carrier struggled with a lack of aircraft and therefore could not cover more than 14 per cent of total passenger transport.[52] Not surprisingly, London wished to revise the bilateral aviation agreement.[53] As was the case with other aviation contacts, KLM's practice of selling tickets for 6th freedom services via Amsterdam was a thorn in London's side. In the autumn of 1950, air attaché Daniël Goedhuis went to great lengths to explain the Dutch view that this was a normal way of conducting business. Still, British concerns about this practice remained.[54] Although there were no direct consequences, Anglo-Dutch talks on the division of traffic between Amsterdam and London dragged on for more than ten years. These added to differences over other Anglo-Dutch aviation issues, such as KLM's commercial stopover at Prestwick on flights across the North Atlantic.[55] The Dutch, like the Scandinavian countries, pursued an air transport regime that was considerably more liberal than London was willing to allow.[56] For years no progress was made on the issue and in 1969 the matter reached the desks of the respective Prime Ministers. By this time the Anglo-Dutch differences had taken on a global perspective, with KLM complaining that London denied access to the British Crown Colony of Hong Kong. Prime Minister Harold Wilson cautiously hinted that Hong Kong rights might be discussed if KLM bought Lockheed Tristar aircraft, a passenger jet that was equipped with British Rolls Royce engines. Rolls Royce was at the time on the verge of collapse because of the cost of development and badly needed extra sales. The Hague rejected this conflation of aircraft procurement and air transport diplomacy.[57] As a consequence Hong Kong remained closed to KLM until July 1971, when Britain's new Prime Minister Edward Heath handed out traffic rights as a present for Joseph Luns on the occasion of his retirement after almost twenty years as the Dutch Foreign Minister.[58] After Britain had

52 Draft MCA report on BEA and their competitors, 2 May 1948: BNA, MCA, BT217, 68. Statistics relating to scheduled air services between the United Kingdom and the Netherlands, August 1950 – July 1951 (MCA paper, undated): BNA, MCA, BT245, 450.

53 Confidential memorandum on amendment of the UK-Netherlands bilateral air services agrt., udated (July/August 1948): BNA, MCA, BT217, 68.

54 Minutes 48th BLV, 4 Oct. 1950; summary of consultations on aviation issues, 7 Nov. 1950: NNA, 2.05.117, Foreign Affairs 1945–1954, inv.nr. 21391.

55 MTCA policy summary by MacGregor, 28 June 1955: BNA, MTCA, BT245, inv.nr. 449.

56 Minutes 89th BLV, 16 July 1957: NNA, 2.05.118, Foreign Affairs 1955–1964, inv.nr. 27493.

57 Minutes 125th BLV, 22 Feb. 1969: NNA, 2.05.313, Foreign Affairs 1965–1974, inv.nr. 25175.

58 Minutes 132nd BLV, 27 Sept. 1971: NNA, 2.05.313, Foreign Affairs 1965–1974, inv.nr. 25175.

initially remained outside the EEC for fear that it would entail a loss of autonomy, Luns had been instrumental from the early 1960s onward in paving the way for British membership of the Community, overcoming French reservations.[59] One of the ways Heath's Conservative government rewarded this was by a change in aviation policy that favored KLM and promised a 'free for all' regime after Britain's accession to the EEC in January 1973.[60]

Flying east, KLM had been dedicated to scheduled its services to and through various cities in Germany. By doing so, KLM competed with other flagship airlines of the Allied occupying powers, which had had free rein in the first ten years after 1945 as a result of a ban on German aviation.[61] However, KLM's hope to operate a scheduled service to Berlin had not materialized. In 1948, the Soviet blockade of West Berlin and the resulting international crisis prevented this.[62]

Things looked different in the Western parts of Germany, where the Federal Republic was founded on 23 May 1949 in the zones occupied by American, British and French forces. By necessity, the new West German nation became involved in the emerging process of European economic cooperation. KLM tried to tap into this by expanding its number of German destinations. In September 1952 Plesman paid a three-day visit to Bonn for high-level discussions on KLM's position in the future West Germany. At the time, initial ideas on the possibility of a European Political Community that might provide a level playing field for general trade between the ECSC members was being investigated in The Hague. In Bonn, Plesman spoke with Chancellor Konrad Adenauer, who was involved in plans for a new German airline through family members. Other interlocutors pointed out that a revival of German commercial aviation was in preparation, possibly on the wings of European cooperation. For the time being, however, the Germans were still looking for funds to found a new airline venture.[63] In this situation various contacts arose, aimed at establishing a bilateral air services agreement that would enter into force once Germany regained its sovereignty, which was projected in 1955. Close cross-border contacts were of great importance to the Dutch. Not only did

---

59 Wendy Asbeek Brusse, Dutch-British Commercial Relations in a European Context, in: Nigel John Ashton, Duco Hellema (eds.), *Unspoken Allies: Anglo-Dutch Relations Since 1780* (Amsterdam: AUP, 2001), p. 214–216. Albert Kersten, *Luns. Een politieke biografie* (Amsterdam: Boom, 2010), p. 362–366, 392–395, 400–408, 431–432, 437–445.

60 Minutes 138th BLV, 1 Aug. 1973: NNA, 2.05.313, Foreign Affairs 1965–1974, inv.nr. 25176.

61 Lutz Budrass, *Adler und Kranich*, p. 444.

62 Minutes 44th BLV, 10 March 1950: NNA, 2.05.117, Foreign Affairs 1945–1954, inv.nr. 21391.

63 Minutes 62nd BLV, 8 Oct. 1950: NNA, 2.05.117, Foreign Affairs 1945–1954, inv.nr. 21391. Lutz Budrass, *Adler und Kranich*, p. 459–480, 494–495.

KLM use its German services as feeder traffic, but a number of the airline's intercontinental flights also made a commercial stop in Germany.[64] Evidently, a bilateral agreement would come at a price. The Germans indicated that they wanted a fifty-fifty distribution of air traffic.[65] This implied that KLM might have to reduce its services to create room for West Germany's new Lufthansa to fly. Discussions on this were difficult. And there were other issues. Bonn was displeased with KLM's scheduled service to Schönefeld airport in Berlin's eastern sector, which the Russians authorized in 1953 after much discussion. Bonn feared that flights to East Berlin, with Soviet consent, could be construed as a prelude to Dutch recognition of a permanent division of Germany.[66]

The need for a Dutch-German air transport agreement became more urgent in 1955 when German sovereignty was restored. Lufthansa began operating experimental services from April that year. In May 1955 the Convention on the Settlement of Matters Arising Out of the War and the Occupation, which had been signed in Paris three years earlier, came into force. This formally ended the state of occupation in the western zones of Germany. In recognition of the new power structures in Europe, the Federal Republic acceded to NATO. The Settlement Convention stipulated that the existing landing rights of foreign airlines in Germany would remain in force for one to two more years.[67] Nonetheless, clouds were gathering for KLM when it became clear in the summer of 1955 that Bonn would retain the fifty-fifty distribution of air transport capacity that had been on the German wish list. The new Lufthansa immediately dug in its heels on this point.[68] The fact that the Dutch did their best to set up services to East Germany at the same time, and operated charter flights on the occasion of the Leipziger Messe, was an additional burden on the talks.[69]

The outcome was a secret exchange of notes, signed on 28 September 1956. KLM was forced to give up its intermediate stops in the Federal Republic on services to Spain and to South America. The airline also had to accept German restrictions on its 5th freedom carriage to the Far East and the number of stopovers in Frankfurt, Düsseldorf and Munich had to be reduced. Bonn wanted to put an end to what the Germans called 'vacuum cleaner services' by which KLM skimmed Lufthansa's home market and siphoned off German

64 Minutes 71st BLV, 23 March 1954: NNA, 2.05.117, Foreign Affairs 1945–1954, inv.nr. 21393.

65 Minutes 75th BLV, 2 Nov. 1954: NNA, 2.05.117, Foreign Affairs 1945–1954, inv.nr. 21393.

66 Minutes 69th BLV, 20 Jan. 1954: NNA, 2.05.117, Foreign Affairs 1945–1954, inv.nr. 21393.

67 Minutes 79th BLV, 13 June 1955: NNA, 2.05.118, Foreign Affairs 1955–1964, inv.nr. 27493.

68 Minutes 81st BLV, 4 Oct. 1955: NNA, 2.05.118, Foreign Affairs 1955–1964, inv.nr. 27493.

69 Code message Van Boetzelaer to Foreign Affairs, 14 Nov. 1955: NNA, 2.05.118 Foreign Affairs 1955–1964, inv.nr. 27500.

passengers.[70] This marked the beginning of years of cumbersome negotiations, but multiple rounds of talks did not bring the parties any closer. In 1960 the problem was still playing out and had become linked to the *Generalbereinigungsvertrag* [General Cleansing Treaty] that had been under negotiation for six years between the Federal Republic and the Netherlands. Minister Luns personally intervened to promote KLM's interests, although without lasting success.[71] In the following years, the Dutch-German talks increasingly focused on giving up commercial stops, which the Dutch tried to defer as long as possible. By 1963 KLM operated 98 flights to and via Germany every week, compared with no Lufthansa flights to Amsterdam, mainly because the Germans did not have enough aircraft for short-haul operations.[72]

In October 1963, the two sides again sat down for talks at the civil service level. As usual the Dutch negotiators tried to obscure and protect KLM's position.[73] Progress appeared impossible. The Hague therefore took the matter to the political level. Discussions were held between State Secretary for Foreign Affairs Leo de Block and the German Ambassador Hans Berger and between State Secretary Mike Keyzer (Transport and Water Management) and the German Transport Minister Hans-Christoph Seebohm.[74] However, a compromise on KLM's position remained out of reach. Bonn insisted that KLM reduce the number of its flights. On the Dutch side, there was a strong incentive to maintain the status quo, as the German services resulted in a positive annual balance of 592.4 million guilders. Against this stood a German surplus on the bilateral balance of payments.[75] As the parties did not get any closer, Bonn increased the pressure by raising specific objections to KLM's stopovers in Frankfurt on flights to Latin America. To accommodate the Germans, KLM offered to reduce the number of flights. However, it soon transpired that KLM's negotiator Henri Wassenbergh held a useful card up his sleeve: the reduction in frequency was to coincide with the deployment of larger aircraft. Such cunning did not improve the atmosphere in the negotiations. Indeed, the Germans

70 Memorandum RLD re. KLM's position in West-Germany, 22 June 1959: NNA, 2.05.118, Foreign Affairs 1955–1964, inv.nr. 8677.

71 Letter Aler to Luns, 24 June 1959: NNA, 2.05.118, Foreign Affairs 1955–1964, inv.nr. 8677.

72 Hans Dienel, Lufthansa: Two German Airlines, in: Dienel, Lyth (eds), *Flying the Flag*, p. 96–97.

73 Memorandum Slotemaker to Albarda, 24 June 1963. Office memorandum VADV to De Block, 25 Oct. 1963: NNA, 2.05.118, Foreign Affairs 1955–1964, inv.nr. 8786.

74 Office memorandum De Block to Van Tuyll van Serooskerken, 25 June 1964. Undated letter Keyzer to Seebohm (June 1964): NNA, 2.05.118, Foreign Affairs 1955–1964, inv.nr. 8677.

75 Office memorandum to VADV, 5 Aug. 1964: NNA, 2.05.118, Foreign Affairs 1955–1964, inv.nr. 8677.

were outraged. It was not until spring 1965 that the parties reached a vague compromise under which KLM was allowed to continue flying for the time being, but was to place its revenues in a pool with Lufthansa.[76] Both parties accumulated their revenues in this pool, after which these would be divided annually on a fifty-fifty basis, meaning that the more efficient or successful airline would transfer funds to the less successful participant. KLM did not rush to implement this deal and signatures were not exchanged until February 1967. By then, the two sides were already embroiled in their next dispute, this time over KLM's handling of freight transport, which, according to German opinion, was one and a half times the agreed weekly volume. Here KLM eventually had to admit defeat.[77]

With Germany divided, KLM also tried to direct some of its attention to the Eastern sector. Despite the Soviet occupation and the constraints of a centrally managed economy, there did appear to be some opportunities here. Since the creation of the two Germanys between 1949 and 1955, the German Democratic Republic (GDR) had tried to break its diplomatic isolation by concluding and expanding trade agreements with several Western countries. These efforts were seriously handicapped by the fact that Western nations did not recognize the GDR.[78] The customary bilateral formalities enabling the operation of scheduled air services also presented obstacles. According to the international standards defined in the Chicago Convention, a bilateral air services agreement should provide the legal basis for such services. However, the fact that the GDR was not formally recognized precluded such agreements and KLM could not progress beyond organizing (private law) charter flights to the annual Leipziger Messe, an activity that started in 1954.

Then, in December 1966, West Germany's Minister of Foreign Affairs Willy Brandt initiated a new policy of rapprochement with the GDR that would become known as the *Ostpolitik*. He set a new course with regard to East Germany that would improve political relations. From KLM's perspective, a new market appeared possible in the shape of charters with cargo and passengers to East Berlin's airport Schönefeld. To get ahead of the competition, KLM quietly struck a deal for flight handling with the East German airline Interflug in the spring of 1969. Cooperation of this kind went beyond the political context

76 Report Wassenbergh to KLM board, 1 Feb. 1965. Letter Borel Rinkes to State Secretary Keyzer (Traffic and Water Management), 10 Feb. 1965: NNA, 2.05.313, Foreign Affairs 1965–1974, inv.nr. 5352.

77 Letter Wassenbergh to Kruys (RLD), 25 March 1968: NNA, 2.05.313, Foreign Affairs 1965–1974, inv.nr. 5352.

78 Jacco Pekelder, *Nederland en de DDR. Beeldvorming en betrekkingen 1949–1989* (Amsterdam: Boom, 1998), p. 149–159.

of the *Ostpolitik*, however, and in Bonn and in The Hague the ministries concerned were not happy.[79] The new West German Foreign Minister Walter Scheel expressed his concern and insisted that Luns should use his influence to keep KLM in check. After all, Berlin's Eastern district had to be shunned by international air traffic to avoid undue questioning of the status of the airports in West Berlin. This approach had been agreed upon within NATO.[80] In Washington, the State Department also found KLM's actions reprehensible, since they could undermine the status of the air corridors to West Berlin over GDR territory. The Americans tried to deflect the issue waving vague commitments on possible KLM landing rights in West Berlin.[81] However, KLM was not to be leashed. Following the Scandinavian airline SAS, the airline asked East Berlin for rights to use Schönefeld as a stopover with 5th freedom rights on flights to Moscow. In Bonn, Ambassador Jacob de Beus failed to see the attraction of the plans: after all, travellers from West Berlin would have to take a bus to Schönefeld from the Funkturm in West Berlin. This meant passing via Checkpoint Rudower Chaussee, located on the border of West Berlin and East Germany. Passengers had to buy a transit visa with which they were allowed into the GDR, subject to a valid passport and a confirmed booking on the flight. The bus ride took a full hour. In Schönefeld, another hour had to be spent waiting before take-off. To compensate for the extra hurdles, fares were much lower than for flights departing from airports in West Berlin.[82] Still, KLM's conduct was not appreciated by the Allied occupying forces, particularly as KLM also held discussions with Interflug on a reciprocal service to Amsterdam.[83] In NATO circles these talks were interpreted as a covert GDR plot to bring diplomatic recognition by Western governments nearer. As a consequence, KLM saw its request to operate a service to West Berlin's Tempelhof Airport rejected in August 1972.[84]

In Bonn, KLM's actions in the GDR met with objections. The issue of curtailment of KLM's rights in the Federal Republic remained explicitly on the agenda. A personal appeal by the new Dutch Foreign Minister Norbert Schmelzer to Walter Scheel failed to change this. The FRG insisted that KLM's German stopovers on various routes must come to an end. Early in 1973 KLM's

79 Letter De Beus to Luns, 3 Dec. 1969: NNA, 2.05.313, Foreign Affairs 1965–1974, inv.nr. 5513.

80 Letter Scheel to Luns, 23 March 1971: NNA, 2.05.313, Foreign Affairs 1965–1974, inv.nr. 5513.

81 Code message Van Lynden (amb. Washington) to Foreign Affairs, 31 March 1971: NNA, 2.05.313 Foreign Affairs 1965–1974, inv.nr. 5513.

82 Code message De Beus (Bonn embassy) to Foreign Affairs, 11 June 1971: NNA, 2.05.313, Foreign Affairs 1965–1974, inv.nr. 5513.

83 Report Wassenbergh of his visit to Berlin, 7 Dec. 1971: NNA, 2.05.313, Foreign Affairs 1965–1974, inv.nr. 5513.

84 Minutes 135th BLV, 29 Aug. 1972: NNA, 2.05.313, Foreign Affairs 1965–1974, inv.nr. 25175.

commercial stop in Frankfurt on the service to Melbourne became a test case. Bonn demanded an end to this, as Lufthansa was also operating on the route. In response, KLM came up with another sly move: the final destination of the flights was moved to Sydney, making Melbourne only a stopover and therefore a seemingly less important intermediate landing. In a letter to Scheel, the new Foreign Minister, Max van der Stoel, clarified the course of action: in the previous ten years KLM had repeatedly surrendered market share in Germany. German policy prevented the free development of international aviation and contravened policy at the European level intended to stimulate trade. Minister of Foreign Affairs Max van der Stoel suggested that the matter be resolved at the ministerial level.[85]

Dutch air transport relations with France were of a different nature. Initially, several options for bilateral cooperation in air services were pursued, although the starting position for KLM was weak due to the size of its home market. While Paris committed to a cooperative structure for European aviation, this was on (protective) French terms and with French interests in mind.[86] In 1950 Air France was designated *chosen instrument* of aviation policy, thus receiving special support. Initially it appeared in The Hague that this would not touch on KLM, which was trying to expand its network by applying for additional commercial stops, as it did in other countries. The main focus was on receiving operating rights for intercontinental flights via Nice. In May 1950 Paris granted rights for services to Rome and Damascus and via Madrid, Lisbon and Dakar to Paramaribo and Caracas. On these routes KLM also made a traffic stop in Frankfurt.[87] Air France, like its British counterparts still suffering from a lack of aircraft, even acted as an advocate for KLM landings in Nice to prevent a PanAm-affiliated company from building a market position there. Such leniency towards the Dutch was, however, temporary. In the spring of 1953 Paris changed its policy after Air France had opened a service of its own to Caracas. Air France now objected to KLM's 5th freedom rights in Nice, although it had been agreed in 1950 that Air France would get a share of the revenues through a pooling agreement.[88]

---

85 Letter Van der Stoel to Scheel, 26 July 1973: NNA, 2.05.313, Foreign Affairs 1965–1974, inv.nr. 5352.

86 Memorandum Goedhuis re. discussions on aviation policy in Paris, 27–29 June 1949: NNA, 2.05.117, Foreign Affairs 1945–1954, inv.nr. 8790.

87 Memorandum RLD to Minister of Traffic and Water Management re. KLM's rights in Nice, 8-4-1953: NNA, 2.05.117, Foreign Affairs 1945–1954, inv.nr. 9890.

88 Minutes 65th BLV 1 April 1953: NNA, 2.05.117, Foreign Affairs 1945–1954, inv.nr. 21392. Office memorandum VADV to Luns re. KLM's rights in Nice (18 April 1953): NNA, 2.05.117, Foreign Affairs 1945–1954, inv.nr. 9890.

Nonetheless, KLM's rights were cancelled. In protest, Goedhuis argued that France treated America's airlines rather better since they were allowed to operate to Nice without too many restrictions. In Goedhuis' view KLM was the victim of discriminatory treatment. Aided by two personal interventions by Foreign Minister Johan Beyen with France's Foreign Secretary Georges Bidault, Goedhuis managed to convince the French Foreign Ministry that curtailment of the Dutch rights did not serve French interests if France wished to promote the Europair idea then under discussion.[89] Beyen's interventions were rooted in the size of KLM's home market, which necessitating 5th freedom services. His was a difficult stance, given KLM's lack of enthusiasm for European cooperation in air transport, for which France was the most vocal advocate. Then, at the end of December, Paris again changed its position. KLM would be allowed to continue in Nice for another year, albeit with restrictions to the number of passengers. Operating conditions deteriorated after Pierre Mendès-France took office as France's new Prime Minister in June 1954. Although formally an advocate of European cooperation, the Mendès-France government invested in protecting French economic interests. KLM's CEO Alphons Aler discovered what this entailed when he tried to promote KLM's interests by organizing a luxury lunch meeting with the new Public Works Minister, Jacques Chaban-Delmas. He had to accept that KLM would not be allowed to take more than five passengers per flight from Nice.[90]

Nonetheless French objections to KLM's flights from Nice remained. In a secret exchange of letters, added to the Franco-German aviation agreement concluded in 1955, it was stipulated that both countries were entitled to terminate third-party air services if these infringed on the agreed bilateral market division. As KLM serviced both Frankfurt and Nice on various intercontinental routes, this would be a problem.[91] The Dutch bargaining position was weak anyhow, as the Netherlands' market was of only marginal interest to Air France. The French carrier did not even maintain a scheduled service to Amsterdam. Instead, French aviation policy focused on the Federal Republic of Germany, with which France also pursued the broader goal of European cooperation.

89 Memorandum Goedhuis re. discussions on aviation policy in Paris, 4-6 May 1953. Office memo Slotemaker to Plesman, 24 Aug. 1953: NNA, 2.05.117, Foreign Affairs 1945–1954, inv. nr. 9890.

90 Office memorandum VADV to Luns re. bilateral aviation relations with France, 23 July 1954. Message KLM Paris office to KLM head office in The Hague, 16 June 1954: NNA, 2.05.117, Foreign Affairs 1945–1954, inv.nr. 9890.

91 Office memorandum VADV to Luns, 14 Dec. 1955: NNA, 2.05.118, Foreign Affairs 1955–1964, inv.nr. 8790.

The French insisted that Air France and KLM should align their interests.[92] One way to bring this about, Paris suggested, would be for KLM to show an interest in the Sud Aviation Caravelle jet airliner that was under development in France. KLM, fixated on American equipment, tried to avoid this, which was not appreciated in Paris. Talks on cooperation remained without substance for years. Relations were not made any easier by the Dutch reservations with regard to the Europair initiative.[93] As a result, KLM continued to be in a tight spot and finally had to surrender the stopover in Nice in October 1958.[94] The Hague was gravely disappointed. Luns personally spoke to his French counterpart Maurice Couve de Murville, but to no avail.[95] Nonetheless, French intentions to open a Caravelle service to Amsterdam in April 1960 were welcomed in The Hague. The Dutch hoped that such a service would make KLM less dependent on unilateral goodwill permits. Still, the first Air France jet did not land at Schiphol until April 1966.[96]

Meanwhile, the general crisis in commercial aviation of the early 1960s led France to adopt a more restrictive policy. For example, France opposed any expansion of capacity for the KLM freight service between Amsterdam and Paris. KLM hoped to replace ageing two-engine DC-3 aircraft with much larger four-engine DC-7F cargo planes. Although KLM was prepared to share part of its cargo capacity with Air France, objections remained. Indeed, French opposition to KLM became stronger when the Dutch decided to purchase six Douglas DC-9 passenger jets, rather than the Caravelle.[97] To underline French discord, KLM's cargo planes were barred from Paris' new Orly Airport.[98] Air France then started a competing freight service from Orly in April 1968.[99] In the end, Orly remained out of bounds for KLM, making it more difficult to transfer goods for shipment beyond Paris.

Although KLM had made tentative efforts after 1945 to start air services to the Soviet Union and the countries in its occupation zone in Eastern Europe,

---

92 Minutes 82nd BLV, 7 Nov. 1955: NNA, 2.05.118, Foreign Affairs 1955–1964, inv.nr. 27493.

93 Memo KLM board re. lunch meeting with Max Hymans and Louis Lesieux of Air France in Paris, 9 July 1957: NNA, 2.05.118, Foreign Affairs 1955–1964, inv.nr. 8790.

94 Minutes 93rd BLV, 19 Oct. 1958: NNA, 2.05.118, Foreign Affairs 1955–1964, inv.nr. 27493.

95 Minutes 99th BLV, 2 Dec. 1959: NNA, 2.05.117, Foreign Affairs 1945–1954, inv.nr. 27494.

96 Letter Louis Lesieux (Air France) to Van der Wal (KLM), 22 Sep. 1965: NNA, 2.05.118, Foreign Affairs 1955–1964, inv.nr. 5361.

97 Summary of conversations on KLM cargo services to Orly, 10 Nov. 1964: NNA, 2.05.118, Foreign Affairs 1955–1964, inv.nr. 8683.

98 Letter Marc Jacquet (French Minister of Public Works and Transport) to KLM, 25 July 1964: NNA, 2.05.118, Foreign Affairs 1955–1964, inv.nr. 8683.

99 Minutes 122nd BLV, 2 Apr. 1968: NNA, 2.05.313, Foreign Affairs 1965–1974, inv.nr. 25174.

these initial plans had run aground in the deteriorating political and military relations of the Cold War. Washington made targeted efforts to discourage services to destinations behind the Iron Curtain and the Russians reciprocated. After the communist takeover in Czechoslovakia in 1948, Moscow forced its carrier ČSA to reduce services to Western Europe.[100] On both sides of the European divide suspicions ran high. KLM, on its part, was drawn into a fabricated espionage case in 1950 in which a Dutch businessman operating in Prague was arrested and put on trial for gathering information and aiding Czech connections to flee the country. KLM was accused of playing a role in this, but no reprisals followed.[101] Even so, KLM wondered if it should reduce the frequency of its services.[102] As before, espionage was the operative word in air connections to and from Prague. In May 1951, Czechoslovak flights ceased entirely when ČSA was hit by an American ban on flights over Western Germany in the aftermath of an espionage affair involving an American journalist imprisoned in Prague.[103]

Under such circumstances, keeping air services going to the Soviet zone was fraught with difficulties. Transport figures showed a downward trend.[104] The few Western airlines that operated to Prague all faced bureaucratic obstacles, such as the need to obtain special permission for each individual flight. In Prague, KLM representative Erik Kloosterhuis, was regularly tailed by Soviet secret agents, who at one point even stole his car and took it apart in search of hidden devices. In The Hague Foreign Affairs advised KLM that Kloosterhuis should be repatriated before something bad happened to him.[105] Following several more incidents, KLM did indeed recall him in the summer of 1951.[106] The situation, however, did not improve. KLM's representative in Hungary, Cornelia Aich, even faced three years of domestic deportation and was forced to forfeit most of her possessions because of her Western contacts.[107] Over

100 Stefan Albrecht, Internationale Luftverkehrspolitik in der Zeit des Kalten Krieges von 1944–1965: das Beispiel Tschechoslowakei, in: *Jahrbuch für Wirtschaftsgeschichte, 2007/1, Verkehrsgeschichte auf neuen Wegen* (Berlin: Akademie Verlag, 2007), p. 93–109. P. Svik, *Civil Aviation and the Globalization of the Cold War*, p. 43–52.

101 Reporting in *De Telegraaf*, 3 March 1950.

102 Letter KLM to RLD, 22 Aug. 1950: NNA, 5.016.5240, RLD, inv.nr. 1508.

103 Letter Czechoslovak legation The Hague to Foreign Affairs, 27 June 1951: NNA, 2.05.117, Foreign Affairs 1945–1954, inv.nr. 9962.

104 Letter KLM to RLD, 22 Aug. 1950: NNA, 5.016.5240, RLD, inv.nr. 1508.

105 Letter Ambassador W. van Tets to Foreign Affairs, 23 June 1950: NNA, 2.05.117, Foreign Affairs 1945–1954, inv.nr. 27304.

106 Code message Stikker to Dutch envoys in Budapest and Prague, 23 Apr. 1951: NNA, 2.05.117, Foreign Affairs 1945–1954, inv.nr. 27304.

107 Code message Posthumus Meyjes to Foreign Affairs, 26 Oct. 1952: NNA, 2.05.117 Foreign Affairs 1945–1954, inv.nr.20856.

time relations became less tense. After Czechoslovakia had suspended the requirement of individual flight permissions in October 1952, Stalin's death on 5 March 1953 seemed to create room for new initiatives, although it was two years before ČSA was able to resume its service to Amsterdam.

In the USSR KLM was one of the first airlines to respond to the new post-Stalin situation. Following aviation discussions between the Soviets and the Scandinavian countries, the Dutch ambassador in Moscow, Pedro Teixeira de Mattos, was instructed in June 1953 to enquire if talks might be held on a KLM service to the Soviet capital. Teixeira was not enthusiastic and reported a month later that Soviet Minister Vyacheslav Molotov had not been either.[108] Still, explorations continued. KLM planned a route to Moscow via Prague or Vienna. Air France was also working on an arrangement in which passengers would change to an Aeroflot plane in Prague that would take them to Moscow. KLM did the same. In October 1955 the Dutch reached an agreement with Aeroflot recognizing each other's tickets in preparation of a joint service. In keeping with the Soviet reluctance to admit foreign aircraft into its airspace, the plans provided for a change of planes in Prague.[109] A little over a year later, relations had crystallized sufficiently that KLM dared enquire about a regular permit to operate to Moscow.[110] However, this effort was lost in the rapidly increasing distrust between East and West as a result of the Soviet suppression of the Hungarian Uprising in November 1956.

Nevertheless, in May 1957, talks started on the possibility of an air link as a first step to improve trade contacts. The Dutch ambassador to Moscow, Daniël von Balluseck and his brother Felix, who had been a member of KLM's executive board, visited Marshal Semyon Zhavoronkov, the director of Aeroflot. Although their conversation got off to a rocky start, the atmosphere improved under the influence of the alcohol, fruit and refreshments that Zhavoronkov ordered to be brought in. There was even talk of a reciprocal KLM/Aeroflot air service via the Baltic Sea. This choice of route made it possible to avoid disputed German airspace. As part of a drive to improve relations with the West, Zhavoronkov hinted that such a service might be feasible.[111] In The Hague, RLD director-general Jan Backer didn't like this one bit. He sent a personal letter to traffic consultant Carel Schaepman at the Ministry of Foreign Affairs: 'Dutch aviation should not be dancing to this tune. We could inadvertently become

108 Minutes 67th BLV, 15 July 1953: NNA, 2.05.117, Foreign Affairs 1945–1954, inv.nr. 21392.

109 Minutes 81st BLV, 4 Oct. 1955: NNA, 2.05.118, Foreign Affairs 1955–1964, inv.nr. 27493.

110 Minutes 85th BLV, 27 Aug. 1956: NNA, 2.05.118, Foreign Affairs 1955–1964, inv.nr. 27493.

111 Report D.J. von Balluseck, 3 May 1957: NNA, 2.05.118, Foreign Affairs 1955–1964, inv.nr. 27551.

the unstoppable lever with which other roads to Russia can be opened.'[112] But when even the Dutch Ministry of Defense did not object, the talks continued. The Russians asked that Aeroflot be granted rights to fly over Denmark on its Baltic route to Amsterdam.[113] With some hesitation, the Danes agreed, after which the talks continued in the wake of other discussions on aviation between the Soviets and Western countries. Moscow declared an interest in a Soviet-Dutch bilateral aviation agreement under which Aeroflot could operate its brand new Tupolev Tu-104 on the route to Amsterdam. The Soviet jets were almost twice as fast as the Douglas DC-6B propeller aircraft KLM used and therefore the question arose whether operation of the reciprocal Dutch service could be at all profitable.[114] This dampened expectations somewhat.

The bilateral agreement was signed on 17 June 1958 and KLM made its inaugural flight to Moscow four days later, with Minister of Transport and Water Management Jacob Algera as a special guest. For the time being, Aeroflot and KLM both operated once a week. Again, the development was not welcomed in Washington, where the Cold War was in full swing. The authorities postponed a bilateral agreement between the United States and the USSR until 4 November 1966.[115] This made the Dutch-Soviet bilateral exceptional as it deviated from the principle of isolation of the Soviet Union agreed to in NATO circles. Foreign Affairs State Secretary Ernst van der Beugel believed that the rapprochement also held opportunities. In his view, the Netherlands might even use the improved relationship with Moscow to press for more American leniency in the ongoing talks in Washington regarding KLM landing rights on the American West Coast.[116]

Even so, the Soviets were not without a hidden agenda. Aeroflot aircraft repeatedly deviated from the prescribed route over the Netherlands on the way from Copenhagen to Amsterdam to make a detour over Leeuwarden air force base.[117] Between October 1958 and August 1960 there were 23 such incidents.[118] This was discussed on several occasions in the context of NATO. Apart from this, bilateral affairs were also under pressure. Relations took a nosedive

112 Letter J.W.F. Backer (RLD) to Schaepman (VADV), 14 June 1957: NNA, 2.05.118, Foreign Affairs 1955–1964, inv.nr. 27511.

113 Minutes 89th BLV, 16 July 1957: NNA, 2.05.118, Foreign Affairs 1955–1964, inv.nr. 27493.

114 Minutes 91st BLV, 13 Jan. 1958: NNA, 2.05.118, Foreign Affairs 1955–1964, inv.nr. 27493.

115 Svik, *Civil Aviation and the Globalization of the Cold War*, p. 81–93.

116 Minutes 92nd BLV, 30 June 1958: NNA, 2.05.118, Foreign Affairs 1955–1964, inv.nr. 27493.

117 Letter State Secretary M. Calmeyer (Defense) to Luns, 6 Aug. 1960: NNA, 2.05.118, Foreign Affairs 1955–1964, inv.nr. 27551.

118 Survey Royal Netherlands Air Force, Sep. 1960: NNA, 2.05.118, Foreign Affairs 1955–1964, inv.nr. 27551.

as a result of the construction of the Berlin Wall in August 1961. Apart from this, bilateral diplomatic tensions also increased. On 12 October 1961, the Soviet ambassador to the Netherlands, Panteleimon Ponomarenko, was declared persona-non-grata after he had hit a military policeman at Schiphol Airport three days earlier. The Soviet ambassador had been on the warpath because military police had confiscated the passport of a Russian citizen, Alexejewa Golub, whose husband Alexei, a chemical engineer, had applied for asylum in the Netherlands earlier that day. Distraught, Mrs. Golub wanted to fly home. After a skirmish and a police siege of the little Aeroflot office at the airport that lasted hours, Mrs. Golub was finally allowed to leave after it had been established that she really wished to depart the Netherlands of her own free will. In retaliation for the incident and Ponomarenko's expulsion, the Dutch ambassador to the USSR, Henri Helb, was deported from Moscow some days later. It was not until May 1963 that the two countries restored relations at ambassadorial level.[119]

Though diplomatic contacts had stalled, KLM and Aeroflot flew on as bilateral trade continued.[120] KLM asked for permission to fly via Siberia on the route to Tokyo, which would mean a significant reduction of about one third in the distance and therefore a substantial cut in fuel costs. The request was based on discussions between the Soviets and Japan on just such routes that had started in 1961 and were as yet undecided.[121] In July 1964, Minister Luns first raised the issue during his visit to the Kremlin. There, the case was referred for consultation between the airlines concerned. In November, a KLM representative came to Moscow offering a package of financial compensations to favor the Russians. This worked and on 14 December 1964 KLM's new CEO Horatius Albarda signed an agreement with Aeroflot under which KLM was promised consent to fly over Siberia – as soon as Aeroflot was granted a Japanese license for a service to Tokyo.[122] The latter condition turned out to be an important caveat when the talks between Tokyo and Moscow stalled. In order to make progress, KLM came up with a remarkable plan in November 1965: perhaps it would be possible to charter an Aeroflot aircraft to operate the KLM service via Siberia? At the end of January 1966, an Aeroflot delegation arrived in the Netherlands, where the Russians were pampered with a program in which food and drink

119 Reporting in *Algemeen Handelsblad*, 9 and 10 Oct. 1961. Janine Jager, *Wilhelmina Triesman, 1901–1982. Een Nederlandse in Leningrad* (Amsterdam: Pegasus, 2012), p. 226.

120 Code messages De Vos van Steenwijk (Ambassador Brussels) to Foreign Affairs, 11 and 18 Dec. 1964: NNA, 2.05.118, Foreign Affairs 1955–1964, inv.nr. 27736.

121 Svik, *Civil Aviation and the Globalization of the Cold War*, p. 96–97.

122 Letter Kruys (RLD) to VADV, 22 Dec. 1964: NNA, 2.05.118, Foreign Affairs 1955–1964, inv.nr. 8727.

very much took a central role, although there were also tourist trips to the Peace Palace and the Mauritshuis Art Museum in The Hague, to Schiphol, to a concert in Scheveningen's Kurhaus and a visit to the Delta Works.[123] At the same time, the Dutch invested in bilateral trade and worked on preparations for a general payments agreement.[124]

In spite of these efforts, an accord remained beyond reach as the case fell victim to a remarkable incident. On 12 April 1967, Aeroflot's chief representative in the Netherlands, Wladimir Glukhov, was arrested in Amsterdam by three Dutch secret service agents on charges of espionage. This happened in a dairy shop near Glukhov's apartment over the local Aeroflot office. The arrest was like a B-movie. Glukov, who was otherwise known as an affable man, resisted fiercely. However, he could not prevent being handcuffed and taken to a car. But his screams caught the attention of a group of youths, who believed a criminal kidnapping was in progress and tried to free the victim. One of the detectives received several fist punches. Hearing the commotion, Glukov's wife also stormed out. Eventually, Glukov was crammed into a car. But when the car tried to drive off, Glukhov's office manager jumped on the bonnet to stop the vehicle. However, the detectives floored the accelerator and the unfortunate Russian ended up hurled onto the street after being 'driven along' for several hundred meters.[125] A diplomatic incident could not be avoided, although Luns and Prime Minister Piet de Jong doubted whether the evidence of espionage was strong enough to lead to Glukov's prosecution. All the same, Glukov was deported a few days later.[126] Repercussions were to be expected, of course. On 27 April, KLM's station manager in Moscow, Ted Donker, was arrested while visiting the theatre, and charged with espionage. He denied this, but was extradited after two days' detention.[127]

Although such incidents put pressure on Dutch-Soviet relations, they had no discernable effect on air services. From April 1968, KLM and Aeroflot began joint operation of the route between Amsterdam and Leningrad.[128] In return Aeroflot received rights to fly to Cuba via Amsterdam, despite NATO objections.

123 Program for Visit of the Management of Aeroflot to the Netherlands, 23–29 Jan. 1966: NNA, 2.05.313, Foreign Affairs 1965–1974, inv.nr. 5418.

124 Code message Minister Roelof Nelissen (Economic Affairs) to Moskow embassy, 10 June 1970: NNA, 2.05.313, Foreign Affairs 1965–1974, inv.nr. 8104.

125 Reporting in *De Tijd : Dagblad voor Nederland*, 13 April 1967.

126 Minutes Council of Ministers, 14 Apr. 1967: NNA, 2.05.313, Foreign Affairs 1965–1974, inv.nr. 25883.

127 Code messages Ambassador Moscow (Beelaerts) to Foreign Affairs, 27, 28 and 29 Apr. 1967: NNA, 2.05.313, Foreign Affairs 1965–1974, inv.nr. 25883.

128 Minutes 122th BLV, 2 Apr. 1968: NNA, 2.05.313, Foreign Affairs 1965–1974, inv.nr. 25174.

Discussions about such a service been proceeding intermittently since 1962.[129] In a sign of improving relations, the Russians hinted at a permit for KLM to fly via Siberia, following a similar permission given to SAS. In June 1969, State Secretary Mike Keyzer arrived in Moscow with a delegation to discuss the matter. It led to a curious agreement under which KLM chartered an Ilyushin IL-62 airplane from Aeroflot, with crew, to operate KLM's flights via Siberia, just as KLM had suggested in November 1966. The Soviets mentioned they were now ready to open an international air route across Siberia, but KLM stuck with the idea of chartering aircraft from Aeroflot. However, because the aircraft used were Russian and operated by an Aeroflot crew, Japan also had to give permission. Discussions took months, but from 6 April 1971, almost seven years since the topic had first been discussed, KLM passengers bound for Tokyo transferred in Moscow to an Aeroflot Ilyushin that was partly painted in KLM livery.[130]

The arrangement was not a success. A lot of time was lost fueling the IL-62 for the long flight to Tokyo. The costs were also found to be much higher than expected, a phenomenon also observed in general trade relations with the Soviets. The service thus showed significant losses.[131] It was not long before the Dutch asked permission to use their own aircraft on the route, an issue that became even more important when it emerged that tickets were being tampered with on the Soviet side.[132] Although the technicalities were complex, the gist of it was that KLM wanted to shed its putative partner Aeroflot. The Dutch hoped to achieve this without ruffling feathers that would put the Siberia permission at risk. Veiled discussions were held about the possibilities of using KLM aircraft and in the end this low-key approach was successful. KLM was allowed to use its own aircraft from April 1972 onwards. In November of that year, the charter agreement with Aeroflot terminated and KLM began operating its own DC-8 aircraft, but by then the orientation at KLM had shifted to the deployment of the Boeing 747, which generated a new set of bilateral issues.[133]

129 Svik, *Civil Aviation and the Globalization of the Cold War*, p. 110–114.

130 Memorandum B. Bugajew (Soviet Minister for Civil Aviation) to State Secretary Keyzer, 5 Feb. 1971: NNA, 2.05.313, Foreign Affairs 1965–1974, inv.nr. 5418.

131 Memorandum RLD, April 1972: NNA, 2.05.313, Foreign Affairs 1965–1974, inv.nr. 5418.

132 Office memorandum VADV to Minister Van der Stoel, 19 Apr. 1974: NNA, 2.05.313, Foreign Affairs 1965–1974, inv.nr. 5418.

133 KLM, *Annual Report 1972-73*. Minutes 138th BLV, 1 Aug. 1973: NNA, 2.05.313, Foreign Affairs 1965–1974, inv.nr. 25176.

3 Asserting the Dutch Position in Indonesia and Australia

In December 1949, when The Hague formally recognized Indonesian independence, preparations were made for a bilateral air transport agreement. In the shadow of the political developments that made headline news, cooperation in the field of aviation was discussed between KLM and representatives of the Republik Indonesia. A new company, Garuda Indonesian Airways, was created under joint Indonesian and Dutch ownership. Garuda was to receive a thirty year concession to operate air services in the Indonesian archipelago. Both parties took an equal number of priority shares for a period of ten years. Ordinary share capital was also distributed on a fifty-fifty basis. After ten years, KLM was to transfer the majority of its shares to Jakarta. Until then, KLM would be responsible for the management of the new airline. KLM's Emile van Konijnenburg, head of KLM's interinsular branch that maintained Indonesian air transport and a personal friend of Sukarno, was appointed as Chief Executive Officer. On 31 March 1950, Garuda's founding papers were signed in Jakarta.[134] A bilateral consortium was set up for international services, Garuda Overseas Airways, which contracted its flights to KLM.

Meanwhile, Indonesian aeronautical institutions needed to be built up. Informal Dutch assistance and advice proved counterproductive, since it encouraged the Indonesians to commit their national aviation interests to paper.[135] Frictions in general Dutch-Indonesian relations added to this. From August 1950 Jakarta changed Indonesia's federal status to that of a unitary state. This strengthened determination in The Hague to cling to a continuation of Dutch sovereignty over the island of New Guinea. The Netherlands-Indonesian Union that had formally been agreed upon at the transfer of sovereignty on 27 December 1949 was increasingly under strain.

With the intention of smoothing out some of the differences as far as they affected bilateral aviation, the Indonesian Minister of Communications, Djuanda, arrived in The Hague in November 1950. At the same time several countries, led by India and Australia, presented themselves in Jakarta to speak about commercial landing rights. Although air services agreements were not immediately forthcoming, such contacts did have an effect on the Dutch position in East Asia. India adopted a more restrictive stance towards KLM and Ceylon also tightened the reins, particularly with regard to KLM's 5th freedom

---

134 Founding Agreement Garuda Indonesian Airways, 21 Dec. 1949: NNA, 2.05.117, Foreign Affairs 1945–1954, inv.nr. 21395.

135 Letter J.H. Crans (KLM representative, Indonesia) to Slotemaker, 28 Dec. 1950: NNA, 2.05.117, Foreign Affairs 1945–1954, inv.nr. 21396.

rights.[136] For The Hague, the question arose as to how to ensure that Indonesia, in its contacts with third countries, would continue to take account of Dutch interests.[137] Disagreements at the political level over the way forward for the Netherlands-Indonesian Union also had an effect on cooperation between the two airlines. On the Indonesian side, distrust of the Dutch who 'dictated everything' at Garuda was growing, which added to Dutch concerns over KLM's role in Garuda's future.[138]

The mutual sensitivities made The Hague focus on concluding a bilateral air transport agreement as a way to bring stability. After all, KLM's operations lacked an international legal basis in the new situation. At the Ministry of Foreign Affairs the matter was treated with urgency, especially because Britain also wished to procure landing rights in Jakarta. If the Netherlands were not the first country to conclude a bilateral aviation agreement with Indonesia, the accords ran the risk of being modelled on the Bermuda Agreement. The Dutch feared this would curtail the freedom The Hague and KLM were standing out for.[139] Nonetheless, a bilateral agreement did not ensue, although the parties agreed that KLM's operating license would be renewable on an annual basis. Before long, however, Indonesian decision-making became linked to the increasing dispute over Dutch sovereignty in New Guinea. In Jakarta, Djuanda saw aviation as a touchstone for the general state of bilateral relations.[140] The prospects for an agreement deteriorated as talks dragged on. In October 1952, anti-Dutch demonstrations and riots broke out in Jakarta, after The Hague had repeatedly said it wished New Guinea to remain under Dutch sovereignty. Angry nationalists took down the Dutch flag from the building of the High Commissariat and telegraph and telephone connections with the Netherlands were cut. The following day flight KL823 was refused permission to land in Jakarta. After much hesitation the captain saw no other option but to fly his Constellation and its 32 passengers all the way back to Amsterdam.[141]

In the meantime, it became clear that the Indonesian nationalists were aiming for the cancellation of the Netherlands-Indonesian Union. This would also

136 Minutes 51st BLV, 20 Feb. 1951; minutes 56th BLV, 23 Nov. 1951: NNA, 2.05.117, Foreign Affairs 1945–1954, inv.nr. 21392.

137 Secret letter Speekenbrink to Foreign Affairs, 20 Jan. 1951: NNA, 2.05.117, Foreign Affairs 1945–1954, inv.nr. 21396.

138 Minutes 57th BLV, 4 Jan. 1952: NNA, 2.05.117, Foreign Affairs 1945–1954, inv.nr. 21392.

139 Minutes 53rd BLV, 14 June 1951: NNA, 2.05.117, Foreign Affairs 1945–1954, inv.nr. 21392.

140 Code message Lamping from Jakarta to Foreign Affairs, 14 Nov. 1951: NNA, 2.05.117, Foreign Affairs 1945–1954, inv.nr. 21397.

141 Code message Beyen and Luns to Jakarta, 17 Oct. 1952: NNA, 2.05.117, Foreign Affairs 1945–1954, inv.nr. 21397. Reporting in *Trouw*, 18 Oct. 1952.

affect aviation and Djuanda brought pressure to bear to break open the contract between KLM and Garuda, ending Dutch participation in the Indonesian carrier.[142] In follow-up discussions, Jakarta used the KLM services as bargaining chips in the broader discussions with the Netherlands on bilateral issues, including threats to curtail the number of KLM flights. In January 1953, these were reduced to five per week. Jakarta steered towards a transfer of ownership and management of Garuda.[143] To the consternation of the government in The Hague, KLM's Board of Control readily agreed. Its members were satisfied with a refund of the investment in Garuda, in exchange for ensuring a future for KLM's services to Indonesia.[144]

In Jakarta, Indonesian national prestige now took center stage. Aviation was seen as an issue second only to the dispute over sovereignty in New Guinea. In talks with Plesman and Van Konijnenburg in Jakarta in early March 1953, Djuanda did not beat about the bush: it was his express wish that Garuda would become entirely Indonesian, because of the importance the airline had for the young country. KLM would be compensated as soon as possible, no later than 1 January 1954.[145]

A cabinet change in Jakarta in July 1953 did not alter the Indonesian position. Hardly any progress was made in the desired disentanglement of the two airlines. Meanwhile, the controversy between The Hague and Jakarta over Dutch rule in New Guinea deepened. Aviation suffered because KLM operated scheduled flights from Amsterdam to New Guinea, a symbol of continued Dutch colonialism in Asia. The service, sponsored by The Hague with 30 million guilders a year, carefully avoided Indonesian airspace by flying from Bangkok via Manila to Biak on New Guinea.[146] This was very unpopular in Indonesia and it was clear that KLM's influence in Garuda would have to end. Jakarta agreed to pay 15 million guilders to buy out KLM's shareholding, but agreed that KLM would continue to provide technical assistance until 1960. After months of discussions, a contract to this effect was signed on 24 March 1954.[147] Four months later Van Konijnenburg was recalled to KLM's head office in The Hague to lead

142 Code message Lamping to Foreign Affairs, 7 Nov. 1952: NNA, 2.05.117, Foreign Affairs 1945–1954, inv.nr. 21397.

143 Memorandum VADV to Luns, 16 Jan. 1953; code message Van Bylandt to Foreign Affairs, 19 March 1953: NNA, 2.05.117, Foreign Affairs 1945–1954, inv.nr. 21397.

144 Dierikx, *Blauw in de lucht*, p. 129–130.

145 Letter Van Bylandt to Foreign Affairs, 3 Apr. 1953: NNA, 2.05.117, Foreign Affairs 1945–1954, inv.nr. 21398.

146 Minutes Board of Control KLM, 8 Nov. 1962: KLM Archive, series R-5.

147 KLM *Annual Report 1953* and *Annual Report 1954*.

the airline's department of foreign cooperation. He was replaced as director of Garuda by his deputy, Dirk van Houten.[148]

Thus KLM's involvement with Garuda continued against the odds, although KLM now also pursued other cooperative ventures in South Asia. In September 1955, the Dutch carrier concluded a joint venture with the Government of Ceylon to found Air Ceylon. KLM participated in exchange for 49 percent of the stock and also provided staff and expertise.[149] Nonetheless, most of the effort remained focused on Garuda, where some 300 KLM staff were still working in 1957. KLM remained apprehensive that its Indonesian landing rights might suddenly be lost and tried to ensure that as few aircraft as possible were on the tarmac at Jakarta's Kemajoran Airport at any given time.[150]

This turned out to be a wise precaution. On Saturday evening, 30 November 1957, an attack was made on president Sukarno when he visited his children's school in Jakarta. The Indonesian authorities immediately assumed that the Netherlands had a hand in this. Sukarno announced that all Dutch assets in Indonesia would be nationalized forthwith. As one of the first sanctions, Indonesia cancelled KLM's landing rights on 1 December. The last flight from Jakarta left empty on Monday 2 December, after a six-hour dispute over whether the aircraft should be allowed to take off at all.[151] What to do? The Hague was quick to approach the British Government in London to ask whether KLM services might temporarily use Singapore as a final destination. The Dutch considered various possibilities for bolstering KLM's position and asked London to grant Garuda a temporary license for a shuttle service between Singapore and Jakarta to take stranded KLM passengers.[152] This emergency provision continued well into 1958. By the end of March, KLM had reached the conclusion that the landing ban in Jakarta was likely to be permanent and applied for permission for three services to Singapore per week. These would then connect to flights to and from Jakarta. However, the British Ministry of Transport and Civil Aviation ruled that such an arrangement was likely to harm the interests of British and Australian airlines. London therefore limited KLM to a single flight per week.[153]

148 Minutes 71st BLV, 23 March 1954: NNA, 2.05.117, Foreign Affairs 1945–1954, inv.nr. 21393.

149 Minutes 81st BLV, 4 Oct. 1955: NNA, 2.05.118, Foreign Affairs 1955–1964, inv.nr. 27493.

150 Code message Luns to Jakarta, 7 Nov. 1957: NNA, 2.05.118, Foreign Affairs 1955–1964, inv.nr. 27528.

151 Code message Hasselman (embassy Jakarta) to Foreign Affairs, 1 Dec. 1957: NNA, 2.05.118, Foreign Affairs 1955–1964, inv.nr. 27522. Reporting in *Algemeen Handelsblad*, 2 Dec. 1957.

152 Telegram Government of Singapore to Foreign Office, London, 2 Dec. 1957; telegram British Embassy Jakarta to Foreign Office London, 2 Dec. 1957: BNA, MTCA, BT245, inv.nr. 444.

153 Telegram British Foreign Office to embassy in The Hague, 2 Apr. 1958: BNA, MTCA, BT245, inv.nr. 444.

Hoping for leniency, The Hague allowed the talks drag on to December 1958, consciously linking the issue to possible Dutch political support for British plans to set up a free trade association in Europe.[154] When this did not produce the desired result and Britain threatened to erode KLM's position in Singapore further, Foreign Minister Luns tried to add the issue to the agenda of the official visit by Queen Juliana and her husband Prince Bernhard to London in January 1959. This too had no effect. For Prime Minister Harold MacMillan, one or two weekly KLM flights to Singapore represented the maximum permissible.[155] However, for KLM one flight a week was not enough to operate the scheduled service profitably, something the deputy head of KLM's Foreign Relations Department, Constantijn Nass, explained at length in a radio interview with the BBC that was picked up by newspapers in Britain and in the Netherlands. Nass appealed for leniency, referring to the liberal nature of Dutch air policy.[156] Such public attention was considered unwelcome by the British Foreign Office. Foreign Secretary Selwyn Lloyd rushed to invite Luns to visit London to discuss matters in person. Luns duly arrived, carrying an extensive memorandum in which he complained, on the basis that KLM had operated in Singapore since 1930, that in his opinion the airline was treated unfairly.[157] His efforts did not yield any results. In a secret session, the British cabinet weighed good relations with the Netherlands against the commercial interests of BOAC and Qantas. Seeking to offer something for all parties, KLM was limited to a single flight per week in Singapore.[158] This was not enough for Luns. In Parliament in The Hague on 18 March, he declared bitterly that a country that had 'so praised free trade, conducts a very narrow, I can almost say, bigoted policy, which brings memories of the Navigation Act of 1651'.[159]

The British were not alone in adopting a restrictive attitude. In April 1960, India took advantage of KLM's desire to start operating DC-8 jets to reduce the number of weekly services from three to two. Later that year Pakistan even wanted to limit KLM to one flight a week, adjusted to two after negotiations.[160]

154 Minute by Prime Minister Harold MacMillan, 31 Oct. 1958: BNA, MTCA, BT245, inv.nr. 445.

155 Letter Macmillan to Luns, 10 Jan. 1959: BNA, MTCA, BT245, inv.nr. 445.

156 Reporting in *Algemeen Handelsblad*, 14 Jan. 1959.

157 British Foreign Office briefing for the Secretary of State (by K.J. Simpson), 23 Jan. 1959: BNA, FO, FO371, inv.nr. 141699.

158 (Secret) extract from Cabinet Meeting and Conclusions, 29 Jan. 1959: BNA, MTCA, BT245, inv.nr. 446.

159 *Handelingen der Staten-Generaal, Eerste Kamer, Verslag, 1958–1959*, 18 March 1959, p. 191.

160 Minutes 100th BLV, 14 Apr. 1960; minutes 101st BLV, 1 Dec. 1960: NNA, 2.05.117, Foreign Affairs 1945–1954, inv.nr. 27494.

But the biggest threat for Dutch air services was Jakarta's attitude with regard to New Guinea. After the failure of negotiations in 1956, Indonesia had terminated the Union Treaty with the Netherlands. In December 1957, the nationalizations of Dutch companies had been added to this. Seemingly oblivious, the Netherlands stuck to its previously agreed long-term plans for New Guinea, which did not include any role for Indonesia. However, for the Indonesians, New Guinea was an inseparable part of the Indonesian archipelago and tensions were running high, with several incidents both on Java and in New Guinea. On 6 May 1960, the chancellery of the Dutch Embassy in Jakarta was attacked by a mob. The Hague decided on a demonstration of force. At the end of that month, a Dutch navy squadron, led by the aircraft carrier *Karel Doorman*, left Rotterdam for the East to underline the importance the Dutch attached to New Guinea. On board was, in addition to a number of Hawker Sea Hawk fighters and Grumman Avenger attack aircraft, the first of two Air Force units equipped with 12 Hawker Hunter fighter jets that were to be stationed in New Guinea. In June 1960, as the Dutch navy squadron sailed east, Sukarno announced the closure of the Indonesian sea area and the airspace between New Guinea and Indonesia.[161] The sea voyage around half the world took nearly three months and the carrier did not arrive until 2 August. Four days later, the Hunters were unloaded at the port of Biak. The 56-man ground crew needed to deploy the fighter jets was transferred from the Netherlands on three KLM flights.[162] This underlined the importance of KLM's services to Biak, now flown with large Douglas DC-8 jets that used the polar route via Anchorage, Tokyo and Manila. A military confrontation with Indonesia seemed at hand when Jakarta formally severed diplomatic relations with the Netherlands on 17 August 1960. However, some level of contact remained. In search of a compromise the mediation of UN Secretary-General U Thant was engaged.[163]

In the meantime, KLM aircraft were quietly used for the transportation of military personnel to New Guinea. This held political risks. In order not to be immediately recognizable and avoid a stir during the intermediate stop in Tokyo, military personnel traveled in civilian clothing and on civilian passports. When the Japanese protested against this practice, The Hague assured

161 Code message Frowein (embassy Jakarta) to Foreign Affairs, 8 June 1960: NNA, 2.05.118, Foreign Affairs 1955–1964, inv.nr. 27523.

162 Duco Hellema, *De Karel Doorman naar Nieuw-Guinea. Nederlands machtsvertoon in de Oost* (Amsterdam: Boom, 2005), p. 113–143. A.P. de Jong (ed.), *Vlucht door de tijd. 75 jaar Nederlandse luchtmacht* (Houten: Unieboek, 1988), p. 171–175.

163 Minutes Council of Ministers, 29 Dec. 1960: http://resources.huygens.knaw.nl/indonesischebetrekkingen1945-1969/Nederlands-indonesischeBetrekkingen1950-1963/Document/16079.

them that no transportation of soldiers was taking place.[164] Nonetheless, KLM was not comfortable with the situation and feared for its operations to Biak and elsewhere in the event of an armed clash with Indonesia. But even without such hostilities, Tokyo revoked its permission for the KLM route to Biak at the end of January 1962. This threatened to interrupt the transportation of military personnel and equipment. The Hague therefore chartered two DC-8 aircraft for flights that would be routed through Anchorage, Honolulu and Wake Island, avoiding Japanese airspace. To engage US cooperation, The Hague invoked Article 5 of the Chicago Convention for these charter flights. It put the Americans on the spot.[165] Washington, ambushed when the first plane took off without prior consultation, refused to cooperate. Luns protested fiercely. He considered this an unprecedented breach of assistance within NATO. In The Hague Prime Minister Jan de Quay also intervened, but to no avail. The Americans stood by their refusal.[166] The atmosphere became tense. Moreover, it did not resolve the issue with Japan. Assuming that there might be soldiers on board, Tokyo withdrew the landing permit for the next regular KLM flight that had Tokyo as its final destination. The flight was stranded in Anchorage and finally had to turn back.[167] The Netherlands suffered a loss of face. But what was worse, the government was unable to follow an unambiguous course: New Guinea was simply too far away and was unreachable in a crisis for soldiers and reinforcements.[168] Meanwhile, Luns traveled to Washington to advocate for Dutch interests, but this too did not have the desired result. In extreme need, the government and KLM jointly decided to allow the army to charter KLM aircraft for flights that would be routed via the Peruvian capital Lima, and Papeete and Noumea in French Polynesia.[169]

164 Office memorandum VADV to Van Tuyll van Serooskerken, 17 Jan. 1962: http://resources.huygens.knaw.nl/indonesischebetrekkingen1945-1969/Nederlands-indonesischeBetrekkingen1950–1963/Document/21746.

165 Memorandum VADV to Luns, 1 Feb. 1962: http://resources.huygens.knaw.nl/indonesischebetrekkingen1945-1969/Nederlands-indonesischeBetrekkingen1950–1963/Document/21749.

166 Telegram Foreign Affairs to Washington and New York, 6 Feb. 1962: http://resources.huygens.knaw.nl/indonesischebetrekkingen1945-1969/Nederlands-indonesischeBetrekkingen1950–1963/Document/21753.

167 Telegram Luns to Tokio, 7 Feb. 1962: http://resources.huygens.knaw.nl/indonesischebetrekkingen1945–1969/Nederlands-indonesischeBetrekkingen1950-1963/Document/21758.

168 Minutes Council of Ministers, 12 Feb. 1962: http://resources.huygens.knaw.nl/indonesischebetrekkingen1945-1969/Nederlands-indonesischeBetrekkingen1950-1963/Document/15633.

169 Telegram Foreign Affairs to Luns in Athens, 5 May 1962: http://resources.huygens.knaw.nl/indonesischebetrekkingen1945-1969/Nederlands-indonesischeBetrekkingen1950-1963

Fortunately for all interested parties, Jakarta ultimately decided not to launch a full-scale military attack. In January 1962 Dutch-Indonesian talks were started under the chairmanship of the American diplomat Ellsworth Bunker, mediated by UN Secretary-General U Thant. The result was that sovereignty over New Guinea would be transferred to Indonesia on 1 May 1963 after a period of transitional administration by the United Nations. Dutch diplomacy suffered its final colonial defeat.

In early September, Garuda announced its intention to start its own scheduled service to Biak. In anticipation, KLM began disposing of personnel and equipment, an operation scheduled to be completed by mid-October 1962. Additional DC-8 aircraft had to be deployed to finish this on time.[170] It was agreed to end the scheduled KLM service to New Guinea after the transfer of sovereignty. The domestic airline on New Guinea, Kroonduif [Crown Pigeon], would be handed over to Garuda. In the end, the relatively calm ending of the conflict opened the doors to a restoration of normal bilateral relations. On 14 November, Djuanda, by now prime minister and acting president in the absence of Sukarno, issued a press statement that hinged on the (preferably early) transfer of New Guinea to Indonesia. A restoration of air connections to Jakarta finally seemed possible. After restoring relations, Djuanda saw no reason to continue to block KLM.[171] Using his own back channels, Van Konijnenburg, a well-known opponent of the Dutch New Guinea policy, applied himself to persuade Djuanda and Sukarno to restore KLM's operating rights. This direct contact with the Indonesian government contravened what was left of the Dutch New Guinea policy. Following orders from Foreign Minister Luns, Van Konijnenburg was reprimanded by KLM president Ernst van der Beugel for meddling. Offended, Van Konijnenburg handed in his resignation in November 1962, but travelled to Jakarta on his own private initiative in January 1963 in a personal – and ultimately successful – effort to restore landing rights.[172] Thanks to his endeavors KLM was again able to land in Jakarta once a week from October 1963 after an absence of nearly six years.

/Document/21289. Minutes 104^{e} BLV, 27 June 1962: NNA, 2.05.117, Foreign Affairs 1945–1954, inv.nr. 27494.

170 Code message governor Platteel to Foreign Affairs, 7 sept. 1962: http://resources.huygens.knaw.nl/indonesischebetrekkingen1945-1969/Nederlands-indonesischeBetrekkingen1950-1963/Document/22374.

171 Memorandum N.S. Blom to Foreign Affairs, 26 Nov. 1962: http://resources.huygens.knaw.nl/indonesischebetrekkingen1945-1969/Nederlands-indonesischeBetrekkingen1950-1963/Document/22687

172 Kersten, *Luns*, p. 288–289. Willem Oltmans, *Memoires 1961–1963* (Breda: Papieren Tijger, 1997), p. 266–277; 292. Also: *Het Parool*, 3 Jan. 1963; *De Volkskrant*, 3 Jan. 1963.

In the wake of this accord, an Indonesian mission arrived at Schiphol in April 1964 to explore the possibilities of normalizing general bilateral relations. In addition to financial support, Dutch aid for improvements to Kemajoran Airport was discussed. The Dutch hoped this could be in exchange for an extension of KLM landing rights.[173] The Hague linked the latter issue to an agreement on the repayment of Indonesia's outstanding debts to the Netherlands, largely triggered by the 1957/1958 nationalizations of Dutch economic interests. In the end, the Netherlands budgeted 18 million guilders for the refurbishment of Kemajoran Airport. In evidence of these improved relations, KLM and Garuda agreed to begin a pooled air service in November 1964. In addition, Garuda was to fly to Amsterdam twice a week from 31 March 1965.[174] Fifteen years after the transfer of sovereignty, the bilateral air services agreement that had been cherished by The Hague for so long, now appeared within reach.

Six months later, on 1 October 1965, relations in Jakarta were suddenly turned upside down by an attempted coup against Sukarno. From the skirmishes that followed, the commander of the strategic reserve, General Suharto, emerged as the new ruler. The subsequent reckoning cost hundreds of thousands of lives.[175] In March 1966, Suharto formally took over Sukarno's position as head of state. He formed a government of technocrats and the military, focusing on a restoration of the economy. The new government was open to an improvement of relations with the Netherlands. After several rounds of talks, an agreement was reached in 1966, whereby Indonesia would repay the outstanding debts over a period of thirty years, from 1973. In exchange the Dutch embraced a coordinating role in providing international aid to Indonesia.[176] This opened the door to a new aviation agreement, signed on 12 July 1966, that laid the foundation for cooperation between KLM and Garuda in the following years.[177]

Since 1945, KLM flights to Sydney had been limited to charters carrying Dutch and Italian immigrants. The aircraft initially had to fly back empty.[178]

173 Minutes 108th BLV, 23 Apr. 1964: NNA, 2.05.117, Foreign Affairs 1945–1954, inv.nr. 27494.

174 Minutes 110th BLV, 17 Nov. 1964: NNA, 2.05.117, Foreign Affairs 1945–1954, inv.nr. 27494.

175 Victor M. Fic, *Anatomy of the Jakarta Coup, October 1, 1965: The Collusion with China which destroyed the Army Command, President Sukarno and the Communist Party of Indonesia* (Jakarta: Jajasan Obor Indonesia, 2005).

176 M.L.J. Dierikx, C.P.M. Klep, E.M.L. Klinkers, M.G.M. Smits, *Nederlandse Ontwikkelingssamenwerking. Bronnenuitgave, Vol. 2, 1964–1967* (The Hague: Instituut voor Nederlandse Geschiedenis, 2003), p. 486–488, 505–509.

177 Agreement, signed 12 July 1966 in The Hague, between the Kingdom of the Netherlands and the Republik Indonesia regarding air services between their respective territories: *Handelingen der Staten-Generaal, 1966–1967, Tweede Kamer*, Kamerstuk 8831, nr. 1.

178 Minutes 47th BLV, 4 Sep. 1950: NNA, 2.05.117, Foreign Affairs 1945–1954, inv.nr. 21391.

The Hague again became interested in extending the air service from Jakarta to Sydney after the transfer of sovereignty to Indonesia. The Dutch found newly appointed Liberal Prime Minister Robert Menzies more receptive than his predecessors and the Menzies government allowed KLM to take return cargo.[179] This raised the question of whether KLM should again seek regular landing rights. However, The Hague was not in a hurry. KLM figures showed that emigrants would make up most of the passenger transport for the time being and the prospects for scheduled flights with normal passengers looked doubtful.[180] Nonetheless, discussions were initiated in the summer of 1951. The Australian government, prompted by BOAC and Qantas who preferred to keep the market to themselves, embraced restrictions. According to Canberra, the air traffic market between Amsterdam and Sydney did not exceed 350 passengers per year anyway. On that basis, KLM could only be permitted to operate one flight per month. In contrast, KLM considered a frequency of one flight per week feasible, a minimum for profitable operations.

At this point the Dutch ambassador in Canberra, Pedro Teixeira de Mattos, a friend of Menzies, managed an intervention. Over a glass of good cognac at the end of an extensive dinner that negotiator Daniël Goedhuis also attended, the ambassador praised Australia's role in the Western alliance, especially its interests in maintaining good relations with its Dutch neighbors in New Guinea.[181] Menzies, in the best of moods, admitted that the Netherlands had been 'unfairly treated by Australia' in the past. He agreed that the Netherlands should be granted rights to fly one service per week via Bangkok, Manila and Biak, but with the restriction that KLM should not deploy larger aircraft than the Lockheed L-749 Constellation that was then in use. Between Biak and Sydney, twenty passengers per week was the maximum admissible.

While there were compliments in The Hague for the tenacity of the Dutch negotiators, no one was satisfied with the 'miserable result' achieved.[182] With these restrictions, KLM's opening flight to Sydney landed on 9 December 1951. In the hope of improvements, Menzies and his wife, visiting London in June 1952, were invited for a two-day visit to the lowlands and on 10 June, Menzies' plane landed at Schiphol Airport. In The Hague he had a conversation with Plesman, who noted that Menzies was positive about the Dutch effort in New

179 Letter Teppema (Envoy Canberra) to Foreign Affairs, 1 Feb. 1950: NNA, 2.05.117, BZ 1945–1954, inv.nr: 9864.

180 Minutes 49th BLV, 18 Dec. 1950: NNA, 2.05.117, Foreign Affairs 1945–1954, inv.nr. 21391.

181 Daniël Goedhuis, *Some Recollections of an International Life* [nagelaten herinneringen – collection of the authors] undated.

182 Minutes 55th BLV, 3 sept. 1951: NNA, 2.05.117, Foreign Affairs 1945–1954, inv.nr. 21392.

Guinea, but nevertheless kept a low profile about KLM's desired commercial rights in Sydney.[183]

Still, the conversation had an effect. In December 1952, the restrictions were lifted, although the Australians remained cautious.[184] A possible second weekly flight was out of the question. Not until February 1958 were Dutch negotiators welcome for talks in Canberra, and even then the delegates returned home without results.[185] However, in July 1959 the Australians were ready for renewed discussions, although a second frequency remained beyond reach. Although flying the big DC-8 jet from October 1960, KLM was restricted to a maximum of 42 passengers per week from Amsterdam, a number that was only increased in 1966.[186] KLM therefore chose to operate the service via the polar route through Tokyo and Manila, hoping to return to the time-honored route via India, Singapore and Indonesia at some future point.

Such an opportunity presented itself when Qantas was allowed to start a service to Amsterdam in April 1968. The Australian carrier was encouraged by the more than 147,000 Dutch migrants who had moved to Australia since 1945. Discussions, which opened in April 1969, resulted in permission for a second weekly flight to Sydney in April 1970.[187] Australia also authorized an additional service via Bali, which had been under discussion for several years.

Also on the Dutch wish list was a service to Melbourne. The Hague hoped that the new Liberal Australian government of John Gorton that had taken office in January 1968 would be willing to do business. However, an agreement on this issue remained beyond reach. Canberra was convinced that Qantas' financial trouble at the time left no room for foreign airlines to operate. Lufthansa also fell victim to this concern.[188] It was only after Lufthansa finally received permission for a service to Melbourne that the Australians were willing to talk to KLM again.[189] For the time being restrictions continued to be favored in Canberra, but when the city of Melbourne opened a new airport they needed additional landing fees to offset costs KLM received permission to fly in February 1973.[190]

---

183 Minutes 60th BLV, 16 June 1952: NNA, 2.05.117, Foreign Affairs 1945–1954, inv.nr. 21392.

184 Minutes 63rd BLV, 2 Dec. 1952: NNA, 2.05.117, Foreign Affairs 1945–1954, inv.nr. 21392.

185 Minutes 92nd BLV, 30 June 1958: NNA, 2.05.118, Foreign Affairs 1955–1964, inv.nr. 27493.

186 Minutes 98th BLV, 24 sept. 1959: NNA, 2.05.118, Foreign Affairs 1955–1964, inv.nr. 27493. Minutes 116th BLV, 9 June 1966: NNA, 2.05.313, Foreign Affairs 1965–1974, inv.nr. 25174.

187 Minutes 126th BLV, 19 Nov. 1969: NNA, 2.05.313, Foreign Affairs 1965–1974, inv.nr. 25175.

188 Minutes 131st BLV, 9 June 1971: NNA, 2.05.313, Foreign Affairs 1965–1974, inv.nr. 25175.

189 Minutes 128th BLV, 28 May 1970: NNA, 2.05.313, Foreign Affairs 1965–1974, inv.nr. 25175.

190 Minutes 134th BLV, 6 Apr. 1972: NNA, 2.05.313, Foreign Affairs 1965–1974, inv.nr. 25175.

4 Attempts to Gain a Foothold in China

Despite a decline in bilateral trade with China due to the postwar political and military instability after 1945, KLM began to develop plans for an air service to Shanghai in 1946. A year later, in June 1947, a Dutch delegation, chaired by the envoy in Bangkok, Abraham Steenstra Toussaint, arrived in the city for talks. An accord was quickly reached and in October received Chinese approval.[191] The Netherlands was one of the first countries to conclude a bilateral aviation agreement with China's Nationalist government. The Chinese were the first to make use of it: even before the treaty had been ratified, a DC-4 of China National Aviation Corporation (CNAC) touched down at Batavia's Kemajoran Airport on Sunday 31 August 1947. However, due to the uncertain situation in China, it took until October 1948 to work out the operational details for a reciprocal service from Batavia. In 1949 both KLM and CNAC offered flights to China's trading metropolis, Shanghai, but had to give these up after a few months in April 1949 due to the entanglements of the Chinese civil war.[192]

In October 1949, Mao Zedong proclaimed the new People's Republic of China after the Communists' victory in the civil war. This necessitated a re-evaluation of policy in The Hague. On 27 March 1950, the Netherlands was the 25th country to recognize the People's Republic, simultaneously withdrawing its recognition of the nationalist government.[193] This move was in keeping with the traditional politics of the Netherlands in East Asia, which was primarily based on economic interests: a feat of *Realpolitik* from The Hague that had no Asian friends left after years of fighting the Indonesian nationalists.

Despite the Dutch recognition of the People's Republic, relations remained at a low ebb, largely because of Chinese support for North Korea and Dutch participation in UN operations in the Korean War. Beijing made improved relations dependent on Dutch support of the People's Republic's claim to the Chinese seat in the UN.[194] The Hague was not prepared to go that far. In the 1950s and 1960s, the Netherlands took a noncommittal position at the United Nations whenever the allocation of a seat to the People's Republic was discussed.

---

191 Vincent K.L. Chang, *Forgotten Diplomacy: The Modern Remaking of Dutch-Chinese Relations, 1927–1950* (Leiden: Brill, 2019), p. 303–308.

192 Minutes 32nd BLV, 20 Oct. 1948: NNA, 2.05.117, Foreign Affairs 1945–1954, inv.nr. 21391.

193 Code message Stikker to Nanking and Beijing, 28 March 1950: NNA 2.05.117, Foreign Affairs 1945–1954, inv.nr. 15534.

194 *Jaarboek ministerie van Buitenlandse Zaken 1950–1951* (Den Haag: Staatsdrukkerij, 1951), p. 130.

Nonetheless, KLM maintained an interest in flying to China. Apart from Beijing, the British Crown Colony of Hong Kong was an obvious destination because of long-standing trading contacts. In London, Anglo-Dutch consultations were held to discuss commercial landing rights, but no results were achieved. The case of the People's Republic was no different: a delegation visited Beijing in 1957 but came back empty handed.[195] It was only after visits by several trade missions that relations began to show signs of improvement.[196] For example, between December 1963 and March 1964 the Chinese government chartered two KLM aircraft for state visits to ten African countries friendly with Beijing.[197]

However, the hoped for progress in bilateral relations did not come about. In July 1966, a visit by Chinese engineers to the Netherlands turned into a tragedy when one fell out of the window of the Chinese embassy in The Hague and was taken to hospital by the police. There he was kidnapped by embassy staff and returned to the legation. The man died and The Hague was outraged, expelling the Chinese envoy from the country. In retaliation, Beijing declared the Dutch envoy persona-non-grata. However, the authorities prevented the envoy from leaving China and he remained more or less locked in the building of the Dutch legation for five months.[198] Beijing froze relations and bilateral trade was scaled back.

It wasn't until the end of the 1960s that there seemed to be room for rapprochement. The Dutch envoy in Beijing cautiously probed whether a KLM service might now be discussed. There was some optimism in The Hague that such an air connection could play a role in promoting trade contacts. Luns, previously a custodian of good relations with Taiwan, the island stronghold of the Nationalists, was now willing to reconsider the Dutch noncommittal

195 Letter J. van der Wiel (KLM) to Schaepman (VADV), 12 Oct. 1957: NNA, 2.05.118, Foreign Affairs 1965–1974, inv.nr. 8783. Minutes 87th BLV, 2 Jan. 1957 NNA, 2.05.118, Foreign Affairs 1955–1964, inv.nr. 27493.

196 Letter M.J. Damme to J.J. Derksen (Chargé d'Affaires Beijing), 19 March 1968: NNA 2.05.313, Foreign Affairs 1965–1974, inv.nr. 6144.

197 Letters Chargé d'Affaires A. van der Willigen, 9 and 24 March 1964: NNA, 2.05.118, Foreign Affairs 1965–1974, inv.nr. 8783.

198 Frans-Paul van der Putten, Van semi-kolonie naar economische wereldmacht: China's toepassing van diplomatieke en economische middelen in de betrekkingen met Nederland sinds het einde van de negentiende eeuw, in: J. Thomas Lindblad, Alicia Schrikker (eds.), *Het verre gezicht. Politieke en culturele relaties tussen Nederland, Azië, Afrika en Amerika. Opstellen aangeboden aan prof. dr. Leonard Blussé* (Franeker: Van Wijnen, 2011), p. 380–381.

policy with regard to the United Nations' membership of the People's Republic.[199] This Dutch U-turn took place against the background of an American policy change towards China. After several years of cautious rapprochement, culminating in the so-called ping pong diplomacy of 1971–1972, Washington accepted the Beijing government as China's international representative, in lieu of Taipei.[200] In November 1971, the Netherlands voted in favor of granting the right to a UN seat to the People's Republic. This improved relations, although the hoped-for Chinese response to the landing rights issue did not materialize. In January 1972, a Chinese trade mission visited the Netherlands, resulting in orders for several Dutch businesses in the field of agriculture.[201] As a sign of improved contacts, diplomatic relations were promoted to ambassadorial level. The Hague even issued a carefully worded communiqué that acknowledged that the Netherlands now recognized the Chinese view that Taiwan was part of China.[202]

The Hague hoped that KLM would be able to piggyback on this momentum. After all, China had already developed aviation ties with other Western countries. Normalization of diplomatic relations took place on 16 May 1972 and at the end of the year a Chinese delegation visited the Netherlands. From a Chinese perspective, however, Amsterdam was not an attractive destination for an exchange of landing rights. In mid-1973, a Dutch concept for a bilateral agreement disappeared in an office drawer in Beijing. It was only when a Dutch delegation, led by Minister of Economic Affairs Ruud Lubbers, visited Beijing in November 1973 that contacts were initiated on shipping and air services.[203] In the expectation that progress might be made on this latter point, The Hague again raised the landing rights issue, but without success. China remained closed to Dutch aircraft.

---

199 Office memorandum (nr. 68/70) Foreign Affairs, re. KLM's relations with China, 28 July 1970: Collection Petit, dossiers VADV.

200 See: Nicholas Griffin, *Ping-Pong Diplomacy: The Secret History Behind the Game That Changed the World* (New York: Simon and Shuster, 2014).

201 Note Foreign Affairs re. contacts Netherlands-China, 22 Jan. 1973: NNA, 2.05.313, Foreign Affairs 1965–1974, inv.nr. 11719.

202 Office memo Foreign Affairs re. Taiwan, 1 Nov. 1983: NNA, 2.06.107, Economic Affairs, Directorate-General Foreign Economic Relations (Buitenlandse Economische Betrekkingen: BEB), inv.nr. 4994. Also: Ko Colijn, Paul Rusman, *Het Nederlandse Wapenexportbeleid 1963–1988* (Den Haag: Nijgh en Van Ditmar, 1989), p. 264.

203 Minutes 139th BLV, 21 Nov. 1973, and 140th BLV, 22 Jan. 1974: NNA, 2.05.313, Foreign Affairs 1965–1974, inv.nr. 25176.

5 Against the Odds: Negotiating with the Americans

After four years of talks and with no bilateral agreement in sight, the mood in the Dutch camp was not good by the end of 1949. Action was called for. In The Hague Plesman contended 'that the US government are bound to take a wait-and-see stance on this issue until we slam our fist on the table.' He sent his head of international affairs, Bert Slotemaker, to Washington to exert pressure.[204] Surprisingly, the wider political effects of the Indonesian drama that had unfolded were barely discussed at the Civil Aviation Meeting in The Hague; international politics and the loss of Dutch prestige in the world were not factored in. That there might be a serious power asymmetry between Washington and The Hague, and that this called for caution, was completely lost on Plesman. He was not alone in this. The Dutch perspective did not extend beyond the field of aviation. Policy discussions focused primarily on the effects of Pan-Am's recent takeover of American Overseas Airlines, which changed competitive conditions on the Atlantic air route. The Dutch ambassador in Washington, Eelco van Kleffens, submitted a request to the State Department in April 1950 for a new round of talks. The Dutch goals remained what they had been all along: strengthening KLM's position in New York and procuring commercial rights for services between New York and Curaçao. On the US side, however, the willingness to enter into discussions was minimal. The Dutch discovered that the CAB, not the State Department, where alliance considerations were written in capital letters, was now leading in this matter, and at the CAB the interests of the American air carriers were paramount.[205]

Simply setting a date for the discussions took months. In the end The Hague decided to send its negotiators to Washington without the usual prior diplomatic consultations – a bad idea. They were instructed to submit a proposal to the CAB for an amended KLM permit. The Dutch were convinced that if they pressed hard enough, the CAB would grant more flights to New York, plus a commercial arrangement to operate between New York and Curaçao. At the beginning of May 1951 Slotemaker and Spanjaard landed in Washington in the company of two advisors. They were shocked to find that the CAB flatly refused to address the Dutch agenda. Instead, the CAB negotiators listed rigid demands that had to be met before anything else could be discussed: if the Dutch wanted to continue operations, KLM must give up its existing practice of 6th freedom transport and significantly reduce the frequency of services

204 Minutes 42nd BLV, 6 Dec. 1949: NNA, 2.05.117, Foreign Affairs 1945–1954, inv.nr. 21391.

205 Minutes informal consultations re. Dutch-American aviation relations, 27 Nov. 1950: NNA, 2.05.117, Foreign Affairs 1945–1954, inv.nr. 21391.

between Amsterdam and New York. The number of flights from New York to Curaçao must also be cut by half. On the Dutch side, disbelief bordered on frustration and the delegation was recalled to The Hague forthwith. KLM and Foreign Affairs drew up a joint memorandum which pleaded for American accommodation on the basis of the centuries-long history of ties between the two countries. The Hague hoped to strike the right note with this, but prospects were bleak. The Dutch were still out of favor in Washington. In parallel discussions with the Netherlands over the procurement of training aircraft in the context of NATO, America used its Mutual Defense Aid Program to kill the prospects of export orders for the Dutch Fokker S-14 jet trainer.[206] The new Dutch ambassador, Herman van Roijen, was convinced that there was no other option for the Netherlands than to 'keep up the fight'. After all, it was conceivable that at some future point better results might be possible.[207] None of this was easy. Despite his best efforts, Van Roijen's consultations with the State Department at the end of 1951 did not produce anything beyond freezing the status quo for KLM for a period of three years.

Parties reconvened in 1954. From the outset prospects for the Netherlands were not encouraging. At the behest of PanAm and TWA, the CAB had in the intervening years dug in further in its opposition to the growing practice of 6th freedom transport by airlines from the smaller European countries. For KLM, this operating practice was vital: 65–75 per cent of passengers on the service to New York had started their journey outside the Netherlands.[208] Passenger transport on the Atlantic route, and hence financial interest, was increasing at a tremendous pace: growing 45 per cent in 1952 and another 23 per cent in 1953.[209]

Given the CAB's strong objections to 6th freedom carriage generally, and KLM's commercial conduct specifically, it was not surprising that the Dutch initiatives to improve KLM's position yielded no results. Even the oft-repeated argument that KLM was one of the main foreign customers of the American aircraft industry failed to open any doors. The 1951 scenario appeared to repeat itself. After a few exploratory talks, Washington postponed actual negotiations. Hoping to effect a breakthrough, The Hague came up with a proposal to link the KLM case to other bilateral trade issues. This, however, was risky and it was

206 Marc Dierikx, *Uit de lucht gegrepen. Fokker als Nederlandse droom, 1945–1996* (Amsterdam: Boom, 2004), p. 70–71.

207 Minutes 52nd and 53rd BLV, 9 and 14 June 1951: NNA, 2.05.117, Foreign Affairs 1945–1954, inv.nr. 21392.

208 Minutes 74th BLV, 23 Sept. 1954: NNA, 2.05.117, Foreign Affairs 1945–1954, inv.nr. 21393.

209 KLM *Annual Report 1952*, p. 10. KLM *Annual Report 1953*, p. 12.

abandoned as it might make aviation an exchange object at other negotiating tables, which could exert even more unfavorable pressure on KLM's interests.[210] It was painful to acknowledge that after years of talking, there was still no way of applying pressure in Washington. Meanwhile, the Americans were handing out landing rights to airlines in other countries in Western Europe, including Lufthansa, BOAC, SAS and Air France – just not to KLM. When visiting Washington in October 1955, Luns and Van Roijen did not even get beyond handing over a note to John Foster Dulles that sought to link Dutch aviation interests to the international situation around the world, which should also concern the Americans:

> The position of KLM, which contributes to the strengthening of Western European Economy, can only be maintained by giving KLM the opportunity to intensify and enlarge its activities. Freedom of air traffic to the United States enables the Netherlands to earn dollars, thus strengthening its economic position in the Western Bloc, which fits in with United States post-war foreign policy.
>
> It goes without saying that the leadership of the United States with regard to a liberal economic foreign policy influences the attitude of other states in this sector and a restrictive air policy would lead to similar repercussions in other countries – a fact which has already manifested itself in various cases. Freedom of air traffic will bind the peoples of the free world and create and preserve friendship, whereas a restrictive policy will cause disunity.
>
> Last but not least, the Netherlands Government wishes to draw particular attention to the fact that in times of international emergency KLM's organization totaling 14,000 men and 97 aircraft would be a considerable asset to the free world. The manner in which Netherlands civil aviation could best be utilized in time of emergency is being studied.[211]

It all made little impression. In the larger game of international politics, the Dutch interests were of minor importance to Washington. It appeared to some in the cabinet, including Prime Minister Willem Drees, that the US was increasingly hostile towards the Netherlands.[212] The Hague could not accept this. Indeed, Dutch-American relations were fraught with difficulties

210 Minutes 80th BLV, 17 July 1955: NNA, 2.05.118, Foreign Affairs 1955–1964, inv.nr. 27493.

211 Memorandum Van Roijen to Dulles, 7 Oct. 1955: US National Archives, State Department, Record Group 59, 611.5694/10-755.

212 Kersten, *Luns. Een politieke biografie* (Amsterdam: Boom, 2010), p. 215.

emanating from the conflict with Indonesia. Unperturbed, KLM now placed commercial landing rights in Chicago and in Houston on its wish list, destinations it hoped to incorporate into the flight schedule of the service to Mexico City. And since Lufthansa, BOAC, SAS and Air France had recently been granted rights in Los Angeles, KLM wanted these as well. To bring more pressure to bear, Aler and Slotemaker flew to the United States. Prince Bernhard, consort to Queen Juliana, was also called upon to help, but he too failed to deliver. The Hague therefore tried to bring in publicity. After the press had been briefed on the issue at the end of 1955, the country's largest newspaper, *De Telegraaf*, began to closely monitor the landing rights controversy, devoting its front page to the matter on Monday 16 January 1956.[213] Other national newspapers followed. In the United States, the *New York Times* covered the topic. The aviation issue thus became a test case for Dutch-American relations. The Hague labelled the denial of landing rights a deliberate obstruction to KLM.[214]

Against this background, it was not surprising that the Dutch delegation in Washington once again came back empty handed. On 26 April 1956, Luns summoned US Ambassador H. Freeman Matthews to complain about American protectionism, saying his government was 'deeply disappointed'.[215] On both sides, incomprehension reigned. In a conversation with Van Roijen, Dulles indicated that the Dutch lacked all sense of realism. With the end of the Korean War, fears of a major global conflict had waned. Could the United States then be blamed for promoting its own national interests in this situation? In The Hague spirits sank.[216] It wasn't until the summer of 1956 that the talks continued. The atmosphere at the negotiating table was as tense as ever, especially because the Dutch still had no results to show for their efforts. Statements of support from local Chambers of Commerce in Los Angeles and in Houston in favor of KLM appeared to have an adverse effect. The frustrations on the Dutch side increased further. In The Hague, the Civil Aviation Meeting contemplated possible countermeasures, including suspension of the ratification of the Dutch-American Treaty of Friendship, Trade and Shipping, concluded

---

213 Reporting in *De Telegraaf*, 16 Jan. 1956 [front page].

214 Memorandum Van Roijen to State Department, 13 Dec. 1955: US National Archives, State Department, RG 59, 611.5694/12-1355.

215 Code message Matthews to State Department, 26 Apr. 1956: US National Archives, State Department, RG 59, 611.5694/4-2656.

216 Memorandum of conversation Van Roijen with Dulles, 25 June 1956: US National Archives, State Department, RG 59, 611.7256/6-2556. Rimko van der Maar, Hans Meijer, *Herman van Roijen, 1905–1991. Een diplomaat van klasse* (Amsterdam: Boom, 2013), p. 302–303.

on 27 March 1956.[217] Luns went so far as to recall Ambassador Van Roijen from Washington for consultations.

It was decided, as the Scandinavian countries had done previously, to send a cabinet-level delegation for the next round of talks. To make sure the Americans understood the weight The Hague attached to the landing rights, Queen Juliana even referred to the aviation issue in her annual speech that opened the parliamentary year in September 1956. This was an additional signal that patience had evaporated in The Hague. At the behest of State Secretary of Foreign Affairs Ernst van der Beugel, the cabinet indeed decided to put the ratification of the Dutch-American Friendship Treaty on hold and delay its parliamentary process.[218] This was considered a signal that could not be ignored. Even so, it took until March 1957 before further negotiations got under way. Van der Beugel, with a personal letter from Prime Minister Drees to President Eisenhower in his pocket, acted as head of the delegation. He was reluctant to commit himself to the task at hand, as the subject was 'not his thing'.[219] To exert additional public pressure, Dutch national newspapers reported on the departure of the negotiators and followed developments closely. Prior to the delegation's departure on 15 March, Van der Beugel outlined the Dutch starting position to US under-secretary of State Christian Herter:

> [The Netherlands is] confronted with a difficult psychological fact of being reduced from a very large empire to a very small metropolitan country. This has tended to increase in the minds of the Dutch people the importance of symbolic indications of Dutch access to the greater world. KLM is one of these symbols. All of these are factors in leading the Dutch government and people to the conviction that the conclusion of a satisfactory air transport agreement is a test to US-Dutch friendship.[220]

Although Van der Beugel privately held doubts on the effectiveness of the Dutch approach, he pulled out all the stops, putting much weight on the fact that KLM had recently bought new American airliners that now needed to earn their keep, an argument that The Hague resorted to over and over, countering American pleas for what Washington called an equitable exchange of

217 Minutes 84th BLV, 20 July 1956: NNA, 2.05.118, Foreign Affairs 1955–1964, inv.nr. 27493.

218 Memorandum Van der Beugel, 10 Sep. 1956: NNA, 2.05.118, Foreign Affairs 1955–1964, inv. nr. 27515.

219 Albertine Bloemendal, *Reframing the diplomat: Ernst van der Beugel and the Cold War Atlantic Community* (Leiden: Brill, 2018) [diss. Leiden, 2017], p. 116–117.

220 Memorandum of Conversation under-secretary of State Christian Herter with Van der Beugel, 8 March 1957: US National Archives, State Department, RG 59, 611.5694/3–1357.

economic benefits. The Dutch position was that KLM should have landing rights in Los Angeles, like its European competitors. Nonetheless, Van der Beugel failed to win his goals. He later remembered how KLM settled for Houston instead, the most the Americans had been willing to offer. The Council of Ministers in The Hague then had to drop Los Angeles in order to avoid further damage to bilateral relations that would result from a break-up of the talks.[221] Two days later, and after a conversation with John Foster Dulles on 3 April, Van der Beugel grudgingly signed the agreement put in front of him by Assistant Secretary of State for Economic Affairs Thorsten Kalijarvi. After 12 years of fruitless pleas, at least KLM's rights were now finally secured in an air transport agreement. For his part, Kalijarvi made a gesture of goodwill and also approved the desired service between New York and Curaçao.[222] It was the maximum result possible. President Eisenhower signed the agreement the same day, but a small storm of protest erupted in Congress, sparked by the American airline industry, which had opposed an extension of KLM rights for years. In a poorly attended Senate meeting, a motion was passed restricting presidential authority on international aviation matters.[223] The Dutch issue was, however, allowed to pass. Van der Beugel was moderately satisfied upon his return to Schiphol Airport, although he thought it wise to 'let the storm subside before we show our faces again.' In his opinion, the Dutch desperately needed 'a better hand of cards in future.'[224] In The Hague the cabinet rushed the treaty through parliament as a matter of priority.

Still, the failure to obtain rights on the US West Coast remained a concern and an annoyance in The Hague. Hope remained that future developments might provide an opening. Various attempts were made to develop an initiative to contact Washington about this, but results were not forthcoming. Several KLM delegations visited Washington in the hope of letting things settle. In 1959 ambassador Van Roijen made another attempt, but the State Department did not budge. The practice of 6th freedom transport stood in the way of any progress.[225] On the other side, the Dutch resentment about the deadlock ran deep. On 9 February 1960, the Lower Chamber of Parliament even passed a motion calling on the government to 'take renewed steps to obtain a review of the

221 Interview Rob Meines and Albert Kersten with Ernst van der Beugel, 1996: NNA, 2.21.183.08, collection Van der Beugel, inv.nr. 63, p.402.

222 Giles Scott-Smith, David J. Snyder, A Test of Sentiments: Civil Aviation, Alliance Politics, and the KLM Challenge in Dutch-American Relations, in: *Diplomatic History* Vol. 37 (2013) nr. 5, p. 917–945.

223 Air-Pact Curbs on Ike Are Voted, in: *The Washington Post*, 5 Apr. 1957.

224 *Het Vaderland*, 12 Apr. 1957.

225 Minutes 96th BLV, 5 May 1959: NNA, 2.05.117, Foreign Affairs 1945–1954, inv.nr. 27494.

US decision.' The Chamber unanimously expressed its deep disappointment at the attitude adopted by the United States Government, which was qualified as a denial of the freedom of air traffic and of the principles of healthy competition.[226] The Hague therefore pinned its hopes on a Democratic victory in the 1960 US presidential election. The idea was that a Democratic president could potentially create new perspectives.

In the hope that his diplomatic skills might push things along, as they had in 1957, Van der Beugel was appointed as the new president of KLM in June 1961. Preparations for his move from politics to corporate interests had been in the works since December 1958. Even before his term at KLM started, he was on the plane to the US to talk to officials. A Dutch negotiating team, headed by State Secretary for Traffic and Water Management Eddie Stijkel, had already been in Washington for weeks, hoping to achieve a breakthrough, but once again an accord on landing rights remained out of sight. Van der Beugel's mission was not made any easier when Stijkel broke off the talks and boarded the next flight home without any results to show for his efforts.[227] Van der Beugel also returned empty-handed. Worse, bilateral relations were again under increasing pressure because of American opposition to the Dutch policy in New Guinea. In Washington, it was even being suggested that the two issues should be linked, making a concession to KLM regarding Los Angeles dependent on a Dutch compromise over New Guinea.[228] Meanwhile, KLM's finances were on a downward track, largely due to the acquisition of new jet aircraft and the ensuing overcapacity in the international airline industry. Before long the Dutch national carrier also had a crisis in the board room to deal with. Differences over the company's strategy, highlighted in a devastating McKinsey report on the airline's management, resulted in the resignation of Van der Beugel and almost all the other executives in December 1962. While the airline tried to sort out its internal problems, the issue of West Coast landing rights temporarily sank behind the horizon.[229]

The situation only began to improve against the background of the 1964 Tokyo Olympics. At the behest of the State of Alaska, KLM and the CAB entered into discussions on commercial landing rights in Anchorage. Alaska was hoping to gain a share of the growth in air traffic to East Asia. In addition to KLM,

226 *Handelingen der Staten-Generaal*, 1959–1960, Tweede Kamer, Verslag, 9 Feb. 1960. Also: *Het Parool*, 9 Febr. 1960 [front page].

227 *Het Parool*, 26 May 1961. Bloemendal, *Reframing the diplomat*, p. 117.

228 Scott-Smith, Snyder, A Test of Sentiments, p. 937.

229 Dierikx, *Blauw in de lucht*, p. 187–195. Bloemendal, *Reframing the diplomat*, p. 130–132.

which already made a stop in Anchorage on the route to Tokyo to take on fuel, Alaska handed out rights to Lufthansa, Air France and SAS. In January 1965, the parties reached agreement and KLM received commercial rights in Anchorage for transportation to and from Amsterdam.[230] Los Angeles was still at the top of the Dutch wish list, however. Knowing full well that this might still be out of the question, KLM expanded its aims to include landing rights in Chicago. Even the diplomats thought this was pushing things too far. At the Ministry of Foreign Affairs traffic advisor Siem Nieuwenhuijsen saw no realistic opportunities for flights to the Windy City, given the American policy of 'equitable exchange of economic benefits' that had now been in place for more than ten years and which left no room to meet Dutch wishes. Moreover, the Americans continued to demand precise figures on the exact nature of KLM's passenger traffic in order to evaluate 6th freedom carriage. For KLM, and thus for The Hague, this was not negotiable.[231] Thus both the West Coast and Chicago remained off limits. Washington made it known that it did not wish to talk about this anytime soon.

In the years that followed Luns repeatedly returned to the case, which finally resulted in informal discussions held in Washington in September 1968. By this time Chicago, the third most populous city in the United States, had become the center of these conversations. In previous years, KLM had promoted Dutch interests by fostering contacts at the municipal level. For a permission to fly to Chicago, KLM was even willing to sacrifice its existing rights in Miami. Three months later, in early December, Luns again referred to the issue during his farewell visit to outgoing President Lyndon Johnson. But if he had hoped the president would hand him the landing rights as a parting gift, he was disappointed.[232]

An unexpected new opportunity to revisit the Chicago issue presented itself early in 1969. In his first European visit, the newly elected President Richard Nixon had not included the Netherlands and Luxembourg – the only two EEC members that were not on his itinerary. Luns, who had suffered significant political damage due to his long-term support for the American war effort in Vietnam, immediately made a scene. To make amends, Nixon invited Luns and Prime Minister Piet de Jong to the White House as his first European visitors on 27 May. However, this did not erase the memory of insult. Indeed, Luns

---

230 *De Volkskrant*, 27-01-1965 [front page].

231 Minutes 111th BLV, 3 Feb. 1965: NNA, 2.05.313, Foreign Affairs 1965–1974, inv.nr. 25174.

232 Kersten, *Luns*, p. 429.

'cherished his grievances', as he called it. Prior to the meeting, he hinted that he expected not to leave the White House empty-handed.[233] De Jong later said:

> I do remember that play: Nixon was with Kissinger and Mr. Schürmann was our ambassador at the time and Luns and I … and we advocated landing rights for KLM in Chicago, among other things. That didn't work out very well at the time, but in the evening there was that dinner at The White House and Nixon had asked me beforehand, to have a drink with him in his room on my own. And up we went and there he said 'those landing rights, that will be all right'. And we went to the table and I quickly said to Mr Luns 'it's in the bag, we have the landing rights in Chicago.' And everyone happy and busy. And a fortnight later, Luns came to me and said, 'Well Piet, now there's something weird: it's a telegram for you and it says if you can please roll back those landing rights, because it turns out he was actually unauthorized to give them.' That there was an autonomous committee in America, which was about landing rights and not Nixon at all. And we – I said, 'Joseph, I can't, I won't. Just make a telegram saying I'm sorry, but a promise is a promise and I'll keep him to his word.' And so: those landing rights materialized.[234]

In any case, Luns and De Jong felt that the aviation issue should be considered in the larger political framework of bilateral relations. In order to cover himself Nixon, prompted by National Security Advisor Henri Kissinger who entertained informal contacts with Van der Beugel via a back channel, stated that the matter would have to be formally negotiated, although the outcome was certain in advance. Thus, the Dutch 'negotiators' sat down in Washington on 14 July to sign the agreement four days later. Discussions also touched on the transfer of American nuclear technology to the Dutch navy, but on this topic no agreement was reached.[235] From 19 May 1970, KLM flew to Chicago three times a week. The KLM service between Curaçao and Miami was terminated.[236]

This did not end all the controversies, however. In the period up to 1974, the number of seats per aircraft increased due to the commissioning of the new, very large Boeing 747 Jumbo Jet, which meant that the average seat occupancy

233 Kersten, *Luns*, p. 432–435. Bloemendal, *Reframing the diplomat*, p. 188–192.

234 Transcript speech Piet de Jong at the presentation of the Luns biography, The Hague, Nieuwspoort, 25 March 2010: http://nos.nl/artikel/146291-biografie-van-een-goddelijke-nederlander.html [2023].

235 Kersten, *Luns*, p. 430–435. Scott-Smith, Snyder, A Test of Sentiments, p. 917–945.

236 Minutes 126th BLV, 19 Nov. 1969: NNA, 2.05.313, Foreign Affairs 1965–1974, inv.nr. 25175.

rate on board airliners decreased. KLM was no exception. Fares and timetables came under increasing pressure. What added to growing concern was the fact that between 1968 and 1973 the share of charter traffic in transatlantic passenger traffic increased from 8.6 to 26.3 percent.[237] On the US side, PanAm and TWA went through years of loss-making operations. In the United States, market share became the backbone of aviation policy.[238]

6 Developments in South America

Not only in North, but also in South America, things did not go the way The Hague would have liked, as indigenous developments affected many of the opportunities pursued by the Dutch. In Argentina, an amalgamation of the existing airlines in 1949 led to the creation of a new national carrier. Aerolíneas Argentinas was set up as a branch of the Ministry of Transport, itself a government department under military supervision.[239] The Perón government fostered the development of aviation as means to demonstrate Argentine modernity, culminating in a new sense of national bonding.[240] For KLM, it meant headwinds at a time when the market for air transport to Buenos Aires was expanding.[241]

There were headwinds in Brazil too. Rio discovered that KLM picked up about 78 per cent of its passengers at stops along the way from Amsterdam. This was not in the spirit of the International Air Transport Agreement signed in Chicago in 1944, the clauses of which implied that such 5th freedom carriage should be marginal.[242] Rio therefore questioned the need for twice weekly services. The discussion about this was particularly difficult, because KLM also operated 35 so-called 'separate flights' to Brazil (outside its official

---

237 IATA figures. For backgrounds, see: Peter J. Lyth, Marc L.J. Dierikx, From privilege to popularity. The growth of leisure air travel since 1945, in: *Journal of Transport History* 15(1994) nr. 2, p. 97–116.

238 H.A. Wassenbergh, *Public International Air Transportation Law in a New Era. Economic Regulation of International Air Carrier Operations* (Deventer: Kluwer, 1976), p. 51ff.

239 Minutes 44th BLV, 10 March 1950: NNA, 2.05.117, Foreign Affairs 1945–1954, inv.nr. 21391. Marc J. Alsina, Aviation for the People: Class and State Aviation in Perón's 'New Argentina' 1946–55, in: *Technology and Culture*, Volume 63, Nr. 1, January 2022, p. 153–181 (p. 176).

240 Melina Piglia, Carry our colors and defend our interests under the skies of other Continents. Argentinian Commercial aviation policy in the Peronista decade (Argentina 1945–1955), in: *Journal of Transport History* 40(2019)nr. 1, p. 44–61.

241 KLM *Annual Report 1949*, p.6.

242 Alan Dobson, *A History of International Civil Aviation. From its Origins through Transformative Evolution* (London: Routledge, 2017), p. 52–57.

flight schedule) that were routed through Rome and for which mainly Italian passengers booked passage. Faced with criticism The Hague adopted a low profile, hoping that Brazilian criticism would blow over without harming KLM's position. Nonetheless, the threat that KLM would have to reduce its services hovered above bilateral contacts for years. In the interest of good relations KLM tried to favor the Brazilians by offering second-hand aircraft at bargain prices. Brazilian aircraft were also offered a discount in KLM's workshops at Schiphol.[243]

Meanwhile, demand for air transport increased as Brazil and Argentina prospered and gradually became more important as trading partners through their food exports to Europe.[244] Argentinian bilateral trade with the Netherlands showed a significant surplus.[245] Perón in particular wished to strengthen the Argentine position on the air route across the Atlantic. In December 1950 Aerolíneas Argentinas began its own European service, to Frankfurt. The Douglas DC-6 used was overhauled by KLM in Amsterdam.[246]

In 1952, several European airlines set about expanding their South American operations, receiving the necessary permissions to extend their routes to Santiago de Chile. KLM wanted to do the same, but encountered opposition in both Rio and Buenos Aires.[247] In Rio, dormant objections to the twice weekly KLM flights stirred back to life – a cause for concern in The Hague. For its part, Argentina demanded that European airlines charge higher fares than Aerolíneas Argentinas for transport between Argentina and neighboring countries. The Dutch considered this a reasonable request, because the trunk services used larger, more comfortable aircraft.[248] Nonetheless, in the civil aviation meeting Plesman was of the opinion that bilateral consultations on the issue should be avoided as long as possible. Negotiations in South America could only cause damage, since the economic rationale of KLM's services was 5th freedom traffic. The Hague aimed for an underhand compromise, which might also take

243 Minutes 44th BLV, 10 March 1950: NNA, 2.05.117, Foreign Affairs 1945–1954, inv.nr. 21391.

244 Personal letter Kleyn Molekamp to Secretary-General Han Boon (16 Feb. 1951): NNA, 2.05.117 BZ 1945–1954, inv.nr. 2351.

245 Trade statistics attached to letter Director-General BEB to Minister of Economic Affairs, 31 Aug. 1951: NNA, 2.05.117 BZ 1945–1954, inv.nr. 24355.

246 Minutes 44th BLV, 10 March 1950: NNA, 2.05.117, Foreign Affairs 1945–1954, inv.nr. 21391.

247 Code message Beyen to Embassy in Rio, 3 Nov. 1952: NNA, 2.05.117, Foreign Affairs 1945–1954, inv.nr. 9867.

248 Minutes 62nd BLV, 8 Oct. 1952. H.A. Wassenbergh, *Post War International Civil Aviation Policy and the law of the air* (The Hague: Martinus Nijhoff, 1957), p. 25.

account of general trading interests.[249] This approach worked. Towards the end of 1952 the Chilean government granted KLM a ten-year license to operate a scheduled service to Santiago de Chile.[250]

While Buenos Aires went along with this, Rio fretted over 5th freedom rights. Yet the stop in Rio was vital for KLM. A direct service from the Netherlands to Santiago precluded profitable operations. In April 1953 KLM again asked its advisor Osvaldo Aranha to mediate.[251] Given that Aranha's name was circulating in connection with a new position in the cabinet at the time, there was hope that a solution could be reached through him. Aranha conferred with Brazilian President Getúlio Vargas and others.[252] However, despite his efforts, Brazil only allowed the KLM service for a probation period of six months. If KLM managed to increase the sale of 3rd and 4th freedom tickets between Amsterdam and Rio, the second frequency might be maintained, however.[253] In the end the case was settled with money, as happened often: KLM proposed to pay all Brazilian airlines a bonus for tickets sold for its services south of Rio. KLM also offered a Lockheed Super Constellation for sale on favorable terms, as well as four of its Convair aircraft.[254]

Thus, an agreement was reached. To celebrate, the Brazilian Aviation Minister, Álvaro Pereira de Souza Lima, offered the Dutch negotiators Daniël Goedhuis, Consul General Jan Voûte and Henri Wassenbergh of KLM, a trip in his private plane to the newly built capital, Brasilia. The plan was to fly early in the morning and make most of the day. After lunch in Brasilia, the company would then return to Rio. But on the flight out the aircraft suffered engine failure over a mountainous, forested area. The captain broadcast a mayday distress signal and made an emergency landing in a clearing in the jungle. One of the wings and an engine tore off. Miraculously, there was no fire and no one was injured. However, the cabin door was jammed. In a panic, Goedhuis tried to kick in a window, but without success. Luckily, the crash landing had also made in a hole in the cabin's ceiling, allowing everyone to clamber out. After some time, another airplane passed low overhead and dropped a message that

249 Minutes 65th BLV, 1 Apr. 1953: NNA, 2.05.117, Foreign Affairs 1945–1954, inv.nr. 21392. Letter H.I. Borel Rinkes to Slotemaker, 18 Apr. 1953: NNA, 2.05.117, Foreign Affairs 1945–1954, inv. nr. 9867.

250 Code message Beyen to Rio, 7 July 1953: NNA, 2.05.117, Foreign Affairs 1945–1954, inv.nr. 9867.

251 Minutes 65th BLV, 1 Apr. 1953: NNA, 2.05.117, Foreign Affairs 1945–1954, inv.nr. 21392.

252 Minutes 66th BLV, 4 June 1953: NNA, 2.05.117, Foreign Affairs 1945–1954, inv.nr. 21392.

253 Minutes 69th BLV, 20 Jan. 1954: NNA, 2.05.117, Foreign Affairs 1945–1954, inv.nr. 21393.

254 Code message Luns to Rio, 2 May 1953: NNA, 2.05.117, Foreign Affairs 1945–1954, inv.nr. 9867.

an ambulance was waiting for the company at the bottom of the mountain where the plane had crashed. Although none were dressed for adventure, the passengers and crew were forced to make their way down on foot. They eventually managed to reach a farm, where the owner had horses available. Hours passed before the men, uncomfortable on horseback and harassed by vultures, reached the road where the ambulance was waiting.[255] Brasilia thus remained unseen, but the promised temporary permit for KLM stood, albeit without 5th freedom rights. In order to reward the Brazilians, several authorities who visited the Netherlands received royal decorations.

Relations as such remained complicated. Brazil, like Argentina, developed problems with foreign payments and erected barriers that made it hard to convert locally earned currency into dollars. Foreign airlines thus faced difficulties, which made the issues over KLM's 5th and 6th freedom carriage resurface. KLM quietly tried to disguise its 6th freedom sales and boost statistics on the Amsterdam-Rio route by registering flight segments separately. A passenger travelling from Frankfurt to Rio would get two tickets: Frankfurt-Amsterdam and Amsterdam-Rio. This was the same approach that KLM used in its dealings with the US authorities.[256]

This satisfied Rio only partially. The Dutch were, however, helped by a reshuffle in the Brazilian government and the civil service that followed the suicide of President Getúlio Vargas in August 1954.[257] Vargas had pursued a nationalist policy, stimulating and protecting domestic industries over foreign investments. His death brought new interlocutors to the table on the Brazilian side, who in December 1954 agreed that KLM could make an extra stopover in São Paulo. Even so, foreign companies continued to suffer from restrictions. In order to preserve SAS's rights, the Scandinavian governments had to promise to import large quantities of coffee to offset Brazilian concessions in air transport.[258] The Dutch did not need to resort to coffee imports, however. Their outlook improved when KLM President Alphons Aler visited Brazil in October 1956. He apparently managed to strike the right note in Rio, because suddenly even a third frequency seemed possible. KLM was also granted permission to move the Brazilian terminus of one of its services from Rio de Janeiro to São Paulo.[259]

---

255 Goedhuis, *Some Recollections of an International Life* [authors' collection].

256 Minutes 76th BLV, 7 Dec. 1954: NNA, 2.05.117, Foreign Affairs 1945–1954, inv.nr. 21393.

257 Minutes 75th BLV, 2 Nov. 1954: NNA, 2.05.117, Foreign Affairs 1945–1954, inv.nr. 21393.

258 Minutes 78th BLV, 28 March 1955: NNA, 2.05.118, Foreign Affairs 1955–1964, inv.nr. 27493.

259 Minutes 86th BLV, 23 Oct. 1956. Letter Dutch ambassador to the Brazilian minister José Carlos Macedo Soares, 18 March 1957: NNA, 2.05.118, Foreign Affairs 1955–1964, inv.nr. 8664.

Dutch aviation relations with Argentina were on par with those with Brazil. A decline in exports resulted in foreign currency shortages and a realignment of Argentine international debt. This, in turn, caused payment problems that also affected KLM's operations.[260] Meanwhile, Perón saw his authority, and that of his government, wane in several scandals and incidents that led to a military coup against him in which he was deposed in 1955. The ensuing disruption in the Argentine government meant that a decision on a third weekly KLM service took time to mature. Argentina preferred air services from Latin American airlines and put the Dutch request on hold. Air France and Alitalia suffered the same fate.[261] Then, in 1958, Argentina indicated that it wanted to grant KLM additional traffic rights after all. It was an offer made against the background of the negotiations with several Western European countries, including the Netherlands, on the refinancing of Argentine foreign debt, talks that had gone on for several years.[262]

A new round of negotiations with Brazil also followed in November 1959. To their relief, the Dutch managed to achieve a satisfactory result, although the delegation had arrived in Rio virtually empty-handed. Building on personal relationships, KLM was now allowed to carry a fair share of 5th freedom transport on its twice weekly flights.[263] The Brazilians accepted the Dutch argument that the geographical position of the Netherlands and the nature of KLM's activities meant that no 'hard' figures could be given to the 3rd and 4th freedom passengers (which meant that KLM was allowed to hide its 6th freedom passengers) .[264]

However, new problems presented themselves in 1960. With the introduction of the new Boeing 707 and Douglas DC-8 jets, airlines saw a sharp increase in aircraft seat capacity. This led Brazil and Argentina to renegotiate the permits for KLM services.[265] On 14 November 1961, Brazil terminated the aviation agreement with the Netherlands. Here, too, the broader framework of trade played a role. Brazil accused the EEC of pursuing an overly restrictive trade policy when it came to imports of raw materials, and aviation was one of the areas

260 Letter Dutch Ambassador London to Foreign Affairs, 17 Feb. 1956 (attached summary of conversation): NNA, 2.05.118, Foreign Affairs 1955–1964, inv.nr. 11526.

261 Letter W.A. Gordinou de Gouberville (KLM representative Buenos Aires) to KLM The Hague, 7 March 1957: NNA, 2.05.118, Foreign Affairs 1955–1964, inv.nr. 8660.

262 Code message Embassy Buenos Aires to Foreign Affairs, 14 Feb. 1964: NNA, 2.05.118, Foreign Affairs 1955–1964, inv.nr. 11528.

263 Minutes 99th BLV, 2 Dec. 1959: NNA, 2.05.117, Foreign Affairs 1945–1954, inv.nr. 27494.

264 Letter VADV to Goedhuis, 4 Jan. 1960: NNA, 2.05.118, Foreign Affairs 1955–1964, inv.nr. 8664.

265 Letter Francisco Clementino de San Tiago Dantas to Ambassador Lewe van Aduard, 14 Nov. 1961: NNA, 2.05.118, Foreign Affairs 1955–1964, inv.nr. 8664.``

which lent themselves to counter measures.[266] Although a compromise on the aviation issues was reached under which KLM received the right to operate the DC-8, KLM saw its flights to Rio cut to one per week. On this basis, the prospects for a successful development of the service were dubious.[267] Added to this, Brazil's aviation policy was becoming more restrictive. In neighboring Argentina, the situation was only marginally better. Here too KLM lost its second weekly frequency and Buenos Aires objected to the KLM practice of offering 5th freedom transport between cities in South America.[268] The Brazilians also made a point of this. Consultations on operating a second weekly flight therefore only began in 1968. To effect a positive outcome, pressure was exerted on The Hague to raise their imports of Brazilian coffee, as the Brazilians had managed previously in the case of SAS.[269]

In the talks with Argentina the broader area of trade was also a recurring point. By the late 1960s, the Netherlands, like the other EEC members, faced a trade deficit with Argentina. One of the ways to mitigate this was an expansion of KLM landing rights. Negotiations were, however, hampered by changes in the Argentine cabinet in 1968.[270] Undeterred, the Dutch reviewed the history of the aviation relation with Argentina, to discover that Buenos Aires had, in effect, promised KLM a future second frequency in 1948.[271] Obviously, the Dutch referred to these promises, but the negative development of the Argentine peso, which went through repeated devaluations, prevented a solution.[272] The matter was overtaken by discussions on the sale of Fokker F27 and F28 passenger aircraft to Argentina, which took precedence in The Hague.[273] However, in 1970 a new round of bilateral air transport negotiations took place. The Dutch managed to land the desired second frequency in the summer of that year, referring to the promises made in 1948.[274] Nonetheless, because Brazil did

266 Letter Lewe van Aduard to Foreign Affairs, 12 Dec. 1961: NNA, 2.05.118, Foreign Affairs 1955–1964, inv.nr. 8664. Minutes 103rd BLV, 20 Dec. 1961: NNA, 2.05.117, Foreign Affairs 1945–1954, inv.nr. 27494.

267 Minutes 105th BLV, 14 Nov. 1962: NNA, 2.05.117, Foreign Affairs 1945–1954, inv.nr. 27494.

268 Minutes 109th BLV, 30 June 1964: NNA, 2.05.117, Foreign Affairs 1945–1954, inv.nr. 27494.

269 Minutes 121st BLV, 8 Jan. 1968: NNA, 2.05.313, Foreign Affairs 1965–1974, inv.nr. 25174.

270 Code message Hagenaar to Foreign Affairs, 19 March 1968: NNA, 2.05.313, Foreign Affairs 1965–1974, inv.nr. 5326.

271 Office memorandum VADV, 27 Sep. 1968: NNA, 2.05.313, Foreign Affairs 1965–1974, inv.nr. 5326.

272 Letter Ambassador Schoch to Foreign Affairs, 4 Sep. 1970: NNA, 2.05.313, Foreign Affairs 1965–1974, inv.nr. 7909.

273 Code message Ambassador Hagenaar to Foreign Affairs, 15 Apr. 1969: NNA, 2.05.313, Foreign Affairs 1955–1964, inv.nr. 5326.

274 Minutes 128th BLV, 28 May 1970: NNA, 2.05.313, Foreign Affairs 1965–1974, inv.nr. 25175.

not allow a second commercial stop in Rio until the end of 1973, it took a long time before the flights generated revenues.[275] Only after the Brazilian airline VARIG announced plans in 1973 to open a service to Amsterdam did a new perspective appear on the horizon.

7 Hurdles on the Route to Southern Africa

By the end of the 1940s, the KLM service to Johannesburg had come under South African scrutiny because of irritations that surfaced when KLM increased its flight schedule without consulting the South African authorities. Beyond the sphere of aviation, other differences also played out. Pretoria's efforts to regulate imports and exports met with criticism from The Hague and relations suffered, which also affected aviation. In South Africa, official displeasure focused on KLM's operations that relied on 5th and 6th freedom transport. Pretoria was not pleased when it learned that KLM was in the market for transport rights between Livingstone (Zambia) and Johannesburg.[276] In addition, South Africa objected to KLM's commercial stops in Rome. In 1950, South African Airways (SAA) and BOAC also operated to the Italian capital, which created a clear conflict of interests. At first government officials in The Hague did not worry too much about such grievances, as the Dutch aloofness at the United Nations regarding condemnation of Prime Minister Daniël Malan's government's racial segregation policy had engendered sympathy in Pretoria.[277]

However, during the course of 1950, South Africa began to exert pressure to cut back KLM's landing rights. The issue was repeatedly discussed at the diplomatic level, with the Dutch trying to soothe and maintain the status quo. At the same time South Africa continued to be in the spotlight at the UN General Assembly. Pretoria needed some degree of sympathy from the Dutch in the shape of abstaining from the votes condemning Pretoria's racial policies.[278] A Dutch-South African cultural accord was under discussion that underlined the

275 Minutes 130th BLV, 17 Dec. 1970: NNA, 2.05.313, Foreign Affairs 1965–1974, inv.nr. 25175.

276 Letter Envoy Cape Town to Foreign Affairs, 15 Feb. 1950: NNA, 2.05.117, Foreign Affairs 1945–1954, inv.nr. 10044.

277 Letter Backer (Director-General RLD) to Foreign Affairs, 22 Dec. 1950: NNA, 2.05.117 Foreign Affairs 1945–1954, inv.nr. 9930. Wider: S. de Boer, Een kwartmaat achter. Buitenlandse Zaken en Zuid-Afrika, in: R.E. van Ditzhuyzen, A.E. Kersten, A.L.M. van Zeeland, A.C. van der Zwan (red.), *Tweehonderd jaar Ministerie van Buitenlandse Zaken* (Den Haag: Sdu, 1998), p. 230.

278 Minutes 49th BLV, 18 Dec, 1950: NNA, 2.05.117, Foreign Affairs 1945–1954, inv.nr. 21391.

old 'special ties of kinship'.[279] But if The Hague hoped such historic ties would work to the benefit of KLM, such ideas proved unfounded.

As was the case in the air transport discussions with the United States and with the South American countries, talks with South Africa came to revolve around 5th and 6th freedom carriage. KLM offered a link from London with a transfer in Amsterdam. South Africa regarded these 6th freedom operations with rising misgivings, fed by irritations over KLM's other African operations, where services to Johannesburg made an intermediate stop in Kano (Nigeria) to pick up passengers for Brazzaville (Congo). Pretoria pointed out that KLM's 5th and 6th freedom transport made up about 70 percent of its traffic, which it found far too high. KLM should reduce its weekly number of flights to one.[280] These demands were presented at the negotiating table time and again, without the beginning of a solution coming into view. The reduction demanded was not acceptable in The Hague, where it was rumored that South African objections were rooted in BOAC's interests.[281] Irritations on both sides meant that bilateral talks were held under a cloud. At the Ministry of Foreign Affairs in The Hague the head of aviation policy, Carel Schaepman, complained about the South African Director-General for Aviation, John Gibson, 'who has spoken out about Holland in the most unmannerly fashion'.[282]

Bilateral relations did not improve when South Africa indicated that it wanted to tighten existing import restrictions to improve the balance of payments. This worked in favor of goods settled in Pounds Sterling. The Hague repeatedly protested against this as the measures affected, among other things, the export of Dutch tulip bulbs, cigars and straw cardboard. KLM tickets were also predominantly in other denominations.[283] The differences remained and in the summer of 1953 the Malan government formally announced that it wished to cut back KLM's operations with the newly delivered Lockheed Super Constellations. Malan decreed that South Africa would limit KLM to 44 passengers per aircraft, a number that precluded profitable operations. This led to an unusually fierce Dutch protest, and also to a surge of interest in

279 Stefan de Boer, *Van Sharpeville tot Soweto. Nederlands regeringsbeleid ten aanzien van apartheid, 1960–1977* (Den Haag: Sdu, 1999), p. 72.

280 Summary of discussions between the Netherlands and South Africa, 19-26 Sep. 1951: NNA, 2.05.117, Foreign Affairs 1945–1954, inv.nr. 9931.

281 Minutes 51th BLV, 20 Feb. 1951: NNA, 2.05.117, Foreign Affairs 1945–1954, inv.nr. 21392.

282 Memorandum Schaepman to Beyen, 27 Feb. 1953: NNA, 2.05.117, Foreign Affairs 1945–1954, inv.nr. 9931.

283 Letter Ambassador J. van den Berg to Foreign Affairs, 9 Feb. 1953: NNA, 2.0.117, Foreign Affairs 1945–1954, inv.nr.: 11329.

the development of possible KLM destinations elsewhere in Africa.[284] Accra (Ghana) became a possibility, for example. In The Hague there was talk of 'a lack of good faith' in South Africa, which called for a high-level response. The matter reached ministerial level when Foreign Minister Johan Beyen was consulted. It was proposed that a cabinet delegation fly with the first Super Constellation to be deployed on the route to Johannesburg.[285] The delegation was given a triple task: tightening mutual bonds, expressing gratitude for South Africa's aid in the North Sea Flood Disaster that had struck the Netherlands in February 1953, and intimating that the South African attitude towards KLM might have repercussions for the Dutch guarded attitude towards critiques of South Africa at the United Nations.[286]

The transmission of this message was not without its problems. On Saturday afternoon 3 October 1953, Prime Minister Willem Drees, his wife Catharina Hent, Minister of Transport and Water Management Jacob Algera and his daughter Tjitske, State Council and Chairman of the Supervisory Board of KLM Bram Rutgers, and Guus de Casembroot, the Queen's Commissioner of the flood-stricken Province of Zeeland, boarded KLM's Super Constellation *Proton* around one o'clock. The company was seen off by several cabinet members. In front of the press, Drees explained the purpose of the trip, carefully avoiding any mention of the thorny point of landing rights:

> The reason for this trip is the first flight, which KLM is carrying out with the new Super Constellation on the route to South Africa. However, I also have an invitation from the South African Government. Last year I have been asked to come to Johannesburg with my wife, which was shortly before the Van Riebeeck festivities. I was unable to respond to that invitation at the time. Now that there is an opportunity, I will seize it with both hands. The South African Government has once again asked me to be its guest. It is not that we are leaving to discuss specific points, but we will probably discuss various issues with several South African authorities as the opportunity presents itself.[287]

---

284 Minutes 67th BLV, 15 July 1953: NNA, 2.05.117, Foreign Affairs 1945–1954, inv.nr. 21392.

285 Code message Van den Berg (Ambassador Cape Town) to Foreign Affairs, 13 Aug. 1953; office memo Schaepman to Van Tuyll van Serooskerken, 21 Aug. 1953: NNA, 2.05.117, Foreign Affairs 1945–1954, inv.nr. 9931.

286 Office memorandum Foreign Affairs, 27 July 1953: NNA, 2.05.117, Foreign Affairs 1945–1954, inv.nr. 14977. Office memorandum to Van Tuyll van Serooskerken, 10 Sep. 1953: NNA, 2.05.117, Foreign Affairs 1945–1954, inv.nr. 9931.

287 *De Maasbode*, 05-10-1953.

Due to fog, the machine left twenty minutes late, but less than five hours later the delegation was back at Schiphol Airport. The plane had suffered an engine breakdown near Frankfurt and was forced to return to base. A new attempt was made the next day with a spare machine. This aircraft did reach Johannesburg. The intention was that Algera would use his meeting with the South African Transport Minister Paul Sauer to discuss the KLM case. Drees planned to raise the issue with Prime Minister Malan. In doing so, the Dutch ministers had to walk a tightrope, avoiding the 'special relations' between the two countries and steering clear of the question of why the Netherlands did not give more evidence of the special relationship by supporting South Africa at the United Nations.

The week-long visit was not a success, despite an enthusiastic crowd that had come to Johannesburg Airport to greet the Dutch travelers. Algera made no progress with Sauer or Gibson towards an agreement on KLM operations and Drees got nowhere with Malan.[288] A second Dutch attempt at improving relations, a carefully arranged weeklong visit to the Netherlands by fourteen South African journalists, paid for by KLM, did not work either. A month later, Pretoria withdrew permission for one of KLM's two passenger services and decreed a maximum of 54 passengers on board its Super Constellations.[289] Pretoria actually withdrew the license for KLM's bi-weekly cargo service to Johannesburg.[290] In The Hague, anger and frustration prevailed: what next? The prescribed maximum of 54 passengers barely allowed for profitable operations and The Hague feared that the service might have to be discontinued. Pretoria's actions set a dangerous precedent.[291]

After several unsuccessful rounds of negotiations, The Hague decided to take the aviation issue to the highest political level, in the form of a renewed personal appeal by Prime Minister Willem Drees to Daniël Malan. Drees appealed to emotion. In his letter, he reminded Malan of their meeting on 6 October in Cape Town, in which Malan had said that 'die Suid-Afrikaanse volk is 'n dogter van Nederland. Ons vergeet daar die feit nie' ['the South African people is a daughter of the Netherlands. We have not forgotten that fact']. Surely such a

288 Code message Luns to Embassy Pretoria, 18 Nov. 1953: NNA, 2.05.117, Foreign Affairs 1945–1954, inv.nr. 9931.

289 Letter Ambassador Pretoria (J. van den Berg) to Foreign Affairs, 21 Dec. 1953: NNA, 2.05.117, Foreign Affairs 1945–1954, inv.nr. 9931.

290 Letter Ambassador Pretoria (Van den Berg) to Foreign Affairs, 17 Dec. 1953: NNA, 2.05.117, Foreign Affairs 1945–1954, inv.nr. 9931.

291 Office memorandum Schaepman to Van Tuyll van Serooskerken, 11 Jan. 1954: NNA, 2.05.117, Foreign Affairs 1945–1954, inv.nr. 9932.

close bond should not be lost? Drees insisted that Malan devote his personal attention to the matter in order to reverse the measures taken against KLM. To make certain that the letter would reach the South African Prime Minister, ambassador Jan van den Berg was instructed to read it out in person and then hand it over to Malan.[292] This approach worked. Malan agreed to renewed diplomatic consultations, but the result was again disappointing: although KLM was allowed to continue to operate to Johannesburg twice a week, it had to forsake 5th freedom rights in Rome, while 6th freedom traffic from Great Britain via Amsterdam was also subjected to restrictions. In addition, South Africa decreed a maximum of fifty outbound passengers per flight from Johannesburg. Nonetheless, Ambassador Van den Berg was satisfied: the scheduled service as such had been saved. In order to keep the route profitable, KLM asked permission to lay in 310 special emigrant flights.[293] South Africa refused permission, contributing to KLM's growing interest in diversifying its operations on the African continent.

Talks were held with Ghana, and also with Ethiopia. Indeed, Ethiopia became the first African country to sign a bilateral aviation agreement with the Netherlands. It gave KLM the right to serve Addis Ababa as soon as the condition of the airport would allow it.[294] Meanwhile KLM countered the effects of the loss of its 5th freedom rights in Rome in an agreement with Switzerland to make a stopover in Zurich to take on passengers for Johannesburg there. KLM also spoke with South African Airways (SAA) regarding the transport of passengers on segments of the route.[295] A two person strong delegation, consisting of Chief Executive Alphons Aler and Commercial Director Jan van der Kloot, made an extensive visit to South Africa, which brought a marked improvement in relations at company level. Meanwhile, The Hague and Pretoria were on diverging courses politically. At the United Nations, Dutch delegates were instructed to lay low in debates where South Africa's race policies were discussed. This lack of support was noted in Pretoria, which worked to KLM's disadvantage.

Meanwhile, KLM had begun actively looking for new destinations on the African continent. In June 1955, the Ministry of Foreign Affairs approached

292 Letter Drees to Malan, 23 Jan. 1954 (handed over 9 Feb.): NNA, 2.05.117, Foreign Affairs 1945–1954, inv.nr. 9932.

293 Code message J. van den Berg (Ambassador Cape Town) to Foreign Affairs, 16 June 1954: NNA, 2.05.117, Foreign Affairs 1945–1954, inv.nr. 9932.

294 Minutes 54th BLV, 29 June 1954: NNA, 2.05.117, Foreign Affairs 1945–1954, inv.nr. 21393.

295 Letter Slotemaker (KLM) to D.H. Robbertze (SAA), 21 Sep. 1954: NNA, 2.05.117, Foreign Affairs 1945–1954, inv.nr. 9932.

London for rights to operate a service via Khartoum (Sudan) to Nairobi (Kenya) and Dar-es-Salaam (Tanganyika). The Dutch envoy in Monrovia (Liberia), Gerard van Swinderen, was enthusiastic: he envisaged a new west coast route from Kano to Lagos, Accra and Monrovia, in direct competition with the services of Air France and BOAC. KLM hoped to stay ahead of the expected decolonizations, but although Aler was receptive to the idea, there were no aircraft available at the time as KLM was also working on plans to operate along the east coast of the continent.[296]

However, the latter option depended on consultations between London and the African territories of the Commonwealth on the organization of air links. Britain made every effort to protect the interests of BOAC and keep foreign companies at bay for as long as possible.[297] In December 1956, a Dutch delegation travelled to London seeking African traffic rights, but came back empty handed. Minister Luns personally intervened and invited the British ambassador in The Hague to his office. All this was to no avail. London felt that the proposed KLM service lacked a 'balance of rights'.[298] For the time being, the Dutch desisted, hoping that the new political conditions arising from the process of decolonization might enable direct negotiations with African nations, thus avoiding British protectionism. In the French-African regions similar issues played out.

While the Dutch negotiators went on an African reconnaissance mission, periodic consultations with South Africa were also kept going. KLM wished to deploy the new DC-8 jets on the route, but the prospects of an air transport agreement with Pretoria were bleak. Once again politics got in the way. At the United Nations South Africa's racial policies had increasingly come under fire, and had been condemned in several resolutions, especially after South African police killed some 250 black anti-apartheid demonstrators in the township of Sharpeville in March 1960. Subsequently, Pretoria had declared a state of emergency under which more than 11,000 people were detained. A wave of protests swept across the globe calling for the isolation of South Africa and an aviation boycott. The Hague was also shocked and indignation was widely shared across the political spectrum. Dutch abstinence when it came to UN resolutions denouncing South Africa changed to votes in support of such public rebukes. It was only a matter of time before the political outcry would have

296 Minutes 80th BLV, 17 July 1955: NNA, 2.05.118, Foreign Affairs 1955–1964, inv.nr. 27493.

297 Minutes 85th BLV, 27 Aug. 1956: NNA, 2.05.118, Foreign Affairs 1955–1964, inv.nr. 27493.

298 Minutes 87th BLV, 2 Jan. 1957 and 88th BLV, 11 March 1957: NNA, 2.05.118, Foreign Affairs 1955–1964, inv.nr. 27493.

repercussions for air transport. In talks held in 1961, South Africa demanded a drastic cut in KLM's weekly passenger carriage, which The Hague interpreted as related to the Dutch opinions on Apartheid. Luns tried to mitigate the quota demands in stressing the historic ties between the two countries, but to no effect.[299]

On 6 November 1962 the United Nations General Assembly passed Resolution 1761 condemning South African Apartheid policies and asking all members to refuse transit and landing rights for South African aircraft. The Netherlands, by now among South Africa's critics, supported this.[300] However, it was evident that there would be a price to pay with regard to KLM's position. That same month KLM was forced to give up one of its two weekly flights to Johannesburg, although South Africa did permit the use of the DC-8. This mitigated the effects of losing one weekly flight as the DC-8 could seat double the number of passengers compared to the Super Constellation. Thus, The Hague grudgingly accepted the reduction, although other airlines continued to fly without restrictions.[301] Nonetheless, the aviation boycott provided the backdrop for a cautious rapprochement of South Africa to the linguistically and culturally related Dutch as South Africa's position in the world became more isolated. In March 1965, South Africa welcomed a Dutch negotiating team which was extensively pampered and flown around by helicopter for tourist outings, although both sides maintained their positions.[302] A settlement came about in November 1966, after extensive UN debates on apartheid condemned South Africa's policy as a crime against humanity.[303] Seeking to maintain its international air connections, Pretoria now welcomed KLM flights provided they were operated under a pool agreement with SAA.[304]

However, in Africa generally KLM's position met with stagnation. Talks on air links along Africa's eastern and western coasts clashed with protectionist

299 De Boer, *Van Sharpeville tot Soweto*, p. 81–85; 105–106.

300 MacKenzie, *ICAO: A History*, p. 231.

301 Letter KLM (Mees) to Director-General RLD, 31 Dec. 1964: 2.05.313 Foreign Affairs 1965–1964, inv.nr: 5452.

302 Letter Ambassador Cape Town (Henri Helb) to Foreign Affairs, 19 March 1965: 2.05.313 Foreign Affairs 1965–1964, inv.nr: 5452.

303 United Nations General Assembly, 21st Session, 1966–1967, Resolution 2202 (XXI) The policies of apartheid of the Government of the Republic of South Africa, 16 Dec. 1966: https://documents.un.org/doc/resolution/gen/nro/005/05/pdf/nr000505.pdf?token=ulqiowwHFKVHPUoIEl&fe=true [accessed 2024].

304 KLM (HAG/DU) memorandum re. South African service, 27 June 1967: 2.05.313, Foreign Affairs 1965–1964, inv.nr: 5452.

influences from London and Paris.[305] Moreover, the new African states did not rush to facilitate discussions. In countries where KLM already operated, such as Nigeria, such services were flown without a bilateral aviation agreement. The acquisition of formal landing rights became a long-term issue due to restrictions on transport quotas and on 5th freedom rights. In the end, the East African Common Services Organization (EASCO), the organizational guise under which Kenya, Tanganyika (Tanzania) and Uganda had been cooperating in the field of transport since 1961, granted permission for a scheduled KLM service commencing in 1965. By then, KLM's interest had waned however. The fear was that the service would generate losses, just as the airline was struggling to shed the losses incurred in the crisis that had hit the industry in the early 1960s.[306] For the time being, an East African route did not appear to be an attractive proposition. Still, a year later the outlook improved and KLM discussed an arrangement with the EASCO countries in the autumn of 1966. However, things were moving slowly. The political and administrative situation of the new states was not stable and restrictions were introduced repeatedly, prompted by London's efforts to maintain the status quo that had existed before decolonization. It was found that a service ending in Dar-es-Salaam would only be profitable if sufficient 5th freedom rights could be exercised.[307]

Even where services were operating, things did not go according to plan. On 27 June 1967, a KLM flight with a delegation of Guinean diplomats on their way home from a visit to the United Nations in New York landed in Abidjan (Ivory Coast). The aircraft had been en route to Monrovia (Liberia) and should have made a stopover in Conakry (Guinea). But bad weather in Conakry and in Monrovia had forced the captain to fly on to Abidjan. There the plane landed just before midnight and passengers were accommodated in hotels. The next morning, however, Ivory Coast, which had a history of conflict with neighboring Guinea, refused to let the Guinean diplomats leave. They were taken as prisoners to the palace of President Felix Houphouët-Boigny and imprisoned there. The KLM plane took off without them. The Ivorian seizure aimed to pressure Guinea to release the crew of an Ivorian fishing boat it had imposed two years earlier. Guinea decided to retaliate. That same day the staff of the KLM office in Conakry were arrested after the representative, H.A. Van Dijck, who doubled as the Dutch honorary consul, had expressed his unhappiness about the imprisonment of the Ivorian diplomats. According to the Guinean government, the Netherlands had a hand in the Ivorian hostage-taking. The

305 Minutes 104th BLV, 27 June 1961: NNA, 2.05.117, Foreign Affairs 1945–1954, inv.nr. 27494.
306 Minutes 113th BLV, 16 Nov. 1965: NNA, 2.05.313, Foreign Affairs 1965–1974, inv.nr. 25174.
307 Minutes 119th BLV, 23 March 1967: NNA, 2.05.313, Foreign Affairs 1965–1974, inv.nr. 25174.

case became increasingly grim when the Guineans withdrew the exit visas of all Dutch nationals residing or working in Guinea. Like an oil spill, the incident fanned out in international diplomatic waters. After fruitless mediation attempts – the special envoy sent from The Hague was refused permission to enter the country – the case became gridlocked when both sides refused to talk about the release of hostages. Meanwhile, the four detained KLM employees in Conakry saw the weeks pass into months in the villa in which they were incarcerated. One mediator after another returned home without success. Finally, Liberian President William Tubman managed to initiate a hostage swap on 28 September. After more than three months, the four KLM employees were allowed to return home on 2 October. The air service, which had been halted as a result of the hostage drama, was not reopened.[308]

KLM flights to West Africa thus came to a complete halt. Services to East Africa did not fare much better. The market for air transport on the continent was relatively small and African nationalism was booming. Tanganyika stated in 1967 that KLM must operate a regular service to Entebbe (Uganda) and Dar-es-Salaam for at least two years before Tanganyika would allow transport rights for a route via the Kenyan capital Nairobi. It took several missions, both from KLM and from Dutch diplomats, to bring the three governments together in October 1968 – only to find that KLM did not have any aircraft available at the time to operate the service.[309] From May 1969, flights were made to Dar-es-Salaam, but the EASCO cooperation platform of the three countries gave little evidence of flexibility when it came to route or timetable adjustments.

The contrast with the situation in South Africa was striking. In the wake of international sanctions and isolation, KLM needed little effort in May 1970 to acquire rights for a third weekly frequency. An unofficial visit by the Minister of Transport and Waterworks, Joop Bakker, to South Africa sufficed. This new, more relaxed attitude resulted from the 1967 pooling agreement with SAA, under which KLM paid the South African carrier a fifty per cent share of revenues.[310] Two years later, however, in February 1972, things got complicated again when SAA started flying its own service to Amsterdam, separate from the cooperation agreement. In order to protect SAA, South Africa put pressure on both Switzerland and Italy to withdraw permissions for KLM's 5th freedom

308 A dossier with details of the hostage crisis is kept in NNA, 2.05.182, Netherlands Embassy in Guinee (Monrovia) 1965–1974, inv.nr. 27.

309 Minutes 120th-124th BLV, 15 Aug. 1967–14 Nov. 1968: NNA, 2.05.313, Foreign Affairs 1965–1974, inv.nr. 25174.

310 Letter Wassenbergh (KLM) to State Secretary Mike Keyzer, 24 June 1970: 2.05.313, Foreign Affairs 1965–1964, inv.nr: 5452.

stops in Zurich and Rome. This needed little persuasion: Italy in particular had long wanted to get rid of these rights.[311] Hoping to develop a new African market KLM then proposed operating Douglas DC-10 wide-body aircraft via Nairobi. This was not to the liking of the South African government, however, and Transport Minister Ben Schoeman, not a fan of the Netherlands, blocked it. The introduction of underlying political frictions in the negotiations was another problem. Hoping to soften the South Africans' attitude, KLM expressed its willingness to make an extra financial gesture to SAA.[312] After all, South Africa was an interesting market for air transport and KLM was keen to keep the economics of travel well away from the political controversies over apartheid.[313] This only partially worked, however, as politics once again got the upper hand in bilateral relations. There was a price to pay for The Hague, now that the Netherlands had for years supported UN resolutions condemning South African racial policies. Air transport was one of the areas in which pressures surfaced.[314]

8 In Conclusion

In the post-colonial era of the 1950s and after, commerce and finances continued to gain in importance in international air transport relations. In the Dutch case, these relationships were complicated by KLM's reliance on the 5th and 6th freedom rights that the airline needed to operate profitably. Pool agreements and money transfers became ever more important instruments to bridge negotiating differences around the globe.

Politics also continued to be a factor, fueled by the tensions of the Cold War. The combination of these forces spelled trouble for the Netherlands. Both the Netherlands' West European partners and countries across the Iron Curtain were increasingly aware that KLM's operations syphoned off traffic that might

311 Minutes 133th BLV, 6 Dec. 1971: NNA, 2.05.313, Foreign Affairs 1965–1974, inv.nr. 25175.

312 Letter Jan de Soet (KLM) to J. Adam (CEO, SAA), 22 Feb. 1973: Collection Petit, dossiers VADV.

313 Office Memorandum Ministry of Foreign Affairs on past and future of Dutch relations with South Africa, 17 Oct. 1975, in: M.L.J. Dierikx, C.B. Feiken, J.H. Gaemers, M.G.M. Smits, *Nederlandse ontwikkelingssamenwerking. Bronnenuitgave. Deel 4, 1973–1977* (The Hague: Instituut voor Nederlandse Geschiedenis, 2005), nr. 167. Stefan de Boer, *Van Sharpeville tot Soweto*, p. 194–204.

314 Letter Spanjaard (RLD) to Foreign Affairs (VADV), 5 May 1972: 2.05.313, Foreign Affairs 1965–1964, inv.nr: 5452. Minutes 136th and 138th BLV, 12 Dec. 1972 and 1 Aug. 1973: NNA, 2.05.313, Foreign Affairs 1965–1974, inv.nrs. 25175, 25176.

have been carried nationally. Contacts with the Soviet Union were especially difficult. In the interactions with Indonesia, too, political echoes lingered, gaining weight as general bilateral relations slid downhill because of the conflict over New Guinea. The Dutch found themselves on their own, since the United States chose not to stand by is ally. In line with this, Dutch wishes for additional landing rights in the USA met with the American insistence on putting the interests of America's airlines first. For the Civil Aviation Meeting in The Hague, one of the few tactics available to defend against such developments was to escalate air transport talks to involve representatives at the highest political level.

FIGURE 1 In 1919 the Paris Convention defined civil use of the air. In the following years the start of commercial air services in Europe depended on bilateral agreements negotiated between governments. Passengers boarding a Fokker F.II airliner at Rotterdam's Waalhaven airport in 1922. (Nederlands Instituut voor Militaire Historie)

FIGURE 2 For the Dutch, the most important incentive for civil air services was speeding up communications with the Netherlands East Indies. Diplomacy was modernized to bring this about. Arrival of the first airliner at Muntok, final stop before Batavia in November 1924. (KITLV, CC BY License)

FIGURE 3 In doubt whether to focus on a national air service to the East Indies or endorse the development of a network in Europe, Dutch diplomacy struggled to provide for KLM's expansion in the 1930s. Arrival of KLM's Fokker F.XX *Zilvermeeuw* at Berlin's Tempelhof Airport in October 1934. (Nationaal Archief, CC0)

FIGURE 4 From September 1939 wartime conditions shrank the civil air services network in Europe. Only airports that could be reached over water remained open. An orange painted Douglas DC-3 marked HOLLAND in black lettering at Oslo's Fornebu Airport, after the German invasion of Norway in April 1940. (Nederlands Instituut voor Militaire Historie)

FIGURE 5
The war brought rapprochement of the British and Dutch positions on rights for air services. In June 1941 an agreement was reached under which KLM carried British mail on its route between Batavia and Lydda (Tel Aviv). An extension of the service to Cairo did not materialize. (Leiden University Libraries, Ephemera Collection, Or. 27.622, nr. 25)

FIGURE 6
With the Douglas DC-4 *Rotterdam* KLM opened its all-important transatlantic service to New York in May 1946, on the basis of a provisional permit. The hoped-for bilateral treaty did not materialize, due to differences over colonial and foreign policy issues. Official baptism of the airplane on 9 May 1946. (Nationaal Archief, CC0)

FIGURE 7 Negotiations on a more permanent settlement of bilateral aviation issues with the USA remained unsuccessful. The American CAB labelled the Dutch claim for services between New York and Curaçao 'preposterous'. Failing agreement, KLM initiated a route via Montreal and Havana in May 1949. Prince Bernhard, KLM's CEO Albert Plesman and corporate lawyer Lambert Slotemaker disembark after the first flight. (Nationaal Archief/Collectie Spaarnestad/ANP)

FIGURE 8 Between 1945 and 1949 the air service between Amsterdam and Batavia (Jakarta) presented a major issue in the Dutch national interest. To circumvent international sanctions against Dutch aircraft, The Hague pursued all options. In 1949, a company of American journalists who the Dutch had tried to win over to their position perished when this Lockheed L-749 *Franeker* crashed on 12 July. (Nationaal Archief, CC0)

FIGURE 9
After 1945, Dutch trade relations with South America expanded. Various talks were held regarding air services. The government sent Prince Bernhard on a goodwill mission in April 1951. Three months later, exporters of herring and gin shipped special gift samples to Uruguay and Argentina to promote trade. Ceremonial handover of the goods before departure on 6 July 1951. (Nationaal Archief, CC0)

FIGURE 10
When talks on an expansion of air services to South Africa stalled in 1953, The Hague mounted a high-level goodwill mission. Queen's Commissionar Guus de Casembroot, Prime Minister Willem Drees, his spouse Catharina Hent, and Minister of Transport Jacob Algera about to board the flight to Johannesburg, 3 October 1953. Algera's daughter Tjitske accompanied them. (Nationaal Archief, CC0)

FIGURE 11 After 12 years of discussions, the Dutch finally managed to wrest a bilateral air transport agreement from the Americans in March 1957. Even the issue of a service between New York and Curaçao was settled. Delegates Nico Slotemaker de Bruïne of the Netherlands Information Bureau in New York and Anton Speekenbrink, head of economic department of the Embassy in Washington (middle) and his wife were met at Schiphol by Arie Jonkers of the Ministry of Overseas Territories. (Nationaal Archief/Collectie Spaarnestad/ANP)

FIGURE 12 The bilateral air transport agreement of 1957 was supposed to placate long-standing Dutch grievances regarding US foreign and aviation policy. To Washington's chagrin The Hague saw it as a step-up to new demands for air transport rights. Arrival of the first KLM machine in Houston on 3 September 1957. (Authors' collection)

FIGURE 13 After an attack on Sukarno, behind which Indonesia suspected Dutch involvement, Jakarta cancelled KLM's landing rights and nationalized Dutch assets in Indonesia on 1 December 1957. The ban lasted almost six years. Arrival at Schiphol of the last passenger flight to leave Jakarta, 2 December 1957. (Nationaal Archief/Collectie Spaarnestad/ANP)

FIGURE 14 Since the 1950s Dutch demands on America focused on acquiring rights in Los Angeles, for which KLM managed to enlist local support. Lambert Slotemaker (left) and Alphons Aler (right) discussing the proposed route with Chairman Charles Detoy of the LA Chamber of Commerce in January 1960. Not before 1978 did the first KLM flight land in LA. (Nationaal Archief/Collectie Spaarnestad/ANP)

FIGURE 15
Diplomat turned aviator, turned academic, Ernst van der Beugel was appointed president of KLM in 1961 in recognition of his efforts regarding the 1957 US-Dutch bilateral air transport agreement. Unhappy at KLM, he left in 1963, but continued to use his diplomatic influence to promote the Dutch cause through his friendship with Henry Kissinger. (Nationaal Archief, CC0)

FIGURE 16
In the early months of 1962 the Dutch-Indonesian conflict over New Guinea climaxed. To move military personnel and equipment to the distant territory the Dutch used KLM, despite protests from Japan and the USA. Inspection in Tokyo of a DC-8 suspected of carrying weapons in February 1962. (Nationaal Archief/Collectie Spaarnestad/ANP)

FIGURE 17 Facing mounting international pressure, The Hague conceded to negotiations over the future of New Guinea in July 1962. Prospects for a settlement with Indonesia did not look good, and Guineans with ties to the Dutch colonial administration left on flights to Amsterdam. Evacuees from Biak arriving at Schiphol, 31 July 1962. (Nationaal Archief, CC0)

FIGURE 18
Celebrating a successful visit to the White House in which they procured KLM landing rights in Chicago from president Richard Nixon, Foreign Minister Joseph Luns and Prime Minister Piet de Jong shared an electric trolley and a good laugh at Schiphol Airport, 30 May 1969. (Nationaal Archief, CC0)

FIGURE 19 After almost seven year of talks and despite incidents that repeatedly upset good relations, KLM and the Soviet-Russian carrier Aeroflot reached an agreement on a Dutch air service across Siberia in April 1971. For the purpose KLM chartered Ilyushin IL-62 aircraft in Moscow with Russian crews. (Authors' collection)

FIGURE 20 After Mao's death, a cautious rapprochement between the Netherlands and China started. On 8 June 1978, Chinese Foreign Minister Huang Hua arrived at Schiphol for talks. His Dutch counterpart Chris van der Klaauw (right) was there to welcome him. (Nationaal Archief/ANEFO, CC BY 4.0)

FIGURE 21 In the 1970s and 1980s State Secretary (later Minister) of Transport and Water Management Neelie Smit-Kroes played a role of major importance in negotiating bilateral air transport agreements, as did Henri 'Or' Wassenbergh, KLM's chief negotiator, depicted here in January 1981. (Nationaal Archief, CC0)

FIGURE 22 On 17 February 1986 Dutch Foreign Minister Hans van den Broek was in Luxembourg to sign the Single European Act, which aimed to liberalize trade and competition and create a Single Market in the European Community by the end of 1992. Air transport was one of the areas that saw profound changes as a result. (Nationaal Archief/Collectie Spaarnestad/ANP)

FIGURE 23 Like all negotiating processes, talks on air transport involved formal exchanges at conference tables and informal gatherings in restaurants. Although agreements were sometimes only reached with difficulty, the results might be celebrated in good spirits. Animated Dutch-Argentine conversation in Buenos Aires, 1993. (Authors' collection)

FIGURE 24 KLM's African network saw many vicissitudes over time as political winds changed. Harare was an example. After the service to Zimbabwe's capital had to be discontinued in 1985, talks were resumed in 1992, resulting in an agreement that permitted a resumption of operations from 13 January 1993. (MAI/KLM Foto Historisch Archief)

FIGURE 25 After fifty years of strenuous diplomatic contacts over air services to China, a Dutch-Chinese bilateral accord was finally signed on 23 May 1996. Over time, services to Taiwan had presented a major stumbling block. As the national carrier, KLM could not fly to Taipei because it would give the impression that the Netherlands recognized Taiwan as an independent state. To placate Beijing a dedicated subsidiary was founded, *KLM asia*, to operate flights to Taipei. (Authors' collection)

FIGURE 26 From 1993 liberalization of the air transport market brought increased competition and important regulatory changes within the European Union, reducing the roles of national governments. Passengers profited from the rapid expansion of low cost carriers, often offering services to and from secondary airports. Passengers disembarking at Eindhoven in 2009. (Authors' collection)

CHAPTER 4

1973–1989: Towards the End of the Preeminence of Politics

1 Introduction

> In 1989, Washington is about an eight hour flight from Amsterdam according to the timetable. But for a passenger arriving late at the airport because of a delayed train, the journey appears much longer. A seat in the middle section of a Boeing 747, sandwiched between two sturdy fellow travelers, arms by necessity tight against the body, is not what one hopes for when booking the ticket. The travel agency already hinted that the plane would be full and advised to show up at the airport early to have a chance for a seat by the window. Nothing comes of this. At the check-in desk, only a few seats on board are left in economy class, of course only in the middle section and not even on the aisle. So this is a *long* flight – and a stuffy one too, because the plane does not have an individually adjustable air supply, but central air conditioning. Fortunately, after an hour or so of flying, there is diversion. A charming flight attendant comes along with nicely printed menu cards offering a choice between various aperitifs, wines, liqueur, beer and soft drinks, three options for the main course of the meal, and a piece of apple pie and coffee after. Once served, consuming the food without spilling requires supreme concentration, since travelers in economy are mangled. After the meal, the lights are dimmed and the small television sets hanging over the aisles offer a special 'airline version' of a recent cinema hit. The sound can be heard with some difficulty via a hollow flexible tube that is connected to each seat's armrest. The movie makes the time tick away slowly and it is a long time before the plane finally begins its descent for landing.[1]

If not entirely relaxing, air transport had become something of a modern commodity since the early 1970s, a travel mode available to a wide cross section of society. Economic growth and rising disposable incomes had created an expanding market as the upward trend of the 1950s continued through the next decade. Between 1960 and 1970, the volume of world trade doubled and worldwide passenger figures for scheduled airlines went up threefold. Chartered

1 Personal recollection by the author.

 | DOI:10.1163/9789004695245_005

air transport, carrying holiday makers from the north of Europe to the sandy beaches of the Mediterranean, showed an even higher growth rate. In the second half of the 1960s international détente had further optimized conditions for this increase in air transport. However, in economic terms all was not well in the world by 1973 as most western countries were experiencing the effects of a stagnating economy that brought inflation and unemployment. In Europe the EEC, looking towards a planned expansion from six to nine members in 1973, hoped to remedy this by extending cooperation between member states from the economic to the political field, coordinated by the Council of Ministers. Such coordination had become all the more necessary in a situation of increasing national deficits. The international economy was losing stability. Two years before, in August 1971, the United States had abandoned the fixed dollar exchange rate and the dollar's convertibility into gold to combat the cost effects of the Vietnam War. Since then, flexible exchange rates had seriously affected transatlantic trade relations.[2] This caused problems for the international airline industry, which was used to conducting its businesses in dollars.

In the political field the improved East-West relations of the late 1960s had been instrumental in taking initial steps to bridge the existing division of Europe. In the wake of the West German government's *Ostpolitik*, six European countries, including the Netherlands, recognized the German Democratic Republic (GDR) in December 1972, followed by eleven more in 1973.[3] For the Netherlands, always interested in opportunities to extend commerce, the GDR became an official trading partner, albeit one with a special status.[4] Contacts across the Iron Curtain were expanded. In a wider sense, the Conference on Security and Cooperation in Europe that convened in Helsinki from 3 to 7 July 1973 confirmed these improved relations. The Helsinki Accords, signed on the 1st of August 1975, laid down that signatory states would refrain from intervention, direct or indirect, in the affairs of another participating state. One of the results of this relaxation was that air services between Western and Eastern Europe could be extended.[5]

While tensions in Europe decreased, a sudden war in the Middle East upset international relations. On 6 October 1973 a coalition of Arab states launched a surprise attack against Israel on the Jewish holy day of Yom Kippur. The war

2 James Foreman-Peck, *A History of the World Economy. International Economic Relations Since 1850* (New York: Harvester Wheatsheaf, 1995), p. 305–307.

3 Marc Dierikx, Sacha Zala (eds.), *When the Wall Came Down. The Perception of German Reunification in International Diplomatic Documents 1989–1990* (Berne: Dodis, 2019), p. 12.

4 Jacco Pekelder, *Nederland en de DDR. Beeldvorming en betrekkingen, 1949–1989* (Amsterdam: Boom, 1998), p. 343–346.

5 Marc Dierikx, Bram Bouwens, *Building Castles of the Air. Schiphol Amsterdam and the Development of Airport Infrastructure in Europe, 1916–1996* (The Hague: Sdu, 1997), p. 312.

raged until 25 October and formed the background for a surge in oil prices of around 70 per cent. The oil dependent world economy headed for a crisis. As a major consumer of fuel, international aviation was immediately affected. Before the end of the year prices for aviation fuel tripled.[6] On 21 October the Organization of the Petroleum Exporting Countries (OPEC) implemented a supply boycott against those countries that supported Israel in the war. The United States was the prime target of this embargo, but it also extended to the Netherlands as Europe's major oil distribution center. Beyond the oil embargo, Dutch air transport was also targeted. Libya, Egypt, Syria, Jordan and Iraq threatened to cancel KLM's landing rights, although only Jordan actually imposed this sanction. In Libya, Syria and Iraq ground crews refused to handle KLM aircraft until January 1974.[7] At several foreign points of call Dutch aircraft had trouble obtaining fuel.

The resulting disruption of supply lines created uncertainty in world air transport. Various airlines studied options to combine services to economize.[8] KLM examined the possibilities for combining several of its North American operations and serving multiple destinations with fewer aircraft. In the end this turned out not to be necessary, however. Despite only meagre support for the Dutch from the other EEC member states, the short term effects of the oil embargo were tempered by Royal Dutch Shell and other oil companies, who maintained their existing distribution channels until the embargos were lifted in the summer of 1974. Supplies to the United States were resumed in March, but the sanctions against the Netherlands were not lifted until July.[9]

In foreign policy terms, dealing with the Oil Crisis was a challenge for all Western nations, but the Dutch position was unusually complicated. The hoped for European solidarity did not materialize and The Hague stood alone until the spring of 1974. The idealist international policy agenda that the cabinet had adopted in May 1973 when parliamentary elections produced a government dominated by parties from the political left did not garner political friends. The corresponding foreign policy agenda, in which human rights and international solidarity played major roles, struck only a limited chord across the border. At the same time the government's plans to cut back on

6 Minutes Supervisory Board KLM, 31 January 1974: KLM Archive, RvC.

7 Duco Hellema, Cees Wiebes, Toby Witte, *Doelwit Rotterdam. Nederland en de Oliecrisis 1973–1974* (Den Haag: Sdu, 1998), p. 72–74, 205–206. Dierikx, *Blauw in de lucht*, p. 255.

8 Minutes 139th BLV, 21 Nov. 1973: NNA, 2.05.313, Foreign Affairs 1965–1974, inv.nr. 25176.

9 Hellema, *Nederland in de wereld*, p. 274–281. Duco Hellema, Cees Wiebes, Tony Witte, *Doelwit Rotterdam. Nederland en de Oliecrisis 1973–1974* (Den Haag: Sdu, 1998), p. 227–260. Hellema, Anglo-Dutch relations in the early 1970s, in: Nigel Ashton, Duco Hellema, *Unspoken Allies. Anglo-Dutch Relations since 1780* (Amsterdam: AUP, 2001), p. 255–272.

military spending reduced Dutch standing with NATO allies, particularly the US. After a new, more conservative government took office in December 1977, The Hague attempted to regain some of its lost influence. However, part of this effort ran aground in a strong domestic public campaign for pacifism. *Hollanditis*, the international term used to describe Dutch public concerns regarding the need to curb the nuclear arms race, did not die away till 1985. Nonetheless, there was more continuity than change in Dutch foreign policy, with economic interests on the rise.[10]

The importance of economics and trade in international affairs were underlined in the aftermath of the second Oil Crisis in 1979, when the revolution in Iran pushed up oil prices, this time by 150 per cent. Once again the economy went into decline, which led to protectionist tendencies that in turn corresponded with a new conservatism in international affairs. Relations between the superpowers deteriorated. In Europe the pace of integration slowed down.

In an attempt to break this trend, the EEC members agreed in 1983 to aim at harmonizing economic policy goals and set course towards a broader European Community. Three years later the adoption of the Single European Act promised a free internal market by 31 December 1992. To coordinate policies, the role of the European Commission grew stronger.[11]

Meanwhile, in Eastern Europe the Soviet-dominated regimes struggled to keep up in economic terms. From 1985 onward, Soviet party leader Mikhail Gorbachev steered a new course, implementing the more liberal politics of *perestroika* and *glasnost* to foster change. To the surprise of all involved, this unleashed a torrent of events that in November 1989 swept away the Iron Curtain and created completely new international conditions.[12]

In the two decades preceding the fall of the Berlin Wall the leisure traveler took over international aviation. The signs for this development were everywhere: highstreets sported an increasing array of travel agencies that advertised colorful tourist destinations only a few hours' flight away. Between 1962 and 1970, the number of Dutch holiday makers boarding airplanes increased twelvefold, with most travelling on charter flights.[13] Traditional airline companies needed time to address these developments and recapture the market share lost to chartered flying.[14] For all who wished to fly, the travel agent was

10 Frank Zuijdam, Dutch left-wing political parties and NATO, in: Krabbendam, Van Minnen, Scott-Smith (eds.), *NL-USA*, p. 652–662. Hellema, *Nederland in de wereld,* p. 282–287.

11 Tony Judt, *Postwar. A History of Europe since 1945,*(London: Heinemann, 2005) chapter XVI.

12 Dierikx, Zala (eds.), *When the Wall Came Down.*, p. 12–21.

13 Annual Reports NV Luchthaven Schiphol, 1962–1970: author's collection.

14 Marc Dierikx, Peter Lyth, From Privilege to Popularity. the Growth of Leisure Air Travel since 1945, in: *The Journal of Transport History*, Vol 15 (1994), nr. 2, p. 97–116.

an indispensable intermediary when booking tickets. Once a ticket had been acquired and the day of departure arrived, the traveler needed an automobile to cover the distance to the airport. Well into the 1970s car travel was the preferred mode of surface transport for airline passengers, although bus services were also available. Railway connections to airports were still in their planning phases. The airports themselves, which had thus far catered to the high paying business traveler, had to be expanded to cope with the increased numbers of users. To keep passengers happy and give them something to do while waiting to board their flight, tax-free shops that offered all kinds of small amenities mushroomed for those who had passed customs.

To partake in such services was, however, becoming more complicated. Commercial aviation, regarded as a symbol of the West's domination over world events, became the target of acts of terrorism. In the 1970s the number of attacks against aircraft, airlines and airports went up spectacularly, bringing the conflict in the Middle East home to the Western world. The Netherlands was not immune. After being accused of secretly facilitating the transportation of arms, ammunitions and even mercenaries to Israel in the Yom Kippur War, a KLM Boeing 747 was hijacked on the evening of Sunday 25 November 1973. Flight KL861, on its way from Amsterdam to Tokyo, had made a stopover in Beirut when three armed, Arabic-speaking men entered the cockpit. The hijackers, who claimed to belong to the National Arab Youth Association, seized the plane and its 247 passengers and crew of 17. Initially it was not clear what the hijackers wanted because of their poor English, but eventually their demands were conveyed: the Netherlands should no longer act as a transit country for the emigration of Russian Jews to Israel; there were to be no Dutch volunteers for the Israeli army; and KLM was to refrain from the transportation of weapons and war material to Israel. While these demands were being discussed, the hijacked plane crisscrossed the Mediterranean. It was midnight before captain Sjaak Risseeuw landed the plane at Nicosia in Cyprus. Here the hijackers demanded the release of seven comrades who were imprisoned on the island. Their action, however, found little support in the Arab world. Only Libya's leader Moammar al-Gaddafi seemed willing to offer support. The plane set off for Tripoli the next morning. By that time Gaddafi had changed his mind and the Libyan authorities gave the hijackers a cold reception. Libya refused to let the plane leave and blocked the runway with fire trucks. Risseeuw, however, managed to get his machine in the air by diverting to an old, decommissioned short runway. Now that the hijacked machine no longer had a destination to go to, an offer from the government of Malta to land there was accepted. It was the first time that a Boeing 747 had ever landed at Luqa Airport and the length of the runway meant that the aircraft could not leave at full take-off weight.

Hence the hijackers found themselves trapped. Malta's Prime Minister Dom Mintoff's negotiations enabled the passengers to disembark, as well as eight flight attendants. In return, Mintoff allowed the plane to be refueled, while a relief crew was flown in from the Netherlands. With only Risseeuw's flight crew and two new volunteer hostages on board, the machine departed from Luqa to land a few hours later in Dubai, where the game of attrition continued. The aircraft was again refueled, but an attempt to divert to Aden in South Yemen met with a firm refusal by the authorities there to let the machine land. For seven hours the Boeing circled over the Persian Gulf before it returned to Dubai due to a lack of fuel. There the hijacking ended through the intervention of the Prime Minister of the United Arab Emirates, Sheikh Maktoum bin Rashid al-Maktoum. The sheikh offered the hijackers a safe passage, but in return demanded their unconditional surrender. Exhausted, the hijackers removed their explosives from the aircraft and came out. The hijack had lasted 68 hours. Finally the crew could go to bed safely. The next day, 29 November, Risseeuw and his people flew the Boeing back to Amsterdam, where they were greeted with relief. The three hijackers remained behind as 'guests of the Ruler of Dubai'. Thus the drama ended without bloodshed.[15] For KLM it was a costly affair: the bills amounted to well over a million guilders, plus – at his request – six riding horses for the Maltese Prime Minister Dom Mintoff as a gesture of gratitude for his mediation effort.[16]

The KLM hijack was just one in a total of ten that occurred in the year after the Yom Kippur War. Together they caused substantial security measures to be implemented at airports throughout the world and to a rephrasing of the clauses of the Convention on the Unlawful Seizure of Aircraft that had been signed in The Hague on 16 December 1970.[17]

For the airline industry, one of the effects of the Oil Crisis was a downturn in general profitability and increased competition. Fuel prices pushed up tickets between thirty and forty per cent in 1974, causing a slump in passenger numbers. To attract customers and increase load factors again ticket prices needed to go down, despite the rising cost of fuel. Controlling costs became of primary importance in airline thinking and planning. Automation, a process that had its origins in the second half of the 1950s, took on a whole new meaning as a way to economize. Airlines not only embraced computer based booking

15 Minutes Supervisory Board KLM, 29 November 1973: KLM Archive, RvC. Dierikx, *Blauw in de lucht*, p. 256–257.

16 Minutes 141th BLV, 16 April 1974: NNA, 2.05.313, Foreign Affairs 1965-1974, inv.nr. 25176.

17 Convention on the unlawful seizure of aircraft, 16 Dec. 1970: https://treaties.un.org/doc/db/Terrorism/Conv2-english.pdf [accessed June 2022].

systems to optimize load factors, but also adopted computer technology to streamline other aspects of operation and administration.

Such ventures into the application of computer technology did not prevent the general downturn of the airline industry in the mid-1970s, however, and in 1974 and 1975 the accumulated deficits ran into hundreds of millions of dollars.[18] On the Atlantic routes protectionism surged. It was increasingly evident that the political nature of international aviation made it difficult for airlines to respond to short term changes in economic and market conditions. Both in the United States and in Europe, critics pointed to the negative effect that regulation had for consumers, in the form of high prices for airline tickets.[19] Initially, such complaints had little effect. Washington even tried to limit the freedom of charter carriers and bring them under the aegis of bilateral agreements. The United States also initiated a renegotiation of the existing air transport agreements, starting with the smaller European countries, primarily the Netherlands, Belgium, and the Scandinavian countries, to adjust the market shares of American and European operators across the North Atlantic. This was part of a wider strategy on the part of the Civil Aeronautics Board to redraw the 'balance of benefits' of air services to and from the United States in favor of America's own loss-making international carriers. In October 1974, the US Department of Transportation launched a Federal Action Plan to improve profitability. The plan was built around a *Fly US Flag* program and was designed to encourage Americans to travel on US airlines. The program also required that any travel associated with government contracts be exclusively on American carriers.[20] The CAB aimed for a substantial reduction of the European market share on the Atlantic routes.

Nonetheless, the desirability of direct government involvement in air transport and the corresponding linkage to high politics became a matter of debate in the mid-1970s. There was reason to redefine the traditional relationship between aviation and the nation state; this gradual process would become known as deregulation. Its international reach was preceded by changes that originated in Britain. In October 1976, James Callaghan's Labor Government unilaterally terminated the 1946 Bermuda I aviation agreement with the United States. This was because 'Bermuda' precluded the entry of privately owned British airlines, such as British Caledonian, to the market for scheduled

18 Rigas Doganis, *Flying off Course. The Economics of International Airlines* (London: George Allen & Unwin, 1985), p. 18

19 For an overview of deregulation incentives, see Paul S. Dempsey, *Law and foreign policy in international aviation* (Dobbs Ferry: Transnational Publishers, 1987).

20 H.A. Wassenbergh, *Public International Air Transport Law in a New Era*, p. 12; 26–36.

services to the United States. By terminating the agreement, London sought to create an opening for private enterprise on the transatlantic routes and at the same time improve the British market share. From the British perspective US carriers were seen as having exploited much more successfully the possibilities of the Bermuda agreement. Negotiations on a new accord took until 23 July 1977, after which Bermuda II came into force in 1978. Washington regarded the new agreement as more restrictive than its predecessor. Although it liberalized tariff provisions, the agreement limited US fifth freedom rights and restricted the number of airports in the United States that could be served directly by British scheduled carriers. At the same time, it permitted non-scheduled airlines to operate to other airports. A set of capacity controls was also agreed on. The British aim was to provide a system under which airlines from either country could compete on more equal terms.[21] The US, however, was not happy with the outcome of the talks, and Bermuda II never became the model agreement its predecessor had been.

While talks on Bermuda were going on, Washington started preparations in February 1977 for a revision of aviation policy. The newly inaugurated Democratic president Jimmy Carter announced that he would sponsor a bill aimed to bring about more competition in the domestic airline market. His Airline Deregulation Act came into effect on 24 October 1978, but even before that date it was clear that deregulation would get an international follow-up. In March of that year the Dutch were the first to put the new American thinking to the test. A protocol amending the existing agreement with the United States established that American carriers could operate to any destination via Amsterdam. Airlines from both parties were allowed to provide unlimited capacity on agreed routes. In the field of tariffs, a more liberal pricing regime was installed. In return, KLM obtained two additional commercial destinations in the US, Los Angeles and Atlanta. In this way 'hard rights' (i.e. frequencies and routes) were traded for 'soft rights' (i.e. pricing). The new principle replaced the strict reciprocity in exchanged benefits that had been Washington's guiding principle in international air transport policy since the 1950s.[22] More competition was to bring lower fares, in the interest of the public. Observing the success of domestic deregulation, President Carter issued a statement in August 1978 that his government was going to promote deregulation in international air transport. This resulted in the International Air Transport Competition Act of 1979.

---

21 Alan Dobson, *A History of International Civil Aviation. From its Origins through Transformative Evolution* (London: Routledge, 2017), p. 65–69.

22 Schreurs, *Positie van Nederland in de internationale luchtvaartpolitiek*, p. 91–94. Doganis, *Flying off course*, p. 57–60.

The underlying idea was to capture a larger market share for American carriers on the routes to and from the United States.[23] Shortly after the Netherlands had done so, Belgium and West Germany became second and third to conclude liberal agreements with the US. These provided for pricing flexibility and increased access to the European air transport market for American carriers, in return for an expansion of the number of US destinations for the European carriers concerned.[24] American aviation policy on the North Atlantic became more liberal.

It thus became inevitable that deregulation or liberalization would cross over to Europe, where competition between the various national airlines, including pool arrangements, had hitherto remained subject to a system of Bermuda-type bilateral agreements and governmental control of market access. In Europe, both Britain and the Netherlands played a role as proponents of change. The European Commission embarked upon a learning curve to develop a community-wide aviation policy. Developing and implementing more liberal ideas took years, as it meant accommodating opposition within the Council of Ministers in which the majority defended the status quo, i.e. the Chicago-based system of bilateral agreements.[25]

In July 1979, the European Commission presented a memorandum that aimed to promote more competition and lower prices. Putting this forward, the Commission wished to strengthen its position in matters regarding air transport policy.[26] Nonetheless, in a period of economic stagnation, effecting policy changes that might bring a more liberal approach toward intra-European air services required both time and patience.[27] It was not until 1982 that ECAC also moved towards liberalization. In May 1982, the ECAC countries signed a Memorandum of Understanding with the United States accepting 'flexibility zones' for tariffs on the North Atlantic. The following year, the European Commission announced steps to extend the competitive scope for interregional air services between EEC members, easing market entry requirements while advancing flexibility towards pricing and capacity. In June 1984 the Netherlands and Great

23 Jacques Naveau, *International air transport in a changing world* (Brussels: Bruylant, 1989), p. 142–151.

24 Minutes 158th BLV, 15 Oct. 1980: NNA, 2.05.330, Foreign Affairs 1975–1984, inv.nr. 24344.

25 Alan Dobson, *Globalization and Regional Integration. The Origins, Development and Impact of the Single European Aviation Market* (London: Routledge, 2007), p. 45–60. Martin Staniland, *A Europe of the Air? The Airline Industry and European Integration* (Lanham MD: Rowman & Littlefield, 2008), p. 64–65.

26 Minutes 156th BLV, 30 January 1980: NNA, 2.05.330, Foreign Affairs 1975–1984, inv.nr. 24344.

27 Minutes 161st BLV, 7 January 1982: NNA, 2.05.330, Foreign Affairs 1975–1984, inv.nr. 24345.

Britain took the lead by introducing route-, capacity-, and tariff freedoms for their respective airlines, thus pioneering the concept of the market as sole 'regulator'.[28] That same year the European Commission began to claim direct authority over the air transport industry in the interest of creating a truly European market and stimulating increased contact between citizens through cheaper air travel.[29]

However, the creation of a liberalized common market for transport required agreement at the European political level, where France and the southern European member countries protected their home markets. Bonn also harbored reservations. The question was to what extent the competition provisions of the 1957 EEC Treaty stretched into the field of air transport, especially after the adoption of the Single European Act in February 1986, which promised to create a single market within the European Community. The two most liberally inclined member states, Britain and the Netherlands, hoped to steer European policy discussions in this direction. While discussions on the liberalization of air traffic were still ongoing at the intergovernmental level, the European Court of Justice in Luxembourg intervened on 30 April 1986. Ruling in a case aptly called *Nouvelles Frontières*, the Court held that the competition provisions of the 1957 Treaty of Rome also applied to air transport.[30] The decision provided the legal basis for the Commission's attack on governmental tariff-setting and anti-competitive practices such as pool agreements between airlines. A political process of liberalization followed. In three intensely debated 'packages' of regulations, the European Commission set its sights on the liberalization of EEC air transport policy and the phased creation of an internal European market for air transport by the end of 1992.[31] In November 1989 the Commission came with proposals for a next phase of liberalization, known as the 'second package', which gave formerly national airlines the new legal status of 'community air carriers': once meeting the Commission's criteria they would be free to offer services on routes between EC member states. This effectively curtailed national roles in exchanging intra-European traffic rights. In addition, the European Commission claimed external competences to pursue a coordinated European aviation policy towards third countries.[32]

28 Doganis, *Flying off course*, 72. Dobson, *Globalization and Regional Integration*, p. 52.

29 Staniland, *A Europe of the Air?*, p. 69–73.

30 F.A. van Bakelen, *'Nouvelles Frontières' – European Court of Justice Decision 30 April 1986* (Groningen: Faculteit der Rechtsgeleerdheid, 1986). E. Giemulla, R. Schmid, W. Mölls (eds.), *European Air Law* Vol. 1 (Deventer: Kluwer, 1994), p. 19–30.

31 Dobson, *Globalization and Regional Integration*, p. 82–148.

32 Minutes 179th BLV, 7 Nov. 1989: NNA, 2.05.392, Foreign Affairs 1985–1990, inv.nr. 126.

This process was enhanced by a fundamental reorientation of the role that national states played in international air transport, brought about by the developments following the collapse of the political, economic and social system in Eastern Europe in 1989 and 1990. It created revolutionary new conditions that would have profound effects on air transport in the next decade and established a competitive framework more compatible with KLM's operations.

2 Defending the Dutch Position in European Air Transport

In 1973 the Dutch role in the process of Britain's accession to the EEC formed the background for London signing a liberal agreement on bilateral air transport across the North Sea.[33] The new ground rules this created came into force in November 1973, allowing services by three British private carriers in addition to BEA: British Caledonian, Dan Air London and Air Anglia. KLM also received options to expand its services.[34] In competitive terms, the Dutch faced increased competition under the new regime: in 1974 London merged BOAC and BEA with two regional carriers North East Airlines and Cambrian Airways into a single large national airline, British Airways (BA). The new bilateral helped create conditions to gradually extend existing services, although government accord was still needed to open new routes. In 1980 the Dutch asked permission to operate to Belfast and to the Channel Islands, but other than this liberalization remained in the works. In January 1983 a provisional arrangement was reached to liberalize bilateral air transport further and give substance to the European policy changes regarding interregional air transport. A more concrete development followed in June 1984 when The Hague and London signed an 'understanding' amending their bilateral agreement, creating complete route and capacity freedom and free pricing.[35] For KLM, this was an opportunity to open additional routes. The new regime also had a downward effect on prices, leading to a traffic increase of over 50 per cent between 1984 and 1990. Britain overtook Germany as the most important country in KLM's European route network.

Meanwhile, the existing differences over KLM landing rights in Hong Kong continued, with no sign that any resolution might be in the works. KLM had wished to operate Boeing 747s on the route, but this was vetoed by London as

33 Minutes 138th BLV, 1 Aug. 1973: NNA, 2.05.313, Foreign Affairs 1965–1974, inv.nr. 25176.

34 Confidential summary of discussions by Dept. Trade and Industry, March 1973: NA, 2.05.313, Foreign Affairs 1965–1974, inv.nr. 5431.

35 Minutes 165th BLV, 19 July 1984: NNA, 2.05.330, Foreign Affairs 1981–1984, inv.nr. 24345.

it would eat into the market share of BA. After several rounds of discussions a solution was found late in 1977, in the form of an arrangement under which KLM paid financial compensation to BA in return for the right to use the Boeing 747 on the route.[36] For the thriving Dutch carrier this increased traffic share was still not enough, however. Before long, KLM asked for a second weekly flight. The request went against British interests and was denied. London then complicated the issue when British Caledonian and Hong Kong's own airline, Cathay Pacific, received British permission to operate services to Hong Kong in 1981, leading to renewed Dutch pleas for a second weekly KLM flight.[37] However, despite the trend towards liberalization between the two countries in the European market, British restrictions on the Hong Kong route remained. Direct contact between Minister Neelie Smit-Kroes and her British counterpart Nicholas Ridley did not resolve the issue.[38] In the end KLM resorted to an arrangement under which it paid BA, British Caledonian and Cathay Pacific compensation for the right to operate two weekly flights. Beyond aviation, the status of Hong Kong itself was up for change. In 1984 diplomatic negotiations between London and Beijing resulted in a Sino-British Joint Declaration, in which the United Kingdom agreed to transfer the colony back to China in 1997. In anticipation thereof, the British government gave Hong Kong the right to conclude its own air transport agreements. Hence, discussions were started early in 1986 between the Dutch and the Hong Kong authorities on a separate agreement with the Netherlands that would continue to cover aviation relations after the British lease on Hong Kong expired. The Netherlands was the first nation to negotiate such an agreement. By the end of 1989 ongoing discussions between KLM and Cathay Pacific were considering possible forms of cooperation.

In the second half of the 1960s and early 1970s West Germany exerted constant pressure on the Dutch to reduce KLM's market presence in Germany. The persistence of these demands was rooted in KLM's considerable passenger and cargo operations, and in the fact that the Dutch ignored German sensitivities about expanding KLM's services to the GDR. Despite the *Ostpolitik*, Bonn's objections against flights to the GDR continued, since the traffic reduced East Germany's isolation, which was part of the general Western Cold War strategy.

KLM's continued practice of making twelve weekly commercial stops in Frankfurt on intercontinental routes, such as the services to Melbourne, to destinations in the Far East, in East Africa and to the Venezuelan capital

36 Minutes 151st BLV, 20 Nov. 1977: NNA, 2.05.330, Foreign Affairs 1975–1984, inv.nr. 24343.
37 Minutes 159th BLV, 19 Feb. 1981: NNA, 2.05.330, Foreign Affairs 1981–1984, inv.nr. 24345.
38 Minutes 165th BLV, 19 July 1984: NNA, 2.05.330, Foreign Affairs 1981–1984, inv.nr. 24345.

Caracas and Lima in Peru, claiming 5th freedom rights between Frankfurt and these destinations, provided a case in point for the German objections. Although the Dutch were not unwilling to reduce the number of stops, they held on to them as negotiating gambits, linking this to an imbalance in overall trade and transport between the two countries.[39] On their side, the Germans aspired to achieve an equal division of capacity and traffic rights. Resolving the issues took time. In January 1974 Foreign Affairs' State Secretary Laurens-Jan Brinkhorst became directly involved. In contacts with Helmut Sigrist of the Auswärtiges Amt, Brinkhorst managed to persuade Bonn to agree to allow KLM to continue a limited number of intercontinental flights via Frankfurt, in exchange for an overall reduction of commercial stops in Germany.[40] To protect its remaining rights, KLM now protested against Lufthansa's commercial stop in Amsterdam on its services to Los Angeles. Because neither party was willing to yield, talks continued into 1974. It looked as if the issue would not be settled, but in October 1974 the Germans gave in after all. In the interest of good neighborly relations KLM was allowed to continue its Melbourne service through Frankfurt – with wide-body aircraft, albeit at a reduced frequency. A new arrangement was formalized in a carefully worded memorandum of understanding, signed in December.[41] Nonetheless, Bonn appeared determined to curb KLM's market presence. The Hague stalled the talks as much as possible and in 1979 parties were still talking about some form of accommodation. That year, thanks to the liberal agreement concluded with the US in 1978, KLM started its own services to Los Angeles. Fearing that KLM would attract additional 6th freedom traffic from Germany on this new route, Bonn put KLM's transit services back on the agenda. At this time Lufthansa withdrew its Amsterdam-Los Angeles service. Convinced there was an imbalance in rights and services, Bonn insisted that both carriers give up their respective 5th freedom rights, possibly in exchange for an arrangement on road cargo transport. Apart from this the Germans again indicated that they had issues with the scale of KLM's remaining 6th freedom operations in Germany.[42] This was a far cry from the principle of 'equal opportunities' embraced in The Hague. To prevent possible encroachment, KLM promised to end its 5th freedom traffic from Frankfurt to Melbourne and Caracas in April 1980. However, the matter of 6th

---

39 Memorandum of Conversation RLD, 3 October 1972; Brief W.F. Pelt (Embassy Bonn) to Foreign Affairs, 3 January 1973: NA, 2.05.313, Foreign Affairs 1965–1974, inv.nr. 5352.

40 Minutes 140th BLV, 22 Jan. 1974: NNA, 2.05.313, Foreign Affairs 1965–1974, inv.nr. 25176.

41 Letter Obermayer to Brinkhorst, 21 October 1974: NA, 2.05.313, Foreign Affairs 1965–1974, inv.nr. 5353.

42 Minutes 155th BLV, 6 Sep. 1979: NNA, 2.05.330, Foreign Affairs 1975–1984, inv.nr. 24344.

freedom traffic, which was of vital importance for KLM, was not easily resolved and actually moved up to the ministerial level. After an exchange of letters between Foreign Ministers Chris van der Klaauw and Hans-Dietrich Genscher a conference was called to discuss bilateral aviation in the context of general economic relations between the two neighboring countries.[43]

Preventing Bonn's rejection of 5th and 6th freedom traffic was no easy matter, however, especially since such rights clearly went against German interests. Transport Minister Kurt Gscheidle in particular voiced his reservations concerning KLM's practices in this field. Genscher even hinted at the possibility of terminating the 1956 bilateral agreement with the Netherlands. The Dutch were shocked by the possibility of such a big step.[44] Terminating a treaty was no small issue between friendly neighbors, partners in the European Community. It took over a year of quiet grassroots diplomacy to try and iron out the differences. The Dutch were helped by a political reshuffle in Germany that put a new Transport Minister in office in November 1980, Volker Hauff. Still, Hauff had to deal with a ministry that defended Lufthansa's interests and did not look kindly on its Dutch competitor. To resolve the situation KLM's chief negotiator, Henri Wassenbergh, suggested that both parties give up their respective 5th freedom rights to save the 1956 bilateral.[45] It was not enough. In June 1981 Lufthansa cancelled all deals with KLM, with immediate effect.[46] One of the reasons given was that NLM, a domestic subsidiary of KLM, had started services to Stuttgart, thus increasing the imbalance in capacity. Germany sought to turn back the competitive clock and start with a clean slate when establishing the equal division of capacity it had wanted for so long.[47] To achieve this, Bonn wished to end all KLM's 5th and 6th freedom traffic. Negotiations linked to general issues in bilateral trade and transit lasted months, but in December Bonn gave in on the issue of 6th freedom rights, provided KLM

43 Minutes 158th BLV, 15 Oct. 1980: NNA, 2.05.330, Foreign Affairs 1975–1984, inv.nr. 24344.

44 Letter Van der Klaauw to Genscher, 15 Sept. 1980: NNA, 2.05.330, Foreign Affairs, 1975–1984, inv.nr. 6742. Minutes 160th BLV, 23 June 1981: NNA, 2.05.330, Foreign Affairs 1975–1984, inv. nr. 24345.

45 Letter Wassenbergh to Schreurs, 10 Feb. 1981 (with draft MoU): NNA, 2.05.330, Foreign Affairs, 1975–1984, inv.nr. 6742.

46 Telex Ambrosius to Wassenbergh, 26 June 1981: NNA, 2.05.330, Foreign Affairs, 1975–1984, inv.nr. 6742.

47 Letter Ambrosius to Wassenbergh, 14 July 1981: NNA, 2.05.330, Foreign Affairs, 1975–1984, inv.nr. 6742.

would henceforth embrace a non-aggressive low profile in Germany.[48] A long standing conflict of interests was thus buried.

After a decade of low-key charter and cargo operations to the German Democratic Republic (GDR) and prolonged discussions on whether accepting Interflug aircraft at Schiphol would be construed as a breach in NATO's policy of isolating the East German regime, the first Interflug machine landed in Amsterdam on 19 January 1973. The flight from East Berlin marked the start of regular air services, possible now that the Netherlands had joined other Western nations in recognizing the GDR the month before. Actual operations preceded a bilateral agreement, which was negotiated later that year but not signed until 1976. This was because the Dutch, on instigation from the Western Allies, asked that KLM be given permission to operate via GDR territory to West-Berlin, rather than via the agreed Allied air corridors to the city.[49] In The Hague everybody knew full well that the GDR would consider this an inopportune solidification of West Berlin's position as an enclave in GDR territory.[50] Nonetheless, this was one of the ways NATO used to put pressure on the GDR to relinquish the enforced use of the Berlin air corridors.[51] Thus, Allied interests in strengthening the status of West Berlin seeped into the bilateral talks with the GDR, to the frustration of East Berlin's Transport minister Paul Wilpert, who had hoped for speedy signatures. When KLM received landing rights in West-Berlin from the Western Allies in January 1975, the issue was pursued anew. Nonetheless, an agreement on overflights of GDR territory remained beyond reach, although a bilateral agreement was signed on 21 July 1976, after which air transport was left to 'fly by itself'.[52] Still, KLM only commenced operations to East-Berlin's Schönefeld in April 1979. The coveted traffic from Amsterdam to West Berlin remained out-of-bounds for KLM. From April 1981, a scheduled service was operated by the British carrier Dan Air.

It had been KLM's long-standing wish to be allowed to operate to Paris' Orly Airport, but ongoing differences over cargo services had precluded French permission. As a consequence, KLM was confined to land at Le Bourget while other international airlines moved to the new facilities at Orly.[53] It appeared there

48 Code message Van Lynden to BZ, 4 December 1981: NNA, 2.05.330, Foreign Affairs, 1975–1984, inv.nr. 6742.

49 Conclusions meeting Foreign Affairs with RLD, 9 October 1973: NNA, 2.05.313, Foreign Affairs 1965–1974, inv.nr. 5351.

50 Minutes 139th BLV, 21 Nov. 1973: NNA, 2.05.313, Foreign Affairs 1965–1974, inv.nr. 25176.

51 Code message Van Lynden (Ambassador Washington) to Foreign Affairs, 20 April 1972: NNA, 2.05.313, Foreign Affairs 1965–1974, inv.nr. 5513.

52 Minutes 147th BLV, 17 Aug. 1976: NNA, 2.05.330, Foreign Affairs 1975–1984, inv.nr. 24343.

53 Minutes 134th BLV, 6 Apr. 1972: NNA, 2.05.313, Foreign Affairs 1965–1974, inv.nr. 25175.

was little The Hague could do to change the French attitude, but in 1973 Paris suggested that if KLM were to develop an interest in the new Airbus airliner the request to move operations might receive a more positive consideration. The Airbus A-300 was partly developed in France and assembled in Toulouse, hence the French suggestion. Firmly committed to American-built airliners, KLM's CEO Gerrit van der Wal would hear none of it.[54] KLM thus remained restricted to Le Bourget, where traffic had been declining since the opening of Orly's new facilities in 1961. Being tied to Le Bourget was not KLM's only problem. As before, there was French pressure to reduce the weekly number of cargo flights.[55] Paris was also unhappy about Dutch attempts to introduce services from Rotterdam under the guise of KLM's domestic subsidiary NLM. The plan was that NLM would operate to the new airport Roissy/Charles de Gaulle, then under construction. KLM also hoped to move to the new airport, but this was not approved by France until 1977. That year relations between the French and Dutch flag carriers improved as KLM and Air France planned to initiate a joint service from Marseilles to Amsterdam via Lyon.[56] Nonetheless maintaining the Dutch presence in France was arduous. The government representatives at the Civil Aviation Meeting were reluctant to push for more services as this might have an effect on bilateral relations.[57]

Such concerns highlighted the fact that no air transport agreement had been signed between France and the Netherlands since 1945. The Hague was doubtful whether an effort to bring about such an agreement would yield favorable results, given the French insistence on a connection between aircraft procurement and landing rights.[58] For years representatives from the Ministry of Transport and Waterworks warned that negotiations might well result in new restrictions for KLM.[59] This became very evident when France blocked KLM's planned new service to Lyon in 1985, which had become possible as a result of liberalizations set in motion by the European Commission three years earlier.[60] KLM's efforts to expand its European network made authorities in France nervous[61] and KLM's practice of 6th freedom carriage caused problems all around. The French Director-General of Civil Aviation, Daniel Tenenbaum, refused to cooperate, as the service to Lyon would syphon off traffic from Air France,

54 Minutes 137th BLV, 22 March 1973: NNA, 2.05.313, Foreign Affairs 1965–1974, inv.nr. 25176.
55 Minutes 143th BLV, 17 Jan. 1975: NNA, 2.05.330, Foreign Affairs 1975–1984, inv.nr. 24343.
56 KLM *Annual Report 1977/78*.
57 Minutes 152nd BLV, 11 April 1978: NNA, 2.05.330, Foreign Affairs 1975–1984, inv.nr. 24344.
58 Minutes 155th BLV, 6 Sep. 1979: NNA, 2.05.330, Foreign Affairs 1975–1984, inv.nr. 24344.
59 Minutes 155th BLV, 6 Sep. 1979: NNA, 2.05.330, Foreign Affairs 1975–1984, inv.nr. 24344.
60 Minutes 166th BLV, 10 Jan 1985: NNA, 2.05.392, Foreign Affairs 1985–1990, inv.nr. 124.
61 Minutes 167th BLV, 9 May 1985: NNA, 2.05.392, Foreign Affairs 1985–1990, inv.nr. 124.

which was struggling to cope with liberalizations.[62] In February 1986 the issue was upgraded to the highest governmental level, when Prime Minister Ruud Lubbers and Foreign Minister Hans van den Broek raised the issue of KLM's proposed Lyon service in exchange for possible Dutch orders for the French nuclear industry on the occasion of their visit to President François Mitterrand in Paris.[63] These differences were, however, not resolved. French policy sought to prevent foreign companies from operating air services to regional destinations that had hitherto been the exclusive domain of Air France. Although KLM had already listed the Lyon service in its timetables, the Dutch had to wait for a year before Air France allowed competition, in return for Dutch agreement on Air France operations between Toulouse and Amsterdam and between Paris and Eindhoven.[64] The Franco-Dutch accord, put into writing in February 1987, represented the first bilateral agreement on air services between the two countries since the war.[65]

Despite the heightened tension due to the Soviet intervention in Czechoslovakia in 1968, air services across the Iron Curtain had continued. As before, Prague featured as the hub for air transport between East and West. Discussions were held on cooperation between KLM and ČSA in a service to New York via Amsterdam. In the spring of 1971 ČSA received permission from the Dutch authorities to operate the route.[66] The service developed into a major hard currency earner for ČSA, which faced mounting annual losses. To counter these, ČSA sold tickets in Western currencies well below the agreed IATA price. This was tolerated by the Dutch Civil Aviation Service RLD, much to the displeasure of KLM.[67] However, the services to and from Prague were not among KLM's most lucrative. Traffic was stagnant, which ČSA also reported, despite the rise in private consumption in Czechoslovakia.[68] Combining Prague and Budapest, KLM operated the services primarily on the basis of 6th freedom traffic, feeding from and into its long-haul flights. To fill the empty seats KLM promoted 'roped off' charter tickets for Dutch passengers travelling to Prague. However,

62 Minutes 168th BLV, 15 Oct. 1985: NNA, 2.05.392, Foreign Affairs 1985–1990, inv.nr. 124.

63 *De Volkskrant*, 07-02-1986.

64 *Het Parool*, 19-02-1987.

65 Minutes 172th BLV, 4 March 1987: NNA, 2.05.392, Foreign Affairs 1985–1990, inv.nr. 125.

66 Letter Raben to Czechoslovakian Ministry of Transport, 11 Sept. 1972: NNA, 2.05.313, Foreign Affairs 1965–1974, inv.nr. 5425.

67 Letter Mees to DG RLD (Raben), 15 Aug. 1972 (with copies of the ČSA tickets): NNA, 5.016.5240, RLD, inv.nr. 427.

68 Svik, *Civil Aviation and the Globalization of the Cold War*, p. 183–184. R.J. Crampton, *Eastern Europe in the Twentieth Century* (London: Routledge, 1994), p. 347.

financial returns remained below expectations and in 1985 KLM transferred part of its Prague services to NLM, which operated smaller aircraft.[69]

Aircraft size had also been an issue in relations with the Soviet Union. In November 1972 KLM terminated the agreement under which it had chartered aircraft from Aeroflot for flights over Siberia to Tokyo. Since then, the Dutch had worked towards a permit to operate the Boeing 747 or the Douglas DC-10 on this route. The Soviets, having no wide body aircraft with which to compete, had dragged their feet in giving the desired permission until the summer of 1973. When it finally came, the permit was only valid for the DC-8 aircraft that had been in use at the time of the Aeroflot charter agreement. Now KLM wished to operate the DC-10, or not use the route at all.[70] Talks did not progress and the issue disappeared from the table during the 1973 Oil Crisis. Not until October 1975 did a new round of consultations start. These were, however, prematurely halted when the Dutch lead negotiator, Rob Schreurs, freshly arrived in Moscow and tired after a difficult mission in Tanzania, slipped and fell from the balcony of his hotel. Miraculously, he survived the drop, but was hospitalized for a week in Moscow before being repatriated. Recuperating from his injuries took several months.[71]

Relations did not improve when the Dutch decided to suspend permission for the Aeroflot service Amsterdam-Moscow-Tokyo while KLM was waiting for a permit to use wide bodied aircraft. The Hague professed that the existing imbalance in transport opportunities between KLM and Aeroflot was the reason for the suspension, but in reality KLM had lost interest in the matter after years of obstruction.[72] The Soviets insisted on the conclusion of some form of 'commercial' agreement between companies operating to Japan via Siberia. They linked the issue to various unresolved questions on rights to overfly Western countries. The matter made little progress.[73] Late in 1976 KLM and Aeroflot signed a fifty-fifty pool agreement encompassing services between Moscow and Amsterdam, but the matter of wide-bodied aircraft flying over Siberia remained on the agenda.[74] The pool agreement itself was marred by differences over payments. In 1983 the Soviets tentatively reopened discussions on the use of the Siberia route, but demanded substantial compensation in the shape of unlimited overflights over the Netherlands and full freedom

69 *Algemeen Dagblad*, 05-03-1985.

70 Minutes 138th BLV, 1 August 1973: NNA, 2.05.313, Foreign Affairs 1965–1974, inv.nr. 25176.

71 Interview with Rob Schreurs, 11 April 2018. Minutes 145th BLV, 1 Dec. 1975: NNA, 2.05.330, Foreign Affairs 1975–1984, inv.nr. 24343.

72 Minutes 146th BLV, 18 March 1976: NNA, 2.05.330, Foreign Affairs 1975–1984, inv.nr. 24343.

73 Minutes 147th BLV, 17 Oct. 1976: NNA, 2.05.330, Foreign Affairs 1975–1984, inv.nr. 24343.

74 Minutes 148th BLV, 8 Dec. 1976: NNA, 2.05.330, Foreign Affairs 1975–1984, inv.nr. 24343.

to sell tickets in Holland.[75] The talks made no progress because aviation relations came under heavy pressure as a result of the downing of Korean Air Lines flight 007 by Soviet fighter aircraft on 1 September 1983. The US compelled its allies to take action against Aeroflot as a form of retaliation. For a period of two weeks all air services to and from the Soviet Union were halted.[76] The controversy over flight KAL007 made the Siberia route significantly less attractive for KLM, whatever the savings in fuel costs, and The Hague let the matter float. Nonetheless, intermittent discussions continued between the two airlines, contacts that led the Soviets to raise their demands for financial compensations. As a result, KLM gradually lost interest.[77] In February 1986 the issue resurfaced after Japan had given KLM permission to operate flights via Siberia. The Soviets now appeared willing to come to an arrangement, given the new political mood in the Soviet Union after Mikhail Gorbachev became General Secretary of the Communist Party in March 1985. The question then was: would The Hague allow Aeroflot freedom of operations and ticket sales in the Netherlands?[78] In June 1986 a new round of talks followed and the Soviets proved more accommodating towards KLM, offering the Dutch two weekly frequencies over Siberia.[79] An accord to this effect was drawn up in February 1987, coinciding with talks on similar rights with Britain. In return Aeroflot received commercial freedom in the Netherlands.[80]

3 Fighting for Friendship in Indonesia and Australia

In 1973 the relations between the Netherlands and Indonesia came under considerable stress. This was largely due to Dutch domestic politics, where the new coalition government coming into office had a significantly left wing signature. The new Minister for Development Cooperation, Jan Pronk, a prominent member of the social democratic party that dominated the new cabinet, threw his weight behind efforts to steer the government away from existing fixes in foreign policy. Pronk had a particular focus on Indonesia, relations with which had improved since the New Guinea crisis of the early 1960s and the toppling of the Sukarno government in 1965. In his first speech as president

---

75 Minutes 163rd BLV, 28 June 1983: NNA, 2.05.330, Foreign Affairs 1975–1984, inv.nr. 24345.
76 Svik, *Civil Aviation and the Globalization of the Cold War*, p. 159–177.
77 Minutes 166th BLV, 10 Jan. 1985: NNA, 2.05.392, Foreign Affairs 1985–1990, inv.nr. 124.
78 Minutes 169th BLV, 12 Feb. 1986: NNA, 2.05.392, Foreign Affairs 1985–1990, inv.nr. 124.
79 Minutes, 170th BLV, 10 June 1986: NNA, 2.05.392, Foreign Affairs 1985–1990, inv.nr. 124.
80 Minutes 172nd BLV, 4 March 1987: NNA, 2.05.392, Foreign Affairs 1985–1990, inv.nr. 125.

of the Intergovernmental Group of countries providing special aid to Indonesia (IGGI), in December 1973, Pronk voiced Dutch concerns over human rights when he referred to the treatment of political prisoners. This invoked serious discord. Indonesia viewed Pronk's statements as neocolonial criticism and as a threat that development aid would be stopped if Dutch conditions were not met.[81]

Bilateral relations took a decisive downward turn, which had an effect on aviation. In a meeting with a senior KLM-official, Garuda's director-general, Wiweko Soepono, expressed his serious disappointment about the apparent change of policy in The Hague, announcing there might well be consequences for the relations between KLM and Garuda.[82] The Indonesians waited until 1976 before partly downgrading cooperation between Garuda and KLM and requiring KLM to pay for the privilege of overflying Indonesian territory on the route to Sydney.[83] Garuda also suggested that the Indonesian carrier might divert to other airports in Europe unless the Dutch became more lenient. Relations took a further downward turn when Indonesia imposed a total ban on KLM flights over Indonesian territory on the route to Sydney in the spring of 1981.[84] The general economic downturn of the early 1980s and the market slump in tourism that accompanied it added to the problems. Relations improved again when a new government in The Hague decided to increase bilateral aid to Indonesia.[85] At Garuda, the appointment of a new CEO, Reyn Lumenta, in November 1984 also helped improve relations. In 1986, KLM and Garuda set up a joint venture to operate a service between Amsterdam and Bali, after which KLM was promised free passage over Indonesian territory for its Australia flights.[86] However, in 1988 Lumenta was replaced by Moehamad Soeparno, who had less of a personal connection with the Netherlands. This had the effect of propelling the new bilateral air transport agreement that had been waiting in the wings for years to the highest political level. It was discussed when a Dutch delegation, led by Prime Minister Ruud Lubbers and Foreign Affairs Minister Hans van den Broek, arrived in Bali for an official visit in October 1988.[87] Although some progress was reported, the issue was only

81 Code message (No. 10184) Chargé d'Affaires in Jakarta to Minister Pronk, 5 June 1974, in: *Nederlandse Ontwikkelingssamenwerking. Bronnenuitgave*. Vol. 4, 1973–1977 (The Hague: Instituut voor Nederlandse Geschiedenis, 2005), p. 233–234.

82 Minutes 141st BLV, 16 April 1974: NNA, 2.05.313, Foreign Affairs 1965–1974, inv.nr. 25176.

83 Minutes 146th BLV, 18 March 1976: NNA, 2.05.330, Foreign Affairs 1975–1984, inv.nr. 24343.

84 Minutes 160th BLV, 23 June 1981: NNA, 2.05.330, Foreign Affairs 1975–1984, inv.nr. 24345.

85 Hellema, *Nederland in de wereld*, p. 329, 335.

86 Minutes 170th BLV, 10 June 1986: NNA, 2.05.392, Foreign Affairs 1985–1990, inv.nr. 125.

87 Minutes 176th BLV, 23 Sept. 1988: NNA, 2.05.392, Foreign Affairs 1985–1990, inv.nr. 125.

resolved in a personal meeting between Indonesia's Minister of Research and Technology Bacharuddin Habibie and the Dutch Transport Minister Neelie Smit-Kroes. This cleared the air and in October 1989 KLM and Garuda drew up a new cooperation agreement.[88]

Beyond the Indonesian archipelago and the Timor Sea, Australia had tabled a proposal in 1975 that Qantas and KLM draw up a pool agreement for air traffic to and from Amsterdam. KLM was not enthused, fearing this might lead to substantial payments to Qantas.[89] Indeed, it was not long before Australia, where the newly elected government under Malcolm Fraser had reorganized the oversight of air transport affairs, began clamoring for a bigger share of the revenues, demanding that Qantas be allowed to operate more flights per week than KLM.[90] Talks about this ran into a stalemate late in 1976, after which Australia decided to steer its own course and introduced cheaper APEX (Advance Passenger Excursion) fares on Qantas flights to boost its market share of traffic to Europe. Canberra pinned KLM to 195 seats per flight. Apart from competing with KLM, Qantas hoped to forestall plans by the British aviation tycoon Freddie Laker to begin extremely low fare operations between London and Sydney with his *Skytrain* air service, outside the normal regulatory framework. The Dutch offer to cooperate on APEX fares in return for a relaxation of passenger quota was rejected in Australia. Canberra was intent on boosting load factors on Qantas' own international flights to improve profitability.[91] This resulted in a deadlock. Next, Canberra embarked on a full review of Australia's civil aviation policy, leading to further restrictions: in future European airlines were to refrain from picking up 5th freedom passengers at stops along the long route to Sydney.[92]

This policy was clearly unattractive for airlines operating the Australia route. In the Dutch case, talks at the political level followed in the spring of 1979 in which State Secretary Neelie Smit-Kroes achieved a breakthrough in a personal discussion with Australia's Transport Minister Peter Nixon. In return for an agreement on lower fares, Smit-Kroes managed to have KLM's quota raised from 195 to 260 passengers per flight.[93] Here the Australians drew the line, however, much to the apprehension of the Dutch. But agreement or no

88 Minutes 179th BLV, 7 Nov. 1989: NNA, 2.05.392, Foreign Affairs 1985–1990, inv.nr. 126.

89 Minutes 144th BLV, 25 June 1975: NNA, 2.05.330, Foreign Affairs 1975–1984, inv.nr. 24343.

90 Minutes 148th BLV, 8 Dec. 1976: NNA, 2.05.330, Foreign Affairs 1975–1984, inv.nr. 24343.

91 Minutes 149th BLV, 5 April 1977: NNA, 2.05.330, Foreign Affairs 1975–1984, inv.nr. 24343. Richard H. Snape, Lisa Gropp, Tas Luttrell, *Australia's Trade Policy. A Documentary History* (St. Leonards: Allen & Unwin, 1998), p. 308–309.

92 Minutes 153rd BLV, 18 Oct. 1978: NNA, 2.05.330, Foreign Affairs 1975–1984, inv.nr. 24344.

93 Minutes 154th BLV, 25 Apr. 1979: NNA, 2.05.330, Foreign Affairs 1975–1984, inv.nr. 24344.

agreement, the fare issue remained a bone of contention. Discussions on the topic continued for over a year without resolution, until the Fraser government moved towards a more liberal aviation policy in 1981.[94] This new course was continued under the subsequent Labor government led by Bob Hawke in 1983. In 1988, after years of friendly prodding, it even appeared that Australia might allow a new KLM service to Perth.[95] To promote the issue, discussions were taken to the highest government level and attached to the agenda for talks during Prime Minister Ruud Lubbers' and Foreign Minister Hans van den Broek's visit to Australia, which was scheduled to follow their Indonesian trip late in 1988.[96] Still, progress was only made after Australia's new Transport Minister, Ralph Willis, put forward policy guidelines that departed from a strict interpretation of reciprocity to incorporate other economic interests, like tourism, in the bilateral equation.[97] And so, after decades of fruitless maneuvers, KLM finally received its coveted second Australian frequency in October 1989. Likewise, Qantas received permission to operate to Amsterdam twice a week.[98]

4 An Air Route to China via Taiwan?

In May 1972, diplomatic relations between the Netherlands and the People's Republic of China (PRC) were upgraded to ambassadorial level. In evidence of these improved relations, The Hague issued a carefully worded statement to the effect that the Netherlands respected the Chinese view that Taiwan was a part of China.[99] The Hague hoped that after more than twenty years of efforts to establish air services KLM might piggyback on this development. After all, China had also established aviation relations with other Western countries. From a Chinese perspective, however, Amsterdam was not a particularly attractive destination for an exchange of traffic rights. A Dutch draft for a bilateral agreement, also intended as an opening to improved trade relations, disappeared into a desk drawer in Beijing in mid-1973. It was only when a Dutch delegation, headed by Minister of Economic Affairs Ruud Lubbers, visited Beijing in November 1973 that renewed contacts about shipping and air

94 Minutes 160th BLV, 23 June 1981: NNA, 2.05.330, Foreign Affairs 1975–1984, inv.nr. 24345.
95 Minutes 175th BLV, 12 Jan. 1988: NNA, 2.05.392, Foreign Affairs 1985–1990, inv.nr. 125.
96 Minutes 176th BLV, 23 Sept. 1988: NNA, 2.05.392, Foreign Affairs 1985–1990, inv.nr. 125.
97 Minutes 178th BLV, 4 July 1989: NNA, 2.05.392, Foreign Affairs 1985–1990, inv.nr. 126.
98 Minutes 179th BLV, 7 Oct. 1989: NNA, 2.05.392, Foreign Affairs 1985–1990, inv.nr. 126.
99 Internal memo Foreign Affairs re. Taiwan, 1 Nov. 1983: NNA, 2.06.107, Economic Affairs, Directorate-General Foreign Economic Relations (further: BEB), inv.nr. 4994.

connections came about.[100] Hoping to make progress, The Hague put aviation high on the agenda, but to no effect.[101]

The situation changed in 1975 as a result of the Sino-Russian conflicts in Southeast Asia, which encouraged Beijing to strengthen its ties with Western Europe.[102] In the first week of September, Dutch negotiators left for Beijing. Shortly before leaving, they received a Chinese draft for a bilateral agreement. The talks, which were held in Beijing on 8 September 1975, were interspersed with trips to the Forbidden City, the Great Wall, Guangzhou and Guilin, but in between tourist trips and culinary outings, discussions were difficult. The Chinese opposed operations with wide body jets, citing insufficient length of the runways in Beijing. Moreover, Beijing would not permit 5th freedom rights between China and Asian destinations such as Japan.[103] This made the route commercially less attractive. In the circumstances, KLM was in no hurry to push things along.[104]

In the spring of 1977, after the end of the Cultural Revolution that had gripped China from 1966 until Mao's death the year before, China put forward an updated proposal for a bilateral agreement. In November 1978 further talks were scheduled, this time in The Hague. China's Minister of Foreign Affairs Huang Hua was received with great respect and personally shown around by his Dutch counterpart Chris van der Klaauw.[105] Nonetheless, discussions were disappointing and no agreement was reached. Although the Chinese said that KLM was welcome in principle, the airline division of the Civil Aviation Administration of China (CAAC) was not interested in flying to Amsterdam.[106] It was not until January 1979 that The Hague and Beijing agreed on an exchange of notes as a commitment to improved relations, but even then the agreements were not fleshed out. Under their new leader, Deng Xiaoping, China was in a phase of ideological and economic reorientation, with agriculture receiving priority. In October 1979, both countries signed a joint declaration on agricultural

100 Minutes 139th BLV 21 November 1973 and 140th BLV 22 January 1974: NNA, 2.05.313, Foreign Affairs 1965–1974, inv.nr. 25176.

101 Minutes 140th BLV 22 January 1974: NNA, 2.05.313, Foreign Affairs 1965–1974, inv.nr. 25176.

102 Annual Report Embassy Beijing on 1975, 29 March 1976: NNA, 2.05.330, Foreign Affairs 1975–1984, inv.nr. 6735.

103 Code message Embassy Beijing re. aviation talks, 16 Sept. 1975: NNA, 2.05.330, Foreign Affairs 1975–1984, inv.nr. 6735.

104 Minutes 145th BLV, 1 December 1975: NNA, 2.05.330, Foreign Affairs 1975–1984, inv.nr. 24343.

105 C.A. van der Klaauw, *Een diplomatenleven. Memoires* (Amsterdam 1995) p. 284–285.

106 Code message Foreign Affairs to embassy Beijing re. aviation talks, 29 Nov. 1978: NNA, 2.05.330, Foreign Affairs 1975–1984, inv.nr. 6735.

cooperation. Direct telephone connections were also established.[107] But in aviation the Chinese authorities were uncooperative. The planned opening of a KLM service again receded into the distance.[108] In the meantime, relations deteriorated in the autumn of 1980 due to developments in the Netherlands.

In the contacts with Beijing, the status of Taiwan had not been mentioned since 1972. The Dutch change of course in the United Nations and the various trade missions that had visited China had raised the expectation that The Hague wanted to strengthen ties with the People's Republic. Outside the spotlight of politics, however, the Dutch trade relationship with Taiwan had also continued. In practice, the People's Republic did not oppose this.[109] This situation changed in 1980. The US, having established diplomatic relations with the People's Republic the year before, revoked its defense treaty with Taiwan, which forced the Taiwanese to look for arms elsewhere. As a result of long-standing informal contacts, the Dutch shipbuilding combination Rijn-Schelde-Verolme (RSV), which was in dire straits, entered into talks with Taiwanese officials about a possible delivery of submarines to the Taiwanese navy. Landing the order was of the utmost importance for the ailing shipbuilding group. Although it was clear from the outset that the acceptance of a Taiwanese purchase would cause political problems, RSV and the Taiwanese navy agreed on the contours of a contract in August 1980.

In The Hague, the ministers of economic affairs and foreign affairs were deliberately only informed late in the process to avoid problems in Dutch-Chinese rapprochement. After all, the issue of a KLM service to Beijing still remained at the top of the bilateral agenda. On 28 October 1980, RSV signed a contract, subject to a government export license. For RSV the permit was of vital importance.[110] Yet the timing of the contract was unfortunate because the next day Prime Minister Dries van Agt and Foreign Minister Chris van der Klaauw were scheduled to visit China to celebrate the rapprochement between the two countries and give the issue of KLM landing rights a push in the right direction.[111]

Eventually, RSV did receive permission to supply two submarines. After a fierce discussion in the cabinet, it was decided that the Taiwanese order was

107 *Jaarboek ministerie van Buitenlandse Zaken 1979–1980* (Den Haag 1980) p. 90.

108 Code message Embassy Beijing re. aviation relations with China and KLM service to Beijing, 20 Nov. 1979: NNA, 2.05.330, Foreign Affairs 1975–1984, inv.nr. 6736.

109 Internal memo Foreign Affairs re. conclusions on 'Chinese perspectives', 9 Jan. 1979: NNA, 2.05.330, Foreign Affairs 1975–1984, inv.nr. 6736.

110 Ko Colijn, Paul Rusman, *Het Nederlandse Wapenexportbeleid 1963–1988* (Den Haag: Nijgh & Van Ditmar Universitair, 1989) p. 275–283.

111 Van der Klaauw, *Een diplomatenleven*, p. 293.

absolutely crucial for RSV's survival in the European shipbuilding industry.[112] But in Dutch political circles there was much opposition, as arms deliveries might be construed as an unfriendly act that could lead to repercussions. In Beijing, the government of the People's Republic expressed its outrage and spoke of an 'act of undermining the friendly Sino-Dutch relations'.[113] Reprisals were inevitable. China recalled its ambassador and lowered diplomatic relations to the level of chargés d'affaires. Chinese shipping in Rotterdam was significantly reduced. A Philips delegation was told that there would be no more follow-up contracts.[114] Shell even saw itself forced to set up a separate subsidiary under British law to trade with China and avoid any appearance of a connection with the Netherlands.[115] And thus ratification of the bilateral aviation agreement of January 1979 was off.[116] Faced with a postponement of services that might prove indefinite, KLM's head of foreign relations, Henri Wassenbergh, concluded that the airline might as well start services to Taipei.[117] The Hague took the view that it had made a binding contractual commitment to Taiwan regarding the submarines, irrespective of the possible Chinese response.[118]

While this was playing out, a second issue had arisen. At the beginning of 1980 both KLM and Martinair, a charter airline that worked closely with KLM, had informally expressed an interest in operating to Taiwan. In contrast to KLM, Martinair was already flying to the People's Republic, where it possessed good contacts. Dealing with the after-effects of the submarine contract, Foreign Affairs Minister Van der Klaauw was not happy with the growing airline interest in Taiwan. While the minister could envision Martinair cargo flights, the suggestion of KLM negotiator Wassenbergh that his airline might also be interested in such flights was to him a harbinger of new problems with Beijing.[119]

112 Colijn, Rusman, *Het Nederlandse Wapenexportbeleid*, p. 286–287.

113 Chinese statement regarding bilateral relations, 27 Febr. 1981: NNA, 2.05.330, Foreign Affairs 1975–1984, inv.nr. 6736.

114 Leonard Blussé, *Tribuut aan China. Vier eeuwen Nederlands-Chinese betrekkingen* (Amsterdam 1989) p. 176–178.

115 Code message Embassy Beijing re. position of Dutch companies in China, 5 May 1981. Code message re. Shell, 3 June 1981: NNA, 2.05.330, Foreign Affairs 1975–1984, inv.nr. 6736.

116 Van der Klaauw, *Een diplomatenleven*, p. 298.

117 Minutes 161th BLV, 7 Jan. 1982: NNA, 2.05.330, Foreign Affairs 1975–1984, inv.nr. 24345.

118 Florentine van Lookeren Campagne, 'Politiek of economisch falen? Het eerste kabinet-Van Agt en de steun aan het RSV-concern. Uit de ministerraadsnotulen van 1980, in: C.C. van Baalen (ed.), *De waan van de dag. Jaarboek parlementaire geschiedenis* (Amsterdam: Boom, 2006) p. 108–118, there 114.

119 Minutes 156th BLV, 30 Jan. 1980: NNA, 2.05.330, Foreign Affairs 1975–1984, inv.nr. 24344. Code message Foreign Affairs to Embassy Beijing re. transport relations with Taiwan, 9 July 1980: NNA, 2.05.330, Foreign Affairs 1975–1984, inv.nr. 6736.

For KLM Taiwan was a commercially interesting market. No other Western European airline offered services to Taipei, although there were extensive trade contacts. Nevertheless, formal diplomatic relations with Taiwan did not exist, since Taiwan was not a recognized state. A bilateral air services agreement was therefore out of the question. At KLM's head office consideration was given to whether a service could be set up on another basis. In the absence of diplomatic channels, KLM might, for example, apply for a 'temporary permit' in cooperation with Taiwan's China Air Lines (CAL). The serial execution of charter flights was also considered. Both options were not without political risk, however, as such a course of action would put renewed strain on relations with the People's Republic. The possibility of repercussions had to be taken into account. Beijing might slam the door on KLM for good.

But problems were also looming beyond the bilateral sphere. KLM was not sure whether the cooperation of other countries along the long route to Taipei could be obtained. Pakistan was a case in point as it maintained friendly relations with China. What made things even more complicated was that in the Netherlands parliamentary elections were planned in May 1981. While the current cabinet had decided to stick to the submarine deal despite the wrath of Beijing, there was reasonable doubt as to whether a new cabinet would dare sign a tainted agreement with Taipei to benefit the Dutch business community.[120]

Concerned about a possible fuss and its political consequences, KLM's management focused on alternatives that would not harm Dutch interests in Beijing. The spotlight shifted to Japan. Since 1975, when Japan and the People's Republic had concluded a bilateral aviation agreement, a peculiar air service had been set up between Tokyo and Taipei that operated outside the framework of bilateral agreements. Japan, too, did not maintain diplomatic relations with Taiwan. The basis for the flights was an agreement between private parties. The Japanese Interchange Association and Taiwan's Association of East Asian Relations had jointly agreed on the desirability of air services between Tokyo and Taipei. This was more or less condoned by Beijing, which turned a blind eye to the situation as long as neither the Japanese nor the Taiwanese authorities were officially involved. All the same, Beijing had said it would under no circumstances condone operations of Japan's national airline, Japan Air Lines (JAL), to Taipei. In Tokyo, the Japanese government was also cautious. Taiwan's China Air Lines was not even allowed to land at the same airport as CAAC. Japan established a special subsidiary to operate flights to Taipei, Japan Asia Airlines (JAA), and as long as no one asked difficult questions, flights went

120 KLM-memo A.J. Ganzeboom to H.A. Wassenbergh re. flights to Taiwan, 1 April 1981: NNA, 2.05.330, Foreign Affairs 1975–1984, inv.nr. 6793.

ahead. From 15 September 1975 onwards JAA operated services.[121] After a look at the Japanese example, KLM hoped to be able to do the same.

Thus, a thorny issue was put on the table in The Hague. Given the existing problems with the People's Republic, Foreign Affairs had to display restraint, although informal relations with Taiwan had shown an upward trend since the submarines agreement. KLM therefore tried to garner support from the Aviation Service RLD, which also held the Martinair file on Taiwan. Because Martinair only took cargo, did not operate a scheduled service and was not the national airline, there seemed to be room for maneuver, provided that the Dutch and Taiwanese governments were kept at bay. This, however, was not to KLM's liking. In August 1982, the airline tried to initiate flights together with China Air Lines as a private endeavor, despite the political objections in The Hague.[122] KLM's CEO Sergio Orlandini took steps to address the government's concerns in a direct conversation with Prime Minister Dries van Agt. It was not enough. At Foreign Affairs, Traffic Advisor Jan van Arkel suggested another option might be to examine the way Japan had approached the issue of the air service to Taipei.[123] A month later KLM signed an agreement with China Air Lines to provide unscheduled flights with passengers.[124]

Meanwhile, Martinair had also remained in touch with Taipei. Now that relations with Taiwan developed – in December 1982 the keels were laid for the first of the two ordered submarines – director Martin Schröder reached an arrangement with China Air Lines. The accord applied to both Martinair and KLM. KLM would fly on behalf of Martinair, with Taipei as the last stop-over of its scheduled service to Tokyo. In exchange for Taiwanese cooperation, China Air Lines would set up a service (sponsored by KLM) to Amsterdam.[125] The newly appointed Minister of Foreign Affairs, Hans van den Broek, was displeased. He feared for the relationship with the People's Republic and was 'very worried about the way in which the Martinair delegation in Taipei

121 Gene T. Hsiao, *The foreign trade of China: policy, law, and practice* (Canberra: Australian National University Press, 1977) p. 68.

122 Memo Foreign Affairs to Prime Minister A.A.M. van Agt re. Dutch airlines and Taiwan, 27 Aug. 1982: NNA, 2.05.330, Foreign Affairs 1975–1984, inv.nr. 6793.

123 Internal memo Foreign Affairs re. Taiwan-KLM, 20 Oct. 1982: NNA, 2.05.330, Foreign Affairs 1975–1984, inv.nr. 6793.

124 Internal memo Foreign Affairs to Minister H. van den Broek re. KLM in Taiwan, 22 Nov. 1982. Confidential letter KLM to Director-General Netherlands Aviation Service H. Raben re. China Air Lines (with text KLM-CAL Inter-Company Agreement: NNA, 2.05.330, Foreign Affairs 1975–1984, inv.nr. 6793.

125 Agreement between China Air Lines Ltd. and Martinair Holland N.V., 11 Jan. 1983. Code message Dutch Consul-General Hong Kong re. aviation relations with Taiwan, 14 Jan. 1983: NNA, 2.05.330, Foreign Affairs 1975–1984, inv.nr. 6794.

has presented things'.[126] The impression had been created that KLM was going to open a scheduled service to Taiwan under the Martinair contract. While this was indeed the case, it was not so *de jure*. Thus, when asked, the Ministry of Foreign Affairs was required to place particular emphasis on the fact that the whole thing was a Martinair operation, the commercial and technical interpretation of which remained outside the government's reach. The Dutch chargé d'affaires in Beijing received strict instructions to maintain that this was nothing but a business deal between private parties and that Dutch approval of China Air Lines landings at Schiphol could in no way be interpreted as a recognition of Taiwanese authorities.[127] Van den Broek hoped that this would counter the expected reactions from Beijing. However, in the Council of Ministers he maintained his objections to the air service as such and to the fact that KLM publicized it.[128] Removing himself as far as possible from the deal he left the details of the implementation of the agreement to the Minister of Transport and Water Management, Neelie Smit-Kroes. The issue came up three more times in the Council of Ministers, as the People's Republic insisted that the government make an effort to undo the Martinair contract. China again threatened general repercussions, but The Hague adopted a wait-and-see attitude.[129]

Some form of reaction from Beijing was inevitable. After all, Taipei proudly announced that China Air Lines, which had had difficulties acquiring foreign landing rights due to Taiwan's status in the world, would shortly start a scheduled service to Amsterdam as its only European destination.[130] On 31 January the Chinese chargé d'affaires Guo Jie reported to the ministry in The Hague carrying an official complaint. By agreeing to an air connection without the consent of the People's Republic, the Dutch had, in Guo's words, again broken away from the international recognition that Taiwan was part of China. This was 'absolutely unacceptable' to the Government in Beijing. Guo called the involvement of KLM under the cover of charter transport a misleading trick

---

126 Letter Van den Broek to Smit-Kroes, 14 Jan. 1983: NNA, 2.05.330, Foreign Affairs 1975–1984, inv.nr. 6794.

127 Code message Foreign Affairs to Embassy Beijing re. Martinair-Taiwan, 25 Jan. 1983: NNA, 2.05.330, Foreign Affairs 1975–1984, inv.nr. 6794.

128 Office memo Foreign Affairs to Van den Broek, 3 March 1983: NNA, 2.05.330, Foreign Affairs 1975–1984, inv.nr. 6794. Cabinet Minutes, 4 March 1983 (3g): NNA, 2.02.05.02, Council of Ministers, inv.nr. 3755.

129 Cabinet minutes, 18 March 1983 (3e), and 25 March 1983 (3f): NNA, 2.02.05.02, Council of Ministers, inv.nr. 3755.

130 Press message Taipei re. Taiwan-Netherlands China Air Lines, 26 Jan. 1983: NNA, 2.05.330, Foreign Affairs 1975–1984, inv.nr. 6794.

and demanded that the case be reversed immediately.[131] Beijing labelled the permission to allow China Air Lines to land in Amsterdam an interference in China's internal affairs and an encroachment on the sovereignty of the People's Republic. Guo even called bilateral diplomatic relations as such into question.[132] For Beijing, aviation was a case *sui generis*, not comparable to other commercial matters.[133]

What could The Hague do without losing face? After consultation between State Secretary of Foreign Affairs Wim van Eekelen and Minister Smit-Kroes, China Air Lines was urged not to present itself as a national airline in any way, under penalty of the loss of the Amsterdam landing permit.[134] Public advertisements planned by KLM to promote Taipei as a new destination were labelled 'not opportune' by the Ministry of Foreign Affairs. But without being able to publicize the service, the question was whether KLM could sell enough tickets to make the flights remunerative.[135] Between KLM and the Ministry of Foreign Affairs, the issue of publicity surrounding the Taipei flights was pushed back and forth several times. Finally, it was decided to announce the service by means of a Martinair advertisement. The text needed precise wording. Martinair held out that 'a weekly scheduled passenger and cargo service will be operated with KLM Boeing-747 aircraft from Saturday 2 April'.[136] Nonetheless, advertising remained a thorny issue. Despite Van den Broek's insistence on keeping a low profile, the first flight to Taipei took off as KL809 on 2 April 1983 with 144 – mostly invited – passengers. As a curtsy to China, the KLM timetable was given a footnote in red ink: 'operated under contract with Martinair'.[137] In the Netherlands, the newspapers reported on the Taipei service as a simple news fact. Thus, the new destination still got its publicity.[138] However, in Beijing, China's foreign ministry spokesman called the connection 'a flagrant violation of Chinese sovereignty.' The link with the submarine deliveries was

---

131 Code message Van den Broek to Beijing re. air service to Taiwan, 1 Feb. 1983: NNA, 2.05.330, Foreign Affairs 1975–1984, inv.nr. 6794.

132 ANP press message re. KLM-flights to Taiwan, 4 Feb. 1983: NNA, 2.05.330, Foreign Affairs 1975–1984, inv.nr. 6794.

133 Code message Embassy Beijing re. air services to Taiwan, 8 Feb. 1983: NNA, 2.05.330, Foreign Affairs 1975–1984, inv.nr. 6736.

134 Office memo Foreign Affairs (DGPZ), 11 Feb. 1983: NNA, 2.05.330, Foreign Affairs 1975–1984, inv.nr. 6794.

135 Memo H.A. Wassenbergh to Foreign Affairs re. air service Amsterdam-Taipei, 28 Feb. 1983: NNA, 2.05.330, Foreign Affairs 1975–1984, inv.nr. 6794.

136 Office memo Foreign Affairs to Van den Broek re. scheduled services Amsterdam-Taipei, 2 March 1983: NNA, 2.05.330, Foreign Affairs 1975–1984, inv.nr. 6794.

137 KLM Timetable 1983, p. 11: Archive KLM, Amstelveen.

138 Example: *Nederlands Dagblad*, 6 April 1983.

underscored and China demanded immediate cessation of the Taipei flights.[139] In Beijing's view, KLM had flown into Chinese airspace without the PRC's permission.[140] By way of reprisal Martinair and KLM were banned from flying the customary route to Hong Kong through Chinese airspace (which meant a costly detour of about 1,100 kilometers) and KLM's never-effected landing rights in Beijing were immediately revoked.[141] The Hague was also forced to express 'regret' that it had not been able to convince the government of the People's Republic of the sincerity of the Dutch one-China policy.[142]

Despite this declaration of regret, the frost was not out of the air, although it did create a basis for some improved contacts. These again came under pressure once again in the autumn of 1983, when information was leaked that Taiwan was considering ordering more submarines from the Netherlands. This time The Hague immediately steered a reticent course, fearful that relations with the People's Republic would be put at risk.[143] This was noted in Beijing. During an informal conversation on 9 November about the economic relationship between the Netherlands and China, Deputy Minister Zhou Nan told his Dutch interlocutor that if The Hague would make an irrevocable and binding statement not to allow new arms sales to Taiwan, Beijing was prepared to restore diplomatic relations at ambassadorial level and to talk about a new aviation agreement. KLM could then still receive landing rights.[144] The airline was quick to claim a service to Beijing, even though its management doubted it would be profitable in the short term.[145]

After the cabinet formally decided on 16 December 1983 not to grant an export license for new submarines, the air cleared further.[146] As early as January

---

139 Telex Embassy Beijing re. air services to Taiwan, 5 April 1983: NNA, 2.05.330, Foreign Affairs 1975–1984, inv.nr. 6736. Also: *NRC Handelsblad*, 6 April 1983.

140 Code message Embassy Beijing re. Chinese protest re. agreement Martinair – China Air Lines, 15 March 1983: NNA, 2.05.330, Foreign Affairs 1975–1984, inv.nr. 6736.

141 Code message Embassy Beijing re. Air service Martinair to Taiwan, 8 April 1983: NNA, 2.05.330, Foreign Affairs 1975–1984, inv.nr. 6794.

142 Press statement re. Chinese reaction to agreement Martinair – China Air Lines, 11 April 1983: NNA, 2.05.330, Foreign Affairs 1975–1984, inv.nr. 6794.

143 Memo Foreign Affairs re. new submarine orders by Taiwan, undated (Jan. 1983); memo G.B. de Grooth (Dir-Gen BEB) to Minister Van Aardenne, 22 Dec. 1983: NNA, 2.06.107, Economic Affairs, BEB, inv.nr. 4994.

144 Code message Embassy Beijing re. consultations with China, 9 Nov. 1983: NNA, 2.05.330, Foreign Affairs 1975–1984, inv.nr. 6736.

145 Letter Orlandini to Van den Broek, 6 Dec. 1983: NNA, 2.05.330, Foreign Affairs 1975–1984, inv.nr. 6736.

146 Cabinet minutes, 16 December 1983 (3g). Export license for Wilton Feyenoord: NNA, 2.05.02, Council of Ministers, inv.nr. 3764. Letter Van Aardenne to Parliament, 21 Dec. 1983: HSG, 1983–1984, 2e Kamer, Bijlage 18207, nr. 1.

1984, chargé d'affaires Guo told The Hague that his government was now committed to take relations to a higher level.[147] Beijing announced that it would be flexible, although the Taiwan issue would not be forgotten.[148] Pending this, relations were normalized on 1 February 1984. State Secretary for Economic Affairs Frits Bolkestein was told he would be welcome in Beijing with a Dutch trade mission; Chinese ships again called at the port of Rotterdam; and Philips was allowed to compete for a contract for the modernization of Chinese telecommunications. There were also opportunities for agriculture, and even for Fokker.[149]

KLM, however, had no intention of leaving Taipei, where operating results were very favorable. On the contrary, CEO Sergio Orlandini trained his sights on a third weekly service. Foreign Minister Van den Broek, meanwhile, stressed that any kind of publicity surrounding additional flights to Taipei was to be avoided so as not to cause further problems with Beijing.[150] In January 1985 Van den Broek visited Beijing. Although the subject was not formally on the agenda, landing rights were also discussed. Beijing now indicated that it was interested in air connections with the Netherlands. As proof of China's good will, Martinair received several charter contracts. It took almost a year before the penny dropped in The Hague that Beijing's more accommodating attitude was intended as an incentive to detach the Netherlands from its aviation relationship with Taiwan.[151]

That Beijing was now serious about strengthening relations was also evident from the invitation for an extensive visit to China by Prime Minister Ruud Lubbers and Foreign Minister Hans van den Broek at the beginning of 1987. Prominent on the agenda was the issue of mutual trade. The Chinese let it be known that they were now interested in formalizing the aviation relationship. Nonetheless, little progress was made with regard to a new bilateral aviation agreement.

In the meantime, the service between Amsterdam and Taipei continued to develop. KLM booked an annual turnover of about 300 million guilders and in

147 Code message Foreign Affairs to Embassy Beijing re. relations with China, 17 Jan. 1984: NNA, 2.05.330, Foreign Affairs 1975–1984, inv.nr. 6736.

148 Memo Wijnaendts to Van den Broek re. consultations in Beijing, 18 Jan. 1984: NNA, 2.05.330, Foreign Affairs 1975–1984, inv.nr. 6736.

149 Report of interdepartmental consultations re. Dutch-Chinese relations on 9 Feb. 1984: NNA, 2.05.330, Foreign Affairs 1975–1984, inv.nr. 6736.

150 Memo Van den Broek to Wijnaendts re. visist by Orlandini and 3rd KLM frequency to Taipei, 6 Nov. 1984: NNA, 2.05.330, Foreign Affairs 1975–1984, inv.nr. 6794.

151 Minutes 169th BLV, 12 Feb. 1986: NNA, 2.05.392, Foreign Affairs 1985–1990, inv.nr. 124.

1988 even considered a fifth weekly flight.[152] The airline also wanted to present itself as the regular partner of China Air Lines. Subsequently, Martinair's role became smaller, which meant that the private law structure underpinning the air connection was eroding.[153] Foreign Affairs traffic advisor Jan van Arkel and the RLD clashed about this. While the former supported Martinair's position as private contracting party, the latter was inclined to let KLM's interests prevail.[154] This was reflected in the issue of a new 'route certificate' to China Air Lines, in which KLM was mentioned as the reciprocal party on the Dutch side. Concerned about the threats to relations with the People's Republic and the potential adverse impact on the interests of other Dutch companies in China, the Ministry of Foreign Affairs insisted that the reference to KLM be removed from the certificate.[155] During a visit to the Netherlands, the Chinese Deputy Minister of Foreign Affairs also indicated that allowing China Air Lines to land at Schiphol remained a stumbling block for the realization of a bilateral air services agreement.[156]

Aviation continued to feature at the highest level in relations with the People's Republic. In May 1989, it was planned that Queen Beatrix and her husband Prince Claus would smooth out the remaining issues during a state visit to China. KLM's new CEO, Jan de Soet, was to travel with them in the retinue. However, two days before departure, The Hague cancelled the visit when martial law was declared in Beijing after anti-government protests in Tiananmen Square. The events surrounding the protests there gave rise to concerted action at the European level to suspend all high-level bilateral contacts. The long sought-after aviation agreement that had, at last, seemed accessible at the beginning of May suddenly disappeared again.

5 At the Hands of the United States Government

In the first half of the 1970s, transatlantic aviation continued to be fraught with problems while competition intensified. On the transatlantic route to the USA,

152 Letter De Soet to Van den Broek, 8 April 1988: NNA, 2.05.392, Foreign Affairs 1985–1990, inv.nr. 162.

153 Letter Martinair to J. van Arkel (Foreign Affairs), 9 March 1988: NNA, 2.05.392, Foreign Affairs 1985–1990, inv.nr. 162.

154 Office memo Foreign Affairs re. Dutch flights to Taipei, 15 March 1988: NNA, 2.05.392, Foreign Affairs 1985–1990, inv.nr. 162.

155 Letter Van den Broek to Smit-Kroes, 15 April 1988: NNA, 2.05.392, Foreign Affairs 1985–1990, inv.nr. 162.

156 Minutes 176th BLV, 22 Sept. 1988: NNA, 2.05.392, Foreign Affairs 1985–1990, inv.nr. 125.

increasing numbers of passengers discovered charter airlines as a cheaper way to fly. Prices were under pressure and traditional airlines saw their margins shrink. To make things worse, the fixed rate between the dollar and the price of gold had been severed in August 1971, leaving the dollar-oriented air transport market vulnerable to the effects of exchange rate fluctuations. The Dutch hoped to reduce the effects of these developments by combining the routes to Montreal, Chicago and Mexico City, 'commingling' in aviation terms.[157] At the negotiating table, the CAB would hear none of this. Rather than accommodating foreign carriers, its representatives focused on prices and helped promote the concept of the Advance Booking Charter (ABC) as a cheaper travel option available for individual purchase if booked at least sixty days before departure.

Then, in the autumn of 1973, the Oil Crisis hit. The United States and the Netherlands, both known for conducting a pro-Israeli foreign policy, were the first nations to be affected by Arab sanctions. Before long, both countries faced an oil embargo, although the effects were not quite as bad as expected since they were mitigated by the big oil companies, which maintained deliveries and stocks.[158] Air transport was an obvious target for the oil boycott. Without substantial subterranean reserves of their own, the Dutch were exceptionally vulnerable. KLM in particular was singled out by several Middle Eastern countries and faced a withdrawal of landing rights.[159]

The Oil Crisis also had an effect on transatlantic operations. Washington implemented a domestic fuel allocation plan to see its own airlines through the crisis, but foreign carriers were told to expect a reduction in fuel supply by as much as 77 per cent, while costs went up by 25 per cent.[160] All the airlines suffered. The Hague tried to exert pressure on Washington to allow 'commingling' to save fuel. As it was, KLM was forced to reduce its frequencies to New York from 14 to 10 flights per week. However, the CAB, prompted by PanAm which vigorously protected its dwindling market share on the Atlantic routes, would have none of this.[161] Air transport relations were in crisis. Not even the end of the oil embargo in March 1974 brought an end to this. In an effort to protect US air carriers that saw their usual customers substituting regular tickets for cheaper tickets for 'roped off' charter seats on scheduled services,

157 Minutes 137th BLV, 22 March 1973: NNA, 2.05.313, Foreign Affairs 1965–1974, inv.nr. 25176.

158 Duco Hellema, Cees Wiebes, Toby Witte, *Doelwit Rotterdam. Nederland en de Oliecrisis 1973–1974* (Den Haag: Sdu, 1998), p. 114–118.

159 Hellema, Wiebes, Witte, *Doelwit Rotterdam.* p. 53–57

160 Letter US Embassy The Hague to RLD, 27 Nov. 1973: NNA, 2.05.313, Foreign Affairs 1965–1974, inv.nr. 5441.

161 Minutes 140th BLV, 22 Jan. 1974: NNA, 2.05.313, Foreign Affairs 1965–1974, inv.nr. 25176.

Washington did its best to bring charter carriage under the restrictions of bilateral air transport agreements.[162]

Aviation relations became even more complicated when the Department of Justice, at the behest of the CAB, started an extensive inquest before a Federal Grand Jury into the competitive practices of PanAm, TWA, Air France, Swissair, Sabena and KLM under allegations of evading antitrust legislation. The action was part of the ongoing campaign the CAB was waging against IATA, which was accused of price fixing and violating antitrust legislation. Both individually and in concert, the European governments involved put pressure on the State Department to halt the procedures in the interest of maintaining good relations and transatlantic air travel in a time of crisis.[163]

But the problems were far from over. In the summer of 1974 PanAm applied for a subsidy of $ 10 million a month to deal with the long term effects of the Oil Crisis. Its competitor, TWA, was not in much better shape.[164] There was considerable political pressure in Congress to restrict European airlines. Washington demanded 'consultations' on the question of the 'balance of benefits' in individual bilateral air transport agreements. In The Hague this was interpreted as a neutral sounding formula to reduce KLM's capacity on the Atlantic route and curb the carriage of 6th freedom passengers. Washington's view was that KLM engaged in unfair competition by providing excessive capacity primarily for 6th freedom traffic. At the same time, the CAB required foreign carriers to 'file' their service schedules, threatening to disapprove these 'if it finds that acts or omissions on part of their governments have the effect of denying US airlines fair and equal opportunity to exercise the operating rights provided for in said agreements.'[165] To apply additional pressure on the Dutch-American talks, Washington made veiled threats that unilateral action was an option, should The Hague refuse to budge. The Netherlands' government instructed KLM not to comply with the request.

Consultations were held in October 1974. In his opening statement Deputy Assistant Secretary of State Raymond Waldmann applied a metaphorical axe to Dutch-American air transport by demanding a capacity reduction of 60–70 per cent. From The Hague, it appeared that Waldmann wanted to keep the

162 Minutes 141th BLV, 16 Apr. 1974: NNA, 2.05.313, Foreign Affairs 1965–1974, inv.nr. 25176.

163 Code message Van Lynden to Foreign Affairs, 16 Aug. 1974. Also: CAB creates its own problems: An Airline Industry Appraisal, in: *The Journal of Commerce*, 4 Dec. 1974: NNA, 2.05.313 Foreign Affairs 1965–1974, inv.nr. 8296.

164 Pan Am asks CAB for emergency aid, in: *Journal of Commerce*, 26 Aug. 1974: NNA, 2.05.313 Foreign Affairs 1965–1974, inv.nr. 5442.

165 Code message Foreign Affairs to Washington, 10 June 1974: NA, 2.05.313, Foreign Affairs 1965–1974, inv.nr. 5448.

airlines of America's smaller allies from landing in the USA at all. Appalled at what they perceived as not just a threat to air transport, but to good bilateral and trade relations in general, the Dutch negotiators asked for a suspension of the consultations.[166] KLM calculated that a reduction of its frequency on the New York route to 8 flights per week, as now demanded by Washington, would amount to a loss of revenue of some 150 million guilders annually.[167] At home there was talk of serious layoffs at KLM, and unions clamored for the conservation of jobs. The major trade unions even petitioned US ambassador Kingdon Gould to allow the Dutch space to fly.[168]

Lacking other means to effect a change in American demands, The Hague reverted to its usual tactics and escalated contacts to Cabinet level. Minister for Transport and Waterworks Tjerk Westerterp announced he would personally head the Dutch delegation when the talks reconvened. Nonetheless, despite Westerterp's involvement and his public warning that American demands could well lead to a general decline in bilateral relations, a second round of talks held in Washington in November 1974 brought no rapprochement. The atmosphere was tense and the parties actually drifted further apart. Westerterp voiced his frustration to Dutch newspaper reporters, saying that 'the Netherland's position in the world has been affected by US policy'.[169] Veiled references to possible consequences for a pending order for new American fighter aircraft to replace the Lockheed Starfighter in the Netherlands Air Force and in other European countries failed to make an impression on the Americans, although the issue was picked up by the *Washington Post*.[170] The mood soured further when the American delegation rejected Dutch proposals for a compromise and broke off the talks. In Dutch circles there was talk of bringing the KLM case before the International Court of Justice.[171] In Washington, Ambassador Age Tammenoms Bakker was at a loss to see how America's aviation policy related to the spirit of cooperation and partnership that Secretary

166 Opening Statement US delegation, 21 Oct. 1974: NNA, 2.05.313, Foreign Affairs 1965–1974, inv.nr. 5442. Minutes 142nd BLV, 29 Oct. 1974: NNA, 2.05.313, Foreign Affairs 1965–1974, inv. nr. 25176.

167 RLD policy paper for Westerterp and the Cabinet, Nov. 1974: NNA, 2.05.313, Foreign Affairs 1965–1974, inv.nr. 5442.

168 *De Volkskrant*, 2 Nov. 1974. *Trouw*, 9 Nov. 1974.

169 *Trouw*, 14 Nov. 1974.

170 KLM Talks Linked with Fighter Sales: KLM Talks Linked to Plane Sales: *The Washington Post*, 16 Nov. 1974.

171 *NRC Handelsblad*, 15 Nov. 1974.

of State Henry Kissinger had repeatedly spoken of publicly.[172] Both NATO Secretary-General Joseph Luns and Foreign Minister Max van der Stoel applied in person to Kissinger, but neither got more than a promise that a third round of talks would precede unilateral action on the part of the US[173] As a last resort, Kissinger's personal friend, former State Secretary and KLM president Ernst van der Beugel, also called on Henry Kissinger. At a private dinner party at Kissinger's house in Washington on 2 December, Van der Beugel managed to extract a promise that he would, if necessary, 'overrule our bureaucracy' in the interests of good relations with the Dutch.[174]

Meanwhile, the CAB demanded that KLM submit its North Atlantic flight schedule. The airline feared such a 'filing' was a tactic that would lead to unilateral action on the part of the CAB, after which only an appeal to the president would be open as a last resort if KLM wished to continue to fly. Not surprisingly, KLM refused to file its operations schedule. In The Hague Foreign Affairs Minister Max van der Stoel was shocked about such a brazen rebuff of the CAB's demands, but the airline's chief negotiator, Henri Wassenbergh, was adamant that filing would result in more trouble than a refusal to do so.[175] The airline even went to court in the US as part of its disagreement with the CAB, but its case was thrown out on technical grounds. In an effort to find some kind of solution, US ambassador Kingdon Gould suggested opening a direct channel with PanAm to discuss a possible compromise that would reduce competitive pressure.[176] Although forbidden under US law, KLM even offered to 'subsidize' PanAm by means of a pool agreement to be concluded between the two airlines. Westerterp also sat down with Waldmann, but to no avail. The Minister summarized the discussions thus:

> Well, I have to say I've felt like a frog these three days; a stork comes up to me and says "I'm going to eat you, but I want to talk to you about how it

172 Code message Tammenoms Bakker to Foreign Affairs, 15 Nov. 1974: NA, 2.05.313, Foreign Affairs 1965–1974, inv.nr. 25193.

173 Letter Luns to Kissinger, 6 Nov. 1974. Letter Van der Stoel to Kissinger, 5 Nov. 1974. Letter Kissinger to Van der Stoel, 26 nov. 1974: NNA, 2.05.313, Foreign Affairs 1965–1974, inv.nr. 5442.

174 Personal letter Van der Beugel to Van der Stoel, 5 Dec. 1974: NA, 2.05.313 Foreign Affairs 1965–1974, inv.nr. 5443.

175 Code message Van der Stoel to Washington, 30 Dec. 1974: NA, 2.05.313, Foreign Affairs 1965–1974, inv.nr. 25193.

176 Giles Scott-Smith, David J. Snyder, A Test of Sentiments: Civil Aviation, Alliance Politics, and the KLM Challenge in Dutch-American Relations, in: *Diplomatic History* Vol. 37 (2013) nr. 5, p. 917–945.

> happens: cooked or raw. What do you prefer?". The frog says "I don't want to be eaten at all". The stork says "yes, but that is not on the menu". And that's how it's actually gone these three days.[177]

Still, the matter did not go away and the Dutch remained extremely apprehensive. Even a second direct personal appeal by Van der Beugel to Kissinger did not allay this anxiety. On 24 February Luns was received at the White House and had a discussion with President Ford and Kissinger on the matter. Again, Kissinger gave off soothing sounds.[178] On Dutch television he admitted:

> Your leaders have convinced me that it is not simply a technical issue, and I have therefore agreed to reopen the negotiations from a wider perspective, and while they're going on I don't want to discuss the outcome except to say that I personally am aware of the particular sensitivity of the KLM-issue to Holland – to the Netherlands – and that I will conduct my discussions on it with your foreign minister (…) with an attitude of being very constructive.[179]

In the Netherlands the issue gave rise to public action. The newspaper *Telegraaf even* initiated a nationwide petition in support of KLM, which collected 110,000 signatures. These were delivered to the White House in March 1975. KLM in the meantime produced a leaflet, 'the truth about KLM's fight against PanAm', that depicted its position as a David versus Goliath struggle for survival against loss-making US carriers and their over-protective civil aviation authorities; it was widely distributed amongst US policymakers and other 'influencers'. The Dutch Parliament also intervened. On behalf of the Second Chamber, its chairman Anne Vondeling sent a letter to President Ford, urging him to 'seek just solutions to the problems risen with regard to civil aviation policy'.[180]

---

177 'Nou, ik moet zeggen ik heb me deze drie dagen gevoeld als een kikvors; er komt een ooievaar op me af en die zegt "Ik ga je opeten, maar ik wil overleg met je hebben hoe het gebeurt: gekookt of rauw. Waaraan geeft u de voorkeur?". De kikker zegt "Ik wil helemaal niet opgegeten worden". De ooievaar zegt "ja, maar dat staat niet op de agenda". En zo is het deze drie dagen eigenlijk ook gegaan.' Transcript of a television interview by NOS Daily News with Westerterp [translation by the author], 29 Jan. 1975: NNA, 2.05.313, Foreign Affairs 1975–1984, inv.nr. 6805.

178 Memorandum Luns on his mediation, 1 March 1975: NNA, 2.05.313, Foreign Affairs 1975–1984, inv.nr. 6805.

179 Transcript interview Kissinger, broadcast 9 Feb. 1975: NNA, 2.05.313, Foreign Affairs 1975–1984, inv.nr. 6805.

180 Letter Vondeling to President Ford, 11 March 1975: NNA, 2.05.313, Foreign Affairs 1975–1984, inv.nr. 6805.

Meanwhile, CAB policy towards the airline industry, along with its history of protectionism, created their own counter forces in the US. Numerous American voices pointed to the negative effects for the consumer of too much regulation. These opinions were especially strong amongst aviation lawyers and transport economists.[181] Such voices eventually carried weight. Late in 1975, the Department of Transportation set the wheels in motion for a fundamental review of air transport strategy. At the international level, Washington came to realize that a policy that fostered resentment with its Atlantic partners reflected poorly on America's position in the world. A new approach was called for.[182] In Washington, President Gerald Ford used deregulation of the domestic airline industry as a major policy incentive in 1975 and 1976, submitting the Aviation Act of 1975 to Congress in October of that year.[183]

Indeed, after further contacts between Van der Stoel, Ambassador Kingdon Gould and Secretary of State Kissinger, who decided to join the talks after the Dutch again professed to harbor 'doubts' about continuing with an order for F-16 fighter aircraft, a third round of bilateral talks resulted in a *modus vivendi* in April 1975. KLM 'voluntarily' gave up three of its weekly services to New York, thus reducing capacity by 11 per cent. It was a frail compromise: both parties agreed that a real accord remained beyond reach.[184] In return, the CAB tacitly suspended its filing order, although it was not formally revoked until December 1978.[185] Thus the wider interests of American foreign policy in fostering good relations with its European allies prevailed over a short term improvement of the competitive position of US airlines. The victim of this outcome was PanAm, which continued to make losses on its services to Europe.

In the sphere of damage limitation after the *modus vivendi* compromise of April 1975, one might have expected KLM to sit tight and wait to see what changes and opportunities a new US aviation policy would bring. This was not the case: in the summer of 1976 the airline unveiled its intention to increase flights once again on the route to New York. In The Hague the government was surprised, given the narrow escape from further curtailment of flights only a

181 See: Paul S. Dempsey, *Law and foreign policy in international aviation* (Dobbs Ferry: Transnational Publishers, 1987).

182 Minutes 144th BLV, 25 June 1975: NNA, 2.05.330, Foreign Affairs 1975–1984, inv.nr. 24343.

183 James W. Callison, Airline Deregulation – Only Partially a Hoax: The Current Status of the Airline Deregulation Movement, in: *Journal of Air Law & Commerce* 45 (1980) 961: https://scholar.smu.edu/jalc/vol45/iss4/7.

184 US statement, 3 May 1975: NNA, 2.05.330, NNA, 2.05.313, Foreign Affairs 1975–1984, inv.nr. 6806.

185 CAB Docket 27186 re. Schedules of KLM Royal Dutch Airlines, 11 Dec. 1978: NNA, 2.05.330, Foreign Affairs 1975–1984, inv.nr. 6809.

year before. Both Van der Stoel and Westerterp stated that they would not stand for the consequences of overoptimistic demands in the future.[186] All the same, the announcement of the new American air transport policy in September 1976 did sustain hope for some form of liberalization. A few months earlier, Britain had renounced the Bermuda Agreement of 1946 because it had become an obstacle that kept privately owned airlines from operating over the Atlantic at lower fares. London wished to reduce the number of US airlines flying to the United Kingdom and curtail their 5th freedom rights. Negotiations on a new Bermuda Agreement followed, the results of which were regarded with suspicion in The Hague, wary that the US might try to use it to curb KLM's rights.[187]

Still, political convictions in Washington were shifting. A consensus was building across government and the airline industry that state regulation of routes, pricing, and market entry should be phased out. Indications were that the age of protectionist policies might come to an end, and that the introduction of lower fares would leave consumers as the big winners. While the domestic Airline Deregulation Bill continued in preparation, the Carter Administration announced a radical change of international air transport policy in September 1977. The basic idea was to open numerous 'gateways' in the US for competitive international air services. It was not long before KLM dusted off its wish list of additional American destinations.

The Airline Deregulation bill was brought before Congress in February 1978. A month earlier, The Hague had silently moved from a position on the sidelines of airline politics to center stage. After informal consultations in Washington, the State Department's Deputy Assistant Secretary for Transportation, Joel Biller, arrived in the Netherlands on 26 January 1978 for secret talks on liberalizing international charter air transport and the implementation of lower fares. The meeting, bringing together two Americans and three Dutchmen, convened in the informal setting of an inconspicuous restaurant at the Denneweg in The Hague. Biller enquired about possible Dutch collaboration to open up the market for these new approaches. Washington wished to create opportunities for carriers like Delta, Northwest and Branniff to develop international services to Europe via Amsterdam. In exchange, Dutch negotiator Rob Schreurs wanted to use this opportunity to expand KLM's access to the American air transport market.[188]

---

186 Minutes 147th BLV, 17 Aug. 1976: NNA, 2.05.330, Foreign Affairs 1975–1984, inv.nr. 24343.

187 Minutes 150th BLV, 9 Sep. 1977: NNA, 2.05.330, Foreign Affairs 1975–1984, inv.nr. 24343.

188 Confidential minutes meeting 26 Jan. 1978: NNA, 2.05.330, Foreign Affairs 1975–1984, inv. nr. 6807. Interview by the author with Rob Schreurs, 11 April 2018.

Three weeks later the US embassy in The Hague indicated that Washington was ready to negotiate a bilateral agreement on the basis of the talks of 26 January, and at short notice. An invitation was extended to convene in Washington on Monday 6 March. A delegation of nine Dutchmen called at the State Department and met with Director of Aviation Michael Styles and his advisers. For the first time since bilateral aviation contacts began in 1929, an accord was reached without difficulties. The Dutch could hardly believe their good fortune. That Friday, the Americans got their freedom for charter traffic through Amsterdam, 5th freedom rights for all points beyond, freedom of capacity on existing routes and a liberalized pricing regime. On the Dutch side, there was also reason to celebrate: the discussions on 5th and 6th freedom traffic were finally laid to rest, while KLM received freedom of capacity and pricing, but also two new destinations in the US, Los Angeles and Atlanta. This protocol amending the 1957 bilateral created a new regime allowing 'free play of normal market forces to the benefit of the consumer'.[189] On both sides of the Atlantic, the tourist industry was the big winner, while KLM, at least temporarily, got ahead of its European competitors by being able to quote lower transatlantic fares, which put pressure on other European aviation authorities to liberalize their agreements with the US as well.[190] Still, the Dutch wanted more. Their room for maneuver remained limited and they pleaded for a fare regime on the basis of 'double disapproval': unless both governments expressly disapproved, all ticket prices would henceforth be acceptable. However, Washington saw no reason to agree, as the US had obtained all the rights they had aimed for. A round of talks in December yielded a document of over a hundred pages defining various rights and clauses.[191] It appeared that both parties were developing second (and third) thoughts, which resulted in postponements. Not before August 1980 did the parties meet again; no further amendment of the bilateral agreement resulted.

In an attempt to build on the discussed liberal principles, the Dutch proposed a blueprint for a multilateral arrangement on air transport rights that entailed freedom of fares. This fit President Carter's international deregulation policy. On the Dutch side, there was some urgency behind this, as there had

189 Press message US Dept. of State, 31 March 1978: : NNA, 2.05.330,Foreign Affairs 1975–1984, inv.nr. 6807.

190 Minutes 152th BLV, 11 Apr. 1978: NNA, 2.05.330, Foreign Affairs 1975–1984, inv.nr. 24344.

191 Summary of aviation talks Netherlands-USA in Washington, 11-20 Dec. 1978: NNA, 2.05.330, Foreign Affairs 1975–1984, inv.nr. 6809.

been growing resistance in Washington against the 'giveaway policy' of air transport rights under the Carter Administration.[192]

The plans ran aground in the outcome of the presidential elections of 1980, with Ronald Reagan and the Republican Party winning the White House. Reagan's more nationalist policy halted developments for several years. Nonetheless, Washington's take on international air transport evolved as the neoliberalist ideas of the Chicago School of Economics on the rule of the market gained ground in policy-making circles. In international air transport, the freedom of airlines to set fares came to be embraced, limited only by 'double disapproval' of the governments involved.[193] The Dutch developed second thoughts, however. The Hague became anxious that this would open the floodgates to cut-throat competition that would eat away at KLM's profit margins. Still, the parties stayed in contact, testing the waters. Then, in 1984, Washington came with proposals for a liberalization drive that would also include freedom of pricing. The latest plans entailed a multilateral deal not unlike the one the Dutch had proposed six years earlier in 1978. The aim was that the deal would include the US, Britain, the Netherlands and possibly Switzerland.[194] However, the proposal fell on infertile soil in London and subsequently disappeared from the agenda.

Another shift in bilateral relations came about in 1985 as a result of changing technological parameters in intercontinental air transport. The introduction in 1984 of two engine aircraft such as the Boeing 767 that were capable of safely crossing the Atlantic brought the possibility of direct point-to-point connections between secondary US airports and non-capital cities in Europe. This changed the old predominance of national capitals and national airlines. The Dutch expected this development would facilitate the expansion of KLM's destinations in the US. Cities such as Boston, Dallas, San Francisco and Seattle came into view.[195] Between October 1986 and March 1987 informal talks focused on the possibility of an arrangement involving code sharing between Dutch and American airlines, a form of cooperation under which airlines virtually expanded their number of destinations served by listing flights operated by their partners under their own flight numbers. At the time, this did not yield results. Nonetheless, The Hague found the matter to be of considerable importance, pressing enough to be put on the agenda for talks that had already been scheduled in Washington for April 1987 between Minister

192 Minutes 157th BLV, 11 June 1980: NNA, 2.05.330, Foreign Affairs 1975–1984, inv.nr. 24344.

193 Minutes 164th BLV, 19 Dec. 1983: NNA, 2.05.330, Foreign Affairs 1975–1984, inv.nr. 24345.

194 Minutes 165th BLV, 19 July 1984: NNA, 2.05.330, Foreign Affairs 1975–1984, inv.nr. 24345.

195 Minutes 166th BLV, 10 Jan. 1985: NNA, 2.05.330, Foreign Affairs 1975–1984, inv.nr. 24345.

for Transport and Water Management, Neelie Smit-Kroes, and her American counterpart, Secretary of Transportation Elizabeth Dole. Their discussions took place against a backdrop of vehement objections from US air carriers and quickly ran aground, although the two ladies got on well at the personal level. This became evident when Dole as a gesture of good will granted KLM landing rights in Orlando, Florida.[196] Dole voiced her commitment to further liberalize air transport. The new destination represented the first direct link between Florida's tourist capital and Europe, and came after many years of efforts by that city to obtain international air services. In return, US carriers got the right to serve any point in the Netherlands. In practice, this meant adding Maastricht, the only airport with a runway long enough for intercontinental operations. Double disapproval of tariffs and a liberal charter regime were also part of the deal. Still, Orlando put KLM in a difficult position as the airline had no aircraft available to operate additional transatlantic flights. For the first time in the long history of Dutch-American aviation, the opening of a new route had to be postponed – in this case until November 1987.[197]

Meanwhile, the British and the Americans were also conducting discussions on code sharing, to be incorporated into an agreement between British Airways and United Airlines. This would offer BA some 90 extra, albeit virtual, destinations in the US. This development was regarded with considerable concern in The Hague, as it would substantially improve BA's market position vis-à-vis KLM. The Dutch position was under some threat anyway, as TWA had recently asked for 5th freedom rights to operate between Amsterdam and Berlin. This request had initially been denied in The Hague, after which the matter quickly escalated to a point where US ambassador Richard Fein was recalled to Washington for consultation. Though not unwilling to agree to the TWA demand, the Dutch did hope to gain extra US landing points in return. To underline the importance of the matter, talks between the Dutch Minister of Foreign Affairs Hans van den Broek and Secretary of State George Schultz were set up. Van den Broek agreed to TWA's new service, hoping this would improve the Dutch negotiating position in Washington in the long term, as KLM was already working on its latest requests for additional US destinations. The Hague hoped to push these along in exchange for lowering Dutch compensation claims to US defense contractors making sales to the Netherlands' armed forces. For the Dutch there was some additional urgency involved because the European Commission was preparing to liberalize the European air transport market in 1992, which would take away the already precarious

196 Minutes 173rd BLV, 15 June 1987: NNA, 2.05.392, Foreign Affairs 1985–1990, inv.nr. 125.

197 Minutes 174th BLV, 7 Oct. 1987: NNA, 2.05.392, Foreign Affairs 1985–1990, inv.nr. 125.

negotiating gambits the Dutch had in allowing 5th freedom operations through Amsterdam.[198]

The above-mentioned deal between British Airways and United Airlines acted as an incentive for KLM to ask for additional US landing points. A connection to Washington DC was high on the list, but rights to add Dulles International Airport, a major hub for United, appeared a bridge too far. Discussions in January 1989 therefore focused on a service from Amsterdam to Baltimore-Washington International Airport (BWI) instead. Local lobby groups claimed BWI to be an 'underserved airport' and strongly supported KLM's request. At the Department of Transportation, Assistant Secretary for Policy and International Affairs Jeffrey Shane was, however, unwilling to sit down and discuss the next package of Dutch demands. To get things moving at the Federal level, Smit-Kroes personally approached her former colleague Elizabeth Dole, then Secretary of Labor, to set up a meeting with Shane's boss, Transportation Secretary Samuel Skinner, who proved equally reluctant to talk. Not until the end of June did the parties meet to review the bilateral air transport situation.[199]

While the diplomats were working to arrange bilateral talks, KLM pursued a plan of its own to improve its competitive position in the North Atlantic. In March 1989 preparations got under way to participate in a takeover of the ailing US carrier Northwest Airlines, together with two American investors, Alfred Checchi and Gary Wilson, and an Australian company. Jointly, they established a special investment vehicle, Wings Holdings. For a total of 3.6 billion dollars, Wings offered to take over Northwest. KLM's participation amounted to 400 million dollars, for which the Dutch airline was to get 20 per cent of the stock, although only 5 per cent of the voting shares.[200] News of this became public when Northwest's shareholders accepted the takeover bid on 19 June.[201] Only then was the government in The Hague informed. Because KLM treated the case primarily as an investment issue, the Civil Aviation Meeting did not convene until 4 July 1989. In the light of the long and close cooperation between KLM and the government, this was surprising. When the members of the Civil

198 Minutes 176th BLV, 23 Sep. 1988; minutes 177th BLV, 25 Jan. 1989: NNA, 2.05.392, Foreign Affairs 1985–1990, inv.nr. 126.

199 Memorandum of conversations, signed Hans Raben and Janice Bay (State Dept. Director of Aviation Negotiations; Chair of US delegation), 29 June 1989: NNA, 2.05.392, Foreign Affairs 1985–1990, inv.nr. 2638.

200 Minutes Supervisory Board KLM, 19 May 1989: KLM Archive, Board of Control (RvC). For background, see: Marc Dierikx, *Blauw in de lucht*, p. 299–303.

201 Consent order Samuel K. Skinner (docket 46371), 29 Sept. 1989: NNA, 2.05.392, Foreign Affairs 1985–1990, inv.nr. 2638. Also: *De Volkskrant*, 20 June 1989.

Aviation Meeting finally met, the government delegates remained passive and silent about the investment in Northwest, instead discussing bilateral aviation issues as if the envisaged cooperation would have no significant impact.[202]

Nonetheless, developments were now picking up speed. In London, British Airways followed KLM's example, exploring the possibility of some level of financial participation in United Airlines. Once more air transport issues reached the highest government levels. On 17 and 18 July, aviation was on the agenda for talks between President George Bush, Secretary of State James Baker, Prime Minister Ruud Lubbers and Minister of Foreign Affairs Hans van den Broek on the occasion of Bush's visit to the Netherlands.[203] Left behind in Washington, Transport Secretary Skinner was not included in this discussion. He was not at all in favor of allowing a foreign entity to acquire control over an American airline company, even if KLM's 5 per cent of voting shares remained well below the US legal limit of 25 per cent foreign ownership. In a talk before the International Aviation Club on 19 September, Skinner made no secret of the fact that he was dead set against the investment deal. In an emotional appeal, he said Northwest should remain 'fit, willing, able, *and* American'.[204] Although Skinner was forced to attach his signature of approval to the KLM-NWA deal, since the Dutch shareholding remained below the legal limits, his reservations subsequently translated into fierce opposition against a new bilateral agreement on air services. This, in turn, led to pressure from The Hague to shield the KLM-NWA deal from a combination of protectionism and discrimination. Van den Broek complained about this to Secretary of State James Baker in so many words.[205] Caught out, Baker replied that 'this action is not a departure from the US policy supporting free flows of investment. The President is committed to maintaining an open investment policy.'[206]

In protest, Skinner dug in and announced in October that the US would henceforth steer a more protectionist course in bilateral contacts, particularly with the Netherlands. Rights to operate new routes would only apply to 3rd and

202 Minutes 178th BLV, 4 July 1989: NNA, 2.05.392, Foreign Affairs 1985–1990, inv.nr. 126.

203 Letter James Baker to Van den Broek, 12 Aug. 1989: NNA, 2.05.392, Foreign Affairs 1985–1990, inv.nr. 2638.

204 Fax message Rob Troost (Dutch Traffic Advisor in Washington) to Den Braven, RLD, 19 Sept. 1989. DOT: Secretary warns of continued vigilance over leveraged buyouts, in: *Aviation Daily*, 20 sept. 1989: NNA, 2.05.392, Foreign Affairs 1985–1990, inv.nr. 2638.

205 Code message Van den Broek to Embassy Washington, 26 Sept. 1989: NNA, 2.05.392, Foreign Affairs 1985–1990, inv.nr. 2638.

206 Quote Ambassador Fein in letter James Baker to Van den Broek, 18 Oct. 1989 (code message d.d. 4 Nov. 1989): NNA, 2.05.392, Foreign Affairs 1985–1990, inv.nr. 2638.

4th freedom traffic.[207] In The Hague, Transport Minister Smit-Kroes was livid. Although she was about to leave office as a change of cabinet was pending, she wrote Skinner an angry personal letter in which she stated:

> It is only fair to say that these developments have left me and my colleagues wondering in what direction United States' policy is developing.' (…) Your recent decisions concerning foreign investment in United States airlines have, I must confess, created considerable confusion about your government's stand on international aviation policy. (…) I feel that it is urgently necessary to clear up any doubts about the treatment the interests of this country may expect to receive at the hands of the US government.[208]

6 Troubles in South America

For a long time after Brazil canceled the 1947 bilateral aviation agreement with the Netherlands in November 1961, contacts about air services had remained inconclusive. This was particularly so with regard to the use of DC-10 wide body aircraft at the beginning of the 1970s. A second weekly DC-10 flight had been on the KLM wish list for years, but the issue had made no progress in the Brazilian capital while the Dutch remained uncooperative in discussions on a general trade agreement between the EEC and Brazil. The situation in Argentina was not much different. Here the same perception of Dutch conduct in trade policy existed. Nonetheless, The Hague hoped to resume bilateral aviation talks in April 1973. The hope was that Brazil might still go ahead with the use of the DC-10, which would benefit talks with Argentina on rights for wide body flights.[209] These discussions soon ran aground, however. Since the Brazilian carrier VARIG had no plans to include Amsterdam in its route network, there appeared to be little reason for the Brazilian authorities to accommodate KLM's wishes. Months passed in which KLM tried to entice the VARIG management to extend their European flights from Madrid to Amsterdam. This appeared to create a tiny window of opportunity. In Brasilia, Ambassador Leopold Quarles van Ufford was instructed to explain to general Edivio Sanctos, the head of the

207 Fax Rob Troost (Embassy Washington) to Den Braven (RLD), 12 Oct. 1989: NNA, 2.05.392, Foreign Affairs 1985–1990, inv.nr. 2638.

208 Letter Smit-Kroes to Skinner, 1 Nov. 1989: NNA, 2.05.392, Foreign Affairs 1985–1990, inv.nr. 2638.

209 Minutes 137th BLV, 22 March 1973: NNA, 2.05.313, Foreign Affairs 1965–1974, inv.nr. 25176.

Comissão de Estudos Relativos à Navegação Aérea Internacional (CERNAI), which regulated Brazil's commercial aviation, the Dutch interest in intensifying trade relations through a second KLM service.[210]

This was a peculiar development, since KLM was already facing a need to economize on its North Atlantic operations to save fuel because of the Arab oil embargo against the Netherlands. But in South America such fuel problems appeared to be absent. A bigger obstacle was that CERNAI dragged its feet and showed little interest in accommodating the Dutch after a temporary VARIG service to Amsterdam started in December 1974. Indeed, the Dutch request for a new round of aviation discussions was categorically denied. In The Hague, this was regarded as an unforeseen consequence of the trade agreement that Brazil had signed with the EEC. Now that the larger Brazilian trading interests were settled, there appeared to be no need to be flexible in the smaller matter of air services. Moreover, the Brazilians shared American objections against KLM's practice of carrying 6th freedom passengers.[211]

After prolonged quiet diplomacy in which Dutch money changed hands and encouraged cooperation, the two delegations sat down at the negotiating table in the spring of 1976.[212] This time an accord was reached and a new Dutch-Brazilian bilateral agreement was signed on 6 July 1976, by virtue of which Brazil agreed to a second weekly KLM flight. The accord also provided for 5th and 6th freedom carriage. This should have pleased everyone in The Hague, but within months the effect of the new settlement was annulled when Brazil introduced severe currency restrictions for passengers on international flights. These currency restrictions cut into KLM's passenger carriage from Rio. The second weekly service, for which The Hague had pleaded for so long, had to be postponed as the market slumped.[213]

Across the border in Argentina KLM was confronted with different problems. On 1 July 1974 President Juan Perón had died, to be succeeded by his wife, Vice-president Isabel Perón. Over the next two years the country, already troubled by surging inflation, sank into economic chaos and increasing political and social unrest. This unstable situation led to a right wing military coup on 24 March 1976. In view of the troubled circumstances the military *junta*, headed by General Jorge Videla, announced it would put an end to what it

210 Minutes 140th BLV, 22 Jan. 1974: NNA, 2.05.313, Foreign Affairs 1965–1974, inv.nr. 25176.

211 Minutes 143rd BLV, 17 Jan. 1975: NNA, 2.05.330, Foreign Affairs 1975–1984, inv.nr. 24343.

212 Interview by the author with Rob Schreurs, 18 April 2018.

213 Aviation agreement Netherlands-Brazil, 6 July 1976: https://wetten.overheid.nl/BWBV0003748/1998-06-19 [2022]. Minutes 147th BLV, 17 Aug. 1976: NNA, 2.05.330, Foreign Affairs 1975–1984, inv.nr. 24343.

called domestic subversion and prepared for a widespread persecution of opponents. International reactions to the military dictatorship were initially moderate. In economic affairs the Videla government embraced liberalism and proclaimed its wish to attract international capital to restore the economy. As an extra incentive, trade barriers were reduced. Yet in contradiction to the policy of economic liberalization, the military imposed rigid state controls in social and political affairs.[214]

When it came to air transport, the *junta*'s nationalistic perspective generated protectionism. The Argentine generals forced foreign airlines to cut back their services to Buenos Aires. Because Aerolíneas Argentinas did not fly to Amsterdam, KLM feared its services would be high on the list, even though bilateral trade continued to flourish.[215] Although The Hague exercised restraint vis-à-vis protests against human rights violations, Dutch-Argentine aviation relations suffered. Buenos Aires spoke out against KLM's long-standing wish to introduce modern wide-body Douglas DC-10 aircraft on its South American route.

The reason for the Argentine rebuff was never officially disclosed, although Aerolíneas Argentinas did not possess similar wide body aircraft, which the generals may have viewed as a loss of face. KLM tried to keep a low profile and avoid discussions about luring passengers away from Aerolíneas Argentinas.[216] Nonetheless, the Argentine military continued efforts to curtail KLM's operations. Repeated Dutch references to the 1948 agreement had little effect. In this context, it was fortunate for KLM's operations to Buenos Aires that the Dutch lost the final of the World Football Championship against the team from the host country, Argentina, in June 1978. Still, by the end of the year maintaining the service to Buenos Aires had become a problem, as KLM was in the process of phasing out its ageing Douglas DC-8 aircraft.

In Brazil, flourishing trade presented problems of its own. In the early 1970s the country had ordered two nuclear reactors from West-Germany. To feed these reactors, Brazil had signed an agreement for the delivery of enriched uranium through the European consortium Urenco, located in Almelo, the Netherlands.[217] In 1977 there was considerable political debate in The Hague over security issues with regard to Urenco's deliveries of enriched uranium to

214 Michiel Baud, *Militair geweld, burgerlijke verantwoordelijkheid. Argentijnse en Nederlandse perspectieven op het militair bewind in Argentinië (1976–1983)* (The Hague: Sdu, 2001), p. 9–31, 135–142.

215 Minutes 148th BLV, 8 Dec. 1976: NNA, 2.05.330, Foreign Affairs 1975–1984, inv.nr. 24343.

216 Survey KLM (Jorge Stabholz, Gerente General para Argentina y Paraguay) [undated] late 1977: NNA, 2.05.330, Foreign Affairs 1975–1984, inv.nr. 6730.

217 *NRC Handelsblad*, 13 Jan. 1977.

Brazil, a country that was not a party to the Non-Proliferation Treaty of 1970. Relations between the Netherlands and Brazil became strained.[218] In evidence the Brazilian Ministry of Foreign Affairs delayed the signing of an amended protocol on a second KLM frequency until the issue of the uranium deliveries was settled. Nonetheless, a formal connection between the two topics was never put on paper.[219] Only after a provisional compromise regarding security concerns had been reached in December 1977 did KLM receive permission to use the DC-10 for its Brazilian service, though again not for the next envisaged stop, Buenos Aires. Meanwhile the issue of the uranium deliveries dragged on, accompanied by heated debates in parliament in The Hague until June 1978, when the Second Chamber provided safeguards surrounding uranium deliveries from 1981.[220] This cleared the air and in the spring of 1979 KLM finally received landing rights for its second service. In the following years relations improved considerably. In March 1980 VARIG saw the festive opening of its scheduled service to Amsterdam, via Lisbon.

Meanwhile, advances in aviation technology and market developments meant that KLM preferred to fly its South American services with Boeing 747s, rather than with the smaller DC-10. Brazil raised no objections now that the Urenco case was settled, but in Argentina things were different as Videla's military regime was facing a collapsing economy. Between 1974 and 1978 the average disposable income declined by half, while unemployment surged. What the generals wanted was some Dutch gesture that suggested friendly bilateral relations, something they could show off in the press. Sergio Orlandini, KLM's CEO, went as far as to suggest to the Argentine ambassador in The Hague that the Dutch Finance minister, Fons van der Stee, might board the opening flight of the second frequency for an official visit to Buenos Aires. Reactions at the Ministry of Foreign Affairs were shocked: a visit by a Cabinet member would surely have political repercussions in Parliament.[221] On the other hand, the *junta* in Buenos Aires insisted that some visible token of good relations was required. Perhaps a celebration of the use of the Fokker F28 executive jet? In The Hague Minister Max van der Stoel, a staunch critic of the *junta*'s human

218 Minutes 149th BLV, 5 Apr. 1977: NNA, 2.05.330, Foreign Affairs 1975–1984, inv.nr. 24343.

219 Minutes 151st BLV, 20 Dec. 1977: NNA, 2.05.330, Foreign Affairs 1975–1984, inv.nr. 24343.

220 *NRC Handelsblad*, 30 June 1978. Hellema, *Nederland in de wereld*, p. 340.

221 Office memorandum Foreign Affairs for Van den Broek, 26 Aug. 1981: NNA, 2.05.330, Foreign Affairs 1975–1984, inv.nr. 6730.

rights record, was appalled by the very idea.[222] In the end, the gesture boiled down to a transfer of funds by KLM to Aerolíneas Argentinas.[223]

But before long relations took a decisive downward turn, as a consequence of the Falklands War between Argentina and the United Kingdom from 2 April till 14 June 1982. Facing European sanctions, Argentina turned to one of the few instruments it had at its disposal to lash out at Britain's allies and terminated the bilateral aviation agreements. The treaty with the Netherlands, dating from 1950, was revoked effective from 29 May 1982. Protests by the Netherlands' ambassador that Argentina should respect the agreed warning period for termination, laid down in the bilateral, were summarily pushed aside by the Argentine Minister of Foreign Affairs Nicanor Costa Méndez. Although completely lacking legal grounds, the Argentinian *junta* expressly forbade the continuation of KLM flights during the agreement's period of notice of termination. No direct explanation was given, but the link to European support for the British war effort appeared obvious. Effective immediately, KLM was forced to re-route its aircraft and use Montevideo as the final stop, with passengers transferring onto regional flights to Buenos Aires.[224] Nonetheless, Buenos Aires publicly stated that the Argentine policy was rooted in the wish of the *junta* to strengthen the international position of Aerolíneas Argentinas.[225]

Despite repeated Dutch requests, bilateral air services were not restored until 2 November 1984, when both parties signed a memorandum of understanding to resume flights.[226] From September 1985 Aerolíneas Argentinas reciprocated with a weekly service of its own to Amsterdam, thus repairing the bilateral balance. But the airline itself fared badly financially and Buenos Aires looked at possibilities for privatization and foreign investment. In February 1988 SAS considered acquiring a 40 per cent interest in the debt-ridden airline, but due to political resistance from the Perónist opposition the deal was never signed. In the end, the Spanish carrier Iberia acquired a majority share in the early 1990s.

---

222 Memorandum 'A.R.' to Van der Stoel personally, 22 Sept. 1981: NNA, 2.05.330, Foreign Affairs 1975–1984, inv.nr. 6730.

223 Telephone note Foreign Affairs, 16 Oct. 1981: NNA, 2.05.330, Foreign Affairs 1975–1984, inv. nr. 6730.

224 Minutes 162nd BLV, 5 Jan. 1983: NNA, 2.05.330, Foreign Affairs 1975–1984, inv.nr. 24345.

225 *NRC Handelsblad*, 1 June 1982.

226 ICAO Aeronautical Agreements, nr. 3340, Memorandum of Understanding relating to Scheduled Air Transport Services for Aerolineas Argentinas and KLM Royal Dutch Airlines, 2 Nov. 1984: https://cfapps.icao.int/dagmar/agr_details.cfm?UserLang=&UserAllowed=Yes&icaoregno=3340%2E0 [2022].

In Brazil, aviation relations were stagnant. Although KLM was allowed to introduce the Boeing 747 on the service to Rio de Janeiro in 1986, its longed for third weekly service remained buried in Brazilian desk drawers awaiting a re-evaluation of bilateral economic and trade policy. In January 1989 a trade mission led by the Dutch Minister of Economic Affairs Rudolf de Korte achieved precious little.[227]

7 A Case Apart: the Route to Southern Africa

When it came to services to Southern Africa, Italy had always been important for KLM. Right from the start, the airline had made intermediate stops in Rome, discharging passengers and taking on new ones under the 5th Freedom regime. Such rights had never been taken for granted and discussions about them sprang up repeatedly. Still, the Netherlands and Italy, both EEC founding members, maintained good relations. Still, in November 1973 Rome indicated the existing arrangements needed revision. This message gave rise to immediate concern in The Hague.[228] As had been the case before the Oil Crisis, Italy conducted a pro-Arab foreign policy, which might have consequences. Indeed, contrary to predictions in The Hague, the matter of the Italian transit and 5th freedom rights escalated over the winter months. Not wishing to alienate Arab nations across the Mediterranean, Italy not only withdrew KLM's commercial landing rights, but also denied the airline's right to make a technical stop in Rome to take on fuel, although such rights had been in force since Italy's ratification of the Chicago Convention in October 1947 and belonged to the realm of good relations between the members of the EEC. Rattled, the Dutch escalated the matter at short notice and sent Ambassador Han Boon, followed by Foreign Affairs' State Secretary Laurens Jan Brinkhorst to plead the Dutch case at La Farnesina, the Italian Ministry of Foreign Affairs. Both missions were in vain. Minister Max van der Stoel then approached his colleague Aldo Moro directly in the halls of a meeting of the European Council of Foreign Ministers in Luxemburg.[229] This had the desired effect: the issue was quietly buried.

Beyond Rome, all appeared to be calm on the African routes, despite the fact that South Africa's membership status in ICAO had been curtailed as a result of

227 *Algemeen Dagblad*, 28 Jan. 1989.

228 Minutes 139th BLV, 21 Nov. 1973: NNA, 2.05.313, Foreign Affairs 1965–1974, inv.nr. 25176.

229 Minutes 141th BLV, 16 Apr. 1974: NNA, 2.05.313, Foreign Affairs 1965–1974, inv.nr. 25176.

motions brought forward by various African nations.[230] Talks were held with three members of the East African Community (EAC), Kenya, Tanzania and Uganda, on an expansion of KLM's services through Nairobi to Johannesburg. Despite African policies towards South Africa, the prospects looked hopeful.[231] Pending formal agreements, the nations involved allowed KLM to operate commercial flights.

On the West-African route things were not as promising. Late in 1975 KLM was instructed to skip its intermediate stop in Congo-Brazzaville to avoid getting mixed up in the conflict with Angola over Cabinda, the Angolan province on Congo's southern border, which was seeking independence. The route was redirected via Kinshasa in Congo, but there airlines faced fuel shortages, which threatened to disturb flight schedules.[232]

Rising international umbrage over South Africa's *Apartheid* policy was potentially more disturbing. For years The Netherlands had tried to remain aloof from the international debate, not wishing to abandon the traditional cultural ties between the two countries. In the shadows of the dispute, Dutch trade with South Africa had increased threefold between 1964 and 1974, although at 0.67 per cent exports were still not very significant as a part of the total Dutch trade volume. Beyond trade, relations were stagnant. Since 1972 The Hague had maintained that apartheid was at odds with human rights.[233] Air services were kept going, though with strict limitations imposed by South Africa on the number of passengers KLM was allowed to carry per week. In these circumstances The Hague continued to steer a middle course in the international debate on Apartheid and in 1975 refused to support a UN resolution calling for an oil embargo against South Africa. The tipping point came a year later, after the bloody suppression of student protests against school reforms in the township of Soweto, near Johannesburg, in June 1976. Against the background of what had happened in Soweto the Netherlands decided not to issue new long term credit guarantees to South Africa. While legal measures to curb private investments in South Africa were not likely to have much effect,

230 David MacKenzie, *ICAO: A History of the International Civil Aviation Organization* (Toronto: University of Toronto Press, 2010), p. 237.

231 Minutes 143th BLV, 17 Jan. 1975: NNA, 2.05.330, Foreign Affairs 1975–1984, inv.nr. 24343.

232 Minutes 145th BLV, 1 Dec. 1975: NNA, 2.05.330, Foreign Affairs 1975–1984, inv.nr. 24343.

233 Stefan de Boer, *Van Sharpeville tot Soweto. Nederlands regeringsbeleid ten aanzien van apartheid, 1960–1977* (Den Haag: Sdu, 1999), p. 176–290; 265–268. Hellema, *Nederland in de wereld*, p. 270.

companies were asked to abide by the codes of conduct agreed on within the EEC as regards dealings with South Africa.[234]

Thus, air services from Europe to Johannesburg continued. Besides KLM, British Airways, Lufthansa and Sabena provided flights. In 1976 several African states spoke out against all intermediate stops in their territories for flights to South Africa.[235] This was a potentially upsetting development for KLM. Because of the airline's pool agreements with SAA, the Dutch carrier was likely to be one of the first to suffer the consequences. SAA itself also felt the impact of being banned from operations over most of South Africa's neighboring countries, as well as needing to steer well clear of the African continent on its flights to and from Europe, which amounted to a considerable detour and corresponding losses due to higher fuel and crew costs and lower traffic.

Politics also impacted KLM's operations in East Africa. In 1977 the East African Community collapsed as a result of political controversy and disputes over each country's influence in the EAC. One of the first victims of this development was the joint carrier East African Airlines, which went into liquidation in February 1977. Following this, a conflict developed between Kenya and Tanzania over aerial sovereignty, leading to a ban on commercial flights between their respective capitals, Nairobi and Dar-es-Salaam. The Kenyan authorities insisted KLM give up its intermediate stop in Nairobi on flights that included landings in Dar-es-Salaam.[236] It thus became imperative that the Netherlands conclude new bilateral agreements with the three former EAC members. For KLM, there was a considerable price to be paid: apart from handing over royalties to the Kenyan government, Tanzania demanded a share of the operational revenues KLM earned between Amsterdam and Dar-es-Salaam.[237] Nonetheless, a new bilateral agreement was signed in February 1978. Aided by the fact that Tanzania featured as one of the prime recipients of Dutch development aid, KLM received considerable operational and commercial freedom under the new agreement, including 5th Freedom rights between Dar-es-Salaam and Johannesburg.[238] Dutch development aid thus facilitated aviation relations with Tanzania. Building on this KLM began providing management assistance

234 Hellema, *Nederland in de wereld*, p. 298–299. De Boer, *Van Sharpeville tot Soweto*, p. 268. Peter Malcontent, Floribert Baudet, The Dutchman's Burden? Nederland en de internationale rechtsorde in de twintigste eeuw, in: Bob de Graaff, Duco Hellema, Bert van der Zwan (eds.), *De Nederlandse buitenlandse politiek in de twintigste eeuw* (Amsterdam: Boom, 2003), p. 89–90.

235 Minutes 148th BLV, 8 Dec. 1976: NNA, 2.05.330, Foreign Affairs 1975–1984, inv.nr. 24343.

236 Minutes 150th BLV, 9 Sept. 1977: NNA, 2.05.330, Foreign Affairs 1975–1984, inv.nr. 24343.

237 Minutes 151th BLV, 20 Dec. 1977: NNA, 2.05.330, Foreign Affairs 1975–1984, inv.nr. 24343.

238 Minutes 152nd BLV, 11 Apr. 1978: NNA, 2.05.330, Foreign Affairs 1975–1984, inv.nr. 24344.

to Air Tanzania. At the same time KLM also invested in the development of a closer relationship with Kenya Airways. A bilateral agreement was signed in Nairobi on 3 May 1979.

This in itself formed a stark contrast with relations with various other countries in Southern Africa. More often than not, the Dutch had to deal with administrative issues, restrictive passenger quotas and hurdles affecting the transfer of revenues that delayed new bilateral agreements. Not all such difficulties were aviation related. In Lagos, Nigeria, the ministry of Foreign Affairs burned to the ground in December 1981, which caused all sorts of administrative problems and procedural delays. In Zimbabwe the authoritarian regime of Robert Mugabe piled up so many barriers for foreign airline operations that KLM, rather than deploying larger aircraft as initially planned, considered abandoning its operations to Harare altogether in January 1985.[239] In contrast, KLM's services to South Africa continued without much interference from The Hague as long as KLM paid SAA for its right to fly. Although respective Dutch governments steered a distinctly anti-*apartheid* course supporting the international political and economic isolation of South Africa, the effects on air transport remained limited, in spite of a 1986 ICAO resolution that called for a ban on air links.[240] One could say that the South African government's fear that it would be isolated if European airlines ceased operating to that country helped KLM maintain its services without burdensome (financial) strings being attached.

8 In Conclusion

The upheaval in international air transport caused by the Oil Crisis of 1973–1974 led to a fundamental re-thinking of the role of the state in this field. While protectionism surged momentarily, ideas regarding a new regime for international air transport also emerged. Next to national states, the market as a force that itself shaped the economic process, assumed a prominent role. While the United States led the way by promoting deregulation policies that extended into the international field, the practice of air transport nonetheless remained highly political well into the 1980s. The Dutch found this to be the case in almost all their bilateral contacts.

In practice, this meant that the agenda of the Dutch negotiators on air transport continued to be characterized by issues similar to those encountered in

239 Minutes 166th BLV, 10 Jan. 1985: NNA, 2.05.392, Foreign Affairs 1985–1990, inv.nr. 124.

240 Minutes 171st BLV, 4 Nov. 1986: NNA, 2.05.392, Foreign Affairs 1985–1990, inv.nr. 125.

the previous decades. Apparently swamped in the many details of individual bilateral negotiating processes, the members of the Civil Aviation Meeting experienced trouble in maintaining their grip. Patterns repeated themselves. The escalation of negotiations to Cabinet level appeared to be one of the few options open to representatives from a small nation hoping to garner results and this course of action became a standard approach. If this failed to bring the anticipated results, only the offer of paying financial compensations remained.

CHAPTER 5

1989—: Liberalism and De-Nationalization as a New Model

1 Introduction

In the late spring of 2022, Amsterdam's Schiphol Airport is overcrowded. The queues of passengers already start on the forecourt outside the terminal. For hours, travelers stand in line for check-in and security. There is not enough staff to handle passengers efficiently. Significant numbers of people miss their flight because all kinds of procedures run aground. The troubles start at check-in. Although the majority of travellers have used the internet to check in at home and already possess boarding passes, those who have luggage that needs to be carried in the aircraft's cargo hold are waiting to drop off their bags. After decades of streamlining aviation work processes and aligning the numbers of employees to match passenger demand for services, the airport does not have enough staff available. The backgrounds to this phenomenon are complex and are characterized by an unexpected collision of developments: decentralization of the airport workflow, lean and just-in-time management, and the effects of a period of two years in which the health risks of the coronavirus reduced the number of passengers, causing lay-offs. Now, with prospects looking up, the travelers are back in numbers too large for the available staff to handle. Passengers are demanding compensation for missed flights, booking changes, upturned travel arrangements and so on.

One floor down from the departures lounge, arriving passengers are also queuing up. They can be found next to conveyor belts that do not bring their luggage. Staff shortages cause a big delay in baggage handling. Endlessly, orphaned suitcases spin on the baggage belts. Along the walls of the arrivals hall many thousands pieces of uncollected luggage pile up. These snags are not unique for Amsterdam, but occur in aviation worldwide. Airports and airlines take draconian measures to bring the problems under control: flights are cancelled and airports announce a maximum number of passengers to be admitted per day. In Amsterdam, Schiphol Airport faces the need to cancel thousands of flights and limit daily capacity till March 2023. That year the hitherto unthinkable

 | DOI:10.1163/9789004695245_006

> happens when the government reconfirms its intention, announced in June 2022, to reduce Schiphol's capacity.[1] After a century characterized by growth, aviation is suddenly reaching its limits.

These were developments no-one could foresee in the early 1990s, when the continued growth of air transport appeared to be self-evident. Between 1989 and 1991 the disappearance of the Iron Curtain and the collapse of the Soviet Union that followed appeared to be harbingers of a new, peaceful world order in which capitalism and liberal democracy would bridge existing political differences between nations. In Central and Eastern Europe, the state's long-term failure to deliver on promises of economic progress led to the overthrow of existing institutions. In the USSR, a new leadership could not prevent the old Union of Socialist Soviet Republics from breaking up into a Commonwealth of Independent States (CIS), asserting rediscovered national identities. The new situation, where the United States appeared to stand alone as the sole remaining superpower, was characterized as 'the end of history'.[2] These changes led to a new capitalist impetus and economic growth based on the liberalization of the market: globalization. Nonetheless, it soon transpired that with the disappearance of the East-West struggle old disputes that had been dormant during the Cold War flared up, as happened in the Balkans, the Caucasus and Africa, for example.[3]

In the former Yugoslavia, another imploding socialist bond, civil war led to a violent break-up. This development in the Balkans exemplified the dangers of the post-Cold War environment. When CIS members flirted with a more independent course later in the decade, Russia reared up in defiance. Nonetheless, Western nations pursued openings in attempts to establish new political and trade relations with the Russian Federation, which in the late 1990s appeared to offer good opportunities for investment, particularly in the oil and gas sectors. Still, such developments did not fundamentally change relations. In December 1997, Russian President Boris Yeltsin described the expansion of NATO, then under discussion, as a threat to Russia. Matters deteriorated with

---

1 *Volkskrant*, 4 March 2023 and 31 March 2023. The decision was later reversed again after international consultations in November 2023: https://nos.nl/artikel/2497812-krimpplan-schiphol-voorlopig-van-de-baan-na-druk-vs-en-eu [14 November 2023].

2 Francis Fukuyama, *The End of History and the Last Man* (London: Hamilton, 1992). Ian Jackson, Jason Xidias, *An Analysis of Francis Fukuyama's The End of History and the Last Man* (London: Routledge, 2017), p. 10–12.

3 Wetenschappelijke Raad voor het Regeringsbeleid, *Aan het buitenland gehecht. Over verankering en strategie van het Nederlands buitenlandbeleid* [WRR-report 85], (Amsterdam: AUP, 2010), p. 38.

the admittance, in 1999 and in 2004, of ten new members to the NATO alliance. That same year the European Union (EU) also expanded eastwards to include a total of 25 countries. A decade later rising tensions and political differences led to war in Ukraine and, ultimately, to the collapse of the peaceful cooperation with Russia that had characterized the 1990s.

Beyond politics, it appeared that trade might become the defining force in world affairs, promoting all forms of transport. In Europe, the EU established in the Maastricht Treaty of February 1992 superseded the earlier European Communities. The EU exemplified the drive towards intensified economic and political cooperation as an answer to the new conditions in Europe. Cooperation in the field of foreign policy was one of the areas where the reach of Brussels was to be extended. Although actual political integration slowed, the launch of the single integrated market on 1 January 1993 and the drive towards a European economic and monetary union fundamentally changed the state of affairs.[4] This process was welcomed by the Clinton Administration in Washington, hoping it would contribute to a further liberalization of trade.[5] Within the European Union the Schengen Treaty of 1993 opened up the borders of the five participating countries to free movement of citizens, bringing a new sense of 'Europeanism' and a boost to integration. The group of Schengen Nations expanded gradually to encompass 27 countries. Economic growth was high in the 1990s and economists predicted the continued development of a 'new economy' based on innovation and technology. In March 2000, at their summit in Lisbon, European heads of government agreed on a strategy to transform Europe into a knowledge-based economy by 2010. Such a transition was facilitated by the European monetary reform process, completed with the introduction of the euro as a new common currency in 2002.[6] As a sign of the times, in 2004 the European Union, then consisting of fifteen members, opened up membership to countries that had formally been part of the Soviet sphere of influence. At the same time, a process was set in motion to bolster common European foreign policy interests, formalized in the Lisbon Treaty in 2009 that established an EU diplomatic branch, the European External Action Service.

Beyond the North Atlantic region the world was, however, unstable. In August 1990 Iraq invaded and occupied neighboring Kuwait. Led by the United

4 Desmond Dinan, *Europe Recast. A History of European Union* (Basingstoke: Palgrave Macmillan, 2004), p. 241–257.

5 Geir Lundestad, *International Relations since 1945: East, West, North, South* (London: Sage Publications, 2017), p. 175–182.

6 Marc Dierikx, Mari Smits, Loes van Suijlekom, Frédéric Clavert, Elena Danescu, Marco Gabellini (eds.), *Common Fate, Common Future. A Documentary History of Monetary and Financial Cooperation in Europe, 1947–1974* (The Hague: Huygens ING and CVCE, 2012).

States, a broad international coalition of forces intervened to 'restore order', celebrating victory in June 1991. For international air transport there was a price to pay: large parts of the Middle East were closed to air traffic and the cost of fuel went up by 30 per cent. The profits of aviation businesses plummeted. But short-term allied success on the battlefield resulted in problems and resentment later: from the sphere of political Islam groups emerged that sought to stop of Western cultural dominance in the world. On 11 September 2001, 9/11 in American parlance, this was part of the background to the unprecedented terrorist airplane attack on the World Trade Centre in New York, one of the symbols of Western dominance. The attack led to an immediate closure of US airspace, as a result of which 238 aircraft en route to the United States had to be diverted to Canada. They ended up at airports that were no longer commonly used in transatlantic traffic, including Gander, Stephenville, Goose Bay and St. John's in Newfoundland. Gander, largely empty since the dawn of the jet age in the early 1960s, accommodated 38 planes that shed 6,500 stranded passengers. It took several days before they could continue their journeys. This disruption generated a worldwide recession in the air transport industry that lasted over a year.

The United States, already embarked under President George W. Bush on a course to emphasize American national interests, responded with force to the 9/11 attacks and struck out against Afghanistan, which was said to harbor and support the al-Qaeda movement that had contrived and carried out the attack. Washington initiated what it called a 'global war on terror'. Western, particularly American, paranoia resulting from 9/11 and a preoccupation with possible threats against the US, led to a renewed American invasion of Iraq in March 2003 and a military occupation that lasted until December 2011. Most of America's European partners, particularly Germany and France, opposed this course of action and refused support. Bridging the ensuing Atlantic gap took several years. In comparison, the military involvement in Afghanistan met with less criticism. America's allies contributed and even sent troops. The intervention itself, extending over a period of almost twenty years, proved ineffective. In August 2021 troops were pulled out in a dramatic airlift, witnessed live across the world.

In the midst of all this Britain decided, following a referendum in June 2016, to leave the European Union after participating in the European experiment for more than 40 years. The negotiations over an exit treaty took years. Not until 31 January 2020 did the parties reach a form of closure. European integration was shown to be a potentially two-way street.

Complicating matters further was the election in 2016 of Donald Trump as America's 45th President – to the surprise and dismay of the European leadership. Trump, no supporter of NATO, announced a new foreign policy built on the slogan 'America First'. In Trump's view the role of the US as protector of the West could no longer be taken for granted. In economics, the new perception encouraged and fed trade disputes across the Atlantic. Trump's ideas were ridiculed at first in the Netherlands through an 'America First, Netherlands Second' video clip that garnered over 29 million views across the world.[7] Nonetheless, Trump's policy forced the Europeans – and the Dutch – to take a new perspective on the age-old transatlantic relationship in an increasingly unstable world.

Coinciding with the political developments of the 1990s, new divisions of labor emerged in the world in a trend towards the internationalization of the production of industrial goods and services, technology and investments, commonly referred to as globalization. All aspects of trade increased rapidly in this period.[8] The developments of the 1980s, in which governments reduced their involvement in the economy in favor of the market as the ultimate organizing force in the social system, gained momentum. Aided by reductions in tariffs on industrial goods, the rise of global value chains and the fragmentation of manufacture across countries enabled the biggest surge of world trade in history.[9] There emerged an increased role for capital streams as forces to shape the international economy. More countries than ever adopted the idea of market economics.

This expanding trade was linked to advances in the realm of computer technologies. The emergence and diffusion of information and communication technology contributed to a reduction of transaction costs in trade and therefore became an important stimulus. It made it possible to fine tune production and delivery chains across the globe. Worldwide information technology services made this possible.[10] Commerce and communication that used the World Wide Web changed the planet. A new information society was in the making. Asian countries, particularly China, profited, experiencing spectacular economic growth. Beijing embraced a political drive to restructure its economy and link it to the world, and even applied to join the World Trade Organization in November 1995. In December 2001, China became a member.

---

7 https://www.youtube.com/watch?v=ELD2AwFN9Nc [accessed 2022].

8 Wetenschappelijke Raad voor het Regeringsbeleid, *Nederland Handelsland. Het perspectief van de transactiekosten* [WRR-report 66], (Den Haag: Sdu, 2003), p. 14.

9 World Bank, Overview, in: *World Development Report 2020: Trading for Development in the Age of Global Value Chains*, at: https://openknowledge.worldbank.org/bitstream/handle/10986/32437/211457ov.pdf?sequence=76&isAllowed=y [2022].

10 Wetenschappelijke Raad voor het Regeringsbeleid, *Nederland Handelsland. Het perspectief van de transactiekosten* [WRR-report 66], (Den Haag: Sdu, 2003), p. 155.

The subsequent influx of Western capital allowed the country to grow into one of the world's most prominent producers of industrial goods. Trade liberalization stimulated economic growth and brought an unprecedented convergence, enabling developing countries to begin to catch up with richer countries. Poverty was reduced.[11] In the wake of these developments new patterns of international transportation emerged. Together with sea container transport, aviation was one of the instruments essential for the new global value chain of production. Physical distances, which in the past had curbed the options for international trade, were, at least partly, negated as more options for air transport became available with the introduction of very long-range jets.

Opening up national markets to international trade became a widely accepted idea. In the provision of public goods and services, more competition was also welcomed. In the early 1990s new and emerging technologies, like email and public access to the World Wide Web, had far reaching effects on the economy, on society, and on life in general. The world experienced a revolution, spurred by computer applications and telecommunications, which ultimately left no area untouched. A 'borderless world' created new business perspectives. People also became more globally orientated. In aviation, this resulted in more air travellers than ever before, with numbers approaching and then surpassing two billion after the turn of the century.[12]

As essential agents driving these developments, governments were increasingly seen as partners, catalysts and facilitators of economic growth originating in the private sector. The combined effect of global integration and the spread of democracy narrowed the scope for arbitrary and capricious government interventions in the economy, according to the World Bank.[13] It was no guarantee against economic mishap, however. Towards the end of the first decade of the new century economic figures plummeted as a consequence of a series of banking crises in the US and in Europe. Problems in the US mortgage finance market in 2007 had repercussions for the global financial system. In 2008, the so-called credit crisis engulfed Europe as well. The Hague was forced to nationalize part of the Dutch banking sector to calm the financial market. In the aftermath of the credit crisis, several countries ran into problems, especially in

11 World Bank, Overview, in: *World Development Report 2020: Trading for Development in the Age of Global Value Chains*, at: https://openknowledge.worldbank.org/bitstream/handle/10986/32437/211457ov.pdf?sequence=76&isAllowed=y [2022].

12 ICAO statistics, in: Marc Dierikx, *Clipping the Clouds. How Air Travel Changed the World* (Westport CT: Praeger, 2008), p. 146–147.

13 World Bank, Overview, in: *World Development Report 1997*, at: https://openknowledge.worldbank.org/bitstream/handle/10986/5980/9780195211146_overview.pdf?sequence=22&isAllowed=y [2022].

southern Europe. In 2010 Greece became the example that stood out as international institutions lost faith in the credibility of the Greek national debt. Starting in March 2010, the European Commission, the European Central Bank and the International Monetary Fund issued a series of bailout loans to rescue Greece from sovereign default and maintain the euro as a common currency. The credit crisis also had a major impact on the real economy. Companies reduced their workforce, or even shut down. It took almost ten years to effect a revival.

The Netherlands struggled with the geopolitical developments of the late 1980s and early 1990s and there was some uncertainty over the aims and the course of foreign policy, now that the Cold War appeared to be over. Hence economic interests assumed more prominence. Initially, the disintegration of the Eastern Bloc supported the idea that the major themes that had dominated the foreign policy agenda for decades could become a thing of the past. However, this view soon turned out to be far too optimistic and most of the topics that had held a permanent place on the foreign policy agenda before 1989 remained there.[14] Although Foreign Affairs Minister Hans van den Broek adhered to the traditional Dutch Atlantic orientation, this cornerstone of Dutch foreign policy became less self-evident. Instead, The Hague appeared to hark back to the older tradition of stimulating the role of international organizations in the interest of stability, peace and prosperity. NATO membership received new emphasis and the Dutch supported the US and Britain in the Gulf War of 1990–1991. Nonetheless, the changes in Europe and in the world beyond gave rise to voices clamoring for a reorientation in Dutch foreign policy – and consequently of the ministry itself. In 1995–1996 this resulted in an extensive recalibration operation to enhance the national economic interest as a guiding principle, related to other foreign policy fields.[15] Although this included the field of air transport, which became part of the new Directorate of Economic Cooperation, aviation initially appeared to escape the reorganization drive. Its tradition of close cooperation with the Ministry of Transport and with the airline sector as such, commonly known as the 'iron triangle' set it apart.[16] Nonetheless, the incorporation of aviation into a new, predominantly

14 Wetenschappelijke Raad voor het Regeringsbeleid, *Aan het buitenland gehecht. Over verankering en strategie van het Nederlands buitenlandbeleid* [WRR-report 85], (Amsterdam: AUP, 2010), p. 38.

15 Nota Herijking van het buitenlands beleid: *Handelingen der Staten-Generaal*, Tweede Kamer, 1994–1995, 24337, nr. 2.

16 Minutes 191st BLV, 7 Dec. 1995 and 192nd BLV, 11 July 1996: Archive Foreign Affairs, VADV, Collection Jean Petit, the Hague.

regionally orientated structure did not improve the effectiveness of Dutch policy.[17] Still, from a wider perspective the changes were perhaps not as significant as intended and the general policy orientation on the United States remained. The Hague embraced American leadership in the war in Yugoslavia and, after 2001, supported the American war effort in Afghanistan and Iraq.

Closer to home, European interests gained in importance. The EU became the dominant arena for cooperation. For the Netherlands, Europe was generally accepted as the most important international arena in which to develop initiatives and bring forward themes. At the Ministry of Foreign Affairs, the architecture of the EU became a priority. Policy towards economic integration in Europe took precedence over progress in political integration. The Dutch became proponents of the Economic and Monetary Union that started out in 2002 as an additional binding structure in a new Europe that looked towards full liberalization of its internal trade and payments. This was a good fit with traditional Dutch interests as it favored free trade. At the same time, The Hague, fearful that its position in the enlarged union would be less prominent than before, appeared to see the EU as a podium for bargaining over its financial contribution, rather than as a supranational order under construction. To compensate for its perceived loss of stature, The Hague favored an increased role for the institutions of the EU with regard to the external relations of the member states as a safeguard against too much weight being assigned to German and French interests. Beyond this, it was in Dutch interests to ensure complete integration of the new Germany in the European structures, although The Hague was critical regarding the effects this had on the German budget – at the expense of neighborly relations. In its own right The Hague embraced its role in providing aid to the Eastern European countries (to the detriment of development aid to the Third World), recognizing that new export markets loomed. In general, economic interests gained in stature in Dutch foreign policy, as evidenced in a government letter to Parliament outlining how diplomacy should primarily be seen as a dedicated public service to represent Dutch interests.[18]

But against the background of the expansions of the EU in 2004, the leeway for an independent Dutch foreign policy was diminished. By 2013 the EU encompassed 23 member states, necessitating an increased role for the central

17 Office memo Petit to Van der Zee, 7 June 1997: Archive Foreign Affairs, VADV, Collection Jean Petit, The Hague.

18 Hellema, *Nederland in de wereld*, p. 391–406. Letter Minister of Foreign Affairs Uri Rosenthal to Parliament, Modernisering Nederlandse diplomatie, 12 Apr. 2011: *Handelingen der Staten-Generaal*, Tweede Kamer, 2010–2011, 32734, nr. 1.

institutions in Brussels. Besides, the European administration saw the emergence of a multitude of formal and informal networks linked to specialist departments, while implementing agencies, local and regional authorities also carved out their own fiefdoms. Specialist ministers and government officials built up direct contacts with their foreign colleagues.[19] A Europe was emerging that was difficult to control, made up of crisscrossing professional networks.

To promote Dutch interests, diplomats and civil service officials exerted themselves to translate national interests into EU agendas on policy or legislation. After all, European laws and regulations were created as a result of interactions between EU institutions and various state and non-state actors. With the institutionalization in 2009 of the European Council as the most important forum in the European political arena, where political priorities were defined, the pressure for commonality increased.[20] The Hague, once a fervent supporter of Europeanism, developed an increasingly critical attitude towards the EU in which the interests of Dutch commerce in the European internal market took central position.[21] It became key to the Dutch position to prevent losing its grip on European foreign policy dominated at the Prime Ministers' level by the major EU members France and Germany. Here, Foreign Affairs combined the tasks of 'gatekeeper' and 'liaison officer': safeguarding and fostering Dutch interests and promote strategic choices that would be to the benefit of the Netherlands and the Dutch through the powers of persuasion.

The collapse of the Iron Curtain did not only change the political landscape in Europe. It also had a major effect on the geography of air transport. In the 1990s the pattern of services, thus far centered on Western and Southern Europe, began a gradual shift to incorporate more East-West operations, a reflection of the new conditions on the continent after 1989. The general relaxation of the political and military environment in Europe led to the closure of several military airbases in Germany, including Lübeck (1990), the American base at Hahn (1993) and the RAF base near Weese (1999). Given the policy of the European Commission in favor of liberalizing air transport in the EU from 1993, this created opportunities for airlines operating between regional airports, offering low-cost, 'no frills' services. This reflected what was already happening in the United States, where budget flying had taken off in the 1980s. Low-cost aviation thrived, based on the concept of very high aircraft

19 Wetenschappelijke Raad voor het Regeringsbeleid, *Aan het buitenland gehecht. Over verankering en strategie van het Nederlands buitenlandbeleid* [WRR-report 85], (Amsterdam: AUP, 2010), p. 79.

20 Wetenschappelijke Raad voor het Regeringsbeleid, *Aan het buitenland gehecht*, p. 11.

21 Hellema, *Nederland in de wereld*, p. 446–450.

utilization, thus reducing costs. Generally, low-cost operators opted to fly only one particular model of aircraft, operated single class seating, and offered no free on board amenities. Tickets were electronic, with no seat allocation and sold according to flexible pricing, with late bookers paying the most. Rather than maintaining a full interlocking network of services, the low-cost carriers opted to treat each service individually as a point-to-point operation. Preferably flying from secondary airports whose terminals did not provide luxuries such as finger piers and covered walkways for boarding, instead using multiple moveable stairs, budget airlines benefitted from shorter turnaround times on the ground. They also focused on operating under advantageous national legal regimes that were advantageous to low labor costs and maximum flexibility in employment contracts. Once it became possible, around the turn of the millennium, to sell tickets directly to consumers via the Internet without the intervention of travel agencies and booking organizations, this led to further improvements in results. The principal victims of this new trend were high street travel agencies and the charter airlines, both of which saw their markets dry up.

In 1991 one of the first to use these new opportunities was the Irish carrier Ryanair. The airline offered flights to regional airports 'near' prime destinations such as London (Luton), Paris (Beauvais), Oslo (Sandefjord) and Brussels (Charleroi), adding 'Frankfurt-Hahn' to its network in 1999. Pressure was exerted on regional authorities to contribute financially to the upkeep of the airport infrastructure. Passengers grew accustomed to journeys via such secondary airports. As long as flights were cheap, the inconvenience of onward bus services to the destination city were taken for granted. As the new opportunities created by the European liberalization packages became clearer more low-cost airline operations were set-up, including Britain's EasyJet in 1995, which initially flew from Luton to Glasgow, Edinburgh and Amsterdam. Across the border in Germany, Lufthansa was one of the founding partners in the low-cost airlines Germanwings and Eurowings, both of which operated from various airports in Germany. This new formula of air transport soon proved to be particularly profitable and the model was copied throughout Europe. In the second decade of the 21st century, budget airlines already accounted for more than a third of the total capacity of aircraft seats in Europe and this advance continued. In 2017, the first transatlantic budget flights appeared. The push for ever lower fares was clearly here to stay and it did not leave the traditional airlines untouched.

In the mid-1990s, as Hungary, Poland, Romania, Lithuania, Latvia, Estonia, Bulgaria, the Czech Republic and Slovenia applied to join the EU, intra-European aviation contacts and travel expanded eastward. Both national and regional airports in the applicant countries saw the potential for traffic growth, generally holiday charters at first. Increased use soon called for modernization and the upgrading of facilities. Around the turn of the century the low-cost airlines discovered a new market transporting young migrant workers from Eastern European countries seeking employment in the West, following accession to the group of Schengen countries in April 2003 and the expansion of the EU in May 2004.[22]

Thus, European air transport underwent a complete transformation. This process could be traced back to December 1987, when the European Commission (EC) first proposed ideas to create more room for a differentiation of fares. The measures discussed encroached on the traditional role of national governments in European air transport. In two 'packages' (1987 and 1990) bilateral capacity controls and tariff restrictions were relaxed. This enabled flexibility in tariffs, which rapidly became one of the prime marketing instruments of the low-cost carriers. In June 1992, the crucial 'third package' resulted in the lifting of all remaining restrictions on European airlines operating within the EU, effective from January 1993. Only cabotage was set apart. The criteria for authorization to fly were coordinated to ensure non-discriminatory operating licenses, thus harmonizing the European air transport market and giving airlines from member states full freedom to fly, subject only to restrictions pertaining to congestion, safety and environmental concerns.[23] Airlines even received the right to operate services within the EU without the flight originating or terminating in the carrier's country of origin, the 7th freedom in aviation legal terminology. Airlines from the member states that complied with criteria, such as being 'majority owned and effectively controlled' by EU citizens or interests (including the State itself), could qualify to receive the newly defined legal status of community air carriers and thus benefit from complete operational and commercial freedom within the European market.

At the beginning of 1990, the European Commission also announced steps towards assuming an autonomous role in aviation matters with regard to the external aviation relations of the member states. In such contacts, the national governments had hitherto retained their sovereign powers. Indeed, airlines had been classified according to the principle of national ownership and effective control of the state designating the carrier in Air Services Agreements.

---

22 Joanna Hawlena, Agata Kobyłka, Anna Mazurek-Kusiak, Low-cost Transport Selection Model on the Polish Airline Services Market, in: *European Research Studies Journal* 25(2022) nr. 2b, p. 3–13.

23 European Parliament, *Air Transport: Market Rules*: https://www.europarl.europa.eu/ftu/pdf/en/FTU_3.4.6.pdf [2022].

This favored airlines from the larger and more populous member states vis-à-vis those from smaller EU states that carried less political clout. The aim of the new policy was to create a level playing field for all European air carriers, allowing them to compete without any need for inter-airline agreements or intergovernmental negotiations. In the new situation under the third EU package of measures airlines received full freedom to set their own fares, subject to the application of EU competition rules. The internal free market would replace the existing agreements between EU states and formed the basis, politically and legally, for the new competence that the European Commission claimed was negotiated in the member states' common interest. For an intermediate period of two years, member states would retain some margin to negotiate their own agreements.[24] With this, the European Commission finally ended the seventy-year-old system of bilateralism in air transport that went back to the Paris Convention of 1919.[25] Even cabotage, the right to transport passengers and freight wholly within another member state, was to be liberated – by 1 April 1997 to accommodate protests from France and Southern European member states in the EU Council of Transport Ministers in 1992.[26]

For obvious reasons, member states were initially not happy with the EC's claim for external competencies. Although the Dutch did not reject the idea out of hand, they believed it was premature.[27] An external air transport policy conducted at the European level would mean the end of the existing order, in which KLM's interests defined Dutch negotiating strategy.[28] Other EU states voiced similar reservations. In 1993 Spain, Portugal, Italy and Belgium opposed talks between the EU and Switzerland on air transport.[29] The question of who had the power to conclude air services agreements with third countries divided the Commission and the member states and the issue took several years to resolve. To arrive at an outcome that would be acceptable to all the governments concerned, a *Comité des Sages* was set up in 1993 by Transport

24 *De Volkskrant*, 27 Jan. 1990. Wider: P.P.C. Haanappel, External aviation relations of the European Economic Community and of EEC member States into the twenty-first century, in: *Air Law* 14(1989) nr.2, p. 69–87 and 14(1989) nr.3, p. 122–146

25 Henri A. Wassenbergh, *External aviation relations of the European Community [Includes the proceedings of two mock negotiations by the 'European Commission' with respectively the 'USA' and 'Czechoslovakia']* (Deventer: Kluwer, 1992).

26 *NRC Handelsblad*, 23 June 1992.

27 Minutes 180th BLV, 25-4-1990: Archive Ministry of Foreign Affairs, VADV, Collection Jean Petit, The Hague.

28 Minutes 185th BLV, 7-7-1992: Archive Ministry of Foreign Affairs, VADV, Collection Jean Petit, The Hague.

29 Minutes 187th BLV, 29-3-1993: Archive Ministry of Foreign Affairs, VADV, Collection Jean Petit, The Hague.

Commissioner Abel Matutes y Juan to report to the European Commission. Chaired by Belgian politician Herman de Croo, the *Comité des Sages* reached the conclusion that an internal European market that harmonized national regulations was badly needed and represented the road forward for the industry, provided an efficient single air traffic management system and a truly European airport network could be set up. More importantly, the Comité also advocated a central role for the EU in external aviation relations.[30]

Finally, the European Court of Justice ruled in November 2002 in the so-called 'Open Skies' cases, that rights exchanged in bilateral treaties of EU members with external parties should not discriminate against carriers from other EU states. Although member states were entitled to negotiate their own agreements, these should respect EU law with regard to the principle of Freedom of Establishment – i.e. the right to pursue activities of a stable and continuous nature, under the same conditions as those laid down by the law of the Member State concerned regarding its own nationals.[31] Despite objections from some of the southern EU members, the European Commission was given a mandate to negotiate so-called 'Open Aviation Area Agreements'. Several such negotiations followed, in each case based on a mandate provided by the Council of Transport Ministers. Talks were held with the US and Canada, and with Brazil and Australia.[32]

As a result of these developments, the established national airline companies were forced to adjust their strategies. Their national identities had been under pressure for some time. In an environment that was becoming ever more competitive, their close relationship to national governments was increasingly seen as a factor that prevented a speedy adaptation to changing market conditions. In the race to lower costs and fares, airlines with a relatively high cost structure were increasingly in danger. Privatization seemed a way out, but the road towards private equity appeared a bumpy one, strewn with potholes. Several national airlines faced a very real threat of liquidation. In November 2001 the first to go under was the ailing Belgian carrier Sabena, followed some months later by its hoped-for savior Swissair in March 2002. Other national carriers were also experiencing heavy turbulence as they needed to cut costs. In February 2012 the Hungarian airline Malév was forced out of business. The

30 Report of the Comité des Sages for Air Transport, published in: *Journal of Law and Economics* Vol. XXIX (1994) nr.2

31 https://www.europarl.europa.eu/factsheets/en/sheet/40/freedom-of-establishment-and-freedom-to-provide-services [2023].

32 https://www.europarl.europa.eu/RegData/etudes/note/join/2013/495849/IPOL-TRAN_NT(2013)495849_EN.pdf [2022].

Italian carrier Alitalia, which had been fighting off bankruptcy ever since 2008, struggled on in various guises until finally suspending its activities in October 2021.

To flourish in this volatile environment, international and even intercontinental partnerships sprang up in response to the competitive necessity to improve economies of scale in a market designed to deliver lower fares. This need determined the behavior of all major airlines. In May 1997, Lufthansa was the first European carrier to embrace a global partnership, joining forces with United Airlines, Air Canada, Scandinavian Airlines and Thai Airways International. Together they formed Star Alliance, the world's first multilateral airline grouping. Their example was followed by the founding of OneWorld in September 1998, bringing together American Airlines, British Airways, Canadian Airlines International, Cathay Pacific and Qantas. A third alliance, calling itself SkyTeam, subsequently united Delta Air Lines, Aeroméxico, Air France, and Korean Air in June 2000. KLM joined this group in 2004.

One of the reasons why this form of cooperation quickly became popular was the ascent of global computer reservations systems, enabling code sharing by airline partners, a marketing arrangement by which one airline attached its designator code to a flight operated by a partner airline, thus creating the impression of operating the flight with its own aircraft. In this way a single airline could appear to take care of the traveler throughout the whole journey. This was seen as a marketing asset because such connections received preference in reservations systems. Gradually, investments and property relations seeped into such alliances. In October 2003 Air France acquired a majority stake in KLM. British Airways did the same with Iberia in 2010. In 2017, Delta Air Lines and China Eastern each took a ten percent stake in Air France-KLM to amalgamate their global joint venture, along with Britain's Virgin Atlantic.

Such developments underlay the spectacular growth in air passenger numbers from 1.4 billion in 1989 to 4.5 billion in 2019.[33] Both the airspace and the airports became ever more congested and the latter, in particular, experienced difficulties keeping up. After all, expanding and improving facilities proceeded according to an entirely different timetable than airline expansion. It was therefore remarkable that all the developments of the past decades ultimately had relatively little impact on aviation security. This was due to the strict enforcement of the international standards and requirements defined in

---

33 ICAO statistics, in: Marc Dierikx, *Clipping the Clouds. How Air Travel Changed the World* (Westport CT: Praeger, 2008), p. 146–147 and https://www.icao.int/annual-report-2019 [2022].

the ICAO security manuals.[34] The need for adequate measures was underlined by the spectacular attacks using hijacked commercial aircraft in the United States on 11 September 2001, which left an indelible impression. More and better controls were implemented, on the ground as well as in the air, to prevent a repeat of '9/11'. The main beneficiaries of this new regime were the passengers: the chance of dying as a passenger in an air disaster decreased to 1:11 million, although such disasters continued to make headlines in the news.[35]

This was certainly the case with regard to the downing of Malaysian Airlines flight MH17, en route from Amsterdam to Kuala Lumpur over eastern Ukraine on 17 July 2014, killing all 298 people on board.[36] The criminal investigation by a Joint Investigation Team of experts from the Netherlands, Australia, Malaysia, Belgium and Ukraine revealed that the flight was shot down deliberately by a ground-to-air missile, provided to regional insurgents by Russia. In May 2018, Russia was held liable for its part in the downing of the plane.[37] Because setting up an international tribunal was politically unfeasible, the Dutch Prosecutor's Office put four suspects on trial under Dutch criminal law in 2020. The Court delivered its verdict on Thursday 17 November 2022, sentencing three of the four accused (in absentia) to life imprisonment.[38]

2 Dutch Air Transport in an Era of European Change

At the beginning of the 1990s policy discussions in The Hague focused on the implications for the Netherlands of the various measures that had been proposed to transform the national air transport markets into a single European market. As noted earlier, The Hague was cautious in relinquishing what control it had over policy, even if experts at the International Institute of Air and Space Law of Leiden University advised policy makers to focus instead on the new regime that was being developed in Brussels.[39] The Dutch policy apparatus

34 ICAO, Doc 10118, *Global Aviation Security Plan*, First Edition, 2017: https://www.icao.int/Security/Documents/GLOBAL%20AVIATION%20SECURITY%20PLAN%20EN.pdf [2022].

35 https://theweek.com/articles/462449/odds-are-11-million-1-that-youll-die-plane-crash [2022].

36 https://www.prosecutionservice.nl/topics/mh17-plane-crash/criminal-investigation-jit-mh17 [2022].

37 https://www.rijksoverheid.nl/onderwerpen/neerhalen-vlucht-mh17 [2022].

38 https://www.courtmh17.com/en/news/2022/summary-of-the-day-in-court-17-november-2022---judgment.html [2023].

39 *Het Parool*, 16 Aug. 1990 and 16 June 1992.

needed time to take in the changed perspective: customarily 'Europe' was the last item on the agendas of the Civil Aviation Meetings, focusing as they did on bilateral issues. Gradually, the old adage of garnering as many landing rights as possible in exchange for access by foreign airlines to Amsterdam was replaced with the conviction that Schiphol, with its many air connections, had become an attractive destination in its own right. At the airport this translated into a new strategic concept, the 'mainport': a large transport junction where different modalities met. The airport was set for growth and policy built on its existing international position.[40] It was, however, not long before a problem arose: how to accommodate the increasing number of aircraft movements, and the associated increased noise nuisance and air pollution, into the societal fabric of the Netherlands.[41] In subsequent years the environmental effects of Schiphol's use became an increasingly important factor influencing Dutch air transport policy – to the chagrin of civil servants at the Ministry of Foreign Affairs.[42] The Netherlands was not the only nation to face such issues. Capacity problems around airports and air traffic control brought so many new regulations that the old restrictions on air transport, motivated by political considerations, were replaced by new ones, resulting from technical limitations of the infrastructure. Air traffic in Europe faced special constraints, both on the ground and in the air.[43]

Under pressure, KLM reoriented itself, trying to improve its position on the new *European* home market. Maintaining its European network in a situation where profit margins were shrinking rapidly was a challenge and no longer linked to the conduct of foreign policy in The Hague.[44] In Europe, KLM was perhaps the loudest proponent of the free market in the air. However, this internationalist view increasingly conflicted with the government's position supporting liberalization while at the same time maintaining that within the Dutch national borders only selective growth was possible because of the external effects of flying. After five decades, Dutch policy coordination

---

40 Government White Paper *Luchtvaartnota Concurrerende en duurzame luchtvaart voor een sterke economie*, April 2009: *Handelingen der Staten-Generaal*, Tweede Kamer 2008–2009, Bijlage 15850.

41 Marc Dierikx, Bram Bouwens, *Building Castles of the Air. Schiphol Amsterdam and the Development of Airport Infrastructure in Europe, 1916–1996* (The Hague: Sdu, 1997), p. 263–273.

42 Memo Petit to Van der Zee, 7 June 1997; minutes meeting between RLD, VADV and KLM, 6 March 1998: Archive Foreign Affairs, VADV, Collection Jean Petit, The Hague.

43 Speech by IATA's Director-General Pierre Jeanniot at the Airports Council International conference, Amsterdam 22 April 1999.

44 Minutes 190th BLV, 6 April 1995: Archive Foreign Affairs, VADV, Collection Jean Petit, The Hague.

began to show cracks.[45] In the years that followed these would deepen. While KLM defended its commercial interests in Europe, Dutch government policy became increasingly entangled in domestic issues to do with airport use. Landing rights, in Europe and beyond, featured less and the frequency of the Civil Aviation Meetings decreased until the meetings as such were abolished in 1997.[46] The ongoing process of liberalization was disconcerting for all those concerned because full liberalization could potentially generate transnational mergers in the European air transport industry that would have a major impact on the ties between KLM and Schiphol. Government policy needed to factor this in, while at the same time fostering free competition.[47]

After 1989, the imminent changes in European aviation gave rise to a series of talks between airlines seeking international cooperation and association. Bilateral discussions between governments on air routes were superseded by contacts between national carriers. In 1990–1991, KLM was involved in discussions on cooperation with Sabena and with British Airways. When these tripartite talks remained unproductive, KLM and BA decided in November 1991 to instead pursue bilateral cooperation. The Hague supported this. However, the respective interests of the two carriers were quite different. While KLM hoped to bolster its market position in Europe, BA's prime incentive was the wish to strengthen its position in the US through KLM's association with Northwest Airlines. The talks moved in the direction of a possible Anglo-Dutch merger following the examples of Shell and Unilever. Given the new conditions in European commercial aviation, the two governments contented themselves with the role of interested council and did not claim a seat at the table, where corporate interests took precedence.[48] However, reaching an agreement on the appreciation of mutual market values, and how to integrate the respective interests into a common corporate structure proved difficult, as was the issue of control over the new endeavor. On 26 February 1992 the talks ran aground.[49]

---

45 Report 'Bosdag' meeting between RLD, VADV and KLM, 22 Dec. 1998: Archive Foreign Affairs, VADV, Collection Jean Petit, The Hague.

46 Report (VADV) on consultations between RLD, VADV and KLM, 14 March 2001: Archive Foreign Affairs, VADV, Collection Jean Petit, The Hague.

47 Letter State Secretary of Foreign Affairs, Ben Knapen, to Parliament, 2 Nov. 2012: *Handelingen der Staten-Generaal,* Tweede Kamer 2012–2013, 22 112, Nieuwe Commissievoorstellen en initiatieven van de lidstaten van de Europese Unie, nr. 1504.

48 Confidential RLD-minute (Cees den Braven) to Minister Hanja Maij-Weggen (Traffic and Water Management) re. possible merger between KLM and BA, 1 Nov. 1991: Archive Foreign Affairs, VADV, Collection Jean Petit, The Hague.

49 Minutes 184th BLV, 3 March 1992: Archive Foreign Affairs, VADV, Collection Jean Petit, The Hague.

In the wake of these developments, the bilateral discussions between The Hague and London moved away from Europe's political arena to focus on 5th freedom rights in Amsterdam for British carriers wishing to operate to airports in the former Soviet Union and the Commonwealth of Independent States.[50] London also worked on a deal that would protect and balance its rights to pursue the interests of British Airways in the context of a wider EU mandate in air transport matters. By April 1997, when the final obstacles for a common European sky were removed, it appeared that the days of government interventions and national policies were numbered.[51] From May 2000 onwards, both governments took a back seat in renewed merger discussions between KLM and BA. But as before in 1992, the discussions stalled on the issue of each airline's relative share in the merged company. On the basis of BA's shareholder value in relation to KLM's, the British claimed full authority over the merged company. This would call KLM's existing foreign landing rights into question, particularly those in the US, and these were vital to the Dutch interests. Also problematic was the legal issue of how to provide for the eventuality of old KLM rights being revoked. In such cases the airline should be able to resort to emergency procedures for intervention from The Hague to secure substantial Dutch ownership and effective control.[52]

In Europe, the role of the national state became even more prominent with Britain's decision in 2016 to leave the EU. This unprecedented step meant that the rights of British airlines to operate services to and from airports in the EU would expire upon leaving the Union. Other bilateral rights would have to be renegotiated, like the all-important treaty with the United States. To avoid chaos, the EU was prepared to hand British airlines landing and traffic rights, although considerably fewer than before Brexit. British Airways was hard hit by the Brexit decision. It would have to transfer existing property rights over European airlines, such as the Spanish carrier Iberia, to a European legal entity to enable these subsidiaries to continue to operate under the legal provisions of the EU.[53]

In 1989, the disappearance of the Berlin Wall had complicated Dutch-German relations. Seen from The Hague, the central issue revolved around the validity of arrangements between KLM and the GDR. As the East-German state was withering, the Dutch were uncertain whether the authorities in

50 Minutes 185th BLV, 7 July 1992: Archive Foreign Affairs, VADV, Collection Jean Petit, The Hague.

51 *Nieuwsblad Transport*, 5 Apr. 1997.

52 Reporting in *NRC*, 22 Sept. 2000.

53 *De Volkskrant*, 13-12-2018.

Bonn would validate KLM's recently obtained rights to operate to Dresden and whether KLM would be allowed to change its Berlin operations and exchange East-Berlin's Schönefeld for West-Berlin's airport Tegel.[54] The Dutch held that German unification meant that the Federal Republic became the legal successor to international agreements signed by the GDR. According to KLM this meant that changing one Berlin airport for another should be no more than an administrative action. The Dutch transport attaché in Bonn was instructed to see this through. After many years of discussions on landing rights that had been dominated by German efforts to contain KLM's market presence, The Hague feared this might entail prolonged discussions. However, Bonn proved more lenient than anticipated and shelved possible restrictive interpretations of the bilateral agreement with the GDR to welcome KLM at Tegel from April 1991.[55] Consequently, Germany proposed in July 1991 to amalgamate the bilateral agreements that the Netherlands had signed with the GDR and with the Federal Republic. However, Bonn did not approve KLM's wish to apply its code sharing agreement with NWA to its German operations, as this would cut into Lufthansa's domestic market. Bonn even went to court over the issue and demanded that NWA's code share services (which were carried out by KLM) be brought under the regime of the US-German bilateral agreement. Fearing this might lead to restrictions from other governments in Europe, especially Italy, Spain and France, the Dutch hastened to open discussions to mitigate this point of view.[56] But even in the new Europe, national interests ran deep. Germany maintained that code sharing was not a marketing tool, as KLM argued, but represented a separate right, apart from the agreed treaty provisions, and had to be contracted specifically. Bonn linked its endorsement of code sharing to ratification of the air services agreement between Germany and the US in 1994.[57] Only when Lufthansa began moving towards an alliance with America's United Airlines, in which code sharing would be a crucial arrangement, did Bonn put its objections aside.[58]

---

54 Code message Foreign Affairs to Bonn Embassy, 7 Sept. 1990: NNA, 2.05.392 Archive Ministry of Foreign Affairs 1985–1990, inv.nr. 5096. Minutes 181st BLV, 27 Sept. 1990: Archive Foreign Affairs, VADV, Collection Jean Petit, The Hague.

55 Minutes 182nd BLV, 3 Dec. 1990: Archive Foreign Affairs, VADV, Collection Jean Petit, The Hague.

56 Minutes 187th BLV, 29 March 1993: Archive Foreign Affairs, VADV, Collection Jean Petit, The Hague.

57 Minutes 188th BLV, 21 Dec. 1993: Archive Foreign Affairs, VADV, Collection Jean Petit, The Hague.

58 Minutes 189th BLV, 6 July 1994: Archive Foreign Affairs, VADV, Collection Jean Petit, The Hague.

The pending liberalization in Europe put the idea of a single market in air transport, governed by corporate rather than national interests, to the test. Developments in France, traditionally inclined to favor a role for the state in air transport, was an example of this. Contrary to past experience, diplomacy only featured on the sidelines. It took Paris a decade to bridge the gap between the old cartel-style system of airline-government collusion and the open market envisaged in Brussels. Thus, France steered a middle course between protecting its air carriers and opening up its home market. The Dutch only found out what this implied after KLM invested in the French regional carrier Air Littoral in 1989. KLM had hoped to take advantage of the liberalization momentum to boost its share in French traffic and use Air Littoral's services to feed into KLM's intercontinental network from Amsterdam. As foreign competition in its home market was not to the liking of Air France, the Dutch initially kept a low profile regarding their investment. The shares in Air Littoral were even kept out of KLM's annual reporting until 1992.[59] Even so, KLM ran up against French national interests. Once KLM held a portion of the shares, Air Littoral began to encounter visibility issues in the French airline booking system. But what was worse for the Dutch: Air Littoral proved to be in a very poor financial state and to keep the airline afloat, KLM was forced to provide a special loan. It did not secure a lasting bond. Continued opposition from Paris was so strong that the Dutch investments had to be written off within four years and in November 1992, KLM sold its interest in Air Littoral to a French aeronautical investment group.[60] Clearly, the French interpretation of free market access did not match that of the Dutch. The British fared little better. After prolonged discussions on access to Paris' Orly Airport for British Airways' French subsidiary Transport Aérien Transrégional in 1994, Paris applied to the European Court of Justice in Luxembourg to avoid having to open up the routes between Orly, Marseilles and Toulouse to foreign competitors. Although the Court ruled in October 1994 that Paris should open Orly to foreign competitors, France initially refused permission for a new KLM service, although agreeing on a solution a month later.[61] Resistance against foreign competition ran deep.

This treatment of foreign airline investments was linked to the development of Air France as it evolved from a lumbering state-owned and prestige-driven airline, characterized as 'an elephant in an evening suit', to become a privately

59 KLM, *Annual Report 1991/92*, p. 34/35.

60 Minutes KLM Board of Control, 6 Feb. 1992: KLM Archive, RvC. KLM, *Annual Report 1992/93*, p. 32. Ties Joosten, *De blauwe fabel*, p. 159.

61 *Trouw*, 21 Sept. 1994; *NRC Handelsblad*, 2 Nov. 1994 and 16 Nov. 1994.

owned, commercial carrier.[62] The process of change was initiated in March 1993 when elections brought a conservative government to office and Air France found itself on a list of state-owned firms to be privatized. The airline reorganized to cut costs and prepare for a complete recreation.[63] This took until June 2002, when Minister of Finance Francis Mer announced the government's intention to reduce its stake in Air France from 54 to 20 per cent before the end of the year. In preparation for this dramatic change of ownership, and to get ready for the new competitive conditions, Air France had participated in the founding of the global SkyTeam airline alliance two years earlier, thus bolstering its international position.

KLM was also experiencing headwinds and was rapidly flying into the red as a consequence of economic setbacks, the SARS respiratory virus in Asia, and the geopolitical instability brought on by the second Iraq War. In the rapidly globalizing airline environment, the alliance with NWA changed from a competitive asset into a constraint on KLM's international development. How should the airline be positioned for truly global competition? In May and June 2003 high-level meetings were held in The Hague in which KLM executives conferred with government officials on whether and how alliance policy could offer a way forward.[64] Two alternatives featured: a link-up with British Airways, or a connection with Air France. Of the two, the possibility of Franco-Dutch cooperation emerged as the best option, not only in terms of finance and operations, but also in terms of aviation policy and landing rights now that responsibilities over these fields were in the process of being transferred to the offices of the European Commission. The word 'merger' was voiced, although caution was urged regarding the legally important impediments of 'ownership and control' that would ensure that KLM remained a Netherlands' air carrier.[65]

From a Dutch government perspective, the status of over 150 bilateral agreements to which the Netherlands was a party were a prime issue to be determined before discussions on a possible merger could proceed. The Hague also wanted French guarantees regarding the future position of Schiphol Airport, which was perceived to be a major factor determining the general Dutch

62 Nicolas Neiertz, Air France: an Elephant in an Evening Suit?, in: Hans-Liudger Dienel, Peter Lyth (eds.), *Flying the Flag. European Commercial Air Transport since 1945* (Basingstoke: Macmillan, 1998), p. 18–49.

63 Robert Espérou, Gérard Maoui, *Air France. Des origines à nos jours* (Paris: Cherche Midi, 1997), p. 106–119.

64 Office memorandum Foreign Affairs (Michiel van der Zee) to Director-General Economic Cooperation, 7 May 2003: Archive Foreign Affairs, VADV, Collection Jean Petit, The Hague.

65 Office memorandum Foreign Affairs, 4 June 2003: Archive Foreign Affairs, VADV, Collection Jean Petit, The Hague.

foreign investment climate.[66] On 30 June 2003, KLM's CEO Leo van Wijk met with a cabinet delegation of Ministers Gerrit Zalm (Finance) and Jaap de Hoop Scheffer (Foreign Affairs) and State Secretaries Melanie Schultz van Haegen (Transport and Water Management) and Joop Wijn (Economic Affairs).The Cabinet members were not enthusiastic about a possible link-up. Words of caution were voiced. After decades of major public investments in Schiphol, The Hague's prime concern was now safeguarding the airport's position as an international hub. Although the Cabinet offered its services to liaise with the highest levels of French government – President Jacques Chirac – and bring all interested French and Dutch parties to the negotiating table, it also warned KLM not to underestimate what it called the 'cultural gap' with the French.[67]

The meeting represented a watershed in the long tradition of government involvement in Dutch air transport in that it placed Schiphol Airport, not KLM, at the heart of policy. At the same time, the cabinet chose to step away from the negotiating table. Although the potential merger was much discussed at the Ministries of Foreign Affairs, Finance, and Transport and Water Management, KLM, as a private venture, would have to fend for itself in its talks with Air France. Foreign Affairs mainly tracked the legal implications regarding substantial (Dutch) ownership and effective control and limited its involvement to participating in a working group to develop an inventory of the possible legal consequences of a merger. Obtaining assurances that would safeguard the hub status of Schiphol Airport and of KLM's network structure was of paramount importance. The wording of the draft merger agreement with Air France was carefully scrutinized in both regards. In subsequent developments, the arrangement and distribution of the shares of the two companies also received attention. Paris privatized 20 per cent of its shareholding in Air France and transferred 15 per cent to KLM. Of its shareholding in KLM, the Dutch government kept only 14 per cent in preferential shares, which in times of crisis could be increased to a majority through a special procedure to prove national ownership.[68] On 30 September 2003, the intended merger was made public by the presidents of the two airlines, Jean-Cyril Spinetta (Air France) and Leo van Wijk (KLM). Over the course of the next month, the agreement was vetted by the Finance Ministers involved, Gerrit Zalm and his French

66 Office memorandum Foreign Affairs (DES) to Minister Jaap de Hoop Scheffer, 25 June 2003: Archive Foreign Affairs, VADV, Collection Jean Petit, The Hague.

67 Report Foreign Affairs of meeting on 30 June 2003: Archive Foreign Affairs, VADV, Collection Jean Petit, The Hague.

68 Office memorandum Foreign Affairs re. KLM alliance consultations, 22 Aug. 2003: Archive Foreign Affairs, VADV, Collection Jean Petit, The Hague. Also: Bram Bouwens, Frido Ogier, *Welcome Aboard! 100 years of KLM Royal Dutch Airlines* (Zwolle: WBooks, 2020), p. 21–23.

counterpart Francis Mer. On 5 May 2004, the founding documents of the new company, Air France-KLM, were signed, formally unifying Dutch and French interests in the air.

In the founding papers, the two airlines agreed to combine their assets and activities under the umbrella of a holding company under French law, with current KLM common shareholders initially owning 19 per cent and the French State 44 per cent. Other Air France shareholders held 37 per cent.[69] Evidently the French side of the new company was poised to be the stronger of the two, although KLM obtained assurances that it could continue to operate under its own name. The brand Air France was also kept. By maintaining the two operating companies, both the French and the Dutch hoped to continue under the existing bilateral agreements that their governments had signed with third countries. At the same time, the EU agreements also allowed them to use their European air carrier status. Although the holding was (and is) a French company, each of the two airlines would fly under its own flag.

At first, the Dutch were keen to stress the benefits KLM gained from the new bond with Air France: network adaptations and code sharing boosted passenger numbers. Traffic results also improved for Air France, but in 2008 the outbreak of a worldwide financial and economic crisis brought complex financial issues to the fore. As a result of the economic downturn, both airlines flew into the red, which put a strain on relations and acted as a magnifying glass for the cultural differences. In the Netherlands, the idea took root that it was a French objective to enhance French elements in Air France-KLM. The deficits subsequently necessitated cost-cutting programs and reductions in the labor force, which in France resulted in violent industrial action. Disgruntled employees physically chased senior Air France managers at Charles de Gaulle Airport on 5 October 2015.[70] In The Hague there was talk of government intervention and of increasing the state's shareholding in Air France-KLM. Similarly, the French government expanded its shareholding, which had been watered down since 2003 to 15.9 per cent, to 17.6 per cent to safeguard France's national interests.[71] In turn, this fed the idea that French and Dutch interests did not run parallel and that Paris was scheming to move flights from Amsterdam to Paris. An added problem was that KLM consistently out-performed Air France, feeding into the chauvinist undertones of discussions on the airline venture. The Dutch Finance Minister Jeroen Dijsselbloem and State Secretary of Infrastructure and Environment Sharon Dijksma travelled to Paris to confer with French

69 Air France and KLM, joint press release Air France – KLM merger, 30 Sept. 2003.

70 http://nos.nl/artikel/2061415, 5 Oct. 2015.

71 http://nos.nl/artikel/2062874, 13 Oct. 2015.

cabinet members regarding how best to effect a solution that would rebuild mutual trust.[72] Meanwhile, voices in Parliament in The Hague worried about Dutch interests and about the durability of the balanced accords signed in 2003. In an effort to silence critics, Air France-KLM announced a special *Trust Together* program in November 2016. This took years and involved dealing with resurging nationalism on both sides, expressed in the form of public critiques regarding the distribution of shares, the differences in profitability and the effects of recurrent labor unrest in Paris.[73] Despite two decades of European liberalization, old national sentiments were still very much present.

This was exemplified by a surprise action of the Netherlands government on 26 February 2019. To the chagrin of Paris, which claimed to have had no prior knowledge, The Hague secretly invested 680 million euros in Air France-KLM shares, increasing the Dutch stake to 12.68 per cent. The two Cabinet members responsible, Wopke Hoekstra (Finance) and Cora van Nieuwenhuizen (Infrastructure and Water Management), stated that it had recently become clear that the government had too little influence on decisions within the holding company, even when major national interests were at stake. Expanding the state's shareholding was therefore called for. There was a need to balance the Netherlands' shareholding with that of the French state. The two ministers referred to the old fear that Air France-KLM might move a substantial part of its operations to Paris to the detriment of Schiphol Airport's hub function, the Dutch investment climate, and employment. There appeared to be some grounds for this fear. Hoekstra stated that The Hague had not been properly consulted when Air France-KLM decided on alliance agreements with Delta Airlines and with China Eastern Airlines. Although some raised doubts on how effective the Dutch move would be to ensure a balance of influence on the decision making processes in the holding company, one thing became clear to observers at a distance: after a century of commercial aviation, the influence of national states was still very much at the heart of international air transport.[74] As if to prove this, each of the two governments injected billions into their own national branch of Air France-KLM in 2020 and 2021 when the airline needed

72 http://nos.nl/artikel/2110040-kabinet-praat-met-fransen-over-air-france-klm.html, 9 June 2016.

73 *De Telegraaf*: 2 Aug. 2017. https://nos.nl/artikel/2230745-franse-minister-toekomst-air-france-klm-is-in-gevaar.html 7 May 2018.

74 *De Volkskrant* (cover story), 27 Febr. 2019. *NRC*, 27 Febr. 2019. https://www.rijksoverheid.nl/actueel/nieuws/2019/02/26/nederlandse-staat-koopt-1268-van-de-aandelen-in-air-france-klm [2022]

rescuing after the collapse of air traffic due to the spread of the deadly corona virus.[75]

In Eastern Europe, the implications for air transport of the political changes that took place in the closing months of 1989 soon became evident. In the wake of the massive transformations, new markets opened. Western airlines were quick to try and develop new eastbound services, even though political circumstances were still in a state of flux. In 1990 KLM planned to increase its number of flights by 70 per cent. The Dutch put out feelers to see if the Czechoslovakian carrier ČSA or the Hungarian airline Malév might be tempted to enter into some form of cooperation.[76] In Budapest the Hungarian government was not enthused and moved to protect the interests of Malév, but bilateral talks with Czechoslovakia resulted in an agreement in Prague in March 1992. This new accord enabled KLM to operate a twice daily service to Prague, which was well above the usual fifty-fifty division of capacity.[77] However, the agreement was soon rendered ineffective in anticipation of the dissolution of Czechoslovakia on 1 January 1993, splitting the country into two independent states, the Czech Republic and Slovakia. Inheriting the aviation treaty from its predecessor, the Czech Republic objected strongly to KLM's capacity entitlement, which left ČSA only limited opportunities to compete. These continued differences gave rise to a Dutch claim for financial compensations to the sum of several million dollars. Only after prolonged discussions was the matter was settled in March 1994, when KLM and ČSA concluded a 'blocked space' agreement that enabled ČSA to sell seats – at a nominal cost – on KLM flights.[78] Nonetheless, in 1996 the Czechs again took issue with KLM's dominance in the bilateral market. Further talks resulted in one weekly flight by ČSA and three by KLM. The 'blocked space' agreement was adapted, providing ČSA with seats on all three KLM services.[79]

Following the Polish political breakthrough in the summer of 1989, the Dutch also initiated talks in Warsaw hoping to increase KLM's weekly frequencies in

75 https://www.rijksoverheid.nl/actueel/nieuws/2020/04/24/kabinet-zet-financiele-steun-klaar-voor-klm 24 Apr. 2020; https://nos.nl/artikel/2375575-air-france-klm-krijgt-4-miljard-aan-steun-franse-overheid-vergroot-invloed.html 6 Apr. 2021.

76 Minutes 180th BLV 25 Apr. 1990: Archive Foreign Affairs, VADV, Collection Jean Petit, The Hague.

77 Minutes 185th BLV 7 July 1992: Archive Foreign Affairs, VADV, Collection Jean Petit, The Hague.

78 Minutes 189th BLV, 6 July 1994: Archive Foreign Affairs, VADV, Collection Jean Petit, The Hague.

79 Minutes 192nd BLV, 11 July 1996: Archive Foreign Affairs, VADV, Collection Jean Petit, The Hague.

exchange for financial support from The Hague: under the old bilateral agreement of 1960 the Polish airline LOT had a virtual veto on any planned KLM expansion, which they and the Polish authorities had used. However, as LOT prepared for a partial transfer of ownership to the private sector, Warsaw found it difficult to come to terms with the liberal ideas promoted in Western Europe, despite signing an Association Agreement with the EU in 1991. Talks progressed slowly as LOT's transition to a joint stock company took more time than anticipated.[80] Nonetheless, the Dutch Transport Minister Hanja Maij-Weggen travelled to Warsaw in December 1992 to sign a memorandum of understanding that covered the expansion of frequencies between the two capitals until the summer of 1997. The Hague hoped to draw up a formal bilateral agreement confirming this, helped along by Dutch funding to provide management assistance to LOT.[81] Nothing came of this. Like Hungary and the Czech Republic, Poland adopted a protectionist course in foreign air transport policy, holding out against the European Commission's efforts to entice Warsaw to adopt EU aviation principles in anticipation of talks on Polish accession to the EU. Relations remained unsettled, as did discussions on a possible increase in the number of weekly KLM flights.[82]

Meanwhile, the three Baltic republics that were part of the Soviet Union clamored for greater freedom, positioning themselves for future independence. This was achieved in August 1991, leading the Netherlands to test the waters for bilateral aviation agreements with the three new European states. Although KLM did not have any aircraft available to operate services, the airline did offer to provide know-how and advice. Thus, the Dutch hoped to attract Lithuanian Airlines, Estonian Air and Latvia Air to begin services to Amsterdam that might feed into KLM's intercontinental network. The Hague, for its part, hinted at possible options for bilateral financial support.[83] While consultations continued with Latvia and Lithuania, a liberal agreement was drawn up with Estonia in September 1991. This allowed Estonian Air to operate twice weekly to Amsterdam. In March 1993 bilateral agreements with Latvia and Lithuania were signed as well.

80 Joanna Filipczyk, LOT: connecting East and West in Poland, in: Dienel and Lyth (eds.), *Flying the Flag*, p. 198–199.

81 Minutes 186th BLV, 4 Dec. 1992; minutes 187th BLV, 29 March 1993: Archive Foreign Affairs, VADV, Collection Jean Petit, The Hague.

82 Minutes 193rd BLV, 25 Febr. 1997: Archive Foreign Affairs, VADV, Collection Jean Petit, The Hague.

83 Minutes 184th BLV, 3 March 1992; minutes 185th BLV 7 July 1992: Archive Foreign Affairs, VADV, Collection Jean Petit, The Hague.

The Dutch also held talks with newly independent Ukraine, hoping to initiate a route to Kyiv once diplomatic relations would be established. These discussions were helped by the establishment of the Commonwealth of Independent States in December 1991, whose members indicated they wished to extend the 1958 bilateral agreement with the USSR to cover future airline operations. Building on this, a bilateral air services agreement was signed on 17 December 1992, evidence of Kyiv's pro-Western course in international politics. Nonetheless, setting up operations was not easy while Ukraine was in the midst of a transition to a market economy and its administration was in flux. KLM had to call in support from the newly opened Dutch embassy to arrange the necessary practicalities and formalities. In Kyiv, the national carrier Ukraine International, founded just a month before in October 1992, saw its first four planes on the Amsterdam route depart completely empty because of insufficient time for marketing preparations.[84] Disappointing commercial results subsequently made Ukraine wary of Dutch desires to extend KLM's flight schedule, even though KLM indicated it would be willing to offer financial compensation.[85] Subsequently, demands for such compensations – disproportionate from the Dutch perspective – became a topic for negotiation. Relations declined in 1997 when Ukraine, suffering a series of economic setbacks, called into question the contents of the December 1992 air services agreement, the basis for KLM's operations. It was a good thing that the European Commission began to manifest itself more prominently in international air transport relations in the 1990s, shifting the discussions away from the bilateral perspective and stimulating the development of Ukrainian ties to the EU. In June 2005, this led to an agreement to liberalize air transport between the EU and Ukraine, a step towards an open skies accord. The process was not helped by the repeated political upheavals that Ukraine went through in subsequent years. Not until 12 October 2021 could a comprehensive air transport agreement be signed during a Ukraine-EU Summit in Kyiv. The agreement opened the way to a 'Common Aviation Area' between the EU and Ukraine and was expected to provide market access and new opportunities. This accord fell victim to the Russian invasion of Ukraine on 24 February 2022 and the subsequent war that closed Ukrainian airspace.[86]

---

84 Minutes 186th BLV, 4 Dec. 1992: Archive Foreign Affairs, VADV, Collection Jean Petit, The Hague.

85 Minutes 191st BLV, 7 Dec. 1995: Archive Foreign Affairs, VADV, Collection Jean Petit, The Hague.

86 https://transport.ec.europa.eu/news/aviation-eu-and-ukraine-sign-milestone-aviation-agreement-2021-10-12_en [2023].

In Russia itself the regime of Mikhail Gorbachev allowed Western airlines more leeway to fly over the Soviet Union in the late 1980s. For example, London and Moscow modified their bilateral air services agreement in March 1987 to permit British Airways and British Caledonian to operate three weekly services to Tokyo over Siberia. A month earlier, KLM had also received such rights, while Aeroflot was granted freedom of action in the Netherlands. It appeared that aviation might be one of the areas in which new forms of cooperation between the Soviets and the West would take shape. Following an agreement between the Soviet Union and Japan, KLM hoped to profit from this momentum and receive additional routes and better operating conditions over Siberia's vast airspace. The latter were much needed. Airline crews flying the route complained about having to provide the aircraft's position to controllers at more than thirty different reporting points, some as close as one minute flying time apart.[87]

Changes would need to be incorporated in the annexes of a new bilateral agreement. Drafting this took time, because the Soviet Union disintegrated at the end of 1991 after an unsuccessful coup attempt in Moscow in August of that year. In its place a Commonwealth of Independent States was set up with the new Russian Federation as its most important constituent. Under the leadership of Boris Yeltsin, a new course was set towards privatization of the economy according to the Western model. Those best positioned to play a role acquired important sectors of the economy. Nudged on by government programs that stimulated private investments and fostered private equity, a number of entrepreneurs became very rich. The influence of these *oligarchs* soon stretched into the field of aviation. It would cost Western airlines dearly.

In the first months of 1992, the Russian Federation took over the international obligations of the former Soviet Union. In aviation terms this meant that the Russian Federation needed to adapt the existing bilateral agreements and negotiate new ones. Western nations hastened to be the first to tap into these emerging new markets, despite reservations concerning air traffic control and flight safety issues.

In the midst of this, the Dutch received a first draft of a new bilateral from Moscow in November 1992. The proposed text appeared to be modelled on the old accord. Not enthused, The Hague asked for consultations, hoping to achieve more operational flexibility under the new political regime.[88] But

87 *De Volkskrant*, 28 Apr. 1990. Further: Svik, *Civil Aviation and the Globalization of the Cold War*, p. 193–194.

88 Minutes 186th BLV, 4 Dec. 1992: Archive Foreign Affairs, VADV, Collection Jean Petit, The Hague.

although in the early 1990s many things were adrift in the Russian Federation and the national airline Aeroflot appeared headed for a break-up into more than 150 different entities, air transport policy continued with its old ways. In four rounds of discussions, in March and September 1993 and February and September 1994, no perspective on increased liberalism came into view. Instead, discussions centered on a financial settlement for transit through Russian airspace above Siberia. If in the past Western airlines had already paid for the right to fly over Siberia, now was the time for serious money transfers. European carriers were obliged to conclude a royalty agreement with Aeroflot. In The Hague this gave rise to considerable concern. Estimates suggested that Western European airlines faced charges amounting to some 200 million dollars annually, a sum unrelated to the actual costs of air traffic control. On top of this, the wording of the new treaty was also a matter of debate. Small wonder then that the Dutch pinned their hopes of achieving a breakthrough on involving the European Commission.[89]

However, such a breakthrough did not come about, despite an agreement in January 1996 between the European Commission and the Russian Department of Transport. It was not in the Russian interest to be transparent about the various charges levied on Western airlines using the Siberia route and talks stalled. KLM itself was looking at a Russian claim of 25 million euros per year. At the Civil Aviation Meeting in The Hague, KLM's negotiator Peter van Fenema saw no signs of a Russian willingness to move towards a reduction in these excessive charges, for the simple reason that it was an ever-increasing source of revenue. The Russian adage was that 'if you don't like to pay, then don't use the route!' Likewise, talks on additional KLM destinations in the Russian Federation did not progress, as Moscow made these conditional on parallel operations by Russian carriers. Moscow also appeared to be testing the mandate and the negotiating skills of the European Commission.[90] The Russians increased their financial demands on Western airlines and linked a settlement of overflight rights to EU funding for a new air traffic control project to oversee the Siberian transit routes.[91] The matter dragged on. Not even Europe's Transport Commissioner Neil Kinnock was able to bring about a settlement. From Montreal, ICAO's president Assad Kotaite tried to mediate, but was equally

89 Minutes 190th BLV, 6 Apr. 1995: Archive Foreign Affairs, VADV, Collection Jean Petit, The Hague.

90 Minutes 192nd BLV, 11 July 1996: Archive Foreign Affairs, VADV, Collection Jean Petit, The Hague.

91 Minutes 193rd BLV, 25 Febr. 1997: Archive Foreign Affairs, VADV, Collection Jean Petit, The Hague.

unsuccessful.[92] Matters became even more complex when the discussion on overflight rights was linked to services to Western Europe by Russian airlines using older Tupolev and Ilyushin aircraft that did not comply with the noise abatement specifications in force in the EU.[93] The EU, on its part, tried to trade off the overflight issue against EU support for Russia's accession to the World Trade Organization, but without success. Over the course of the decade Russian airlines gradually began using Western equipment, which resolved the noise issues, but the issue of overflight rights was never settled and discussions continued. In 2004 Moscow promised to abolish payments by December 2013, but did not ratify the underlying agreement. Although an understanding was reached on a deal that linked the EU's green light for Russia's accession to the WTO to a promise to put an end to the enforced royalty payments as of January 2014, the deadline passed without any sign of a change.

Meanwhile air transport between the Netherlands and Russia expanded as economic and tourist ties became firmer. Bilateral trade, not just in oil and gas but also in agricultural products was growing, albeit against the political tide that showed signs of a widening gap between Russia and the West. In evidence of this, the planned celebration in 2013 of long-standing bilateral relations between Russia and the Netherlands ran aground in a series of incidents. Aviation also represented a contentious topic. Plans made by Europe's Commissioner for Climate Action, Connie Hedegaard, to enforce payment for CO_2 emissions from all airlines flying over the EU met with Russian threats to withdraw the operating rights of European carriers over the Russian Federation.[94]

A year later, a much more serious conflict arose when Russia occupied and annexed the Crimean peninsula in March 2014. Four months later, on 17 July 2014, Malaysia Airlines flight MH17, was shot down over eastern Ukraine. Investigations revealed that the plane was hit by the explosion of a ground-to-air missile, provided to Ukrainian insurgents by Russia. The disaster led to a package of European sanctions against Russia.[95]

The effect was a general deterioration of relations between the Netherlands and the Russian Federation, in which air transport became one of the eye-catching factors. In October 2017, an issue with operating slots at Schiphol for Russia's AirBridgeCargo that forced it to reduce its operations led to retaliatory

92 Minutes discussion between RLD, VADV and KLM, 4 Sept. 1998: Archive Foreign Affairs, VADV, Collection Jean Petit, The Hague.

93 Minutes discussion between RLD, VADV and KLM, 30 Jan. 2002: Archive Foreign Affairs, VADV, Collection Jean Petit, The Hague.

94 *De Volkskrant*, 4 Apr. 2014.

95 https://www.rijksoverheid.nl/onderwerpen/neerhalen-vlucht-mh17 [2022].

threats to close Siberian airspace to KLM flights.[96] Although the issue was resolved between the two airlines involved – KLM 'lent' slots at Schiphol to AirBridgeCargo – bilateral aviation relations continued their downward trend. The potential use of the 'Siberian overflight weapon' remained a risk for all European airlines operating on the route.

Rising political tensions between Russia and the West were highlighted in 2021 when Russia's remaining European ally, Belarus, instigated a state hijack of a commercial airliner. On Sunday 23 May 2021, a Ryanair flight from Athens to Vilnius in Lithuania was forced to land in Minsk after a fake warning from Belarus' air traffic control about 'a security risk on board'. Once on the ground in Minsk, Belarus' security officers arrested and abducted journalist Roman Protasevich, a known critic of the regime and held and questioned all the other passengers on the flight for seven hours. The following day, discussions at an (already planned) EU summit in Brussels resulted not only in a sharp denunciation of the hijack, but also to a ban on all flights between the European Union and Belarus, and further political sanctions. As was to be expected, Russia stood alone in its defense of the Belarus' action.[97]

Relations hit rock bottom when Russia invaded Ukraine on 24 February 2022. In protest against the unprovoked attack on a neighboring country, the EU implemented a series of sanctions aimed at crippling the Russian economy. One of the first of these was a complete ban on all flights by Russian airlines to and across EU territory, followed by a ban on the export of spare parts for (Airbus) aircraft built in the EU. On 25 February, KLM had its scheduled flights to Moscow and St. Petersburg turn around.[98] In an act of retaliation, Russia did the same for flights from 36 countries, including the Netherlands.[99] Politics and war had brought air services to a complete halt.

3 New Perspectives in Indonesia and Australia

In October 1989 KLM and Garuda had drawn up a new cooperation agreement after years of discussion. This boosted hopes that an accord on a new bilateral between the Netherlands and Indonesia was within reach. Indeed, a settlement

96 *De Volkskrant*, 31 Oct. 2017.

97 *De Volkskrant*, 25 May 2021.

98 Mario Barbano, Turbulence in the air and space industry: EU sanctions against Russia, 29 Apr. 2022, at: https://www.leidenlawblog.nl/articles/turbulence-in-the-air-and-space-industry-eu-sanctions-against-russia [2022].

99 https://nos.nl/collectie 28 Febr. 2022.

was initialed in June 1990 that laid the groundwork for an expansion of KLM's services to Bali from two to four flights a week. The Hague and Jakarta also settled the long-standing issue of overflight over Indonesia by KLM aircraft on their way to and from Australia. The formal exchange of signatures took place on 23 November, when the Indonesian Transport Minister Azwar Anas visited the Netherlands.[100] The sky seemed clear for smooth cooperation carried by the economic boom Indonesia was experiencing in the early 1990s. However, relations remained touchy and easily upset by incidents. At this particular point in time the powder keg was East Timor. On 12 November 1991 the Indonesian military opened fire on people protesting against Indonesia's occupation of the former Portuguese colony, allegedly killing over a hundred people. Reports and film images of this clash reached the international media, leading to political pressure on Indonesia to stop the violence. The Netherlands was amongst the nations protesting, in accordance with a policy whitepaper that the incoming Minister for Development Cooperation, Jan Pronk, had sent to parliament in the autumn of 1990. The Dutch policy guidelines stressed the importance of freedom, democracy and human rights as preconditions for development and aid.[101] With a personal history of discord with Indonesia since the 1970s, Pronk was under pressure from Parliament to take action and restructure relations with Jakarta. After some debate, Dutch bilateral aid was indeed paused on 21 November 1991, pending inquiries into the violence.[102]

This brought a marked deterioration of contacts. In March 1992, Indonesia unilaterally ended their development relationship with the Netherlands.[103] Aviation also suffered. The ratification of the bilateral accord was put on hold in Jakarta and KLM President Pieter Bouw was forced to postpone his planned visit to the country. Rebuilding bilateral relations took time, but was helped by Indonesian promises of a full investigation into the events in East Timor. Improvements also came in April 1992, with senior Indonesian aviation officials visiting the Netherlands, nurturing relations with KLM and with Schiphol Airport. These discussions resulted in extracting a promise of a profit-sharing

100 Minutes 182nd BLV, 3 Dec. 1990: Archive Foreign Affairs, VADV, Collection Jean Petit, The Hague.

101 J.J.P. de Jong, A Challenge Ignored. The Netherlands and the Asian Tigers, 1985–1993, in: J.A. Nekkers, P.A.M. Malcontent (eds.), *Fifty Years of Dutch Development Cooperation, 1949–1999* (The Hague: Sdu, 2000), p. 289–305 (296–297).

102 *De Volkskrant*, 20 Nov. 1991; *Algemeen Dagblad*, 22 Nov. 1991.

103 Peter Malcontent, Floribert Baudet, The Dutchman's Burden? Nederland en de internationale rechtsorde in de twintigste eeuw, in: Bob de Graaff, Duco Hellema, Bert van der Zwan, *De Nederlandse buitenlandse politiek in de twintigste eeuw* (Amsterdam: Boom, 2003), p. 91. Hellema, *Nederland in de wereld*, p. 376.

arrangement for traffic to Denpasar on Bali from KLM.[104] The Dutch Minister of Foreign Affairs Hans van den Broek subsequently paid an official visit to Indonesia, in July 1992, but found that a deal on aviation remained beyond reach. Progress appeared to depend on moves made by Indonesia. Jakarta provided an opening when the Indonesian Transport Minister Haryanto Dhanutirto visited the Netherlands in September 1993. He proposed a 'limited open skies agreement' to end the long history of disputes between the two countries. In February 1994 a new air transport agreement was signed, ending a series of differences that dated back to 1968. The parties agreed on an extension of Garuda's route schedule by six intermediate points with 5th freedom rights. KLM, on its part, was allowed to incorporate Denpasar, Surabaya and Medan in its route schedule, but without such 5th freedom rights. From 1 April 1994 both carriers were free to add an extra weekly flight up to a total of 14 in April 1999. Combining points in Indonesia was, however, subject to restrictions. Still, The Hague was pleased. The new agreement would enable an expansion of services, keeping pace with Indonesia's economic boom and expanding tourism. On the other hand, The Hague was uncertain about the longevity of the deal and, by extension, of the Suharto regime, which was marred by persistent corruption.[105] Both sides were content, therefore, when in December 1994 KLM and Garuda translated their accord into long-term strategic cooperation. On the surface all looked fine, but behind closed doors KLM's Peter van Fenema and others complained about Garuda's diffuse management structure, which made practical cooperation difficult and opened the door to all sorts of problems. What was worse, KLM's new service to Surabaya needed 5th freedom rights to be economically viable in the long term, rights Indonesia was unwilling to give.[106]

Queen Beatrix's official state visit to Indonesia in August 1995 had a positive effect on the bilateral contacts and aviation was one of the areas to profit. Indeed, relations improved to the point that The Hague was prepared to facilitate a settlement of Indonesian debts. After decades of troublesome relations that went back to colonial times, bilateral air transport was increasingly determined by economic factors, rather than the sensitivities of politics. These were easier to build on, which also had a beneficial effect on politics. In August 2005, Foreign Minister Ben Bot was the first Dutch Minister to be present at

104 Minutes 187nd BLV, 29 March 1993: Archive Foreign Affairs, VADV, Collection Jean Petit, The Hague.

105 Minutes 189th BLV, 6 July 1994: Archive Foreign Affairs, VADV, Collection Jean Petit, The Hague.

106 Minutes 192nd BLV, 11 July 1996: Archive Foreign Affairs, VADV, Collection Jean Petit, The Hague.

the annual celebration of Indonesia's declaration of independence. Relations calmed further.[107]

On 19 August 2009, a new round of bilateral talks took place in The Hague, resulting in the amendment of the Air Transport Agreement of 23 November 1990. Reflecting European policies, rates were liberalized. A new clause on code sharing was adopted that created leverage for additional agreements. This was formalized in a diplomatic exchange of notes on 29 December 2011.[108] Soon after, the European Union stepped in, which widened the scope of the air transport agreement to eventually encompass a comprehensive accord between the 27 member states of the EU and the 10 members of the Association of Southeast Asian Nations (ASEAN) in October 2022.[109]

KLM had, after years of discussions, received Australian permission in October 1989 for a second weekly flight to Sydney. The Dutch were very pleased with this unexpected concession and showed this in a letter congratulating Transport Minister Ralph Willis with this 'bold and courageous step forward'. Nonetheless, in keeping with the Dutch pattern of continuously knocking on all doors, The Hague's chief air transport negotiator Irene Albers hinted that the result held no finality and left room for wider development.[110] Still, both parties agreed to maintain the status quo for the time being while Australia readied itself for a new election in March 1990. To the relief of the Dutch, these brought a new term in office for Labor – and a continuation of Australia's liberally inspired air transport policy. Indeed Canberra continued the policy adopted in 1989, allowing KLM to fly to 'any four points in Australia'.[111] This fit Willis' promise to the House of Representatives that emphasized the interests of consumers and industries such as tourism in future international airline negotiations.[112] In June 1996, Canberra widened possibilities even further, giving permission to KLM to lay on two additional weekly flights to Sydney and Melbourne, while also promising two further Australian destinations to

107 Hellema, *Nederland in de wereld*, p. 420, 432–433.

108 *Handelingen der Staten-Generaal*, Tweede Kamer 2012–2013, 33 225, nr. 2: https://zoek.officielebekendmakingen.nl/kst-33225-2.pdf [2022].

109 https://ec.europa.eu/commission/presscorner/detail/en/ip_22_6126 [2023].

110 Letter Albers to Willis, 3 Oct. 1989: Archive Foreign Affairs, VADV, Collection Jean Petit, The Hague.

111 Minutes 185th BLV, 7 July 1992: Archive Foreign Affairs, VADV, Collection Jean Petit, The Hague.

112 Statement Ralph Willis to House of Representatives, 15 June 1989, in: Richard H. Snape, Lisa Gropp, Tas Luttrell, *Australia's Trade Policy 1965–1997. A Documentary History* (St. Leonards: Allen & Unwin, 1998), p. 355–356 [doc. 8:42].

boost bilateral tourism and trade.[113] It appeared that after decades of restrictions, liberal air ideas had taken root. Australia even initiated steps towards the implementation of 'open skies' in its external relations. Initially, this approach focused on several European countries, but by the dawn of the new century Canberra was developing a keen eye for a treaty at the European level.

This latter policy was evidenced in the talks between the European Commission and Australia's Labor Government under Prime Minister Kevin Rudd in April and June 2008 on an 'open skies' agreement to supersede the existing bilateral accords. Modelled on the 'open skies' agreement between Australia and the United States that had been concluded earlier that year, the treaty aimed to remove most of the existing limitations for Australian and European airlines operating between Australia and the EU.[114] No agreement materialized, but Australia signed a so-called horizontal agreement with the EU in 2008, recognizing the EU provisions on Community carriers and accepting the principle of non-discrimination on the basis of nationality.

4 Turbulence on the Air Route to China

After the suppression of the demonstrations in Tiananmen Square in May 1989 and the ensuing cancellation of the royal state visit to China, relations between the Netherlands and China remained lukewarm. Beijing put the issue of a bilateral air transport agreement on hold. A year and a half later there was some movement in the case file when China Eastern Airlines expressed an interest in opening a service to Amsterdam.[115] This message came as a surprise for KLM. In the economic impasse caused by the Gulf War the airline had no plans for new routes and preferred to focus on an expansion of its services to Taipei.[116]

Talks with Beijing took place in August and September 1991 in the framework of a Dutch trade mission led by the State Secretary for Economic Affairs

113 Minutes 192nd BLV, 11 July 1996: Archive Foreign Affairs, VADV, Collection Jean Petit, The Hague.

114 Open-sky pact with the EU: *The Australian*, 1 May 2008. Also: https://parlinfo.aph.gov.au/parlInfo/search/display/display.w3p;db=CHAMBER;id=chamber%2Fhansardr%2F2008-06-17%2F0020;query=Id%3A%22chamber%2Fhansardr%2F2008-06-17%2F0000%22 [2022].

115 Minutes 182nd BLV, 3 December 1990: Archive Foreign Affairs, VADV, Collection Jean Petit, The Hague.

116 Office memo acting VADV to Van den Broek re. flights to Taipei, 16 May 1991: Archive Foreign Affairs, VADV, Collection Jean Petit, The Hague.

Yvonne van Rooy and resulted in a provisional accord. The ink on the documents was barely dry when relations took another nosedive, however. At the beginning of October, the newspaper *NRC* had got wind of the visit of yet another Taiwanese mission to the RDM shipyard in Rotterdam. Urged on by Foreign Affairs after informal consultations in Beijing, the Ministry of Economic Affairs issued a public veto.[117] A new Taiwanese submarine order was out of the question. Nonetheless relations with the People's Republic cooled.[118] A request from KLM to use a specific route for overflight over China was left unanswered in Beijing. After all, China was not a party to the 1944 International Air Services Transit Agreement and was thus under no obligation to cooperate. Hoping to effect an improvement in relations, Minister of Economic Affairs Koos Andriessen visited Beijing in April 1992. He returned with a contract for the sale of seven Fokker airliners.[119] In the matter of landing rights, however, Beijing reiterated the existing complaints against air traffic between the Netherlands and Taiwan. Once again, it turned out to be impossible to achieve progress. The People's Republic insisted on a veto regarding the operations of China Airlines at Schiphol, while The Hague maintained that this was an arrangement under private law on which the government could exercise no influence.[120]

Before this, KLM's profitable operations to Taiwan had not gone unnoticed in international aviation. Other major airlines had approached their own governments in an effort to develop opportunities in Taipei without ruffling feathers in Beijing. In 1990, Australia's Qantas was the first to pioneer a new approach. Qantas Hotels established a subsidiary in Taiwan, Australia Asia Airlines, which offered a scheduled air service from Sydney. To operate the reciprocal service whilst sparing Chinese sensitivities, Taiwan founded a new carrier, Mandarin Airlines. Mandarin operated with no display of the Taiwanese flag on its aircraft. This set an example. In March 1993, British Airways set up a dedicated subsidiary to fly to Taiwan, British Airways Asia, while Air France and Lufthansa also worked on similar constructions that made it possible to fly to Taipei. This brought pressure on Beijing. In a meeting with the Dutch ambassador Dirk Jan van Houten, CAAC director Lu Ruiling hinted that China might

117 Interview with Henry Wijnaendts, 2 March 2022: https://diplomatieke-getuigenissen.huygens.knaw.nl/ [2023].

118 *NRC Handelsblad*, 2 Oct. 1991. Ingrid d'Hooghe, The 1991/1992 Dutch debate on the sale of submarines to Taiwan, in: *China Information*, 6.4 (1992) p. 40–54.

119 Office memo VADV, 6 Nov. 1991: Archive Foreign Affairs, VADV, Collection Jean Petit, The Hague.

120 Code message Embassy Beijing re. air services to China, 3 Dec. 1992. Also: minutes 186th BLV, 4 Dec. 1992: Archive Foreign Affairs, VADV, Collection Jean Petit, The Hague.

now be willing to condone services between Amsterdam and Taipei, as long as national emblems were not shown on the aircraft.[121]

The new conciliatory position taken by Beijing gave the Netherlands and Taiwan reason to think about alternative forms for the air services. In The Hague, both KLM and charter carrier Martinair forwarded proposals. To avoid arousing sensitivities in Beijing by sending an official Dutch negotiating team, The Hague sent two 'private delegates' to Taipei in June 1994, Schiphol's director Hans Smits and Jan-Willem Weck in his capacity as Vice-President of Schiphol's Supervisory Board. The aim of their mission was to safeguard future flight connections between Amsterdam and Taipei.[122] A second visit followed in September 1994. The Dutch now proposed a scheduled air service on the basis of a private contract between the airports of Amsterdam and Taipei. This would be drawn up in lieu of the customary bilateral treaty. Following other examples of such accords, the airports each designated airlines of their choosing to maintain the service.[123]

This alternative arrangement met with vehement criticism from the People's Republic. After all, China Airlines carried the Taiwanese flag on its planes. Beijing was adamant that the arrangement with Taiwan made talks about an agreement between the Netherlands and the People's Republic impossible. The Dutch, by now really hoping to reach an accord with Beijing as well, were most concerned. Referring to the new practice developed for other Taiwanese air services to Europe, they insisted that Taiwan should designate Mandarin Airlines to operate the route to Amsterdam, rather than China Airlines.[124] In this way they hoped to address Beijing's objections, while at the same time safeguarding opportunities for KLM in mainland China. It was a bitter pill for the Taiwanese. After all, KLM and China Airlines had operated scheduled services for over ten years.[125] But for The Hague, breaking the deadlock in relations with the People's Republic carried the highest weight. To arrive at a satisfactory final solution Taipei was forced to trade in China Airlines for Mandarin. But this in itself

121 Code message Embassy Beijing re. air services to China, 2 Febr. 1993: Archive Foreign Affairs, VADV, Collection Jean Petit, The Hague.

122 Fax message VADV to Michiel van der Zee in Strasbourg, 18 May 1994: Archive Foreign Affairs, VADV, Collection Jean Petit, The Hague.

123 Memorandum Gerrit Draai (Martinair) to Nelleke Don (RLD), re. Taiwan, 5 May 1994: Archive Foreign Affairs, VADV, Collection Jean Petit, The Hague.

124 Fax message Jan Willem Weck (RLD) to Mao Chi-Kuo, 19 Oct. 1994. Fax Nelleke Don (RLD) to VADV, KLM, Martinair and NVLS re. letter to Mao Chi-Kuo, 19 Oct. 1994: Archive Foreign Affairs, VADV, Collection Jean Petit, The Hague.

125 Fax message Jaap Mol to Jan Willem Weck, 7 Oct. 1994: Archive Foreign Affairs, VADV, Collection Jean Petit, The Hague.

was not enough to pacify Beijing. The People's Republic insisted that the Dutch should also remove their flag carrier symbol. As a price for a bilateral aviation agreement with the People's Republic the elements that visibly connected KLM to the Dutch state – the designation 'Royal Dutch Airlines' and the crown above the KLM logo on the tail of its aircraft – would have to go from planes operating to Taipei.[126] After some hesitation KLM agreed to this cosmetic procedure. With effect from 21 October 1995, flights to Taiwan used aircraft that carried the simple marking 'KLM asia'. KLM founded a 'paper subsidiary' for the service to Taipei.[127] The flights were thus no longer visibly carried out by the national airlines from either side and operated under private law agreements to which neither the Dutch nor the Taiwanese government were a party.

In return for these adjustments, Beijing was prepared to abandon its political objections to the Taipei service and, after almost 50 years, sign an agreement with the Netherlands that gave KLM access to China. Given the rapid development of the Chinese economy and the fact that mutual trade between the Netherlands and the People's Republic had tripled since 1989, this was of considerable economic importance.[128] Nonetheless further consultations were necessary between The Hague and Beijing to work out the details. Foreign Affairs' Traffic Advisor Michiel van der Zee was requested to travel to Beijing to demonstrate that the Taiwan arrangement did not breach The Hague's official one-China policy. In particular, this referred to the asterisk in KLM's official timetable that stated that KLM's flights to Taipei were actually carried out under contract with Martinair. Beijing demanded that Weck and Van der Zee, as government representatives, travel to Beijing to reconfirm this arrangement. China made the visit a condition of signing the bilateral air services agreement. In the end talks were held in The Hague on 6 December 1995. The minutes contained the final text of the Treaty with the People's Republic, specifying a single Dutch airline to operate as the designated carrier. For Martinair, a separate charter package was drawn up. In The Hague the Cabinet approved the accord on 2 February 1996, while the Chinese Deputy Prime Minister Qian Qichen endorsed the agreement during his visit to the Netherlands on 20 April. Signatures were finally exchanged in Beijing on 23 May 1996.[129] The agreement

---

126 Email message Peter van Fenema to the author, 14 July 2016.

127 Letter KLM to Tsay Ching-yen (Head China's Civil Aeronautics Administration), 20 Oct. 1995: Archive Foreign Affairs, VADV, Collection Jean Petit, The Hague.

128 Letter Prime Minister Wim Kok to China's Prime Minister Li Peng, 13 June 1995: Archive Foreign Affairs, VADV, Collection Jean Petit, The Hague.

129 Treaty between Koninkrijk der Nederlanden and People's Republic of China re. commercial aviation, with annexes, Beijing, 23 May 1996: https://officielebekendmakingen.nl/trb-1996-149.html [2022].

entered into force immediately, bypassing the usual parliamentary ratification. A month later, on 26 June 1996, the first KLM flight finally took off for Beijing, in time for the rapid expansion in bilateral trade that would characterize relations in the following years.[130]

While bilateral trade continued to expand, air transport interests were gradually taken over by the European Commission in conformity with its policy of assuming a coordinating role regarding the external aviation relations of the member states. Between 2008 and 2017, the traffic between the EU and China doubled, requiring new regulations on air transport. In 2016 the Commission received a mandate to negotiate 'horizontal' aviation agreements with China and a number of other countries. This resulted in the signature of an initial accord between the EU and China, although the parties did not conclude a formal air transport agreement. Individual EU member states continued to regulate their aviation relations with China bilaterally, but in May 2019 the EU and China signed their 'horizontal' agreement. 'Horizontal', in this case, meant that the internal EU accords would be incorporated in the air transport relation with China. Under this agreement, EU 'Community carriers' received equal rights to operate. Up to that point, only airlines owned and controlled by an EU member state or its nationals had been allowed to fly. Now carriers from any EU member state that had a bilateral air services agreement with China with unused traffic rights could operate.[131]

5 Opening up the Skies with the United States

Late in 1989, it appeared that US international air transport policy might be leaning towards adopting a new protectionist attitude. Although Washington was, in principle, willing to open additional airports for international services, it announced that foreign operating rights would be strictly limited to 3rd and 4th freedom traffic.[132] At the same time, the Department of Transportation attached new conditions to KLM's participation in Northwest Airlines, effectively curtailing KLM's share in the NWA take-over investment and limiting its – perceived – control over the airline. This gave rise to considerable

130 Hellema, *Nederland in de wereld*, p. 379; 433–434.

131 Memo European Commission re. EU – China aviation agreements, 20 May 2019: https://transport.ec.europa.eu/system/files/2019-05/2019-05-20-aviation-china-memo.pdf [2022].

132 Fax message Rob Troost (Embassy Washington) to Den Braven (RLD), 12 Oct. 1989: NNA, 2.05.392, Foreign Affairs 1985–1990, inv.nr. 2638.

concern in Dutch government circles. The answer, as before in history, was a surge forward and a new push for additional landing rights. KLM's 400 million dollar investment in Northwest meant that a concerted Dutch effort swung into action. The idea, developed by KLM's Vice-President of Foreign Relations and Co-operation Henri Wassenbergh, was to move away from applying to the administration in Washington and instead build on the earlier approaches to 'underserved airports' such as Baltimore-Washington International (BWI) for rights to fly, an idea to which Transportation Secretary Samuel Skinner was now sympathetic. Resonating with such views, American cities aspiring to develop international air connections set up the United States Airports for Better International Air Services (US-BIAS) coalition. The idea was to offer 'underserved' business communities access to the global marketplace. To achieve maximum impact, KLM joined forces with Schiphol Airport, the Ministry of Transport and Water Management and the Ministry of Foreign Affairs. Meanwhile, the airline called on Foreign Affairs Minister Hans van den Broek to sound the alarm on the possible curtailment of KLM's influence in NWA. The Hague asked for a new round of bilateral talks on air transport, to be scheduled for early 1990.[133]

Held in March 1990, the talks presented the Dutch with a new disappointment: as always, their delegation arrived with proposals for a liberal air services agreement, this time along the lines that the Americans had already discussed with Britain, France and Germany. However, the larger European nations had not been receptive.[134] Against this background the Americans put the issue of liberalism on hold. It appeared that the Netherlands were considered too small a player in the international arena to act as a key for the implementation of a major policy switch. Nonetheless, the rights for Baltimore-Washington International were offered, although KLM's application to open a service to Detroit was turned down later that year as it conflicted with the interests of PanAm. However, a request for a service to Minneapolis was granted.[135] With these decisions, it appeared likely that American policy-making would come to a halt, but in fact Transportation Secretary Skinner was preparing to take liberalism to the next level. An outline for a new 'open skies' policy that would liberalize international air transport and open up 'underserved' airports to the world was in the making.

Bilateral discussions with the Dutch resumed in November 1991. In the best of traditions, delegations aimed for an equitable exchange of economic

133 Minutes 179th BLV, 7 Nov. 1989: NNA, 2.05.392, Archive BZ, 1985–1990, inv.nr. 126.

134 Minutes 180th BLV, 25 Apr. 1990: NNA, 2.05.392, Archive BZ, 1985–1990, inv.nr. 126.

135 Minutes 182th BLV, 3 Dec. 1990: NNA, 2.05.392, Archive BZ, 1985–1990, inv.nr. 126.

benefits: the US confirmed permission for KLM to serve Baltimore-Washington, Minneapolis and also Detroit, plus one additional point to be selected later. Furthermore, the Dutch received 5th freedom rights in Orlando and Houston. In return, US carriers got freedom of pricing and extra cargo possibilities in the Netherlands. Building on these new concessions KLM set its sights on San Francisco.[136]

A few months earlier, in December 1991, Skinner had left the Department of Transportation to become White House Chief of Staff. It was his successor Andrew Card's task to formalize American thinking in an Open Skies Policy document that saw the light of day in March 1992. This document fitted Republican Party thinking on the role of the government in the economy. Following this line, Card indicated that he was considering discussing open skies with the smaller European countries, since Britain, France and Germany had thus far shown little interest. The Hague, on the other hand, hastened to send a positive reply.[137] There was some urgency to the matter now that European aviation was heading for a more liberal environment from January 1993, while upcoming elections in the US in November made the long term prospects of American policy uncertain. Additionally, KLM and Northwest were looking for a political regime that would allow for more opportunities to cooperate.

The Final Open Skies Order was published on 5 August 1992, despite reservations in the American civil service apparatus and in the US airline industry. Four weeks later American and Dutch delegations met in Washington. Since June, the Dutch had been preparing the various points they wished to bring up. This time things moved smoothly. After only four days of talks the parties were able to sign an accord on 4 September. Dutch participants would later comment that this was the first time in their negotiating careers that they felt they sat on the same side of the table as their counterparts. Both sides were intent on creating a historic agreement that could change the nature of international air transport. The outcome was confirmed in an exchange of diplomatic notes on 14 October 1992.[138] For the airlines of the two contracting parties, all air services between the United States and the Netherlands, and points beyond, would henceforth be at liberty to operate as they wished. KLM and other Dutch carriers were henceforth free to fly to any destination in the US and set

136 Minutes 184th BLV, 3 March 1992: NNA, 2.05.392, Archive BZ, 1985–1990, inv.nr. 126.

137 Office memo VADV to Van den Broek, 4 Apr. 1992: Archive Foreign Affairs, VADV, Collection Jean Petit, The Hague.

138 H.S. Rutger Jan toe Laer, Kick-starting Cross-border Alliances: Approval and Clearance; the Past, the Present and the Future, in: *Air&Space Law*, Vol. xxxii/4–5 (Sept. 2007), p. 287–325.

their own prices; the US intended to use the bilateral agreement to pry open the European market in advance of the new situation that would exist from 1 January 1993.[139] After 63 years of air transport contacts, American and Dutch carriers finally received full access to each other's markets. The advantages for KLM were enormous: the barriers to its expansion on the important American market were removed at a stroke of the pen.

Only a single point now remained to be settled: for KLM and NWA to be able to operate as a single entity and gain the full benefits of their cooperation, they would need an exemption from the provisions of American anti-trust legislation that banned virtually all forms of cooperation between competitors. The Dutch attached particular urgency to this after George Bush lost the presidential elections to his Democratic rival Bill Clinton in November 1992. Through the embassy in Washington, The Hague put pressure on the Bush Administration to sign an exemption order before the government's term expired at the end of January 1993.[140] Indeed, on 11 January 1993, the Department of Transportation concluded that competition on the North Atlantic would not be materially affected if the fourth biggest airline in Europe joined forces with the fourth airline in the US and granted final approval and antitrust immunity.

The nature of the Dutch-American Open Skies agreement generated concern in Europe. France, Germany, Britain, Italy and Spain reasoned that their national carriers ran the risk of being overrun by US competition should they go for a similar accord. Warning sounds also came from the European Commission. To apply pressure, the US announced its intention to negotiate Open Skies agreements with the smaller European states. Indeed, by 1995 Washington was in discussion with nine countries. Eventually sixteen bilateral Open Skies agreements were signed. Nonetheless, the Open Skies approach was not without its critics. In politics and in commerce the wisdom behind liberalism in the air was questioned. Repeatedly, US voices clamored to attach more weight to America's national interests in dealing with international air transport, harking back to protectionist traditions. This fed anxieties in The Hague about the longevity of the 1992 agreement.

On 3 June 1995, the European Commission presented a draft mandate to negotiate EU air transport relations with the US. The Hague was not enthused, stating that such a course of action offered no additional benefits over bilateral consultations and could actually harm Dutch interests.[141] Policy in The

139 *NRC*, 7 Sept. 1992.

140 Office memo VADV to Directorate Western Hemisphere at Foreign Affairs, 18 March 1993: Archive Foreign Affairs, VADV, Collection Jean Petit, The Hague.

141 Minutes 191st BLV, 7 Dec. 1995: Foreign Affairs, VADV, Collection Jean Petit, The Hague.

Hague instead focused on a liberal transatlantic air transport regime that would safeguard the existing KLM-NWA partnership.[142] Defending these interests, KLM opposed any mandate for the European Commission to act in aviation relations, as long as it remained uncertain that Commission negotiations would create added value. Nonetheless, in June 1996 the European Transport Ministers approved a phased mandate for the Commission to act on aviation in the common interest. Thereafter, a first round of EU-US talks was scheduled late in October 1996, with a second round planned in February 1997.

Right from the start the European Commission was handicapped by its limited mandate. A number of EU member states questioned the Commission's jurisdiction when it came to negotiating external aviation agreements. Its team could thus only discuss 'soft' issues like competition policy, state aid, computer reservations, slots, ownership and control, and code sharing. Across the table, the American side wanted to discuss 'hard' issues, such as market access. Since this was not in the Commission's mandate, both parties left empty-handed. The second round of talks went the same way. For the Commission, it was clear that the unwilling member states would not voluntarily provide it with a full mandate for a comprehensive air transport agreement with the Americans. The Commission therefore decided to resort to legal action against all member states that had signed an open skies agreement with the US since January 1993, the entry into force of the third and final package of liberalization. This included Denmark, Sweden, Finland, Belgium, Luxembourg, Austria and Germany. For legal reasons, the UK was added to the suit. Though Britain had not signed an open skies agreement with the US, its bilateral agreement of February 1997 contained the same discriminatory national ownership and control clause, which the Commission regarded as a violation of the 1957 EEC Treaty.

On 18 December 1998 actions were brought before the European Court of Justice in Luxembourg. Apart from the charge that the agreements contained an illegal clause, the Commission also claimed that the Open Skies agreements of the arraigned nations infringed on the European Community's new competence to negotiate agreements with third countries. After lengthy consideration, the Court ruled in favor of the Commission on 5 November 2002.[143] Most important for the follow-up was that the Court regarded as illegal all nationality clauses in the bilateral agreements concluded after January 1993.

142 Kees den Braven, Dutch draft position on possible EU mandate in EU-US aviation, 13 Febr. 1996. Foreign Office memo (VADV), 27 June 1996: Foreign Affairs, VADV, Collection Jean Petit, The Hague.

143 https://eur-lex.europa.eu/legal-content/EN/ALL/?uri=CELEX%3A61998CJ0466 [2022].

This decision gave the European Commission the legal basis to demand that all member states concerned amend or even terminate their agreements with the US, or face further infringement procedures. Consequently, the European Council of Transport Ministers, realizing that the individual member states would not be able to amend their agreements accordingly, had no choice but to give the Commission a full mandate for aviation negotiations with the US that would cover and bind all EU members.

Negotiations with the US opened in Washington in February 2003. Both parties aimed at Open Skies. Topics discussed included issues like free market access and fair competition. There were two new demands from the European side: the right to invest in or take over US carriers, and cabotage rights within the US. The role of computer reservation systems and practicalities such as security protocols also featured. At the behest of the Dutch, possible environmental impacts were added to the agenda. In view of these wide-ranging topics progress was slow, and on the European side all subjects needed to be vetted by the European Council.[144] In 2003 and 2004 further rounds of talks followed in Washington, under the chairmanship of John Byerly, Deputy Assistant Secretary for Transportation at the Department of State. As before, much time was needed, partly because of the divergences in legal regimes on both sides of the Atlantic, partly because of differences of opinion between the EU member states, partly because of the need for Congressional and European Parliamentary consent. It took over four years before these partial accords could be combined into a full agreement on an Open Aviation Area. One of the major bones of contention was the desire of European air carriers to extend possible ownership and control rights in the United States. Washington's inability to move on these issues delayed and nearly derailed a final accord. In the agreement reached in November 2006 the issue was left unresolved and remained so when the final text was signed on 25 April 2007 in Brussels and on 30 April in Washington.[145] Even so, the Open Aviation Area was a landmark agreement for both sides, removing virtually all restrictions on market access, pricing, capacity and frequencies. It also dealt with regulatory cooperation in such areas as competition, subsidies, and environment. For the first time, European airlines could fly without limitations from any point in the EU to any

144 Report by René Fennes on US-EU discussions in February 2003, 27 Febr. 2003: Foreign Affairs, VADV, Collection Jean Petit, The Hague.

145 Charles A. Hunnicutt, US-EU Second Stage Air Transport Agreement: Towards an Open Aviation Area, in: *Georgia Journal of International and Comparative Law*, Vol. 39 (2011) nr.1, p. 663–725. Official signed text of US-EU Air Transport Agreement, 18 Apr. 2007: https://eur-lex.europa.eu/legal-content/EN/TXT/PDF/?uri=OJ:L:2007:134:FULL&from=EN [2022].

point in the US and beyond, while American carriers received the same rights across the European Union. Nonetheless, since not all issues had been settled, the parties continued their conversations. Over the course of the next decade and beyond, detailed practical issues arising from the agreement would be discussed by increasingly large delegations, totaling 89 members in June 2022.[146]

The new role for 'Brussels' in international aviation policy meant that the Dutch had to come to terms with the fact that European Transport commissioners Ignacia de Loyola de Palacio and Jacques Barrot assumed a leading role in the political negotiations with the US. This reduced the direct influence of the member states, which in turn translated into an increased focus on various underlying legal issues in air transport policy. To enrich and bolster Dutch legal opinions, The Hague sought and relied on the expertise, research and advice of the International Institute of Air and Space Law at Leiden University on matters such as 7th freedom, cargo rights and cabotage, the latter of which remained heavily disputed in Washington.

6 Expanding Air Services to South America

At the beginning of the 1990s South America's largest economies, those of Brazil and Argentina, were in a state of crisis resulting from hyperinflation, poor governance and mounting national debts. In terms of air transport, a capital-intensive economic sector, both countries were looking for fresh investments to keep their national airlines operating. While Brazil's VARIG struggled with its finances and accepted competitors in the international market as a consequence of deregulation, Aerolíneas Argentinas followed older patterns in the Spanish speaking world and looked towards Spain for possible assistance from the Spanish national air carrier Iberia.

These financial struggles meant that there was little room to maneuver in international contacts over landing rights and flight frequencies. Consequently, Brazil dragged its feet regarding KLM's request – already granted in June 1989 – to operate a third weekly service. Nonetheless, the Dutch hoped that the process of democratic reform that was underway in the country might help build an atmosphere that would work in their favor.[147] Indeed, after a further year of delay, the extra frequency was accorded and commenced in October 1991.

146 https://www.state.gov/twenty-third-meeting-of-the-u-s-eu-joint-committee-record-of-meeting/ [2023].

147 Minutes 182nd BLV, 3 Dec. 1990: Archive Foreign Affairs, VADV, Collection Jean Petit, The Hague.

With three weekly flights to Rio, KLM applied in Buenos Aires for an additional third service to Argentina early in 1992. The request reflected Aerolíneas Argentinas' troubles. Earlier that year the airline had been forced to withdraw its operations to Amsterdam due to the dire state of its finances. Despite a history of experiences to the contrary, the Dutch were hopeful that Argentina, markedly different since the return to democratic governance in 1982, might allow a third weekly flight. However, Aerolíneas Argentinas' financial dependence on Iberia, which offered onward European connections in Madrid on flights from Buenos Aires, prevented a quick accord. Objections were still on the table late in November 1992 when State Secretary of Economic Affairs and Foreign Trade Yvonne van Rooy visited Buenos Aires. She managed to melt some of the Argentine resistance and the two parties agreed on a new memorandum of understanding that offered a provisional green light to KLM, pending negotiations over a new bilateral agreement in 1993 that, KLM hoped, might include freedom of capacity and liberal 5th freedom rights.[148] Signed on 23 November 1993, the occasion of an official visit to the Netherlands by the Argentine President Carlos Menem, the third frequency was incorporated in the new bilateral. KLM, always on the lookout for network expansion, tried to use the spirit of the moment by bringing up the question of a possible fourth frequency to Buenos Aires in 1994. That KLM did not have the aircraft capacity to actually operate the extra flights was prudently left out. Talks did not start until April 1996, however. They ended without accord, pending the long-delayed development of a new Argentine international air transport policy based on the liberal ideas of the Menem government.[149] Talks continued into November 1998, when the Dutch Prime Minister Wim Kok visited Argentina and neighboring countries for a combined political and trade mission, hoping to harvest some of the possibilities created by the spectacular economic growth of the country in the preceding years.[150] In personal discussions with Kok, Menem indicated he would consider KLM's wish for an extra frequency.[151]

Meanwhile, in 2000 the EU had entered into discussions with the Latin American group of Mercosur countries (among whom were Brazil and Argentina) on a comprehensive free trade agreement. These talks took almost two

148 Minutes 186th BLV, 4 Dec. 1992: Archive Foreign Affairs, VADV, Collection Jean Petit, The Hague.

149 Minutes 193rd BLV, 25 Febr. 1997: Archive Foreign Affairs, VADV, Collection Jean Petit, The Hague.

150 Jan Edward Craanen, *Ooit hadden we een vaderland: het verdriet van Argentinië* (Amsterdam: Uitgeverij Podium, 2017).

151 Minutes meeting RLD-VADV-KLM, 4 Dec. 1998: Archive Foreign Affairs, VADV, Collection Jean Petit, The Hague.

decades and complicated discussions on air transport.[152] Progress on this latter issue proved exceptionally difficult as Buenos Aires made the future of KLM's 5th freedom rights dependent on reaching a new overall aviation accord.[153] However, as had been the case in past contacts in Buenos Aires, scheduling a meeting with Argentine senior civil servants proved difficult. At the start of the new millennium Argentina struggled with yet another economic and political crisis. As a consequence of the economy collapsing after a bank run in November 2001 and a ban on foreign money transfers, KLM suspended its four weekly flights to Buenos Aires. Services resumed in 2002 when bilateral contacts expanded again in the wake of the developing personal bond between the Netherlands' Crown Prince Willem-Alexander and Máxima Zorreguieta, an Argentine-born business lady. Their marriage in February 2002 caused more than a stir of interest in things Argentinian, which translated into business opportunities and a renewed interest in air services. KLM picked up where it had let off.[154] Since then, Dutch-Argentine air services have continued to develop with ups and downs.[155] In October 2016, a new bilateral agreement was negotiated in Buenos Aires, signed on 27 March 2017.[156]

By comparison, aviation relations with Brazil were complex. In the context of a wider process of democratic reform, the Federal Government in Brasilia initiated a gradual deregulation of the air transport market. Brazil's prime international carrier VARIG had to accept competition on the home market from VASP (Viação Aérea São Paulo) and Transbrasil. Domestic airlines received authorizations to try out international routes. They expanded rapidly under the liberal model that Brazil now subscribed to. The new entrants to the market complicated bilateral aviation relations with the Netherlands and the advances in transport rights that The Hague hoped for disappeared from view. Brazil proved unwilling to lift the passenger and cargo quota that had been imposed on Dutch flights under the bilateral treaty of 6 July 1976. It was, therefore, somewhat unexpected when talks in Maastricht in May 1994 produced rights for KLM to increase its Brazilian services to five flights per week

152 Progress report on EU trade agreements, Febr. 2019: *Handelingen der Staten-Generaal*, Tweede Kamer, 2018–2019, doc. 21501-02, nr. 1957, 21 Febr. 2019.

153 Minutes meeting RLD-VADV-KLM, 27 March 2001: Archive Foreign Affairs, VADV, Collection Jean Petit, The Hague.

154 KLM *Annual Report 2002/2003*, p. 20.

155 Office memo VADV to DES re. conference *The future of airline alliances and mergers*: 29 March 2004: Archive Foreign Affairs, VADV, Collection Jean Petit, The Hague.

156 Treaty on Air Transport between Kingdom of the Netherlanden and the Argentine Republic; Amsterdam, 27 March 2017: *Tractatenblad* 2017, 54. *Handelingen der Staten-Generaal*, Tweede Kamer 2016–2017, 34 772, nr. 1.

after the summer of 1995.[157] Although it was not yet clear what the price of these additional rights would be, the Dutch hoped to confirm the new arrangements through an amendment of the bilateral agreement of 1976. Scheduling discussions on this issue took until April 1996, when delegations met in Rio de Janeiro. To the surprise of the Dutch, customarily the demanding party, Brazil indicated it wished a considerable expansion of landing rights in Amsterdam. The Dutch initial reaction was lukewarm and the issue was referred for further consultation.[158] The parties agreed to meet again in February 1997, by which time the Brazilian interest had shifted towards expanding air services to Frankfurt.[159] The picture was complicated further when the domestic airline TAM (Transportes Aéreos Meridionais) initiated international services to the United States, followed by flights to Europe two years later.

Given the complexity of the Brazilian situation, talks on modifying the 1976 bilateral with the Netherlands were difficult. The Hague therefore decided to escalate its contacts and sent a trade mission in March 2002 chaired by State Secretary for Economic Affairs Gerrit Ybema.[160] In the wake of this, KLM and TAM came to an agreement on code sharing on flights between São Paulo and Buenos Aires, connecting to KLM's intercontinental service.[161] This set the stage for untrammeled operations by carriers from both nations. Meanwhile, the EU negotiated intermittently with Brazil and the Mercosur group of South American countries on a comprehensive free trade agreement. The Hague also sent several national trade missions, but air transport issues were seldom mentioned. Not until 2019 did Brazil and the Netherlands find it necessary to re-address the old question of updating the 1976 air transport agreement. This resulted from low-key contacts that were kept going on minor topics. On 8 July 2019 a new treaty was signed in Brasilia, stating in its route schedule annex that the contracting parties allowed designated Dutch and Brazilian airlines to freely determine capacity in order to support fair competition operations.[162]

157 Minutes 190th BLV, 6 Apr. 1995: Archive Foreign Affairs, VADV, Collection Jean Petit, The Hague.

158 Minutes 192nd BLV, 7 Nov. 1996: Archive Foreign Affairs, VADV, Collection Jean Petit, The Hague.

159 Minutes 193th BLV, 25 Febr. 1997: Archive Foreign Affairs, VADV, Collection Jean Petit, The Hague.

160 Confidential report on consultations between DGL, VADV and KLM, 30 Jan. 2002: Archive Foreign Affairs, VADV, Collection Jean Petit, The Hague.

161 Confidential report on consultations between DGL, VADV and KLM, 22 Oct. 2002: Archive Foreign Affairs, VADV, Collection Jean Petit, The Hague.

162 Treaty regarding Air Services between the Kingdom of the Netherlands and the Federative Republic of Brazil, 8 July 2019: *Handelingen der Staten-Generaal*, Tweede Kamer 2019–2020. Nr. 35 330 nr. 2.

7 Soft Landings in Southern Africa

In air transport terms, political changes on the African continent expanded the market for air services. In October 1988, representatives of forty member states of the African Union gathered at Yamoussoukro, Ivory Coast, where they drew up a declaration 'to promote a climate of cooperation and solidarity which is necessary for the safeguarding and development of international air transport activities in Africa'.[163] The declaration embraced the idea of liberalizing African air traffic, following similar trends in Europe and in the Americas.

Although the Yamoussoukro Declaration had as its principal aim the need to bring air transport between its signatory states to a higher level, its general spirit had a considerable impact on air transport to South Africa as well. In February 1990, South Africa's president Frederik de Klerk announced that opposition movements who were against the Apartheid system were to be legalized. In preparation, the country's opposition leader Nelson Mandela was released from prison. De Klerk's government embarked on a series of political reforms, including a negotiated transition to a participative democracy and an end to Apartheid. These changes fostered new international relations with South Africa that brought an end to the isolation of the country.

A process of rapprochement got under way to reconnect South Africa with the rest of the continent. In evidence of emerging possibilities, Kenya Airways contemplated opening a service to Johannesburg in 1990. In the light of the new situation, KLM hoped to intensify its own services. Even so, the Dutch faced difficulties in Southern Africa, stemming from the previous decades. After 43 years of Dutch air services, Nigeria threatened to revoke KLM's landing rights in Kano as of April 1993 to add pressure to an existing dispute over financial claims. Talks on a resumption of services to Harare in Zimbabwe, which KLM had discontinued in 1985 after a series of conflicts, ended without result.[164] Even escalation of the talks, going as far as a personal discussion between Prime Minister Ruud Lubbers and Zimbabwe's Robert Mugabe on the occasion of the Global Panel on Social and Political Development in the World that convened in The Hague in May 1992, did not resolve the issue.[165] Finding a compromise took time, but in January 1993 the Dutch air service was finally reinstated. The problems were not entirely unique to Zimbabwe; in both Kenya

163 Declaration of Yamoussoukro on a new African Air Transport Policy, 7 Oct. 1988: https://repository.uneca.org/handle/10855/13773 [2022].

164 Minutes 182nd BLV, 3 Dec. 1990: Archive Foreign Affairs, VADV, Collection Jean Petit, The Hague.

165 Minutes 185th BLV, 7 July 1992: Archive Foreign Affairs, VADV, Collection Jean Petit, The Hague.

and Malawi questions on royalty payments by KLM also posed problems. In the Civil Aviation Meeting in The Hague chairman Michiel van der Zee even spoke in terms of 'milking KLM to the extreme'.[166]

Bilateral relations between the Netherlands and the new South Africa, on the other hand, picked up. Both countries invested in discussions on a revised air transport agreement now that an expansion of South Africa's economic and tourist contacts with the Netherlands was viable in the international arena. These consultations tied in with the process of recalibrating South Africa's external aviation policy that had been ongoing since 1990.[167] In Pretoria, restrictions imposed on foreign airlines were reduced. In January 1992, the parties reached a new bilateral accord on additional reciprocal services by both KLM and SAA. This was signed by Transport Minister Piet Welgemoed and his Dutch counterpart Hanja Maij-Weggen on the occasion of her visit to South Africa in May 1992.

In the first half of the 1990s the political situation in South Africa was changing rapidly. In April 1994 South Africa held its first free general election, resulting in a black majority government led by Nelson Mandela of the African National Congress party. These developments marked the end of legislated apartheid. These political changes acted as a stimulus for South Africa's international contacts. That same year, South Africa joined the development alliance of southern African states, aimed at furthering the cross-border development of the region. Such extended contacts translated over the next few years into new air services. After so many decades of bilateral air transport politics conducted by governments, a general atmosphere of liberalism appeared to be pervading the southern skies, just as it had done in the Northern hemisphere in the previous decade. Consequently, airlines were left to fend for themselves, without immediate recourse to politics and diplomacy. Meanwhile, the new relationship between the two countries manifested itself in Queen Beatrix's state visit to South Africa in October 1996 that fostered new contacts in trade and tourism. In the new memorandum of understanding on air transport KLM and SAA received permission to increase their frequencies between Amsterdam, Johannesburg and Cape Town to seven flights per week.[168]

The prospects for KLM's African services were looking up generally. Promoted by the African Union, spreading ideas on liberalism combined with improved economic prospects and generated a rising demand for air services.

166 Minutes 188th BLV, 21 Dec. 1993: Archive Foreign Affairs, VADV, Collection Jean Petit, The Hague.

167 Minutes 183rd BLV, 25 Apr. 1991: Archive Foreign Affairs, VADV, Collection Jean Petit, The Hague.

168 Memorandum of Understanding between the governments of South Africa and the Netherlands, 13 Nov. 1996: Archive Foreign Affairs, VADV, Collection Jean Petit, The Hague.

In this situation KLM's cooperation with Kenya Airways developed further, leading to an agreement under which KLM invested 26 million dollars in January 1996 to acquire a 26 per cent share in Kenya Airways. Plans were hatched to develop the airport in Nairobi into a new African hub. Cooperation in the form of code sharing was also extended.[169] KLM's African development continued to build on this model. The Dutch air services to Zimbabwe expanded as well, after a relaxation of the mandatory royalty payments to Air Zimbabwe. Provided only passenger aircraft were used, KLM was exempted from royalties on cargo, an arrangement that suited the airline.[170] Nonetheless, putting an actual end to existing 'royalty practices' took time and was not achieved until 1996.[171] By that time the earlier difficulties regarding flights to Kano in Nigeria had been resolved and the frequency of services to the capital Lagos increased.[172]

With all the various bilateral contractual and legal issues settled, KLM continued to gradually increase its services to Southern Africa, following an increased awareness of Dutch commercial interests in relations with African countries. The Dutch carrier mainly relied on direct dealings with its partner Kenya Airways, but contacts with African aviation authorities also intensified. This tied in with the African Union's Yamoussoukro Decision of 14 November 1999 that established a framework for liberalization of air transport services between 44 African countries.[173]

For the Netherlands, the African liberalization process meant that mediation by The Hague's diplomatic representatives became less necessary. Given the changing circumstances, they acted more as a go-between, conveying information on practicalities between airlines and their respective governments.[174] Diplomatic attention turned instead towards aviation security issues and the financial management of airports.[175] This was a development that tied in with the rapid expansion of international airline alliances in the first decade of the new century, which also brought closer contacts between Western and African air carriers.

---

169 Minutes 192nd BLV, 11 July 1996. Minutes meeting RLD-VADV-KLM, 6 June 1999: Archive Foreign Affairs, VADV, Collection Jean Petit, The Hague.

170 Minutes 188th BLV, 21 Dec. 1993: Archive Foreign Affairs, VADV, Collection Jean Petit, The Hague.

171 Minutes 192nd BLV, 11 July 1996: Archive Foreign Affairs, VADV, Collection Jean Petit, The Hague.

172 Minutes 189th BLV, 6 July 1994: Archive Foreign Affairs, VADV, Collection Jean Petit, The Hague.

173 https://digitallibrary.un.org/record/579810?ln=en [2022].

174 Office memorandum VADV, 11 June 2003: Archive Foreign Affairs, VADV, Collection Jean Petit, The Hague.

175 Email exchange Netherlands Embassy Nairobi with Foreign Affairs in The Hague, 28 Dec. 2014 and 7 Feb. 2015: Archive Foreign Affairs, VADV, Collection Jean Petit, The Hague.

Following this, in 2015 23 members of the African Union launched a declaration calling for the establishment of a Single African Air Transport Market, the treaty for which was signed in Addis Ababa, Ethiopia, on 28 January 2018. This established the framework for a liberalized air transport market across large parts of the African continent to boost trade and tourism, promote lower fares, ease passport restrictions and abolish existing barriers rooted in sovereign and protectionist traditions.[176] As one of the signatory states, South Africa joined the trend to open the skies.

8 In Conclusion

After 1989, expectations were that the political aspects of air transport relations would be overtaken by economic and financial aspects. Indeed, the economic, financial and technological aspects of airline operations became much more prominent in shaping the international arena, as did the role of corporate interests. The transatlantic market featured as the major indicator: between 1992 and 2007, open skies agreements followed by the EU-US pact on an Open Aviation Area confirmed that states would henceforth play second fiddle to market forces. In Europe, these processes were deeply influenced by the regime changes at the EU level in 1992–1993, which reserved center stage for economic and corporate interests in air transport. However, this did not imply that the role of the state was on an exit trajectory, as was evidenced in various bilateral contacts – and ultimately in the responses to the Russian invasion of Ukraine in 2022.

In the Netherlands, these developments coincided with the outcomes of policy discussions at the Ministry of Transport and Waterworks that recognized the prime importance of Schiphol for the Dutch economy. To emphasize this, the airport's management coined the catch-phrase *Mainport* Schiphol. For the development of an international aviation policy, the interests of KLM could no longer be seen as preeminent, a watershed development. To build up its competitive position in Europe's post-1992 common aviation market, KLM would have to fend for itself. The ultimate effect of this was that the government largely stayed away from the merger of Air France and KLM in 2003, although this amalgamation in itself gave rise to periodic surges of national sentiments, leading to government interventions that often seemed to refer back to historical traditions.

176 *De Volkskrant*, 29 Jan. 2018.

CHAPTER 6

Concluding Remarks

> I begin my flight, steady and sure, towards the coast of England. I have no apprehensions, *pas du tout.* (…) The moment is supreme, yet I surprise myself by feeling no exultation. Below me is the sea, the surface disturbed by the wind, which is now freshening. The motion of the waves beneath me is not pleasant. I drive on. Ten minutes have gone. I have passed the destroyer, and I turn my head to see whether I am proceeding in the right direction. I am amazed. There is nothing to be seen, neither the torpedo-destroyer, nor France, nor England. I am alone. I can see nothing at all – *rien du tout!* For ten minutes I am lost. It is a strange position to be alone, unguided, without compass, in the air over the middle of the Channel. I touch nothing. My hands and feet rest lightly on the levers. I let the aeroplane take its own course. I care not whither it goes. For ten minutes I continue, neither rising nor falling, nor turning. And then, 20 minutes after I have left the French coast, I see the green cliffs of Dover, the Castle, and away to the west the spot where I had intended to land.[1]

Thus French aviator Louis Blériot described the first ever flight across the Channel from Baraques just outside Calais to Dover on Sunday, 25 July 1909. It was not only the very first sea crossing by plane that earned him his place in the history books. His was also the first recorded international airplane flight. The event was front page news, described as a major sporting achievement. At the same time, it was also a legal première: for the first time an airplane had flown across a border and landed in another country. And although the flight attracted little attention from government legislature, the feat, and others that followed, created the necessity to define airspace in legal terms. It galvanized early philosophies about national sovereignty in the air and of the roles of

1 Account by Louis Blériot of his cross-Channel flight on 25 July 1909, in: *The Times*, 26 July 1909.

 | DOI:10.1163/9789004695245_007

states regarding international aviation. Such roles created national interests in the air and provided feeding ground for attention in foreign politics to the development of aviation that would remain to this day.

The ease with which aircraft were able to cross borders meant that flight needed an international legal regime. The use of the air medium in the First World War added urgency to this. After 1918, the necessity of developing a generally accepted set of basic principles was underlined by the inception of international civil air transport. In October 1919, the need for such a common regime resulted in the Paris Convention, establishing national sovereignty in the air. The Netherlands was not a party to this treaty.

Following examples across its borders, Dutch foreign policy concerns with regard to civil air transport originated in the 1920s, when the first international air services were set up. Initially, the government's role was limited: in tune with the general approach to foreign relations of the civil service apparatus of the Ministry of Foreign Affairs, and of the Dutch diplomatic corps, a wait-and-see attitude prevailed. Continuing a long tradition, Dutch diplomacy focused on the representative aspects of international relations.

The pursuit of economic interests entered Dutch foreign policy practice towards the end of the decade, a time in which calls for a more pro-active diplomacy were voiced. Air transport was one of the new topics that required diplomats' attention. Although civil aviation at the time hardly represented a major national interest in economic terms, the public's fascination with airplanes as a new technology, representing modernity and prestige, propelled air transport into the international spotlight.

From the start, international aviation experienced restrictions that originated in state sovereignty. The Paris Convention required explicit prior government permission for border-crossing air services. A system emerged in which states negotiated and exchanged rights for national airlines to carry commercial traffic to and from other countries. Since their inception, thousands of such agreements have been concluded worldwide. The Hague was slow to engage in these exchanges. The task of maintaining the necessary contacts with foreign governments and conducting negotiations regarding permission for air services belonged to the realm of diplomatic envoys. It was left to these professionals in diplomacy to arrange accords. The Hague took a long time to develop an overarching policy. This only became problematic around 1930, when the first serious encounters with adverse foreign interests in the air left Dutch administrators bewildered. Ignoring the larger foreign policy aspects that might play a role in issues to do with air services, Dutch diplomats were late to recognize the long-term consequences of the bilateral accords the Netherlands concluded, such as the agreements with Britain and with the United States.

The outbreak of the Second World War meant that experiences gained from diplomatic skirmishes in the previous decades merged with current difficulties the Dutch had over international air services that involved Britain and the US. The government-in-exile gradually came to embrace liberal ideas on postwar commercial aviation. At the Chicago international civil aviation conference in 1944, the first aviation gathering the Dutch sent an actual delegation to, the representatives from the Netherlands expressed wholehearted support for the perceived common interests with the United States in pursuing liberalism in international air transport. The Dutch statement reflected the importance the government-in-exile attached to the commercial interests of the national airline KLM, wishing to advance its global presence. Pending the confirmation of liberalism as a guiding principle for international air transport, the Dutch hoped the new Chicago regime, would work in their favor and give KLM opportunities to play a leading role in postwar air transport. This meant that to develop new international air services, any bilateral accord, however provisional, was acceptable. The Hague expected that such agreements would consolidate over time. Decades ahead of the rest of the world, liberalism became engrained in Dutch aviation diplomacy.

When the United States abandoned their position on liberalism in July 1947 by withdrawing from the International Air Transport Agreement that had been signed at the Chicago conference, this left the Dutch in a difficult position as supporters of liberalism in a world that embraced sovereignty and restrictionist ideas on national protection. Moreover, political developments around the world began to have a direct impact on Dutch air transport. KLM was banned, in July 1947 and again in December 1948, from the skies over India and Pakistan as the Dutch colonial war in Indonesia expanded. Initially, the understanding in The Hague that the war in Indonesia would have an effect on the Netherlands' international position in air transport was limited. To the chagrin of the Dutch negotiators, who were expecting to reach easy agreement with the United States, the Americans used the international rejection of the Dutch Indonesia policy to restrict KLM. Rather than acknowledging this, the Dutch engaged in a policy of escalating the bilateral talks, raising the discussions from the diplomatic level to Cabinet level to exert pressure, a recurring pattern in air transport negotiations ever since. At the top of the escalator delegations would henceforth be chaired by a Cabinet member. This involvement of the highest political level pushed air transport higher up the foreign policy ladder. Increased safety, comfort and speed of air transport made it possible to send such political delegations. If even these failed to deliver, The Hague brought in royalty.

World politics had other consequences for Dutch air transport. In particular, the Allied military occupation of Western Germany was of major significance.

A ten-year ban on German air activities translated into market opportunities for KLM, offering worldwide air services to and from as many as nine German cities, albeit with a change of plane in Amsterdam. Germany developed into KLM's most important European market. Over the next few decades, KLM applied itself to copying the model elsewhere, particularly in Britain. In international aviation, the practice of operating between different countries with a change of plane at the airline's home airport came to be identified as 6th freedom carriage. This became the backbone of KLM operations, but also one of the bones of contention for The Hague in many air transport negotiations. The first and most important case in which this played out was in contacts with the United States. Washington was dead set against the way KLM welcomed passengers from abroad. Countries in South America also objected to the practice, as did South Africa. For KLM, and for the Dutch negotiating position, it was of paramount importance to deny any such thing or practice as 6th freedom even existed, for fear of creating a new bargaining topic that might bring restrictions. The airline therefore organized its administration in such a way that tickets and travel were documented as combinations of 3rd and 4th freedom traffic. In more than a few cases differences could not be overcome and KLM ended up handing out financial compensations to be allowed to operate. This was not the only form of paying for rights. Up to the liberalizations of the 1990s, many bilateral air services were operated 'in pool' with the airline of the other contracting state, meaning revenues were split according to agreements between the airlines involved. In such cases, the more efficient airline subsidized the less efficient pool partner.

Thus, the liberalism the Dutch had aspired for to build KLM's intercontinental network did not come about. On the contrary, as time passed Dutch negotiating delegations found the air KLM wished to fly into increasingly unfree. To obtain the coveted traffic rights The Hague needed to present the strongest possible case. To promote a unified point of view in negotiations, the Civil Aviation Meetings that had been set up in The Hague in 1945 were important for policy coordination between KLM and the government departments involved. Here, differences in policy perception were ironed out. Nonetheless, some of the Dutch negotiating goals remained out of reach. In the all-important contacts with the US, it was only after prolonged, serious conflict and involving the highest political circles that The Hague managed to procure a bilateral air services agreement in 1957. Meanwhile, ongoing controversy over the continued Dutch colonial presence in Asia – in particular, the Dutch-Indonesian conflict over New Guinea – lay at the heart of several encounters in which KLM saw its landing rights revoked, or its commercial operations curtailed.

At the same time, KLM's European business model came under strain after Germany had its aerial sovereignty reinstated in 1955 and re-founded its own national airline. West German governments were unhappy with the market position KLM had built up. The ensuing push for a re-division of European market shares led to initiatives to found a pan-European air transport venture, Air Union, built on an intergovernmental agreement on respective national market shares. The Dutch did their utmost to steer clear of this development and focused instead on bolstering KLM's own position in Europe. In this they were aided by a crisis in general European political cooperation that evolved from 1965 and on which the Air Union plans ran aground.

Over the course of the 1960s, economic issues became increasingly important in Dutch foreign policy, air transport being one of them. The number of bilateral air services agreements expanded, as did the links with general trade policy. This reflected the growth of international air transport, fueled by the increase of disposable incomes. The Dutch applied themselves to garner additional air transport rights despite increasingly restrictive international sentiments, finding that their negotiating position often depended on whether or not a foreign carrier was interested in serving Amsterdam. Nonetheless, new rights and routes were accumulated. By the end of the decade these developments had landed KLM, despite the relatively small size of its home market, among the select group of the most prominent air carriers in the world. This steady development was interrupted by the Oil Crisis of 1973, bringing dire times to air transport. In the highly regulated environment of commercial aviation, dealing with this crisis proved difficult and losses were substantial. Beginning in the US, voices called for a greater focus on the market, with less regulation increased competition and lower fares to boost passenger numbers. Within a few years this new trend spread across the Atlantic and set the wheels in motion for a fundamental reorientation regarding the role of national states in air transport.

In 1978, the Netherlands profited from the new American market outlook in signing a liberal protocol amending the 1957 bilateral air services agreement. Both sides built on this. During the 1980s, policy gradually moved towards a notion of air transport as a normal economic activity that could (and should) operate beyond the scope of direct government attention. In an international economic environment that favored the rule of the market, the US and the Netherlands cleared the final hurdle in October 1992 with the signature of a bilateral Open Skies agreement, the first of its kind in the world. Open Skies introduced a new regime in international air transport, in which market forces, not states, determined competitive opportunities. Two-and-a-half months later, the EU completed its own trajectory towards liberalization. In January

1993, the results of three packages of reform measures created a single integrated market for air transport within the EU, giving the airlines of the member states full freedom to fly. At KLM, there was reason to party: after decades of struggles with restrictionism, the brakes were released.

As a result of these developments, the role of the European Commission in air transport diplomacy became more important, superseding the previous national government policies of the individual EU member states. In April 2007 this led to the agreement on an Open Aviation Area between the US and the EU. Other such agreements followed, including an agreement with Australia in 2008 and another a decade later with China, in 2019. A century after international aviation had been officially established as a matter for foreign policy, subject to national sovereignty, The Hague's role at the negotiating table appeared to be receding.

These developments moved the center of gravity in Dutch aviation policy away from the issues that had in the past been dictated by the interests of KLM. In policy matters, domestic affairs gained weight. The role of Schiphol Airport as a 'mainport' and its significant impact on the Dutch economy made it a focus of national and international policy and a factor in its own right. This reduced the need for any direct involvement of the Ministry of Foreign Affairs. As a consequence, KLM grew less interested in the Aviation Meetings as the 1990s progressed. The frequency of the gatherings decreased until they were disbanded completely in 1997. No new institution emerged to continue the role. The period in which KLM shaped Dutch aviation policy was coming to an end. A watershed moment in this development took place in 2003, when the government stepped away from the tradition of treating KLM's interests as paramount for Dutch civil aviation policy and instead identified Schiphol Airport as the new center of interest. Although the KLM-Air France merger issue was much discussed that year at the Ministries of Foreign Affairs, Finance, and Transport and Water Management, the airline would henceforth have to fend for itself. That, at least, was the new proposition. However, as was the case with flag carriers in other European countries, the ties between the government and the national airline proved difficult to sever. This was a recurrent problem for the Air France-KLM venture. National sentiments surfaced repeatedly and the two governments each sailed their own course. In 2020–2021 both Paris and The Hague came to the rescue of their 'own' part of the joint company to prevent its collapse as a consequence of the disastrous effects on air transport of the corona pandemic. After a century of commercial aviation, and decades of international liberalization in the air, national governments thus showed they still played an essential role in international air transport.

Bibliography

Adriaansen, Wim, *Jons Viruly. 1905–1986. Vlieger en schrijver* (Zaltbommel: Aprilis, 2008)

Albrecht, Stefan, Internationale Luftverkehrspolitik in der Zeit des Kalten Krieges von 1944–1965: das Beispiel Tschechoslowakei, in: *Jahrbuch für Wirtschaftsgeschichte, 2007/1, Verkehrsgeschichte auf neuen Wegen* (Berlin: Akademie Verlag, 2007), p. 93–109

Alsina, Marc J., Aviation for the People: Class and State Aviation in Perón's 'New Argentina' 1946–55, in: *Technology and Culture*, Volume 63, Nr. 1, January 2022, p. 153–181

Altrudi, Soledad, *Of Personalities and Democratization in US Public Diplomacy: The Case of the Blue Book on Argentina*: University of Southern California, Center on Public Diplomacy, 2015)

Asbeek Brusse, Wendy, Dutch-British Commercial Relations in a European Context, in: Nigel John Ashton, Duco Hellema (eds.), *Unspoken Allies: Anglo-Dutch Relations Since 1780* (Amsterdam: AUP, 2001)

Ashton, Nigel John, Hellema, Duco (eds.), *Unspoken Allies: Anglo-Dutch Relations Since 1780* (Amsterdam: AUP, 2001)

Bakelen, Frans van *'Nouvelles Frontières' – European Court of Justice Decision 30 April 1986* (Groningen: Faculteit der Rechtsgeleerdheid, 1986)

Baud, Michiel, *Militair geweld, burgerlijke verantwoordelijkheid. Argentijnse en Nederlandse perspectieven op het militair bewind in Argentinië (1976–1983)* (The Hague: Sdu, 2001)

Bloemendal, Albertine, *Reframing the diplomat: Ernst van der Beugel and the Cold War Atlantic Community* (Leiden: Brill, 2018)

Blussé, Leonard, *Tribuut aan China. Vier eeuwen Nederlands-Chinese betrekkingen* (Amsterdam 1989)

Boer, Stefan de, *Van Sharpeville tot Soweto. Nederlands regeringsbeleid ten aanzien van apartheid, 1960–1977* (Den Haag: Sdu, 1999)

Bouma, Tjalling, *Naar een federaal Indonesië. De geschiedenis van de totstandkoming van de Republiek der Verenigde Staten van Indonesië en de bijdrage van federale Indonesische nationalisten aan de Indonesische onafhankelijkheid 1917–1949* (Hilversum: Verloren, 2020)

Bouwens, Bram, Ogier, Frido, *Welcome Aboard! 100 years of KLM Royal Dutch Airlines* (Zwolle: WBooks, 2020)

Budrass, Lutz, *Adler und Kranich. Die Lufthansa und ihre Geschichte 1926–1955* (München: Blessing, 2016)

Callison, James W., Airline Deregulation – Only Partially a Hoax: The Current Status of the Airline Deregulation Movement, in: *Journal of Air Law & Commerce* 45 (1980)

Chang, Vincent K.L., *Forgotten Diplomacy: The Modern Remaking of Dutch-Chinese Relations, 1927–1950* (Leiden: Brill, 2019)

Colijn, Ko, Rusman, Paul, *Het Nederlandse Wapenexportbeleid 1963–1988* (Den Haag: Nijgh en Van Ditmar, 1989)

Craanen, Jan Edward, *Ooit hadden we een vaderland: het verdriet van Argentinië* (Amsterdam: Uitgeverij Podium, 2017)

Crampton, R.J., *Eastern Europe in the Twentieth Century* (London: Routledge, 1994)

Davies, R.E.G., *A History of the World's Airlines* (London: Oxford University Press, 1964)

Davies, R.E.G., *Airlines of Latin America since 1919* (London: Putnam, 1984)

Dekker, Ariëtte, *Leven op krediet: Anton Kröller, 1862–1941* (Amsterdam: Prometheus, 2015)

Delepierre-Nys, Christiane, *Air Europe. La politique de coopération entre les compagnies aériennes de l'Europe des Six* (Bruxelles: Éd. de l'Université, 1975)

Dempsey, Paul S., *Law and foreign policy in international aviation* (Dobbs Ferry: Transnational Publishers, 1987)

Diederiks-Verschoor, I.H.Ph., Dr. J.F. Lycklama à Nijeholt (1876–1947), in: *Air & Space Law*, Vol. XIX, 1994, nr.1, p. 8–9

Dienel, Hans, Lyth, Peter (eds.), *Flying the Flag. European Commercial Air Transport since 1945* (Basingstoke: MacMillan, 1998)

Dierikx, Marc, *Bevlogen Jaren. Nederlandse burgerluchtvaart tussen de wereldoorlogen* (Houten: Unieboek, 1986)

Dierikx, Marc, *Begrensde Horizonten. De internationale burgerluchtvaartpolitiek van Nederland in het interbellum* (Zwolle: Tjeenk Willink, 1988)

Dierikx, Marc, Shaping World Aviation: Anglo-American Civil Aviation Relations, 1944–1946, in: *Journal of Air Law and Commerce* 57 (1992) nr. 4, p. 795–840

Dierikx, Marc, Bouwens, Bram, *Building Castles of the Air. Schiphol Amsterdam and the Development of Airport Infrastructure in Europe, 1916–1996* (The Hague: Sdu, 1997)

Dierikx, Marc, *Blauw in de lucht. Koninklijke Luchtvaart Maatschappij 1919–1999* (Den Haag: Sdu, 1999)

Dierikx, Marc, *Uit de lucht gegrepen. Fokker als Nederlandse droom, 1945–1996* (Amsterdam: Boom, 2004)

Dierikx, Marc, Hoofd in de wolken of benen op de grond? De ontwikkeling van het toezicht op de luchtvaart, in: *150 jaar toezicht Verkeer en Waterstaat. Rampen, wetten en inspectiediensten* (Den Haag: Sdu, 2004)

Dierikx, Marc, Een spel zonder kaarten: KLM-landingsrechten als nationaal belang, 1945–1957, in: D.A. Hellema, C. Wiebes, B. Zeeman, *Derde jaarboek voor de geschiedenis van de Nederlandse buitenlandse politiek in de twintigste eeuw* (Den Haag: Sdu, 1996)

Dierikx, M.L.J., Klep, C.P.M., Klinkers, E.M.L., Smits, M.G.M., *Nederlandse Ontwikkelingssamenwerking. Bronnenuitgave, Vol. 2, 1964–1967* (The Hague: Instituut voor Nederlandse Geschiedenis, 2003)

Dierikx, M.L.J., Feiken, C.B., Gaemers, J.H., Smits, M.G.M., *Nederlandse ontwikkelingssamenwerking. Bronnenuitgave. Vol. 4, 1973–1977* (The Hague: Instituut voor Nederlandse Geschiedenis, 2005

Dierikx, Marc, Frappez Toujours. De diplomaat en het luchtvervoer, in: Bob de Graaff, Duco Hellema (eds.), *Instrumenten van buitenlandse politiek. Achtergronden en praktijk van de Nederlandse diplomatie* (Amsterdam: Boom, 2007)

Dierikx, Marc, *Clipping the Clouds. How Air Travel Changed the World* (Westport CT: Preager, 2008)

Dierikx, Marc, Smits, Mari, Suijlekom, Loes van, Clavert, Frédéric, Danescu, Elena, Gabellini, Marco (eds.), *Common Fate, Common Future. A Documentary History of Monetary and Financial Cooperation in Europe, 1947–1974* (The Hague: Huygens ING and CVCE, 2012)

Dierikx, Marc, The Dutch 'Contribution' to the Werner Plan, in: Elena Danescu, Susana Muñoz (eds.), *Pierre Werner et l'Europe : pensee, action, enseignements: Pierre Werner and Europe: His Approach, Action and Legacy* (Brussels: P.I.E. Peter Lang, 2015), p. 217–230

Dierikx, Marc, Zala, Sacha (eds.), *When the Wall Came Down. The Perception of German Reunification in International Diplomatic Documents 1989–1990* (Berne: Dodis, 2019)

Dierikx, Marc, *Vliegende Hollanders. Het ware verhaal van Anthony Fokker & Albert Plesman* (Amsterdam: Boom, 2020)

Dijk, Ruud van, Kruizinga, Samuël, Kuitenbrouwer, Vincent, Maar, Rimko van der, *Shaping the International Relations of the Netherlands, 1815–2000: A Small Country on the Global Scene* (London: Routledge, 2020)

Dinan, Desmond, *Europe Recast. A History of European Union* (Basingstoke: Palgrave Macmillan,2004)

Ditzhuyzen, R.E. van, Kersten, A.E., Zeeland, A.L.M. van, Zwan, A.C. van der (eds.), *Tweehonderd jaar Ministerie van Buitenlandse Zaken* (Den Haag: Sdu, 1998)

Dobson, Alan P., *Peaceful Air Warfare. The United States, Britain and the Politics of International Aviation* (Oxford: Oxford University Press, 1991)

Dobson, Alan P., *Globalization and Regional Integration. The Origins, Development and Impact of the Single European Aviation Market* (London: Routledge, 2007)

Dobson, Alan P., *A History of International Civil Aviation. From its Origins through Transformative Evolution* (London: Routledge, 2017)

Documenten betreffende de buitenlandse politiek van Nederland, 1919–1945. Periode C : 1940–1945, Vol. 7 (The Hague: Instituut voor Nederlandse Geschiedenis, 2004)

Documenten betreffende de buitenlandse politiek van Nederland, 1919–1945. Periode C : 1940–1945, Vol. 8, (The Hague: Instituut voor Nederlandse Geschiedenis, 2004)

Doganis, Rigas, *Flying off Course. The Economics of International Airlines* (London: George Allen & Unwin, 1985)

Dongen, Luc van, *Un Purgatoire Très Discret. La Transition Helvétique d'Anciens Nazis, Fascistes et Collaborateurs après 1945* (Paris: Perrin, 2008)

Edmonds, Leigh, Australia, Britain and the Empire Air Mail Scheme, 1934–1938, in: *Journal of Transport History* 20 (1999), p. 91–106

Escudé, Carlos, US Destabilization and Economic Boycott of Argentina, in: Guido di Tella, Donald C. Watt (eds.), *Argentina between the Great Powers, 1939–46* (Basingstoke: Macmillan, 1989)

Espérou, Robert, Maoui, Gérard, *Air France. Des origins à nos jours* (Paris: Le Cherche Midi, 1997)

Eysselsteijn, Ben van, *Naar breeder vlucht. Van vrede tot vrede,* (Den Haag: Leopolds, 1946)

Fic, Victor M., *Anatomy of the Jakarta Coup, October 1, 1965: The Collusion with China which destroyed the Army Command, President Sukarno and the Communist Party of Indonesia* (Jakarta: Jajasan Obor Indonesia, 2005)

Filipczyk, Joanna, LOT: connecting East and West in Poland, in: Dienel and Lyth (eds.), *Flying the Flag. European Commercial Air Transport since 1945* (Basingstoke: MacMillan, 1998), p. 195–222

Foreign Relations of the United States: Diplomatic Papers, 1945, The American Republics, Volume IX, (Washington: United States Government Printing Office, 1969)

Foreign Relations of the United States, 1946, The American Republics, Volume XI, (Washington: United States Government Printing Office, 1969)

Foreman-Peck, James, *A History of the World Economy. International Economic Relations Since 1850* (New York: Harvester Wheatsheaf, 1995)

Fukuyama, Francis, *The End of History and the Last Man* (London: Hamilton, 1992)

Giemulla, E., Schmid, R., Mölls, W. (eds.), *European Air Law* Vol. 1 (Deventer: Kluwer, 1994)

Goedhuis, Daniël, *National Airlegislations and the Warsaw Convention* (The Hague: Nijhoff, 1937).

Graaff, Bob de, *Kalm temidden van woedende golven. Het ministerie van Koloniën en zijn taakomgeving, 1912–1940* (Den Haag: Sdu, 1997)

Graaff, Bob de, Hellema, Duco, Zwan, Bert van der (eds.), *De Nederlandse buitenlandse politiek in de twintigste eeuw* (Amsterdam: Boom, 2003)

Graaff, Bob de, Hellema, Duco (eds.), *Instrumenten van buitenlandse politiek. Achtergronden en praktijk van de Nederlandse diplomatie* (Amsterdam: Boom, 2007)

Griffin, Nicholas, *Ping-Pong Diplomacy: The Secret History Behind the Game That Changed the World* (New York: Simon and Shuster, 2014)

Haanappel, Peter P.C., External aviation relations of the European Economic Community and of EEC member States into the twenty-first century, in: *Air Law* 14(1989) nr.2, p. 69–87

Hagens, G.J., *De KNILM vloog door…* (Haarlem: Uitgeverij Bakkenes, 1972)

Hagens, Jan, *Londen of Berlijn? De KLM en haar personeel in oorlogstijd,* Vol. 1, *1939–1941* (Bergen: Bonneville, 2000)

Hagens, Jan, *Londen of Berlijn? De KLM en haar personeel in oorlogstijd,* Vol. 2, 1942–1945 (Bergen: Bonneville, 2005)

Heinrich-Franke, Christian, From a Supranational Air Authority to the Founding of the ECAC, in: *Journal of European Integration History* 13(2007)nr. 1, p. 69–89

Hellema, Duco, Wiebes, Cees, Witte, Toby, *Doelwit Rotterdam. Nederland en de Oliecrisis 1973–1974* (Den Haag: Sdu, 1998)

Hellema, Duco, *De Karel Doorman naar Nieuw-Guinea. Nederlands machtsvertoon in de Oost* (Amsterdam: Boom, 2005)

Hellema, Duco, *Nederland in de wereld. Buitenlandse politiek van Nederland* (Utrecht: Het Spectrum, 2016)

Higham, Robin, *Britain's Imperial Air Routes 1918–1939. The Story of Britain's Overseas Airlines* (London: G.T. Foulis, 1960) [reprint: Fonthill Media 2016]

Hofstee, M.L.J., *Nederland en het luchtverkeer in de toekomst* (Amsterdam: Swartsenburg, 1918)

Högselius, Per, Kaijser, Arne, Vleuten, Erik van der, *Europe's Infrastructure Transition. Economy, War, Nature* (Basingstoke: Palgrave Macmillan, 2016)

Hsiao, Gene T., *The foreign trade of China: policy, law, and practice* (Canberra: Australian National University Press, 1977)

Hunnicutt, Charles A., US-EU Second Stage Air Transport Agreement: Towards an Open Aviation Area, in: *Georgia Journal of International and Comparative Law,* Vol. 39 (2011) nr.1, p. 663–725

Jackson, Ian, Xidias, Jason, *An Analysis of Francis Fukuyama's The End of History and the Last Man* (London: Routledge, 2017)

Jager, Janine, *Wilhelmina Triesman, 1901–1982. Een Nederlandse in Leningrad* (Amsterdam: Pegasus, 2012)

Jong, A.P. de (ed.), *Vlucht door de tijd. 75 jaar Nederlandse luchtmacht* (Houten: Unieboek, 1988)

Jong, J.J.P. de, A Challenge Ignored. The Netherlands and the Asian Tigers, 1985–1993, in: Nekkers, J.A., Malcontent, P.A.M., (eds.), *Fifty Years of Dutch Development Cooperation, 1949–1999* (The Hague: Sdu, 2000), p. 289–305

Jönsson, Christer, *International Aviation and the Politics of Regime Change* (New York: St. Martin's Press, 1987)

Joosten, Ties, *De Blauwe Fabel. Waarom we de KLM al een eeuw lang tegen elke prijs in de lucht houden* (Amsterdam: Follow the Money, 2022)

Judt, Tony, *Postwar. A History of Europe since 1945,*(London: Heinemann, 2005)

Kassim, Hussein, Stevens, Handley, *Air Transport and the European Union: Europeanization and its Limits* (Basingstoke: Palgrave Macmillan, 2010)

Kersten, Albert, *Luns. Een politieke biografie* (Amsterdam: Boom, 2010)

Klaauw, C.A. van der, *Een diplomatenleven. Memoires* (Amsterdam 1995)

Klemann, Hein, Een handelsnatie in de twintigste eeuw, in: Graaff, Bob de, Hellema, Duco, Zwan, Bert van der (eds.), *De Nederlandse buitenlandse politiek in de twintigste eeuw* (Amsterdam: Boom, 2003)

Klemann, Hein, The 'Tommies' or the 'Jerries': Dutch Trade Problems in the Inter-War Period, in: Ashton, Nigel John, Hellema, Duco (eds.), *Unspoken Allies: Anglo-Dutch Relations Since 1780* (Amsterdam: AUP, 2001)

Krabbendam, Hans, Minnen, Cornelis A. van, Scott-Smith, Giles (eds.), *NL-USA. Four Centuries of Dutch-American Relations* (Amsterdam: Boom, 2009)

Laer, H.S. Rutger Jan toe, Kick-starting Cross-border Alliances: Approval and Clearance; the Past, the Present and the Future, in: *Air&Space Law*, Vol. XXXII/4–5 (September 2007), p. 287–325

Leeuw, René de, (ed.), *Fokker Verkeersvliegtuigen. Van de F.I uit 1918 tot en met de Fokker 100 van nu* (Amsterdam: NV Koninklijke Nederlandse Vliegtuigenfabriek Fokker, 1989)

Lieftinck, Pieter, *Herinneringen* (Utrecht/Antwerpen: Veen, 1989)

Lindblad, J. Thomas, Schrikker, Alicia (eds.), *Het verre gezicht. Politieke en culturele relaties tussen Nederland, Azië, Afrika en Amerika. Opstellen aangeboden aan prof. dr. Leonard Blussé* (Franeker: Van Wijnen, 2011)

Lookeren Campagne, Florentine van, 'Politiek of economisch falen? Het eerste kabinet-Van Agt en de steun aan het RSV-concern. Uit de ministerraadsnotulen van 1980', in: C.C. van Baalen ed., *De waan van de dag. Jaarboek parlementaire geschiedenis* (Amsterdam: Boom, 2006) p. 108–118

Luchtvaart gebonden. Een institutioneel onderzoek op het terrein van de burgerluchtvaart, 1945–1993 (The Hague: Rijksarchiefdienst/PIVOT, 1994)

Lundestad, Geir, *International Relations since 1945: East, West, North, South* (London: Sage Publications, 2017)

Lycklama à Nijeholt, J.F., *Air Sovereignty* (The Hague: Martinus Nijhoff, 1910)

Lyth, Peter J., Dierikx, Marc, From privilege to popularity. The growth of leisure air travel since 1945, in: *Journal of Transport History* 15(1994) nr. 2, 97–116

Lyth, Peter, Chosen Instruments: the Evolution of British Airways, in: *Dienel and Lyth (eds.), Flying the Flag. European Commercial Air Transport since 1945 (Basingstoke: MacMillan, 1998)*

Maar, Rimko van der, Meijer, Hans, *Herman van Roijen, 1905–1991. Een diplomaat van klasse* (Amsterdam: Boom, 2013)

Maare, Leo van, *De Mauritius Route. KLM Constellations in het kielzog van Abel Tasman* (Hilversum: All Media Productions, 2005)

MacKenzie, David, *ICAO: A History of the International Civil Aviation Organization* (Toronto: University of Toronto Press, 2010)

Malcontent, Peter, Baudet, Floribert, The Dutchman's Burden? Nederland en de internationale rechtsorde in de twintigste eeuw, in: Graaff, Bob de, Hellema, Duco, Zwan, Bert van der (eds.), *De Nederlandse buitenlandse politiek in de twintigste eeuw* (Amsterdam: Boom, 2003)

Mantegazza, Amilcare, Alitalia and Commercial Aviation in Italy, in: Hans-Liudger Dienel, Peter Lyth, *Flying the Flag. European Commercial Air Transport since 1945* (Basingstoke: Macmillan, 1997)

Masson-Zwaan, Tanja L., Mendes de Leon, Pablo (eds), *Air and Space Law: De Lege Ferenda. Essays in Honour of Henri A. Wassenbergh* (Dordrecht: Martinus Nijhoff, 1992)

Matte, N.M., *Treatise on Air-Aeronautical Law* (Toronto: Carswell, 1981)

Meijer, Hans, *Den Haag-Djakarta. De Nederlands-Indonesische betrekkingen 1950–1962* (Utrecht: Spectrum, 1994)

Mendes de Leon, Pablo, *Introduction to Air Law* (Alphen aan den Rijn: Kluwer Law International, 2022)

Meurs, Wim van, Bruin, Robin de, Hoetink, Carla, Leeuwen, Karin van, Reijnen, Carlos, Grift, Liesbeth van de, *Europa in alle staten. Zestig jaar geschiedenis van de Europese integratie* (Nijmegen: Vantilt, 2013)

Middelaar, Luuk van, *De passage naar Europa. Geschiedenis van een begin* (Groningen: Historische Uitgeverij, 2009)

Moll, J.J., *Langs de hoge weg. Herinneringen uit een vliegersleven* (Den Haag: Van Hoeve, 1959)

Naveau, Jacques, *International air transport in a changing world* (Brussels: Bruylant, 1989)

Neiertz, Nicolas, Air France: an elephant in an evening suit, in: Dienel, Hans, Lyth, Peter (eds.), *Flying the Flag. European Commercial Air Transport since 1945* (Basingstoke: MacMillan, 1998)

Nekkers, J.A., Malcontent, P.A.M. (eds.), *Fifty Years of Dutch Development Cooperation, 1949–1999* (The Hague: Sdu, 2000)

Officiële bescheiden betreffende de Nederlands-Indonesische betrekkingen, 1945–1950, Vol.7 (The Hague: Nijhoff, 1978)

Officiële bescheiden betreffende de Nederlands-Indonesische betrekkingen, 1945–1950, Vol. 10 (The Hague: Nijhof, 1982)

Officiële bescheiden betreffende de Nederlands-Indonesische betrekkingen, 1945–1950, Vol. 16 (The Hague: ING, 1991)

Oltmans, Willem, *Memoires 1961–1963* (Breda: Papieren Tijger, 1997)

Omissi, David E., *Air Power and Colonial Control. The Royal Air Force, 1919–1939* (Manchester: MUP, 1990)

Pekelder, Jacco, *Nederland en de DDR. Beeldvorming en betrekkingen 1949–1989* (Amsterdam: Boom, 1998)

Piglia, Melina, Carry our colors and defend our interests under the skies of other Continents". Argentinian Commercial aviation policy in the Peronista decade (Argentina 1945–1955), in: *Journal of Transport History* 40(2019) nr. 1, p. 44–61

Pirie, Gordon, *Air Empire. British Imperial Civil Aviation 1919–1939* (Manchester: Manchester Univ. Press, 2009)

Proceedings of the International Civil Aviation Conference Chicago, Illinois, November 1 – December 7, 1944, [2 volumes] (Washington DC: United States Printing Office, 1949)

Putten, Frans-Paul van der, Van semi-kolonie naar economische wereldmacht: China's toepassing van diplomatieke en economische middelen in de betrekkingen met Nederland sinds het einde van de negentiende eeuw, in: Lindblad, J. Thomas, Schrikker, Alicia (red.), *Het verre gezicht. Politieke en culturele relaties tussen Nederland, Azië, Afrika en Amerika. Opstellen aangeboden aan prof. dr. Leonard Blussé* (Franeker: Van Wijnen, 2011)

Rapoport, Mario, Foreign and domestic policy in Argentina during the Second World War: the traditional political parties and the military regime, 1943–1945, in: Tella, Guido di, Watt, Donald C. (eds.), *Argentina between the Great Powers, 1939–46* (Basingstoke: Macmillan, 1989)

Roper, Albert, *La Convention Internationale du 13 Octobre 1919 portant Réglementation de la Navigation Aérienne. Son Origine, son application, son avenir* (Paris: Recueil Sirey, 1930)

Saint Sauveur-Henn, Anne, Die deutsche Migration nach Argentinien (1870–1945), in: Birle, Peter (ed.), *Die Beziehungen zwischen Deutschland und Argentinien* (Frankfurt: Vervuert Verlag, 2010)

Sassen, Saskia, *Globalisering: over mobiliteit van geld, mensen en informatie* (Amsterdam: Van Gennep, 1999)

Schot, J.W., Lente, D. van, Techniek, industrialisatie en de betwiste modernisering van Nederland, in: *Techniek in Nederland*, Vol. 7 (Zutphen: Walburg Pers, 2003)

Schreurs, R.L.M., Positie van Nederland in de internationale luchtvaartpolitiek, in: Bakelen, Frans van (ed.), *Teksten vervoerrecht* (Zwolle: W.E.J. Tjeenk Willink, 1985).

Scott-Smith, Giles, Snyder, David J., "A Test of Sentiments": Civil Aviation, Alliance Politics, and the KLM Challenge in Dutch-American Relations, in: *Diplomatic History 37*(*2013*)

Segers, Matthieu, *Reis naar het continent. Nederland en de Europese integratie, 1950 tot heden* (Amsterdam: Bert Bakker, 2013)

Seyer, Sean, *Sovereign Skies. The Origins of American Civil Aviation Policy* (Baltimore: Johns Hopkins University Press, 2021)

Snape, Richard H., Gropp, Lisa, Luttrell, Tas, *Australia's Trade Policy. A Documentary History* (St. Leonards: Allen & Unwin, 1998)

Societé des Nations, *Etudes sur la Situation Economique, Administrative et Juridique de la Navigation Aérienne Internationale* (The Hague: Martinus Nijhoff, 1930)

Staniland, Martin, *Government Birds. Air Transport and the State in Western Europe* (Lanham : Rowman & Littlefield, 2003)

Staniland, Martin, *A Europe of the Air? The Airline Industry and European Integration* (Lanham MD: Rowman & Littlefield, 2008)

Svik, Peter, *Civil Aviation and the Globalization of the Cold War* (Cham (CH): Palgrave Macmillan, 2020)

Tella, Guido di, Watt, Donald C. (eds.), *Argentina between the Great Powers, 1939–46* (Basingstoke: Macmillan, 1989)

Vanthemsche, Guy, *La Sabena. L'Aviation commerciale Belge 1923–2001. Des origines au crash* (Brussel: De Boeck, 2002)

Vidal Olivares, Javier, *Las Alas de España. Iberia, Lineas* Aéreas (1940–2005) (Valencia: Universidad de Valencia Press, 2008)

Vleck, Jenifer van, *Empire of the Air. Aviation and the American Ascendancy* (Cambridge: Harvard UP, 2013)

Wassenbergh, Henri A., *Post-War International Civil Aviation Policy and the Law of the Air* (The Hague: Martinus Nijhoff, 1957)

Wassenbergh, Henri A., *Public International Air Transportation Law in a New Era. Economic regulation of international air carrier operations* (Deventer: Kluwer, 1976)

Wassenbergh, Henri A., *External aviation relations of the European Community* [*Includes the proceedings of two mock negotiations by the 'European Commission' with respectively the 'USA' and 'Czechoslovakia'* (Deventer: Kluwer, 1992)

Wetenschappelijke Raad voor het Regeringsbeleid, *Nederland Handelsland. Het perspectief van de transactiekosten* [WRR-report 66], (Den Haag: Sdu, 2003)

Wetenschappelijke Raad voor het Regeringsbeleid, *Aan het buitenland gehecht. Over verankering en strategie van het Nederlands buitenlandbeleid* [WRR-report 85], (Amsterdam: AUP, 2010)

Wielenga, Friso, *West-Duitsland: partner uit noodzaak. Nederland en de Bondsrepubliek 1949–1955* (Utrecht: Spectrum, 1989)

Zweers, Louis, *De crash van de Franeker. Een Amerikaanse persreis naar Nederlands-Indië in 1949* (Amsterdam: Boom, 2001)

Index

Printed in the United States
by Baker & Taylor Publisher Services